To Liz

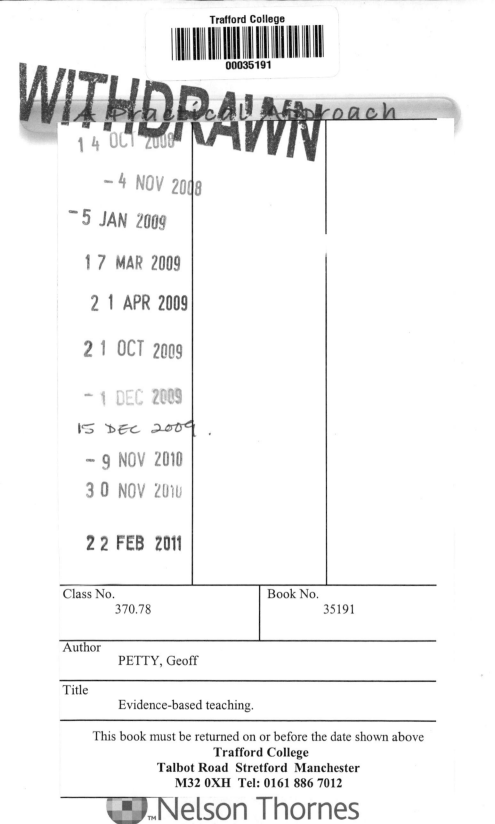

Nelson Thornes
a Wolters Kluwer business

Published in 2006 by:
Nelson Thornes Ltd
Delta Place
27 Bath Road
CHELTENHAM
GL53 7TH
United Kingdom

08 09 10 / 10 9 8 7 6 5 4 3

A catalogue record for this book is available from the British Library

ISBN 978 0 7487 9594 9

Illustrations by Liz Singh

Page make-up by Florence Production Ltd
Stoodleigh, Devon
Printed and bound in Spain by GraphyCems

Acknowledgements

The Publishers gratefully acknowledge the following for permission to reproduce copyright material:

Crown copyright material is reproduced with the permission of the Controller of the HMSO and the Queen's Printer
for Scotland; 'Dweck's Questionnaire' from SELF THEORIES: Their Role in Motivation Personality and Development by
C. S. Dweck, published by Psychology Press 2000; Text relating to Feuerstein's Instrumental Enrichment. Reprinted with
the kind permission of Professor Reuven Feuerstein; Do, Review, Apply and Learn, from LEARNING BY DOING: A
Guide to Teaching and Learning Methods by Graham Gibbs, 1989 reprinted with the kind permission of the author;
Violinist's Graph, from THE ROLE OF DELIBERATE PRACTICE IN THE ACQUISITION OF EXPERT PERFORMANCE
by K. Ericsson, R. Krampe and C. Tesch-Romer. Psychological Review, 1993 vol 100 no 3 pp 363–406 published by
American Psychological Association; Extracts of dialogue taken from 'Reciprocal teaching of comprehension-fostering and
comprehension-monitoring activities' by A. S. Palincsar and A. L. Brown 'Cognition and Instruction' 2 117–175 1984
published by Lawrence Erlbaum Associates. Reprinted with permission of A. S. Palincsar and the publishers; Table from
'FRAMEWORKS OF THINKING' David Moseley, Vivienne Baumfield, Julian Elliott, Steven Higgins, Jen Miller and Douglas
P. Newton. Published by Cambridge University Press 2005. Rperinted with permission of Cambridge University Press;
Graph based on one from TEACHING FOR QUALITY LEARNING AT UNIVERSITY by John Biggs, published by Open
University 2003. Reprinted by permission of the Open University.

Effect sizes throughout this book are from:
Professor John Hattie in a personal communication of his latest table dated Nov 2005
Robert Marzano (1998) A theory-based Meta-Analysis of Research on Instruction Mid-continent Regional Educational
Laboratory Aurora, Colorada;
H.Cooper (1989) Homework. White Plains, NY: Longman;
H. Cooper: (1989) Synthesis of research on homework. Educational Leadership 47 (3) 85–91. Alexandria VA:
Association for Supervision and Curriculum Development.

Whilst every effort has been made to trace the copyright holders, in cases where this has been unsuccessful or if any
have inadvertently been overlooked, the Publishers will be pleased to make the necessary arrangements at the first
opportunity.

Contents

Part 4: Seven principles for evidence-based teaching

In which we extract from the research seven general principles that seem to explain what makes teaching methods work, and use them to improve our teaching

Part 5: Choosing and using teaching methods

In which we look in detail at an ideal plan to teach a topic, looking at alternative teaching methods and how to use them

Part 6: Teaching intelligence

In which we see that intelligence is a range of skills that can be taught, and consider strategies to teach them

Part 7: What do the best teachers, schools and colleges do?

In which we see how expert teachers and the best schools get their incredible pass rates

Part 8: Your own evidence

In which we see how to improve our teaching, and find it's a bit scary, but fun

Part 9: The rational curriculum _____

In which we see what 'they' ought to tell us to teach, and find that if we teach it anyway, students do much better. But we find teachers have an awesome responsibility. You create the future

Part 10: Management and leadership _____

In which we find out how to improve the teaching of others in our team

Preface and acknowledgements

I spent 28 years teaching, but now I realise I was doing much of it wrong. It's not that I was doing it badly either. (My A-level physics students, for example, did two grades better than their GCSE scores predicted.) But ten years studying research on what works in classrooms has shown me what I did right, and what I did wrong.

When I first published *Teaching Today* in 1993, I found remarkably little research that helped us make real-life teaching decisions. Since then there has been a revolution in how research is done, creating an avalanche of information on what works and why. This research is very practical, and if we put it all together, very, very persuasive. In fact we would be quite crazy to ignore it just from the point of view of our own interests. The most effective methods expect teachers to do less, and the students to do more, so as well as being more effective, these methods make teaching less tiring and more enjoyable. Students enjoy these methods much more, too, though some will have to get used to actually doing something!

I have tried to write the book I craved in my first few years of teaching, one that skated over the basics but gave ideas known to work. I hope it doesn't stay on your shelf, but enlivens your planning, and spurs you to experiment with your teaching, and your students' learning.

Good teachers touch people's lives for ever. If you teach well, some of your students will only succeed because of your excellent teaching. Then they might go on to get more advanced qualifications and skills, again just because of your expert teaching. Then they might get a career, indeed a whole life, built on your excellent teaching. No other profession is that consequential and enabling.

Teaching is just too damned difficult to get right. It is always possible to improve. I am supposed to know about these things but I am still changing what I do. If you step out of your comfort zone and experiment with new methods you will find this enormously rewarding, just so long as you are in control of the change, and doing it at a comfortable pace that gives you some time for reflection.

Experimenting can be great fun, especially if you do it for your teaching team and share your findings with others, and if they share their findings with you, as described in Chapter 23. Look out too for the target icons [🎯] in the margin which mark strategies worth trying. Better ways to teach can enliven your career, and your life, as well as meeting your professional responsibility to do the best job you can for your students. In any case why waste our efforts on teaching methods that don't work, when we can use the ones that do? Evidence-based practice has swept traditional practice away in agriculture and medicine, and it is only a matter of time for the broom to sweep through teaching.

More even than that, as I hope to show in Chapter 24 on the 'rational curriculum', teachers now have a role to help shape the thinking of present and future generations. This is an awesome responsibility, especially as environmental and other ethical decisions made by the people that you have taught to think, could make a huge difference to the prospects for life on the planet. If the near-unanimous cry of environmental experts is half right, then effective thinking could make the difference between creative flourishing, bare survival, or even the near extinction of our species. I know that sounds apocalyptic, and we might both wish that teachers were not so influential, but we are, and we do not live in ordinary times. I will argue that whether we like it or not, teachers make the future, so we had better do it well.

I hope this book will furnish you with a host of practical and useful ideas to enliven the learning and the lives of you and your students! Evidence-based practice is here to stay; I hope you make it welcome.

Acknowledgements

The errors are mine, but I would like to thank:

Professor John Hattie for his pioneering work, for allowing me to use his tables of effect sizes, and for answering my queries; without him this book could not have been written.

Professor John Biggs for perusing my explanation of his SOLO taxonomy.

Robert Marzano for asking and answering some questions every teacher asks, and for answering my queries.

Janice Evans and her history department at Solihull Sixth Form College for their pioneering work and their willingness to explain their thinking to me.

Jim Judges of Sutton Coldfield College for his ideas on the use of the mini-whiteboard.

Keith Cole for insisting that I read Steven Pinker.

Liz Singh for her drawings, her editing, her rigorous insistence whenever I wasn't making sense, and also for her unwavering support and patience.

Geoff Petty, 2006

Part 1 What is evidence-based teaching?

1 We need evidence-based practice, not custom and practice

Some medieval farmers used to sprinkle ox blood on their fields at full moon, in the mistaken belief it increased soil fertility. What made them think it would work? If you had asked them they would have said, 'Everyone does it!' People often mistake common practice for best practice, and seem to prefer the comfort of the crowd to thinking for themselves using hard evidence.

Medicine was once the same: doctors bled patients suffering from anaemia, and administered bee stings to arthritic joints. Why? Because everyone else did, and all those doctors couldn't be wrong – could they?

Medicine and agriculture are now both 'evidence based', and it is time for education to follow their example. It is no shame to follow them; it is easier to work out how a liver works or how a plant grows than how a person learns. But we do know a great deal about how people learn now, and we need to change our practice accordingly.

> *Very successful procedures have been discovered without science in medicine, agriculture and education. We mustn't abandon our intuition or our own evidence; this is the final court of judgement, as we see in Chapter 23.*

But isn't educational practice evidence based already? Hardly. For example, there are many teaching strategies that enable learners to do a grade or two better in assessments than more customary teaching methods. These highly effective methods don't take more time, though some require more skill from the teacher. Yet many of these methods are almost unknown in this country, and others are only rarely used, because teachers are unaware of their exceptional power. If education were evidence based experienced teachers would be using these methods frequently. They wouldn't be taken in by the initiative described just below either.

If the use of just *one* of these top performance methods can improve students' achievement by as much as two grades, imagine what would happen if an evidence-based teacher routinely used many of these highly effective methods in every lesson.

So what would teaching look like if we dropped the snake oil,* and took up the evidence? That is what I hope to show you in this book. I am convinced that by

---

*Snake oil – useless 'medicine' sold as a cure all

the end of this century people will look back at our present 20th-century practice and laugh – or groan – just as we do when we hear of 19th-century teaching. And they may envy us that we were born in a time when old methods were abandoned for exciting new and powerful ones, and when teachers had the challenge and fun of working out the teaching of the future. And seeing the results.

The future is in sight, but the path is not yet clear, and it is the present generation of teachers who will forge these new ways. That's you! Our students have a lot to gain, and so will the economy and social inclusion. We teachers have a lot to gain too, as the new methods often make teaching less tiring, and much more interesting.

What is evidence-based practice?

First let's look at what evidence-based practice is *not*.

Not long ago I had a very common experience that many of you will have shared, often many times. Someone with excellent educational credentials was describing a new educational initiative to me and to others. As I describe this below it may seem like an evidence-based approach, but it is little better than disguised snake oil.

The initiative was introduced with great enthusiasm by a man who fair-mindedly described both the advantages and disadvantages of the new approach in terms of the improvement in learning quality it could bring about. He persuasively and accurately argued that the advantages would outweigh the disadvantages. He quoted some acknowledged authorities citing a piece of research that had found a qualitative and quantitative improvement in students' learning when the initiative was tried in a pilot. He ended by exhorting us to join in with the initiative on the basis of the information he had just outlined.

Even if all the claims he made were true, this is not evidence-based practice, and implementing the initiative could be a wasteful distraction of the very limited time and energy available to teachers. What's wrong with this man's argument?

> *The mistake of evaluating something while forgetting to seriously consider its alternatives is extremely common in every walk of life. Those at the meeting will probably have made it very many times, with who knows what negative results. Had they been taught the 'rational curriculum' outlined in Chapter 24 they would not have made this mistake, and both they and their students would have been a great deal better off.*

Let's use the methods that work best

As we will see later, syntheses of research by international experts like Professor John Hattie and Bob Marzano have shown us that the great majority of educational initiatives have positive effects on learning. Improving your handouts, team teaching, tutorials, peer assessment, computer-based instruction, and painting the classroom can all have a positive effect on achievement. But if you don't have the time to do them all, which will have the *greatest* effect? (Can you guess which ones? We will find out later.)

We are knee deep in strategies that could improve things for our students, so the question is not 'Will this strategy work?' but '*Which* are the most productive strategies to adopt?' Answering this last question has been the life work of academics such Hattie and Marzano. Thanks to them teachers can direct their precious time and energies to the variables, and the methods, that make the biggest difference to student achievement.

The 20–80 rule
Twenty per cent of what you do makes 80 per cent of the difference, so let's work smarter, not harder, by concentrating on the factors that make this difference.

Let's try to understand the learning process

It is one thing to know what methods work, quite another to understand why. Without understanding why they work we are most unlikely to use them effectively. We will also be unable to criticise constructively our own and others' practice.

Thanks to ingenious theorising backed up by rigorous experiments in neural physiology, psychology, social psychology, cognitive science and elsewhere, we now understand a great deal about why we learn, how we learn, and consequently what can help us to learn.

Let's find the problems and fix them

Using the teaching methods that are known to work best, and understanding how they work in terms of brain science, is only part of evidence-based practice. Research reviews can only tell us how the *average* student learns best. But this ignores the contexts in which you teach, and the problems these can cause.

Each of our students is unique, and while they will benefit from the methods that work best they will also have unique needs. Other contextual factors also come in to play: your subject, your institution's tutorial system, the prior learning required for success in your subjects, your favourite teaching methods, and so on. These introduce factors that need addressing if your students are to learn at their best.

For example, if your guidance and selection system sets the bar too low when deciding which students are allowed on to your A-level course, then you may get poor attainment almost no matter what teaching methods you use, and no matter how well you understand the learning process. No initiative will fix this poor attainment, except improvement to your selection procedure. We need to find the contextual factors that most contribute to success on your courses, diagnose any problems you are experiencing with them, and fix these. This is another arm of evidence-based practice that we will look at.

Principles of evidence-based practice

There are four principles of evidence-based practice; at least one of these is often ignored in most arguments that attempt to justify educational practice. *All* these principles need to be taken into account in evidence-based practice.

1 You need all the evidence to make sound decisions

    a In order to evaluate an educational initiative or strategy, *you must compare it with any alternatives* that might achieve the same goals. However good a strategy, there may be another that is even better! As we will see, it is now possible to compare the effectiveness of strategies using average 'effect sizes' and other approaches.

    b You need the views of *experts* who have looked at *all* the research and weighed *all* the arguments to reach their conclusions. This is necessary because one piece of research is often contradicted by another.

2 It is not enough to know what works, you need to know why

If you use a highly effective teaching strategy blindly you are most unlikely to get the best out of it. You must understand *why* it works to mine its full potential. When you teach you react constantly to the situation in the classroom, and it is your understanding of the teaching situation and what your methods should achieve that guides these crucial decisions.

... react constantly ...

3 You need to find the critical success factors that are failing in your teaching context and fix these

'Context is all' in understanding many problems that inhibit attainment. This is considered mainly in Chapter 25.

4 You need to review your teaching constantly in the light of the evidence above

The final court of judgement is not academic research, but what works in your classroom. Trust your own judgement! Try a new strategy a few times, learn from these experiments and adapt, but in the final analysis the best evidence you have is your own experience. So you must keep your practice under continual review and become a 'reflective practitioner'. This is considered mainly in Chapter 23.

. . . experiment with
graphic organisers . . .

Evidence-based teaching does not dictate what you should do; it just shows you how best to achieve your own values, priorities and goals. You will still need to provide the creativity and judgement needed to decide on the best methods, and how to apply them within the context of your own teaching. Evidence-based practice re-professionalises teachers, giving them control over initiatives to improve learning, even giving them control over the most important part of the curriculum – thinking skills – as we will see in Chapter 24.

It makes sense to adopt the strategies that are known to have the greatest average effect on student achievement and to understand why these methods work, and to adopt strategies that meet the unique needs of our learners, our subject, and other important contextual factors. To do this effectively we need evidence. Let's look at what evidence is available to us now.

We want the truth . . . (evidence rather than tradition, hard sell from those with power or financial interest, or personal opinion, even authoritative personal opinion)

The whole truth . . . (all the evidence, e.g. research reviews from all schools of research)

And nothing but the truth (no exaggerations, bandwagons, unexamined prejudices, and certainly no snake oil!)

But getting the truth is far from easy, so we need to keep an open mind. Thanks to more effective research we are learning fast, and the best evidence available can only give us the best guess so far. Medical and agricultural practice changes as new evidence becomes available; education should be the same.

Contradictions and agreement between our sources of evidence

Different sources of evidence sometimes lead to different conclusions, as we will see in Chapter 9. However, we need the whole truth, so we need to listen to *all* these sources, and take what we find useful from each.

This situation is reminiscent of the Indian parable of the six blind men examining an elephant:

> One feels his side and says 'an elephant is like a wall'.
> One feels his tusk and says 'an elephant is very like a spear'.
> One feels his trunk and says 'an elephant is very like a snake'.
> One feels his leg and says 'an elephant is like a tree'.
> One feels his ear and says 'an elephant is like a fan'.
> One feels his tail and says 'an elephant is like a rope'.

The moral, of course, is that if we only look at part of the evidence we are bound to get a partial and so inaccurate view. A fun poem by John Godfrey Saxe (1816–87) tells this tale and concludes:

> And so these men of Indostan
> Disputed loud and long,
> Each in his own opinion
> Exceeding stiff and strong,
> Though each was partly in the right,
> And all were in the wrong!

(The full poem by John Godfrey Saxe can be found at Duen Hsi Yen's site: www. noogenesis.com/pineapple/blind_men_elephant.html.)

In practice good researchers often ignore the neat boundaries between different sorts of evidence and different approaches to research. We will find remarkable agreement between different schools, for example in Chapter 22.

How this book is organised

Please have another look at the contents page of this book, and read it right through, especially the italics. It will really help you to understand how this book is organised.

Further reading

Brown, G. and Atkins, M. (1988) *Effective Teaching in Higher Education*, London: Routledge.

Gibbs, G. (1992) *Improving the Quality of Student Learning*, Bristol: Technical & Educational Services.

Hattie, J. A., 'Influences on student learning'. This can be downloaded from Professor John Hattie's staff home page: www.arts.auckland.ac.nz/staff/index.cfm?P=5049.

Muijs, D. and Reynolds, D. (2000) 'School effectiveness and teacher effectiveness in mathematics: some preliminary findings from the evaluation of the Mathematics Enhancement Programme (Primary)', *School Effectiveness and School Improvement*, 11, 3, 273–303.

Muijs, D. and Reynolds, D. (2001) *Effective Teaching: Evidence and Practice*, London: Paul Chapman.

Petty, G. (2004) *Teaching Today: A Practical Guide* (3rd edition), Cheltenham: Nelson Thornes. See also www.geoffpetty.com.

Ramsden, P. (1992) *Learning and Teaching in Higher Education*, London: Routledge.

Westwood, P. (2003) *Commonsense Methods for Children with Special Educational Needs: Strategies for the Regular Classroom* (4th edition), London: RoutledgeFalmer.

Review of reviews: a report by Charles Desforges can be downloaded from: www.tlrp.org/pub/acadpub/Desforges2000b.pdf.

For publications and research on education issues and evidence-based practice: www.ascd.org.

2 Learning is making sense, not just remembering

A common misconception sees the brain as a container, and learning as retaining what has been poured into it. But the mind is much more than a bucket. Much more even, than a hard disk where discrete facts are filed in English. What I explain in this chapter challenges many common conceptions, it might seem puzzling at first, and you might need to be patient and read it more than once to get the idea. Understanding it, however, is crucial to teaching well.

The theme of this chapter is that learning is an active process of *making sense* that creates a *personal interpretation* of what has been learned, rather than a perfect representation of what was taught. This involves not just storing personal interpretations of facts and ideas, but also *linking* them in a way that relates ideas to other ideas, and to prior learning, and so creates meaning and understanding. A dictionary links the word you look up with other words you already know, the brain does something similar, but the links are physical connections between concepts.

Meaning is not enough; the learner must know the conditions when ideas are relevant or useful to make the learning functional. They must learn ways to use this knowledge to solve problems, make judgements and carry out other useful tasks. It is this productive thinking that is the main purpose of education – and knowledge is often just a means to that end.

I hope to show that, again, it is the 'structure' of knowledge, the links between discrete bits of knowledge in the brain, that enables this productive thinking. Active learning on challenging reasoning tasks is required to create this structure.

How the brain learns

The human brain, of which you are a proud owner, has been evolving for about six million years, but we have only had language for about the last quarter of a million years at most. So for 95 per cent of its evolution, the brain thought in a language called 'mentalese' (rhymes with Japanese). This language is rather like a computer code or computer language. It expresses meaning non-linguistically.

Then evolutionary pressure 'bolted on' to the brain a remarkably small language module, but the brain continued running with the same 'computer code', 'software' and 'operating system'. It still thought and remembered in mentalese. But the brain could now translate mentalese into spoken language, enabling us to express our thoughts. It could also translate spoken language into mentalese when trying to comprehend someone else's speech. (Throughout this account I am going to assume you and your students converse in English but the same goes for any language.)

Time line of our past in millions of years

| 6 | 5 | 4 | 3 | 2 | 1 | now |

The brain of the nomadic hunter-gatherer, thought in a wordless language called 'mentalese'

We have had language for only the last 200,000 years, but we still think mainly in 'mentalese'. The modules of the mind communicate with each other in mentalese too.

All the modules of the brain still communicate in mentalese. So classroom learning requires the learner to translate the language of instruction into the language of meaning and understanding: mentalese. When students achieve this they sometimes experience the 'penny dropping' or 'I get it' feeling. The instruction has not changed, their interpretation of its meaning has.

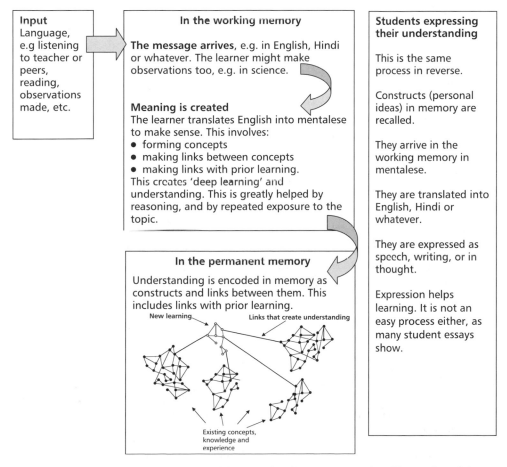

Input
Language, e.g listening to teacher or peers, reading, observations made, etc.

In the working memory

The message arrives, e.g. in English, Hindi or whatever. The learner might make observations too, e.g. in science.

Meaning is created
The learner translates English into mentalese to make sense. This involves:
- forming concepts
- making links between concepts
- making links with prior learning.
This creates 'deep learning' and understanding. This is greatly helped by reasoning, and by repeated exposure to the topic.

In the permanent memory

Understanding is encoded in memory as constructs and links between them. This includes links with prior learning.

New learning   Links that create understanding

Existing concepts, knowledge and experience

Students expressing their understanding

This is the same process in reverse.

Constructs (personal ideas) in memory are recalled.

They arrive in the working memory in mentalese.

They are translated into English, Hindi or whatever.

They are expressed as speech, writing, or in thought.

Expression helps learning. It is not an easy process either, as many student essays show.

The learning process (see also the chart of 'The teaching/learning process' in Chapter 8, p. 84). Adapted from Marzano (1998).

> *We do label our concepts with words, of course, but what we label is a meaning in mentalese. Remember also that much of our thought is unconscious.*

The brain consists of a vast array of about 11 billion brain cells called neurones that can be connected or disconnected. To form a concept, which you do in mentalese, your brain creates a *construct*, which is a little network of interconnected brain cells. This is your personal meaning for the concept. Everything you know you have encoded in your brain in this way. So if I ask you 'What is a fraction?' your brain will use the word 'fraction' to lead it to where it has stored the idea of what a fraction is. This idea is 'written' in the brain's language of interconnected neurones. However, this construct has a label – the word 'fractions'.

You have written this 'construct' for fractions yourself, in response to instruction, and particularly in response to your own efforts to use this idea and make sense of it. Your construct for 'fraction' will be connected by neural links to other constructs for related ideas such as 'half' or 'quarter'. If you are good at maths your construct for 'fraction' will also be neurally linked to more distantly related ideas such as 'percentage', 'proportion' and 'ratio'. You will also have linked all these ideas to very general mathematical principles. This will all become clearer later.

Your construct, and its connections to other constructs, differs at least in matters of detail from everyone else's. You have not passively recorded what your maths teacher told you, but have interpreted it in a unique way, made a meaning for it, and encoded it in your brain. This is not to say that an actor cannot 'learn lines' verbatim; they can. But most learning is not like this.

Some evidence that we think in mentalese

Many teachers are easily persuaded that their students have the ancient, language-free brains of tribal savages! Others find it hard to believe that people do not think primarily in their mother tongue. The evidence for this lies well outside the scope of this book, mainly in the painstaking experiments of cognitive science. But have you or your learners ever experienced any of the following, which suggest we think in  mentalese? (Again I will assume that you and your students use English.)

Having a clear thought, that nevertheless you find hard to express

How could this be if the *thought* was in English? Actually the thought was in mentalese and you were having trouble translating it into English. Writing often involves struggling with this translation: 'What I've written is not what I meant.'

Have you had the similar 'tip of the tongue' experience of having a concept in mind (in mentalese), but being unable to recall the word for it? This couldn't happen if the concept were in English.

'Getting it': Have you ever read or heard a sentence and not understood it first time, then read it again and 'got it'?

If understanding were expressed and remembered in English you would not experience this change. This was you having difficulty translating the English sentence into the language of meaning: 'mentalese'.

Experiencing ambiguity

A convicted US murderer called Bundy was thought to be due for execution when a newspaper headline read 'Bundy beats date with chair'. Hopefully readers choose the right meaning from the context! But if meaning itself were in English how could you have an ambiguity like this? And in what language are these two meanings? Mentalese of course.

Remembering the gist but not in English

Suppose I asked you for the story of a film that you saw last week, and you gave me an account. If I asked you to recount it again a few days later, you would do so using different sentences even if the account was otherwise identical. But if your memory of the film were in English you would just 'read it off' from this memory and it would have the same wording each time.

People who were born deaf and dumb, and who have not gone on to learn any language (even sign language), are able to think very effectively. So can babies before they develop language. The absurd notion that the electrical and chemical signals that bat about the brain when we think are alphabetical and in English must be dropped if we are to understand thinking and learning!

Mentalese records deep meaning. For example, look at this sentence: 'Colourless green ideas sleep furiously.' You understand all the words, and the sentence obeys all the laws of grammar, but it has no meaning, so it cannot be translated into mentalese. Notice that meaning is not about individual words all of which you understand. It is a property of whole sentences, paragraphs and chapters. It is a holistic property.

Permanent memory

Once the meaning has been deduced by the working memory, it can be sent to and stored in permanent memory, still in mentalese, not English.

Permanent memory is split into two main parts.

The *declarative* memory stores *facts* and is in the hippocampus. This part of the brain was originally used to store a map of a creature's territory, and though it has evolved from this it still keeps its map-like characteristics. The declarative memory has two parts:

- the *episodic* memory which stores 'stories' or episodes: what happened first, second and third, and so on
- the *semantic* memory, which stores information about words and their meanings.

Desert mice that hoard food have a larger hippocampus than closely related species that don't hoard. We humans also keep knowledge of facts in this map-like memory system in the hippocampus, which may partly explain why mind-maps and other visual methods mentioned in Chapter 10 work so well.

There is also a *procedural* memory that stores skills and processes; this is in the neo-stiatum. Notice that procedural and declarative memory are quite distinct, which might explain why it helps to review content and skills in two separate procedures as described in Chapter 21.

Misconceptions

Creating meaning in mentalese is not straightforward; it is usually a process of trial and error. For example, the psychologist M. Bowerman (1978) observed her daughter form the concept of 'ball'. Let's call her daughter 'Jo'. Aged 13 months, Jo saw a ball, said 'ball' and then immediately went to pick it up. Despite appearances, Jo had not understood the concept. During the next month or so she used 'ball' to describe a balloon, an Easter egg, a small round stone, and so on. Like all learners Jo needed feedback to learn to use 'ball' correctly. Vygotsky (1962) reported a similar process during language acquisition.

Misconceptions are not peculiar to infants; all learning requires us to 'have a stab' at expressing an understanding in mentalese, and this will often be imperfect. For example, a student might find that 5, 7, 11 and 13 are all examples of prime numbers, and incorrectly conclude that all odd numbers are prime numbers. Misconceptions like these are integral to the very process of learning, which is to guess a meaning, and then use feedback of some kind to improve it.

Common errors in Advanced English language papers in 2003 showed similar errors in concept development. For example, 'alliteration' occurs when words begin with the same *sound*, such as the phrase '*b*right *b*lue *b*ird' or '*g*hostly *g*alleon'. But students quoted 'capacious ceiling' and 'grand giraffe' as alliterative though the *sounds* are not the same in these cases. (The *c* and *g* sounds are soft in one word, but hard in the other.) They would probably not spot 'rough wrought' as alliteration either, though both words start with an *r* sound.

Students also confused what are called 'complex' sentences (which require sub-ordinate clauses), with long sentences that did not have subordinate clauses; and they confused 'metaphor' with 'simile'. Concept development requires students to see examples, but also to see *non-examples*, so they can see the boundaries of the concept.

'Decisions decisions' is a great way to teach concepts without such misconceptions. See Chapter 11. If students confuse two concepts use 'same but different', page 117.

Misconceptions are common in the classroom:

'Earthworms may only see another earthworm every five years because they have no eyes.'

'During the birth of a baby, first of all the mother becomes pregnant . . . later her hips will dislocate.'

'The mother experiences labour pains because the baby is turning itself round and getting in position for its head-first exit.'

Disadvantages of asexual reproduction: 'You don't have sex.'

'We worked it out by a process of illumination.'

Not all howlers are misconceptions, however; most are just spelling mistakes (hopefully):

'We held the crucible with our thongs.'

'The early Britons made their houses of mud, and there was rough mating on the floor.'

From www.biotopics.co.uk/howl/howl01.html

Reasoning not reproduction helps meaning making

Reasoning tasks encourage deep learning

Tasks fall into two types, reproduction tasks and reasoning tasks.

Reproduction tasks

Here the student repeats back knowledge or skills that have been directly taught by the teacher or directly explained in resources. For example:

– copying a labelled diagram
– recalling a definition or a simple explanation given earlier
– completing a calculation in a way shown earlier.

These tasks are lower on Bloom's taxonomy (see below). They do not require the learner to process the material, or to apply the learning, or even to understand it. This makes the task simple, but has the disadvantage that it does not require learners to create a meaning in mentalese and to connect it to their existing learning.

Reasoning tasks

Here the student must process and apply what they have learned, linking it with existing learning and experience. They must think with it. The task is relatively high on Bloom's taxonomy. As a consequence of the reasoning involved the task requires the learner to form a mentalese construct linked with existing learning. Assuming the answers to the following questions have not already been given, then the following tasks are reasoning tasks.

For students of low attainment:

Which of these six knives would be best for slicing the apples, and why?

How could we make sure we don't forget something when we go shopping?

For students of higher attainment:

How could this business plan be improved?

Which of these factors most influenced Harold Macmillan's political thinking?

Why must x^2 always be positive?

Teachers who must 'cover' a great deal of material in little time, or who teach students whose reasoning skills are weak, often stick to reproduction tasks. The problem with this is that students do not create their own meanings. There is more detail on this in *Teaching Today* (2004), where I show that a student can get correct answers to questions on a piece of nonsense text such as Lewis Carroll's 'Jabberwocky' poem, without of course understanding it.

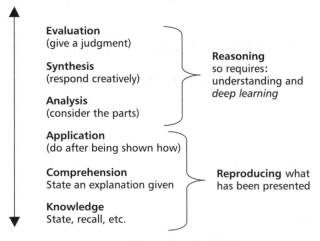

High cognitive demand – reasoning required

Evaluation
(give a judgment)

Synthesis
(respond creatively)

Analysis
(consider the parts)

Reasoning
so requires:
understanding and
deep learning

Application
(do after being shown how)

Comprehension
State an explanation given

Knowledge
State, recall, etc.

Reproducing what
has been presented

Low cognitive demand – little reasoning required

Bloom's taxonomy.

Reasoning questions are required for differentiation

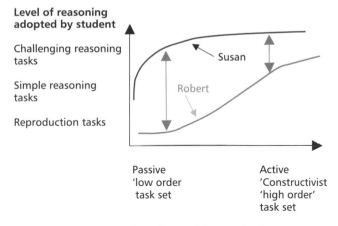

John Biggs (2003) imagined two students sitting next to each other in the same class: Susan who is academic and a good learner, and Robert who is not. Let's assume they are both reasonably well motivated.

If their teacher used a passive method such as teacher talk, demonstration, or showing a video, Susan would reason during this presentation asking herself *'Why is it like that?'*, *'But what would happen if . . .'*, *'How could that be used in practice'*, and so on. In order to answer her own questions she would have to make a meaning for what she was being taught, and relate it to her previous knowledge. Robert, however, would just be trying to remember what he had been told. He would not be trying to make rigorous personal sense like Susan.

The reason Susan learns well, and Robert badly, is not to do with intelligence, or even necessarily motivation. The difference is that Susan habitually goes through the cognitive processes required for good quality learning: making meanings related to what is already known, and reasoning with this. She has the habits that create deep learning. Robert only learns deeply when he is set reasoning tasks, or other tasks that *require* him to go through these cognitive processes. Differentiation requires that learners are set reasoning tasks, whatever their attainment. We will return to this at the end of this chapter.

Reasoning develops relations between constructs

Imagine our little girl Jo learning division for the first time with a teacher who adopts 'constructivist' methods that encourage deep learning. Rather than teaching her to punch in numbers into a calculator without understanding, he tries to build Jo's understanding out of what she already knows.

Before starting work on division, he uses a method called 'relevant recall questions' (see Chapter 16) . He asks Jo to recall her experiences of 'cutting things up' and he starts to relate this to division. 'So if you cut up the cake like this, how many pieces would you *divide* it into?'

In a similar way he relates 'sharing out' to division. 'If there were six sweets, to *divide* between two children, how many would each child get?'

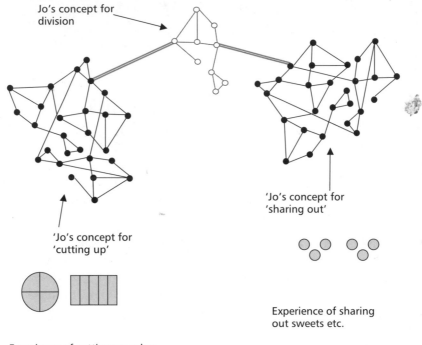

Jo's concept for division

'Jo's concept for 'sharing out'

'Jo's concept for 'cutting up'

Experience of sharing out sweets etc.

Experience of cutting up cakes, cutting up paper, etc.

Jo must establish relationships between concepts.

Jo already has constructs for 'sharing out' and for 'cutting up', and the teacher is getting her to construct her concept for division, out of and onto this existing learning. The teacher gives Jo some activities to cut up paper and share out bricks, and keeps using the term 'divide'. Without these links to previous experience the concept of division would not be connected to her prior learning.

These links between constructs are most important for two reasons. First of all they create 'meaning'. When we understand something it means we can explain it in terms of something else. If you looked up 'division' in a children's dictionary it would probably say something about 'sharing out' and 'cutting up'.

Secondly, these very links make our learning 'functional'. When we problem solve we think along these relational links. If Jo learned division well, building it firmly on her existing learning and experience, then when she was asked a question such as 'If a gardener has 225 bulbs to place equally in 15 flower beds, how many would be in each bed?' she could think for a bit and say 'Hey, this is a cutting up question so I divide', or 'This is a sharing out question so I divide.'

The links between new learning and her previous learning and experience have made her learning both meaningful and 'functional'.

Some teachers only set reproduction tasks. They show students 'how to do it' on the board, and then ask them to reproduce the method by rote. When students get the right answer to these 'Jabberwocky' questions they incorrectly assume students have an understanding. But understanding means 'linked with prior learning', not 'able to reproduce'.

Quality learning requires reasoning to develop relations between constructs

Many problems in learning and teaching are due to surface learning, and can be traced back to the nature of the tasks that students are set. Only active tasks and reasoning tasks create deep learning, especially for the 'Roberts' of this world.

I mean tasks of any kind, including verbal questions, tasks requiring students to work practically or on paper, assignment tasks; even an elaborate project can be seen as a large task or sequence of tasks. It often helps to build a 'ladder' of tasks as shown.

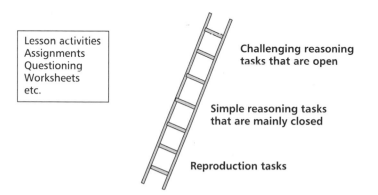

Lesson activities
Assignments
Questioning
Worksheets
etc.

Challenging reasoning tasks that are open

Simple reasoning tasks that are mainly closed

Reproduction tasks

Learning quality and the SOLO taxonomy

John Biggs, one of the great educationalists of our time, wanted an objective measure of learning quality. A measure of how *well* students had learned or understood something, rather than how much they could recall. He and Kevin Collis looked at students' work of widely differing quality, and began to recognise that a measure of the quality of the work was its *structure* as explained below.

This gave rise to a taxonomy (hierarchy of types) called the SOLO taxonomy, with higher quality 'deep learning' at the top, and lower quality 'surface learning' at the bottom. SOLO stands for the 'Structure of the Observed Learning Outcome', i.e. the structure of students' work.

Let's look at the SOLO taxonomy by considering an example. Suppose some catering students had been given an assignment that required them to write about the foods used in salads from the perspective of catering establishments. It is important to remember that SOLO rates the work, not the student, and as a student learns a given topic better, their work should gradually climb the taxonomy shown diagrammatically on page 22.

One student's work might give a very weak response to this task, giving irrelevant information such as his personal tastes in salads. This Biggs calls a *prestructural* response. The student has entirely missed the point of the exercise.

A slightly better piece of work might list the ingredients that could be used in salads, and explain a little about each one. Another weak response would be to write about salads solely from one point of view, say costs. This Biggs calls a *unistructural* response, because the student sees the topic from just one perspective, such as 'list the ingredients', or 'write about their costs'. The learner often 'closes' on a conclusion – 'iceberg lettuce is best because it's cheapest per pound' – and may stick to this in debate, overlooking or even denying other ways of looking at the question of 'best ingredients', such as taste or preparation time.

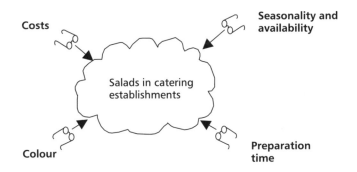

A better student might use a number of perspectives, creating a *multistructural* response. They might, for example, write about the ingredients in salads from the points of view of flavour, texture, costs, seasonality and availability, colour, nutrition, common serving practices, and so on. They might also do as the unistructural student has done, and list the possible ingredients, but they have gone beyond this. Indeed every level of the SOLO taxonomy tends to contain, but go beyond, the levels below it.

Multistructural work uses different aspects, but is compartmentalised, concrete, and jumps from one aspect to another. Conflicts and inconsistencies in the different points of view are not noticed, or are denied, or ignored in an attempt to seek 'closure', by a single 'right answer'. The learner can't weigh the pros and cons of alternative viewpoints to come to a balanced view.

With better learning and more thought another student, or the same student some time later, might give a *relational* response. Here, they give the detail of a multistructural response, but go beyond this to consider relationships between factors (or 'spectacles') within the topic, and between the topic and elsewhere. For example, one student might see a relationship between the 'spectacles' (perspectives), and explain that when ingredients are local and in season this causes the costs to be lower, and the flavour better. Another 'relational' point is that when salads are stored in a certain way they have a better texture and colour. Here the student has considered cause-and-effect relationships, but any meaningful and important relationships will do to make the response relational. Relationships between the perspectives may be particularly important here. On page 22 relations show up as links between concepts.

A relational response will strive to recognise and reconcile conflicts in the information and between the different perspectives. In the example above, the student has considered what to do about the conflict or difficulty that high-quality ingredients are often high in cost. This is reconciled by advice to buy locally and seasonally. Notice that a more holistic view is taken than in a multistructural response, where the different perspectives were just described, but not related to each other. The student is beginning to see the wood for the trees but still sticks to the topic, to the given data, and to concrete experience. Most adults operate at this level after learning, even in areas of some expertise, and it can serve very well for most practical purposes.

The highest response is rare and takes a great deal of time and effort to attain. Biggs calls this *extended abstract*. Here the student delivers a relational response, but then goes beyond the immediate context and the factors given, and sees the situation from the vantage point of general principles and, if relevant, values. One can imagine a student writing from the point of view of culinary styles, originality of ingredients, or the environmental impact of the choices made by the caterer. These subject principles range much further than the given topic and act as 'helicopters' enabling the learner to look down on the topic from a great conceptual height. Clearly the subject principles need to be well chosen, and to be relevant to the task.

There can of course be many extended abstract responses: another student might take the subject principles of multicultural catering, another some gourmet principles, for example. Another might take the principle 'look after the customer and the business looks after itself' and use this to develop an approach to salads. Sometimes more than one principle will be necessary to do justice to the task. The approach is 'holistic', that is it looks at the subject as a whole rather than looking at parts of it in turn.

> *In English literature students may begin by looking at a poem line by line, or verse by verse (atomistic); only then might they be able to look at the work holistically, searching for a number of meanings and for universal themes in the poem.*

Extended abstract requires study of all the important evidence, from all important points of view, and an acceptance of conflict and contradiction in this evidence. There is no attempt at that dash to a 'right answer' that is called 'early closure'. There is a recognition that context counts: 'Most gourmet salads involve high-cost ingredients and some have long preparation time, and so are rarely suitable for budget meals.' Alternative hypotheses, explanations and principles are made and tested; for example: 'There are probably several causes for the increase in interest in Mediterranean dishes in recent years.'

Hypothesis testing works well if you follow this sequence:

If . . . (hypothesis)

Then . . . (stating logical consequences if the hypothesis were true)

Looking for evidence that these logical consequences really occur, then:

If the evidence is found, a tentative acceptance of the hypothesis

If this evidence is not found, a tendency to reject or modify the hypothesis.

Biggs and Collis used an empirical approach, unlike any other taxonomy I know of, including Bloom's. Their research showed that SOLO can be used to assess mathematics, modern languages, English literature, geography and history. They found also that the 'gut feelings' of teachers assessing work in all these subjects were guided by an intuitive SOLO approach. (Teachers tended to give higher grades for higher SOLO responses, even if they had never heard of SOLO.) Biggs and Collis also found that teachers could be trained to use SOLO accurately to assess work, and that the judgements of trained assessors agreed very well indeed.

They also suggested some pedagogical implications of the taxonomy. These include that we should teach up the taxonomy, not down it. That is, we learn – and so should teach – from concrete to abstract.

Regrettably, even A-level exam essays are not assessed with the SOLO taxonomy. Instead, students get marks if certain points are made, so even if their overall argument is confused or even self-contradictory, they may get top marks or very nearly top marks if they mention the crucial points. This is because SOLO measures *quality* while conventional marking schemes measure *quantity* (marks for 'points'). In other words, students can get an A grade with just a multistructural response as long as it is sufficiently detailed.

The SOLO taxonomy was developed from studying school-based assessment but is now very influential in higher education, where some departments use it to decide on the level of degree a student will be awarded.

The greatest value of SOLO is that it shows how our learning in a given topic area *develops*. When we learn a new topic we start near the bottom of the taxonomy (however bright we are), and as our learning improves we climb the taxonomy, adding detail, but also relations.

The most complete description of SOLO can be found in Biggs and Collis's seminal work *Evaluating the Quality of Learning* (1982).

In the diagram (shown on p. 22) I have tried to represent SOLO visually, and also to depict how the learning might be represented in the brain at different SOLO levels. The latter is highly diagrammatic. Though when you understand a relation between two constructs, this does involve a *physical* link between them in your brain.

A student's understanding may be at a higher SOLO level than the work they produce, due to poor writing skills or lack of effort, for example. But it is hard to imagine how a student's work could be at a higher SOLO level than how they represent it in their brain! If it is, suspect copying!

The main source for this chapter is the biggest review of research on learning ever undertaken: Bransford et al. (2000). This comes down heavily in favour of a deep learning approach, which I believe is best explained by Biggs's SOLO taxonomy.

How experts structure their understanding

Biggs's ideas were confirmed in a vivid and persuasive manner when researchers in the USA discovered how experts differed from novices in their learning. These researchers, who appear not to have been familiar with SOLO, found that experts don't just know more, they structure their understanding around principles rather than around topics (Bransford, 2000). This is exactly the difference between extended abstract and relational learning in the SOLO taxonomy. (Recall that moving from relational to extended abstract takes a great deal of time and effort on the part of the learner.)

The research was not without some false starts and surprises, however. It was well known for example that a chess master could look at a chessboard in the middle

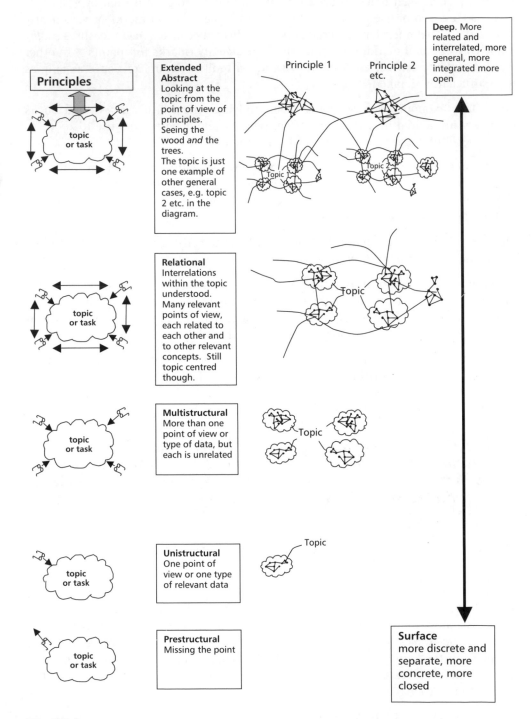

Principles

Extended Abstract
Looking at the topic from the point of view of principles.
Seeing the wood *and* the trees.
The topic is just one example of other general cases, e.g. topic 2 etc. in the diagram.

Principle 1   Principle 2 etc.

Deep. More related and interrelated, more general, more integrated more open

topic or task

Topic 1   Topic 2

Relational
Interrelations within the topic understood. Many relevant points of view, each related to each other and to other relevant concepts. Still topic centred though.

topic or task

Topic

Multistructural
More than one point of view or type of data, but each is unrelated

topic or task

Topic

Unistructural
One point of view or one type of relevant data

topic or task

Topic

Prestructural
Missing the point

topic or task

Surface
more discrete and separate, more concrete, more closed

The SOLO taxonomy.

of someone else's game for five seconds, and then recall the positions of the pieces on the board four times better than a non-player, and twice as well as a good player. Was the exceptional ability of the chess master due to their exceptional memory? Someone thought to test this by showing a chess master a chessboard with pieces arranged in a meaningless way that could never occur in a real game. The performance of the master slumped to that of the non-player. Also, chess masters are no better at remembering shopping lists or other non-chess details than the rest of us. What was going on?

The expert chess players were not seeing the pieces individually; they were recognising relations and *patterns*. They were noticing clusters of pieces with certain relative positions that they had seen many times before: 'White is deploying the Slav defence but with an unusual use of his bishop . . .' (The chess players would not need such a running commentary; they would be observing and thinking in mentalese, which is much faster than language.)

Chunking

When we see something enough times, even if it is complicated like a pattern of chess pieces, we begin to recognise this 'pattern', and it gets established in our long-term memory. When we see the pattern again we recognise it (re-cognise means 'think it again'). We might even give the pattern a name – the 'Rosberg defence'– though this is not necessary for recognition. (I recognise the pattern of roads in a nearby town that I have often visited, but I can't remember the road names.)

From then on we don't need to remember *all the individual pieces*, just the *pattern*. This is called 'chunking', because individual bits of information are put together into one chunk or pattern, and remembered like this. Recalling the pattern enables us, should we need it, to go to permanent memory, and 'look up' the constituents of this pattern.

The only way of chunking details into patterns in permanent memory is to gain sufficient *familiarity* with the individual pieces of information through *repetition*. Telling is not enough. Experiencing the pattern once or twice is not enough either. One long experience with a pattern is nowhere near as effective as the same total time arranged in many short exposures. Memory is strengthened by repetition rather than total time.

A great deal of chunking is done without conscious effort, but it clearly helps if you *concentrate* on the pattern, for example *reason* with it, so that you notice its constituent parts and their relations, and become familiar enough with it for it to go through the automatic unconscious process of being lodged in permanent memory.

If patterns are complicated or not easily noticeable then it helps if someone *points the pattern out to you*, and points out other occurrences of this pattern in the past, and when you might come across it again in the future: 'We get this pattern whenever . . .' This pointing out of patterns is sometimes called *mediation*. For example, a chess teacher might say to a learner: 'Notice how she evaded your attack, it's a classic defence, very useful if you can protect your queen.'

Chunking has immense relevance to learning and teaching. We will draw some principles from it soon, but first let's look at some other studies of experts.

Principles first

Physics experts and novices were given questions to sort (Bransford *et al.*, 2000). The novices sorted them by surface features; for example, they put together all the questions that involved an object on an inclined plane. The experts grouped the problems according to the subject *principle* that would be used to solve it: conservation of momentum, or Newton's laws, and so on. The experts were at the extended abstract level of SOLO, while the students were not. This is also a major difference between expert and experienced teachers, as we will see in Chapter 22.

Expertise is not just knowing more. Experts structure or organise their knowledge around deep subject principles, and understand the conditions when these principles apply. Their memory is indexed so that relevant knowledge can be retrieved. When solving a problem they look to see what conditions apply, and so retrieve all the information that is relevant to that task. They don't need to search the whole of their permanent memory. That is, they can transfer their knowledge, which makes it fully 'functional'.

Bransford's review shows that textbooks cover such subject principles, but often leave out the vital knowledge of *when* these principles are useful. The same is true of much teaching. See 'question typing' in Chapter 11 for a great method to teach students when to use what principle.

Sometimes the drive to 'deliver' the syllabus content means that important principles and methods are left out entirely. In another study quoted in Bransford's review, a group of history experts were given the same task as a group of gifted high school students. However, the task was related to knowledge that the high school students had been studying (American history), but the history experts specialised in Asian and medieval history so the task lay well outside their fields of expertise.

As one might expect, the high school students did much better than the history experts at a test on the area of American history that was the background to the task. The experts knew only one-third of the answers for the test and were outscored by the high school students. However, the task involved making sense of historical documents, and the experts excelled at this, approaching it in a dramatically different way from the students. The students made snap decisions without qualification, and often got things wrong.

The experts did much better, despite much less background knowledge. They examined the documents minutely, noticed contradictory claims, realised no single document could tell the whole story, considered alternative hypotheses, tested these, sorted out a reasoned interpretation, and then made their judgement on the task

. . . high school students did much better . . .

given. In short, the experts understood the methods of enquiry or 'epistemology' of their subject – the most general of all history principles.

Every subject has its epistemology or theory of knowledge and enquiry, and John Hattie has found that a crucial distinction between the very best teachers and average teachers with the same experience is that the best teachers teach these 'modes of enquiry' principles very deliberately and carefully, because they are so important and generally applicable. Bransford gives an example of a history teacher who put up a poster early on in their course entitled 'Rules for determining historical significance'. The poster was referred to throughout the course, and as more was learned about historical significance it was adapted and improved. The abstract principle was learned by seeing many concrete applications.

> *Could you itemise general principles in your subject, and create a poster for them, and add to this through the teaching year in the same way?*

Crucially if learning is structured around principles this enables the learner to transfer their learning to entirely new contexts. This was also illustrated earlier when 'Jo' learned that division is a principle related to 'cutting up' and 'sharing out'. The more general a principle the more widely it can be applied. So the organisation of the knowledge is at least as important as the knowledge itself. An encyclopaedia with no index and all the pages in the wrong order would be nearly useless.

Feedback

Students' constructs have errors and omissions and must be improved. This requires feedback to the learner and to the teacher so that both can improve the constructs. Dialogue is an excellent way to do this. Have a look at the diagram on the teaching and learning process in Chapter 8 (page 84).

Structuring takes time

I showed in *Teaching Today* that even very appropriate teacher talk can deliver material at least 20 times faster than it can be learned. If content is delivered too fast the working memory and short-term memory soon get swamped. Key points, relations and subject principles get obscured by the detail. Students need time to familiarise themselves with the new content.

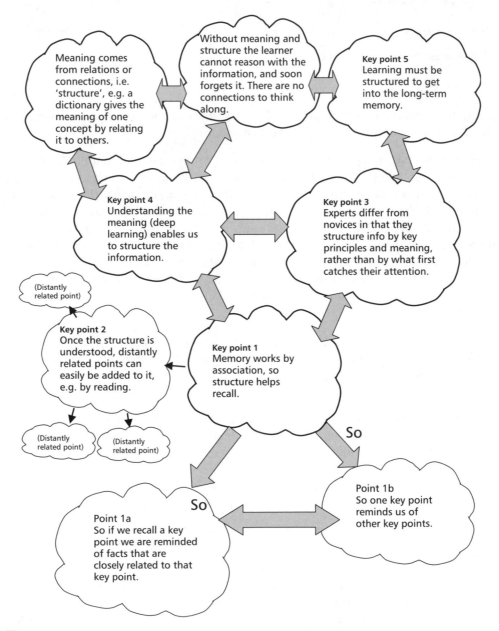

The importance of structure to understanding.

Reasoning tasks are a good way of creating this familiarity as the learner will h to concentrate and create constructs (understandings of concepts) and relatio links between them. As the learner gets familiar with material they 'chunk' bits of it together, thereby saving space in the working memory. This chunked material takes less space in the working memory, which in turn creates the space in working memory to allow the learner to create relational links between constructs. Sense making takes time.

But if time is allowed for reasoning tasks, there is less time to deliver the details. The best strategy to overcome this problem is to cut the content to the bare bones, and teach this skeleton for deep understanding by setting challenging reasoning tasks. Then add the detail to this skeleton later by reading homework or assignments. Many teachers know far more than they can hope to explain in the time they are allowed. Even if they could explain it all, students would lose the key points in the detail unless reasoning tasks were set.

This strategy is explained more fully in Chapter 18 under 'Myth 1', and in Chapter 21 under 'Help! There's too much content to teach skills as well'.

Which teaching methods are most constructivist?

This chapter has reviewed the 'qualitative' research on learning which tries to answer the questions 'What is learning?', 'Why does it happen?', and 'How can we teach for high-quality learning?' We have seen that learners don't just *remember* what we tell them, but must make their own *sense* of what they are learning, and *relate* it to what they already know.

With the theoretical account of learning outlined in this chapter still ringing in our ears, let's return to planet earth and ask ourselves how we could create deep learning in a real classroom on a wet Wednesday in Wigan. We need to use 'constructivist' teaching methods that:

- *Require the learner to make a construct* (not just enable this if they want to). If students are required to explain their understanding then even the 'Roberts' of this world must make their own sense of the topic.
- *Require reasoning not just reproduction.* Students can reproduce material they don't fully understand, but reasoning requires the learner to make sense.
- *Give the student thinking time.* It takes time to reason and to create meanings.
- *Give the student feedback* on their understanding (construct). Students will make errors when they form constructs and these must be discovered and corrected, preferably by the student themselves. Dialogue with other students can do this well.
- *Ensure teacher feedback* on student understanding. If the teacher knows a student or a class haven't 'got it' then they can fix this.
- *Have a high participation rate.* We want teaching methods that do not allow students to become 'passengers' leaving others to do the work.
- *Are fun.* Fun teaching methods create engagement and so help deep learning.

Score the following teaching methods on the above criteria as 'good' or 'poor'.

'Present' methods

These involve explaining new information and demonstrating new skills, etc.

1 *Teacher talk/lecture.* The teacher gives a verbal input, explaining and describing, etc., perhaps with OHP or board to assist.
2 *Reading.* Students read appropriate texts.
3 *Students watch a video or film.* This simply involves watching the video or film; no other activity is set.
4 *Students look at a website.*
5 *Teacher demonstration.* The teacher shows students how to do something. This could be a practical or an intellectual procedure. It could also be showing students how to do something on the board/OHP, for example a teacher showing students how to punctuate a sentence or solve a mathematical problem.

'Apply' methods

6 *Buzz group.* Students work in a small group for a few minutes to answer a question or complete a task. The teacher asks the group for its answer.
7 *Students create a leaflet, poster or handout.* Students are given a 'design brief' such as 'Design a leaflet/poster summarising the main means of ensuring effective dental care', and work alone or in pairs to create this using their own words.
8 *Experiment/practical 'recipe style'.* Students are given a task to do along with the materials needed, and are also given a detailed description of how to do the task.
9 *Experiment/practical 'discovery style'.* Students are given a task to do but not told how to do it. Students plan a method, then check this with the teacher before starting. Students who cannot work out how to do it are given a 'recipe' style help sheet or helped in some other way.
10 *Pair checking.* Students check each other's work. For example, they check each other's calculations, punctuation, etc., after this work has been done individually.
11 *Explaining tasks.* Students explain the key points of a lesson to each other at the end of that lesson. *Maths/science:* Students study worked examples and then explain the 'how' and the 'why' of the method to each other. In both cases the teacher then gives model explanations.
12 *Case studies.* Students are given a case study with graded questions. For example, PSHE students are given scenarios involving teenage pregnancy and asked to describe the practical or the emotional ramifications. Both reproduction and reasoning questions are included.

You can download a card-sorting game based on this exercise from www.geoffpetty.com. It is called 'teaching methods game'.

If you evaluate the above teaching methods in terms of how constructivist they are, those in the 'present' category are weak. We will see ways of fixing this in Chapter 17.

Misconceptions of the deep and surface approach

Let me point out a few common misconceptions that you might create while conceptualising your own version of Biggs's ideas. 'Surface' and 'deep' are characteristics of the approaches that students make, not characteristics of the students themselves. The same student might adopt a deep approach while learning fly fishing and a surface approach when learning mathematics, or vice versa. If we teach well, we can virtually require all our learners to adopt a relatively deep and then deepening conceptualisation of what we are teaching. Students often adopt both approaches, making their choice depending on the assessment and their teacher's requirements. A small proportion of students seem only to adopt a surface approach (Gibbs, 1992).

Another misconception is that because constructivism requires students to make their own meaning, we mustn't tell them anything. Many criticisms of constructivism are based on this misconception. If Sir Isaac Newton took many years to work out his laws of motion, 'physics 3' won't manage it on Friday afternoon without considerable guidance!

The deep-surface approach is widely accepted, but not adopted

Bransford's review, and Frank Coffield's review of learning styles (see below), both stress the vital importance of deep learning. The idea is as close as you can get to a consensus in education. Yet Gibbs (1992) summarises research showing a shockingly surface approach:

- High school pupils have been found to progressively *abandon* a deep approach over the four years of their studies!
- Students who pass courses have been shown to have little idea about basic concepts.
- Surface learning produces marginally higher scores on tests of factual recall immediately after studying. However, surface learners forget quickly, and as little as a week later deep learners score *higher* even in tests of factual recall. They can show little forgetting even over 11 years.
- Coursework grades are a better predictor of long-term recall than exam grades.

- However, the good news is that some courses have been shown to develop a deep-learning approach even if students arrive with a surface-learning habit. This is done by learner activity on intrinsically interesting tasks, by student interaction, and by building new learning onto old.

The nature of knowledge

Most students think that knowledge is just the way things are. They need to know instead that knowledge is a personal meaning that attempts to *represent* the way things are, that a topic, and a piece of knowledge about that topic, can both be seen from different perspectives. That knowledge is improvable, and like anything else we make, can be evaluated.

Students also need to know how knowledge is created in your subject, the methods of enquiry that are used, and how ideas, theories and principles are tested and improved. They need to know that science, experts, religious and other authorities all create their own meanings and that history shows they have all made mistakes. This is called the 'epistemology' of your subject, and theorists like Hattie and Carl Bereiter put heavy emphasis upon its importance for learners. In Chapter 22 we find that the very best teachers also put emphasis on epistemology, though it is rarely on the syllabus as such.

I will publish more on this on my website as it is crucial to thinking skills. You can download Bereiter's 'Beyond Bloom's Taxonomy' from www.ikit.org/people/bereiter. html.

Learning styles

It is tempting to believe that people have different styles of learning and thinking, and many learning style and cognitive style theories have been proposed to try to capture these. Professor Frank Coffield and others conducted a very extensive and rigorous review of over 70 such theories (Coffield *et al.*, 2004a and 2004b). They used statistical methods such as 'factor analysis' to see whether any of the models corresponded to reality, and they tested the validity of learning-style questionnaires to see if they really measured what they claimed. They found remarkably little evidence for, and a great deal of evidence against, all but a handful of the theories they tested. Popular systems that fell down at these hurdles were Honey and Mumford, Dunn and Dunn, and VAK (visual, auditory and kinaesthetic).

The learning style systems for which Coffield *did* find good evidence all considered a person's cognitive or learning style as adaptable to the *context*, and to be at least partly learned and modifiable. Those theories that assumed style to be innate, god given and fixed all failed his tests. Consequently Coffield's advice is:

- Don't type students and then match learning strategies to their styles; instead, use methods from *all* styles for everyone. This is called 'whole brain' learning.
- Encourage learners to use unfamiliar styles, even if they don't like them at first, and teach them how to use these.

Left brain, right brain

Coffield's report rated very highly the theory of 'surface' and 'deep' approaches to study, which is the main focus of this chapter. He also rated highly two developments of the 'left brain/right brain' idea. One was Herrmann's whole-brain model; have a quick look at the diagram on page 32 to get the general idea.

The box below shows the general idea of 'left-brain' and 'right-brain' approaches; the diagram shows Herrmann's development of this. The physiology of the brain was thought to explain 'left' and 'right' styles, but 'left brain' functions have been found in the right brain and vice versa, so the left and right functions are now thought of as metaphors for different thinking styles and functions.

LEFT-BRAIN LEARNERS (verbal sequential, or serialist learners)

You have a preference for learning in a sequential style, doing things logically step by step. You like to be organised and ordered in your approach, and like to break things down into categories and to consider these separately. You are good at deductive thinking in terms of cause and effect. You like to do 'one thing at a time'. You like attending to detail.

Serialist strategy (left-brain students tend to adopt this approach)
• a step-by-step approach doing things 'in order'
• a narrow focus dealing with parts of the whole in isolation
• working from the parts to the whole in small steps
• likes rules and structure and is logical rather than intuitive
• uses facts rather than their own experience

RIGHT-BRAIN LEARNERS (visual or holistic learners)

You like to see things in the round, and consider the whole. You focus on similarities, patterns, and connections with former learning. You like to get a 'feel' for the topic, and see how it all fits together. You prefer to follow your intuition rather than work things out carefully. You can use lateral thinking. You are flexible, and like to use your imagination and be creative.

Holist strategy (right-brain approach)
• a broad, global approach
• idiosyncratic, personalised and intuitive
• likes to jump in anywhere
• impatient with rules, structures and details
• likes anecdotes, illustration and analogy that show the whole in context

---

Imagine a serialist and a holist were each making a bedside table from an Ikea flat-pack. How would they proceed?

Herrmann's 'whole brain' model

Theorist – the rational self
(males often prefer this)

Likes: Logical, rational, and mathematical activities *(as opposed to:* emotional, spiritual, musical, artistic, reading, arts and crafts, introvert, or feelings activities)

Learns by:
Acquiring and quantifying facts
Applying analysis and logic
Thinking through ideas
Building cases
Forming theories

Learners respond to:
Formalised lecture
Content which includes data
Financial/technical case discussions
Textbooks and bibliographies
Programmed learning
Behaviour modification

Innovators – the experimental self

Likes: Innovating, conceptualising, creating, imaginative, original, artistic activities *(as opposed to:* controlled, conservative activities)

Learns by:
Taking initiative
Exploring hidden possibilities
Relying on intuition
Self-discovery
Constructing concepts
Synthesising content

Learners respond to:
Spontaneity
Free flow
Experiential opportunities
Experimentation and exploration
Playfulness
Future-orientated case discussions
Creating visual displays
Individuality
Aesthetics
Being involved

Organisers – the safe-keeping self

Likes: Order, planning, administration, organisation, reliability, detail, low level of uncertainty *(as opposed to:* holistic thinking, conceptualising, synthesis, creating or innovating)

Learns by:
Organising and structuring content
Sequencing content
Evaluating and testing theories
Acquiring skills through practice
Implementing course content

Learners respond to:
Thorough planning
Sequential order
Organisational and administrative case discussions
Textbooks
Behaviour modification
Programmed learning
Structure
Lectures

Humanitarians – the feeling self
(females often prefer this)

Likes: Interpersonal, verbal, people-orientated, emotional and musical activities. *(as opposed to:* analytical technical, logical, mathematical activities)

Learns by:
Listening and sharing ideas
Integrating experiences with self
Moving and feeling
Harmonizing with the content
Emotional involvement

Learners respond to:
Experiential opportunities
Sensory movement
Music
People-orientated case discussions
Group discussion
Group interaction such as jigsaw
Empathy and role play
Reflection

Herrmann's 'whole brain' model: each person likes two styles, but can use them all.

Herrmann developed this model in 1982 for use with adults in business; over one million profiles have been created using a questionnaire called the Herrmann Brain Dominance Instrument (HBDI). It is assumed that the model works outside of business, and this seems very likely.

He identifies four learning styles related to right-brain and left-brain styles, and each person is dominant in any *two* of these.

The styles are seen as *complementary* ways to understand a topic, rather than as *alternative* approaches that the learner can choose from. So teachers should try to help students to work effectively in all styles, even if this requires students to move beyond their 'comfort zones'. Teachers may also help students to use each style effectively by explaining and discussing effective strategies in each style. We should aim for 'whole-brain learning': using teaching methods from all styles for each learning objective.

The work of Herrmann (and Apter, also reviewed positively by Coffield, 2004b) shows that learners greatly enjoy moving between opposite styles, even if they are initially resistant to this. Working with opposites helps learners to become more creative, and to see their work as more varied and interesting. Herrmann positively encourages change and growth, by getting students to work on their weak styles. He tells us not to stereotype learners but to encourage everyone to use all styles.

Who has what style?

Everybody has a preference for two out of the four Herrmann styles:

- Sixty-two per cent of people are 'harmonious' with preferences for *either* the two 'left' quadrants (theorist organisers) *or* the two 'right' quadrants (humanitarian innovators).
- Thirty-one per cent of us have a preference for either the 'upper' quadrants (theorist innovators) or the two 'lower' quadrants (organiser-humanitarians).
- Only 7 per cent of us prefer styles on the diagonal or 'conflicting' quadrants of the brain (theorist humanitarians or innovator organisers).

Herrmann found that perhaps as many as 75 per cent of theorists are male, and 75 per cent of humanitarians are female. However, this preference may be learned, or simply a reflection of the learner's own cultural assumptions being expressed in the questionnaire. No ethnic differences were found between Black, Hispanic, Native American, Asian or White learners. The HBDI questionnaire can be downloaded from www.HBDI.com, but it costs to have it scored. A post-16 version of the questionnaire is in production.

Allinson and Hayes' learning-style system

This is closely related to Herrmann's system, and it was also positively reviewed in Coffield (1992b). There are just two styles:

Intuition: This is a right-brain approach, making immediate judgements based on feeling and the adoption of a global perspective

Analysis. This is a left-brain approach, making judgements based on mental reasoning and a focus on detail.

Like Herrmann, Alinson and Hayes believe that cognitive style is shaped by culture, altered by experience, and overridden for particular purposes. They worked with adults in business, and found some startling results.

Effectiveness in organisations:

- Entrepreneurs were strongly 'intuitive'.
- Senior managers were mainly 'intuitive'.
- Workers in subordinate positions in organisations tended to have an 'analytical' style.

Critical thinking and academic success:

- 'Intuitive' students were found to be better at critical thinking.
- 'Analytical' students were found to get better degree results.

So we have an educational system that penalises people who are good at critical thinking and business, the majority of whom are women! Some of us are amazed.

It is thought that 'intuition' is the capacity to consider a number of factors simultaneously and to use experience to make a judgement. 'Analytics' are likely to oversimplify and just consider a few factors at once, or in extreme cases, only one. The use of 'spectacles' (see Chapter 24) may well help 'analytics'.

It is easy to see that Alinson and Hayes' system is like a simplification of Herrmann's, but research evidence and factor analysis show that Herrmann's model is strongest.

How should teachers use learning styles?

Herrmann's 'whole-brain learning' exploits all the strengths and addresses important weaknesses in all your learners. It also helps to ensure enjoyment, variety and high-quality learning. It should be a key factor in the design of teaching. Consider it with special care in the teaching of challenging concepts and topics.

Case study: whole-brain mathematics

A mathematics teacher is planning a lesson on percentages. Her students have studied this in earlier years with limited success. Her natural approach is to explain the theory logically and in a careful sequence, and for students to work alone on problems. This is an 'analytic organiser' or 'left-brain' approach. To make her teaching 'whole brain' she adds some 'right-brain' or 'innovator-humanitarian' activities to her lesson.

- She gives each student a different percentage calculation. She asks them to represent the calculation visually using a pie chart, a 10 × 10 chessboard-like pattern that she provides, or preferably in some other way (innovator). Each

---

Are you a whole-brain teacher?

Have a look at the diagram of Herrmann's 'whole brain' model a few pages earlier. Look at the methods suitable for each style and decide how often you use those methods, or other methods appropriate for each style. In the box at the bottom right-hand corner of each style, write the percentage of the time you use methods appropriate for that style. Ideally every lesson should score 25 per cent for each of the four styles, but this would be most unusual! Now look at the styles you satisfy least. Can you make more use of the methods for this style? In the next chapter we will isolate some highly effective teaching methods compared to conventional teaching. Most are right brain, suggesting that conventional teaching is rather left brain.

---

student is then asked to explain his or her own calculation with the help of their diagram to others in his or her group (humanitarian).

- She asks students in groups to make up percentage sums that relate to the real world (innovator). These are then passed on to another group to solve. The original group then marks their attempt (humanitarian).
- She uses a 'peer assessment in groups' activity (humanitarian) (see Chapter 19).

The activities turn out to be very popular and effective with her students, and she displays the diagrams that students think most useful on the wall.

See also www.berkshiremathematics.com/marhesh.asp.

Case study in English

Andy is preparing a lesson on a short story. His natural style, which he does well, is to get students to work in groups to empathise with characters and use their intuition and imagination, and to synthesise the main themes and meanings in the story in whole-class discussion. This is an 'innovator-humanitarian' approach. He adds a 'theorist-organiser' activity to make his lesson 'whole brain'.

He provides each student with one of four short 'hypotheses' or interpretations of the story, which claim to explain the meaning of the story, or the nature of one of the characters. He asks students to work alone, and to use the text to confirm or deny their hypotheses. Students with the same hypothesis then work together to develop their argument. They are then asked to highlight the evidence in the text that they used to test their hypothesis. They explain this to the class.

He finds the activity to be remarkably productive, and he uses it to demonstrate that there can be more than one interpretation of a story, and to stress the importance of quoting text to support an argument. He finds that students enjoy the task much more than he expected, and that some students in the group shine for the first time.

Some right-brain teaching strategies

These help *all* students as everyone has a 'right brain'!

Methods that show the holistic structure and key points

- 'Advance organisers' or even better 'graphic organisers'. See Chapters 10 and 16.
- Get students to state meaning in their own words by writing summaries, reviews, overviews, etc. See Chapter 6.
- Case studies, demonstrations, anecdotes, etc., which show 'the whole' in context.
- Planning writing or an argument with thinking frames, writing frames or graphic organisers.

Visual methods

- Creating a visual representation, especially a graphic organiser such as a flow diagram. Designing posters, leaflets, handouts, pictures, images, graphs, charts, etc. Displaying these on the classroom wall.
- 'Same and different' analysis, for example with overlapping Venn diagrams. See Chapter 10.
- Visual essay planning; see Chapter 10.
- Creating a website, computer or interactive whiteboard presentation, exhibition, etc.

Emotional, metaphorical and imaginative methods

- Creating and/or exploring metaphors, analogies, similes, symbolic representations, etc.
- Imagining and emphathising: 'What would it have been like to be a monk in an Abbey?' or 'Imagine you are a water molecule in a heated saucepan . . .'
- Creating a short role-play or drama.
- Writing a story that illustrates a teaching point, or expresses the learner's personal emotional reaction.

Direct experience

- Doing things physically, hands on: examining or manipulating, real objects and primary sources, etc.
- Research, explorations, experiments finding out for oneself.
- Trips, visits, visitors, 'shadowing' etc.
- Role-play and simulations.

Some left-brain teaching strategies

- Creating, or being given hypotheses or theories, and then testing them with evidence.
- Problem solving, decision making, etc. (though this is often whole-brain).
- Analysing the detail and giving reasons, e.g. case studies, worksheets, highlighting text, teaching without talking methods. See Chapters 24 and 21.
- Evaluating by using evidence and creating detailed arguments. See Chapter 24.

Multiple modes of representation

As we have seen, Biggs's SOLO taxonomy shows that both weak and very effective learners learn every new topic from concrete to abstract. I believe that combining this idea with Coffield's finding that we should explain and experience new topics in both 'left' and 'right' brain ways leads to a specific form of 'multiple representation'. Look at the diagram on the next page.

If a concept or topic is hard for students it helps them to see a number of concrete examples of it and to reason with this. The more varied the examples the better. The learner then begins to express the new learning in terms of their *existing learning and experience* and/or *new concrete experience* (such as a game or a teacher demonstration they have observed).

It helps the learner to express these ideas, or to hear them expressed in terms of 'everyday' language: 'voltage is the push on the electrons' rather than 'electromotive force produces a potential gradient'. Visual representations both literal and diagrammatic can help greatly here. This allows the ideas to be represented in both a right- and a left-brain way.

If the learning goes well, then the learner is eventually able to understand abstract and symbolic representations of this new learning.

The Standards Unit ICT project

This project involved discovering the topics that students found most problematical, and one of these was databases and relational databases. In order to teach these difficult concepts the team of teachers devised a simulation. Students were asked to pretend they ran a sandwich shop and had to take orders on paper, which would eventually be computerised. They found, for example, that when one person ordered more than one sandwich they had to write the address more than once, which was clearly redundant. This led them to understand what a database was, how it could be used, and some of the difficulties in storing data.

The project is still in its pilot stage but initial feedback shows that students have found the simulation very helpful in learning the abstract concepts involved, such as data redundancy.

How could you make use of multiple representations to teach a difficult concept in your subject?

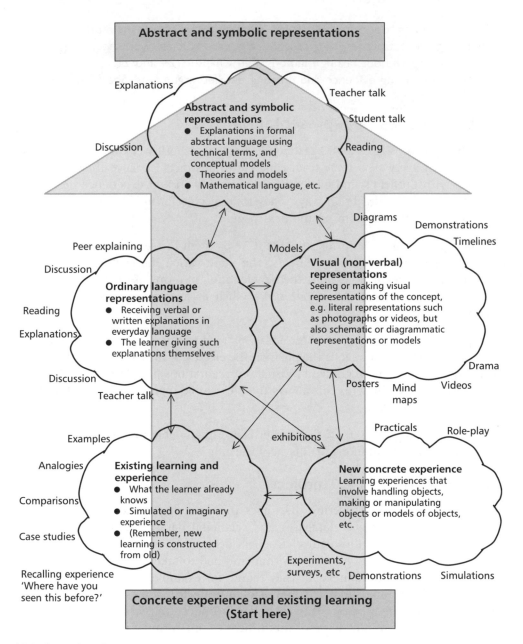

Multiple modes of representation.

Conclusion

The research summaries of qualitative descriptions of the learning process such as Bransford *et al.* (2000) suggest some highly interrelated general principles: high-quality learning requires:

- *Structure.* Students must be aware of the purpose, key points and key principles in what they are learning. Expert and high SOLO learning is structured like this; see page 22. Also we saw, in the simple 'Jo example' of learning division, that it made learning transferable and functional. We need to establish structure and meaning first, *then* add the detail.
- *Deep understanding.* Students must make their own meaning and understanding, not just try to remember. This requires seeing relations between constructs and building new learning on old. We learn from known to unknown and from concrete to abstract.
- *Reasoning*, not just reproduction, requires learners to connect new concepts to what they already know, and so create meaning. We need to set 'challenging goals'.
- *Feedback.* Students' constructs have errors and omissions and must be improved. This requires feedback to the learner and to the teacher so that both can improve the constructs. Dialogue is an excellent way to do this.
- *Time and repetition.* Students need familiarity with material to 'chunk' it into meaningful bits. Six encounters at least. Students do not simply 'write' concepts and logical relations onto their hard disk. Much learning is intuitive and below consciousness. To assist this, students need to see examples and non-examples of concepts and principles in many different contexts in order to 'get' them.
- *Multiple perspectives and multiple representations.* Students need right- and left-brain representations, that is 'whole-brain learning', to aid understanding. SOLO shows that students need to look at material in more than one way, and more than once.

References and further reading

Bereiter, C. and Scardamalia, M. (1998) 'Beyond Bloom's taxonomy: rethinking knowledge for the knowledge age', in A. Hargreaves, A. Lieberman, M. Fullan and D. Hopkins (eds), *International Handbook of Educational Change* (pp. 675–92). Dordrecht: Kluwer. Download from: ikit.org/people/bereiter.html.

Biggs, J. (2003) *Teaching for Quality Learning at University*, Maidenhead: Open University Press/McGraw Hill.

Biggs J. and Collis, K. (1982) *Evaluating the Quality of Learning*, New York: Academic Press.

Bransford, J. D. *et al.* (2000) *How People Learn: Brain, Mind, Experience and School*, Washington: National Research Council.

Coffield, F., Moseley, D., Hall, E. and Ecclestone K. (2004a) 'Learning styles and pedagogy in post-16 learning: a systematic and critical review' (LSRC reference). Download from: www.lsda.org.uk/research/reports.

Coffield, F. Moseley, D., Hall, E. and Ecclestone, K. (2004b) 'Should we be using learning styles? What research has to say to practice' (LSRC reference). Download from: www.lsda.org.uk/research/reports.

Dienes Z. P. (1960) *Building up Mathematics*, London: Hutchinson Educational.

Donovan, M.S. and Bransford, J. D. (2005) *How Students Learn: History, Mathematics, and Science in the Classroom*, Washington: National Research Council.

Gibbs, G. (1992) *Improving the Quality of Student Learning*, Bristol: Technical and Educational Services.

Herrmann, N. (whole-brain approach) See: www.leonardconsulting.com/Whole%20 Brain%20Learning2.htm.

Vygotsky, L. S. (1962) *Thought and Language*, Cambridge, Massachusetts: MIT Press.

3 Motivation

I will restrict myself here to looking at expectancy-value theory, and attribution theory in the form of Dweck's theory of motivation. I will also consider Maslow's theory of motivation, still the richest theory of motivation in my view, as this is so useful in itself, and relates directly and very usefully to expectancy-value theory. *Teaching Today* looks at other theories of motivation and deals with the topic in more detail.

The expectancy-value theory of motivation

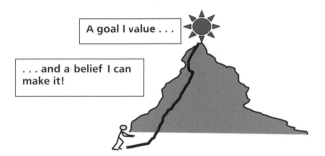

According to the 'expectancy-value theory' a learner's motivation is determined by how much they value the goal(s) you or they are setting, and whether they expect to succeed. The motivation is given by the following formula:

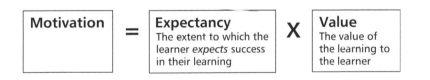

| Motivation | = | Expectancy
The extent to which the learner *expects* success in their learning | X | Value
The value of the learning to the learner |

Value and expectancy are said to multiply, not add (Feather, 1982). This means that if a student gives the course an 'expectancy' score of zero, then motivation is zero however large the 'value' score. Similarly, motivation is zero if the student scores 'value' as zero, however high their 'expectancy' score.

How would your students score value and expectations of success? Why not ask them?! Get them to score both value and expectation of success on a scale of zero to ten, ten being the highest score. You can then multiply to find their motivation score as a percentage. A motivation of 50 per cent is a fairly high motivation on this scale.

Let's look at how we might increase motivation according to this theory.

Do your students have a low value score?

Then sell the value of your lesson, your subject and your course to your learners.

Some learners come from families or cultures that do not value education. If no one in a learner's family got a job or some other advantage out of education then that family may not believe education improves their children's opportunities in life. We need to 'sell' the value of our courses to our students.

One way of doing this is to get students to calculate the monetary value of the course they are studying, in terms of the extra lifetime earnings it gives them. On p. 43 is a handout which describes an activity carried out during course induction to do just this.

Don't show students the following worked examples, or the answers. Let them work them out for themselves – this will have much more impact. Here is a worked example for your eyes only to give you the idea of the figures involved. It relates to a student who already has a level 1 qualification, and is about to do a level 2 qualification. This student gains the least, and all other calculations will give a *larger* gain. Here are the figures for the tasks given in the box earlier.

Task 1

a. £225 per week
b. £208 per week

Task 2

a. 225 − 208 = £17 (in a week)
b. 52 × 17 = £884 (in a year)
c. 40 × 884 = £35,360 (in 40 years)

So the gain in my lifetime earnings for doing a level 2 qualification is £35,360.

Task 3

I am in college 36 weeks on my level 2 qualification so the amount I am adding to my lifetime's earnings per week will be:

   £35,360 ÷ 36 = £982 per college week

It will be more if I go on and get a level 3 qualification of course.

The amount I am adding to my lifetime's earnings per college day is:

> Does this mean that every day I'm absent I lose £196?

   £982 ÷ 5 = £196

That makes it about £40 per lesson.

You're earning while you're learning!
How much is your qualification worth? Work out how much the qualification you are working towards will earn you over a lifetime.

The following table uses official government figures to show the average weekly earnings of people with qualifications at different 'levels'.

- **Level 1:** e.g. Foundation
- **Level 2:** e.g. GNVQ Intermediate, GCSEs, etc.
- **Level 3:** e.g. A level AVCE, National Diploma, etc.
- **Level 4:** Degree or equivalent
- **Level 5:** Postgraduate or professional qualifications

Earning and unemployment rates for people with different qualification levels

	None	Level 1	Level 2	Level 3	Level 4	Level 5	Average
Average weekly wage in pounds	190	208 (est.)	225	280	410	(not known)	(not known)
Unemployment rate (%)	12.2	8.8	9.2	6	4.3	3.6	7.5

From a DfEE leaflet created in the late 1990s called 'Learning pays: the value of learning and training to individuals'. Figures were researched by the National Advisory Council for Education and Training Targets

Task 1
Using the figures in the table, how much would you earn a week if:

a. you *did* get your qualification(s) at the end of your course?
b. you did *not* get the qualification(s)?

Task 2
If you got your qualifications, how much *extra* would you earn

a. in a week?
b. in a year of 52 weeks (assume you get paid when you are on holiday)?
c. in a lifetime of 40 years' working?

Task 3
Work out how much you are adding to your lifetime's earnings every day, and every week you attend college.

Other calculations

The increase in lifetime earnings per college week for some other students is given below:

> Level 1 qualification aim but no qualifications at present: £1040 per college week

> Level 3 student who already has level 2: £1589 per college week if both years are counted as 36 weeks

All figures are averages; some individuals will of course do much better. You could argue that as our society gets more technologically advanced, and as the market requires a more adaptable and more easily trained workforce, the gains in earnings for qualifications will increase markedly in the future. Not everyone values education, and encouraging students to work in their own long-term interests is an equal opportunities issue.

Other ways to get students to value your course

You can of course get students to value your course and your lessons in other ways, and in the long run these, being more short term, will be more motivating. You will think of others, but here are some ways to see a purpose in their learning:

- Set goals and targets that are meaningful and interesting.
- Persuade students of the importance and relevance of the topic you are teaching. This will often be obvious to you, but is it to them?
- Make the process of learning interesting and rewarding. This can be done by making use of Maslow's theory of motivation below.

Do your students give a low score for expectancy of 'success'?

Then make use of role models
Talk to students about students in past years who have gone on to be successful, or better still get these past students to come to the class and to talk to them. Stress that the prior achievement of these role models was not exceptional when they arrived.

Make sure that tasks allow students to gain early success
Make sure there is a mixture of reproduction and reasoning tasks for students. See Chapter 2.

Arrange for them to get an early qualification or certificate
Arrange for the students to gain an intermediary qualification very early on in the course. This could be a nationally accepted qualification like a first-aid certificate, or it could be a college certificate.

Looking back to the diagram on page 41 we have considered how to make learners value learning goals; now let's see how to foster the belief that this goal is achievable.

Dweck's theory of motivation: giving students a belief they can make it

Carol Dweck is Professor of Psychology at Columbia University. She is a leader in the field of student motivation. Over many decades she has developed a highly influential theory of student motivation building on the idea of 'attribution theory' – which focuses on the reasons we give for our failures and successes. We are more likely to provide effort if we believe it will make a difference. So if we attribute success to factors *in our control*, then we are more motivated, and more successful, especially in challenging situations. If we attribute success to factors outside our control, like our genes or luck, then we are less motivated, and less successful.

She divides students into two types, based on the *student's own theory* about their own ability.

Fixed IQ theorists
These students believe that their ability is fixed, probably at birth, and there is very little if anything they can do to improve it. They believe ability comes from talent rather than from the slow development of skills through learning. 'Its all in the genes'. Either you can do it with little effort, or you will never be able to do it, so you might as well give up in the face of difficulty. For example, 'I can't do maths', 'I'm useless at essays.'

Untapped potential theorists
These students believe that ability and success are due to learning, and learning requires time, effort, help and practice. So in the case of difficulty one must try harder, try another approach, or seek help, etc.

Fixed IQ theorists	15% are undecided	Untapped potential theorists
Ability comes from talent, 'it's in my genes'.		Ability comes from time and effort spent learning.
In the face of difficulty the student gives up, declines learning support, guesses, etc.		In the face of difficulty, the student tries harder, asks for help, etc.

About 15 per cent of students are in the middle; the rest are equally divided between the two theories. Amazingly there is no correlation between success at school and the theory the student holds. Differences in performance only show when the student is *challenged* or is *facing difficulty*, for example when they move from school to college, or probably from GCSE to A level. Then research has shown that the untapped potential theorists do very much better, as one might expect. The reasons for this are shown in the table on page 46 which defines the types in more detail.

FIXED IQ THEORIST

Beliefs

Intelligence and ability are **fixed.**

You can't change your basic ability however hard you try.

Ability is in your genes, as are gifts and talents. You are born with them.

(Nearly half of learners at *every level* of attainment have this belief.)

Goals – 'proving myself'

I try to 'look smart' by beating others, or succeeding with little effort.

If I succeed especially with little effort, this proves I am a high-ability person.

If I fail this proves I am a low-ability person (so failure is shameful).

I avoid situations that might make me look stupid or where I have to try hard.

Meaning of difficulties

Difficulties mean that you are not bright.

Setbacks even more so.

Response to difficulties . . .

Judgementalism: 'I'm no good at this'. Feeling of worthlessness and despair, etc.

Blaming: myself, or protecting my ego by blaming elsewhere.

Maladaptive learning strategies: I try guessing, copying, remembering what I don't understand, etc.

Distraction: I seek distractions to make myself feel better, for example ego-boosting distractions.

Depression: I have strong negative emotions and negative thoughts: 'I'll never get this right.'

If despite all this I *am* successful I underestimate how much I achieved and overestimate my errors.

. . . leads to the withdrawal of effort

Helpless response: I withdraw effort, and this leads to the failure I expected (so it's self-fulfilling).

Defensive withdrawal of effort: If I deliberately don't try, I can blame my failure on lack of effort (not lack of ability). 'I didn't pass because I didn't

UNTAPPED POTENTIAL THEORIST

Beliefs

Intelligence and ability can **grow.**

Ability is due to learning, and learning requires effort over time. If I haven't learned it yet, then I need to try harder for longer, seek help, take risks, or change my strategy, it certainly doesn't mean I'm stupid.

(Nearly half of learners at *every level* of attainment have this belief.)

Goals – 'improving myself'

I seek interesting challenges and an opportunity to learn.

I seek validation through my effort to learn, not giving up, taking risk, etc.

The knowledge and skills I gain are more important than the grades I achieve.

I enjoy putting my learning to good use.

Meaning of difficulties

Difficulties can be an enjoyable challenge and mean you are *really* learning.

Difficulties are a cue to think, and to try harder for longer, change strategy, get help, etc.

Response to difficulties . . .

Difficulties and mistakes are inevitable, and are a natural part of the learning process.

I have a 'no blame' policy – I just want to know how to do it better.

If you are not having difficulties, the task is too easy to really learn from, and may even be not worth doing.

I feel positive and have a hardy 'can do' mentality.

I think positive, task-centred thoughts, e.g. 'I need to find out more about . . .'

. . . leads to an increase of effort

Difficulties make me try harder for longer.

Responsiveness: the greater the difficulty, the greater my effort.

Difficulties mean I should consider changing my strategy. Maybe I should take a few risks and see what happens.

An active, thoughtful, problem-centred approach. I focus on the task, and or effort.

Attitude to help and support: I am happy to accept support if it is needed, but would like first to try by myself. I ask appropriately for help.

Note that the increase in effort occurs precisely when it is needed, and so it is productive and self-fulfilling.

Attitude to challenges
Challenges are an opportunity to learn.
I enjoy engaging fully with challenges.
I adopt meaningful strategies towards deep learning rather than seeking short term 'quick fixes'.

Performance
I learn well in almost all circumstances.

Mottos
When the going gets tough – the tough get going.
You are not a failure until you give up.
Think positively.
No gain without pain.
Work hard, and you'll get smart – so if you're smart, you'll work hard.
Why worry about looking stupid, if you can get smarter?
My future is not in my genes.
The brain is a muscle – the more you exercise it, the stronger it gets!

---

revise.' If despite this defensive withdrawal of effort I am successful, then this will prove that I am very bright! (So my ego is protected in both success and failure.)
The greater the difficulty, the less likely I am to try.
Learned helplessness: The repeated withdrawal of effort and subsequent failure teaches me that nothing I can do makes a difference, so I might as well give up. I learn I am helpless.
Attitude to help and support: I refuse support and don't like help because I believe I can't benefit from it, and I don't want to fail during this help.

Note that withdrawal of effort occurs precisely when effort is needed, and so it is counterproductive and self-fulfilling

Attitude to challenges
Challenges are a threat to my self-esteem.
I fear failure, so I want to stay within my 'comfort zone'.
If I fail this *proves* my low ability for ever (so give me something simple to do that protects me from this).

Performance
I do much better than you would think, especially if I am able – until I meet challenges.

Mottos
When the going gets tough – you must be stupid (so give up).
Either you're good at it or you're not.
If you are really good at something, you don't need to try.
If you have to try, you must be stupid.
Watch out for tasks that might humiliate you. If you are given one, don't try.
Don't risk trying hard. If you don't try you have a ready excuse for failure.

What is evidence-based teaching?

It *is* possible to move students from the fixed IQ theory to the untapped potential theory. We will see in Chapter 21 that teaching students to attribute success to factors within their control has a huge 'effect size' (large effect on achievement).

As well as teaching attribution directly, it can be taught more indirectly by showing students that it is the *strategies* that succeed, not their *ability*. This can be done with:

- Feedback methods (see Chapter 8), especially self, peer and spoof assessment. When students compare what they did with what they should have done they realise why marks were gained or lost, and that this is not to do with ability, but with doing it the right way.
- Reciprocal teaching (see Chapter 13).
- Learning loops (see Chapter 8).

Many teachers, myself included, thought that 'it's obvious' that learning is worth the effort and can produce improvement. But almost half of our students, at every level, do not share this view. Changing their minds is known to produce a huge effect on achievement.

Dweck's questionnaire

The following questionnaire, devised by Carol Dweck, can be used to type students as fixed IQ theorists or untapped potential theorists. The questions do look very similar, but the questionnaire has been fully validated as set out below. Students who score low should be considered to be at risk of withdrawing and failing on a course they find challenging.

	1 Strongly agree	2 Agree	3 Mostly Agree	4 Mostly disagree	5 Disagree	6 Strongly Disagree
1. You have a certain amount of intelligence, and you really can't do much to change it						
2. Your intelligence is something about you that you can't change very much						
3. You can learn new things, but you can't really change your basic intelligence						

Establishing an unfulfilled potential ethos

Here are some ways to increase the number of unfilled potential theorists amongst your students – which is a very productive task.

Stress that:

- intelligence and ability can be cultivated
- effort is required for learning
- effort grows connections in your brain which make you smarter
- the brain is like a muscle which strengthens with exercise and you need to 'work out' to get bright.

In addition:

- Don't attribute difficulty to fixed intelligence.
- Warn students about the defensive withdrawal of effort, stressing it is counter-productive.

How?

- Use induction activities to teach the unfulfilled potential theory.
- Use the Dweck questionnaire and mark fixed IQ theorists 'at risk'.
- Use course mottos, logos, posters, etc., on analogies for learning:

  - gym workout ('the brain is a muscle')
  - learning a musical instrument
  - learning as rock rolling
  - learning a computer game, getting stuck at a level, and then finding the way up a level by persistent trial and error. Skills come from practice.

- Get second-year students to teach the growth ethos to first-year students.

Give role models as evidence

- Some of the most creative people have average IQs.
- Some of the highest attainers have average IQs.
- Einstein did badly at school and at college. His teacher said in a report: 'You will never amount to very much.'
- Thomas Eddison was thrown out of school for being 'educationally subnormal'.
- Education has been shown to increase IQ.

Use self-assessment and peer assessment. These methods have been found to make huge differences to students 'attributions', and have doubled attainment in mathematics and related subjects.

Use feedback methods. The methods in Chapter 8 have been shown to be among the best ways to teach students that they can succeed; see Chapter 9 to find out why.

Making use of Maslow's hierarchy of needs

Abraham Maslow's idea is that we are motivated by just five needs, and as the lower needs are met they become less pressing and higher needs take their place. His *Motivation and Personality* is still the most commonly referenced book in

If the need is not met the person feels . . .	*Needs*	*If the need is met the person feels . . .*
• restless and bored, with a lack of zest for life • life is meaningless, boring and without purpose • a tendency to avoid growth and development • listless	**The Self-Actualisation Needs** To make actual what you are, potentially. Personal growth and development by following one's own passions and interests. Self-expression, creative action, need to search for identity, and meaning in life.	• a desire to grow and develop in the direction of their higher values • creative, positive and energetic • unselfish desire to make a useful contribution • curious, and open to new experiences • a desire to think for himself or herself • a growing sense of identity
• fearful of criticism • inferior, weak and helpless • fearful of failure, and of risks (e.g. fear of new situations or learning activities, etc.) • fearful, frustrated, or angry toward those who withhold respect, e.g. a teacher, school or college • envy and bitterness Persistent thwarting leads to neurotic compensation • e.g. chronic showing off; attention seeking; arrogance • or shyness and withdrawal	**The Esteem Needs** *Self-esteem:* desire for achievement, strength, and confidence. Adequacy: to be able to cope by oneself. *Respect:* desire for recognition, reputation, prestige, status and dignity.	• self-confident, content, • self-belief and self-respect • prepared to take risks and try something new, e.g. to learn • cooperative, generous and kindly • esteem needs become less and 'higher' needs take their place
• lonely, rejected, and rootless • strong conformity to group norms • dislike or hostility towards 'out-groups': racism, etc. Persistent thwarting leads to neurotic compensation • e.g. maladjustment and hostility . . . or withdrawal	**The Belongingness and Love Needs** The need to give and receive love and affection. To 'belong', to have roots.	• they can love themselves, and others • they can trust friends and loved ones, and give them freedom • these needs become less and 'higher' needs take their place
• anxiety, dread, • fight-and-flight behaviour	**The Safety Needs** Freedom from pain and injury, security, stability, etc.	• physical security • safety needs become less, and 'higher' needs take their plac
craving for food, water, etc.	**The Physiological Needs** Food, water, air, etc.	• no physiological craving • these needs die away and 'higher' needs take their place

Maslow said these needs are rather like vitamins in that:
• we can never be healthy without them
• a long term deficiency causes 'disease'
• there are no substitutes for them. That is, a child who is aggressive or attention seeking can only be 'cured' of this behaviour by getting their esteem and belonging needs met. Punishment can never produce a long term 'cure'.

Maslow's hierarchy of needs.

psychology. Below I give just a few ways in which these needs can be met; there are very many more. Maslow's theory predicts the basic idea behind this whole book: that students learn by challenging goals, by active learning, and by feedback on the extent to which their goals have been met. In particular, esteem needs suggest that we pay great attention to the audience for students' work; an audience of peers may motivate them more than you marking it.

Meeting self-actualisation needs

This is about the search for identity and a search for a meaning to one's life: through work; through making use of your own talents and abilities; through exploration of what interests you . . .

* Creative tasks
* Work towards personally set targets
* Curiosity: answering a puzzling or interesting question; exploring something that is interesting; solving a puzzle
* Fun
* Expressing personal values, beliefs, and priorities in discussion or in writing; evaluation; discussions and debates about issues
* Tasks that allow learners to express their own values, e.g. helping a peer, artistic or expressive work, collecting for charity
* Making choices to control your own development in the direction of your own values.

Esteem needs

Self-esteem

* Striving towards independence, adequacy: to be able to cope by oneself
* Satisfaction from finishing a good job on something you are interested in, especially creative tasks
* Becoming more capable in a direction the learner values, e.g. being able to service a car, or for someone with learning difficulties being able to cook themselves a meal.

Esteem of others

* Respect: a desire for dignity through reputation, prestige, and status
* Recognition of your successes by peers, teacher, college: telling the group your ideas; having your work displayed or used as a model
* Certificates, special jobs, and other symbols of respect.

Belongingness and love needs

* To give affection and regard to others; to help others
* To belong: to my team, class, group and college

- To get affection and recognition from others
- To be valued as a person, not just for what I do for others
- To be wanted as a person.

Don't underestimate the power of *symbols* that show that esteem needs and belongingness needs are being met. For example:

- My name being remembered and used positively
- A welcome when I come in the class
- My work on the classroom wall
- A star earned for effort on the classroom wall or on my work
- Teacher recognition in the form of competences signed off, comments on work, etc.

Summary of key principles on motivation

A goal I value: it allows me to self actualise.

Motivation	**=**	**Expectancy** The extent to which the learner *expects* success in their learning	**X**	**Value** The value of the learning to the learner

References and further reading

Dweck, C. S. (2000) *Self-Theories: Their Role in Motivation Personality and Development*, Philadelphia: Psychology Press.

Feather, N. (ed.) (1982) *Expectations and Actions*, Hillsdale, New Jersey: Erlbaum.

Maslow, A. H. (1970) *Motivation and Personality* (3rd edition), New York: Harper Collins.

Part 2 What methods work best?

Effect sizes: finding what works

Effect-size studies

How can teachers find out which teaching methods or learning activities work best? Effect-size studies are a brilliant source of evidence. They are a 'suck it and see' research method, based on the question: 'Never mind the theory – does it work in practice?'

The experimental approach is the same as that used to test medical treatments, and to test fertilisers. One group has the treatment you are testing, and another does not, but is otherwise identical. You then compare how the two groups do to see if the treatment has had an effect.

The studies are carried out by real teachers in real schools and colleges, and the best are rigorous 'randomised control group studies'.

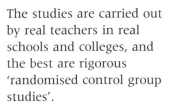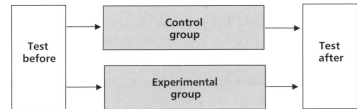

Hundreds, or even thousands, of students are divided between two groups:

'Control' group
This group is taught with conventional methods.

'Experimental' group
This group is taught for the same amount of time as the control group, and by the same teachers in the same way, except for one difference. The experimental group experiences a 'treatment', such as a teaching strategy that is the focus for the study. For example, the experimental group might be taught using 'mind maps' to summarise topics (see Chapter 10). While this happens the control group will be summarising the same topics using conventional means, such as a teacher summary.

The control and experimental groups are carefully composed to be identical in their mix of students' ability, social background, and so on. This is can be done by randomly assigning students to the two groups. If the groups are above a certain size, and this size can be determined statistically, then random assignment ensures that there will be just as many, say, dyslexic students in one group as there are in the other. So any differences between the groups are negligible. Another method of ensuring that the control and experimental groups are near identical is to pair students up with students of similar ability, ethnicity, gender, maths score, and any other factor thought important, and then to assign one of each pair to the control group and the other to the experimental group.

Imagine that an experimenter wants to test out the effectiveness of an instructional activity where students create their own mind maps to summarise topics and subtopics. The researcher finds a school or college and a group of teachers prepared to carry out the experiment. The researcher trains the teachers in mind-mapping techniques, and then assigns a large group of students to control and experimental groups.

The two groups are given a 'pre-test' to discover what they know about the topic they will be taught before they are taught it. They might know next to nothing of course! Then the control and experimental groups are taught this topic for the same length of time, by the same teachers, or by teachers of the same ability, using the same methods and resources and so on, except, of course, that the experimental group uses student-created mind maps to summarise topics and subtopics, while the control group uses a conventional method, for example teacher summaries. Only the experimental group experiences the 'treatment' of student mind mapping; the control group is just for comparison purposes.

Once the topic has been taught both groups are given another test on the topic called the 'post-test'. For each student, the difference between their pre-test and post-test scores is a measure of how much he or she has learned.

The test results of the two groups can be shown graphically as shown in the figure below.

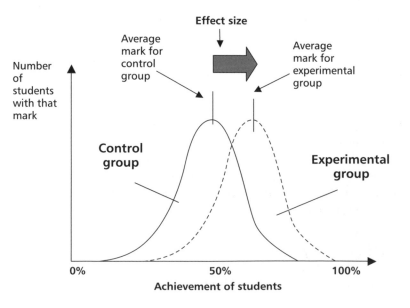

In the better studies (experiments) that get into the research reviews the group sizes are large. Many groups have over 100 students, so many classes are needed to form the control and the experimental groups. Consequently, if the researchers plot the number of students (N) that get a mark in a certain band (e.g. between 55% and 60%) they can create a graph like that shown. Many students get a middling mark for their group, and only a few in each group do very well, or very badly compared to the others in their group. This creates the 'bell-shaped' curve you can see in the figure.

Suppose this graph is the one we get for our mind-map experiment. You can see that the average mark for the control group is about 45%, but for the experimental group it is about 65%. If the experiment is well designed, then this improved achievement can only be attributed to mind mapping, as it is the only difference between the two groups.

So the difference between the average marks is a measure of the effectiveness of mind mapping during this experiment, called the 'effect size'.

It is a sad reflection on conventional teaching strategies that the experimental group nearly always does better than the control group. Custom and practice gets a very bad press from these studies!

Can we generalise from this experiment?

Now it is misleading to say that the experimental group has learned 20% more than the control group, even though this is true in this one case. If we did the experiment again with tests that were twice as hard, then students would get half the marks, and so the difference in the average marks would also be half as much, that is 10% instead of 20%. How is this improvement we call the 'effect size' to be expressed? Statisticians get over this problem of the test difficulty, and other problems, by expressing the effect size in units of 'standard deviation'.

Standard deviation is explained in any good statistics textbook, and can be shown to be a much fairer scale to compare the control and experimental groups. However, 'an effect size of 0.5 standard deviation' means very little to non-statisticians, so let's compare it to a scale we are very familiar with: GCSE grades, or A-level grades. The difference between two adjacent grades at GCSE or A level just happens to be about 0.5 standard deviation. If you improve by two grades this is 1.0 standard deviations. So:

Compared to conventional teaching:

- A teaching method with an effect size of 0.5 gives a one-grade leap.
- A teaching method with an effect size of 1.0 gives a two-grade leap.

In other words, suppose that I find that in my mind-map study that the effect size of mind maps is 1.0 standard deviation. Suppose also that in my study I grade the tests in the same way that GCSEs or GCE A levels are graded. Suppose I put one average student, Jason, in the control group, and he gets a C grade at the end of the study. Then, if I had put Jason in the experimental group instead he would have got two grades better: an A grade. Mind mapping alone has created this improvement, even though it might have only been one activity of many carried out during the teaching.

If you were Jason's parent, you would certainly want that method used, wouldn't you! Yet most teachers and most parents are not aware of the effect sizes of teaching methods.

What effect size is necessary to improve a pass rate from, say, 80% to 100%? This can be statistically estimated and the table below gives figures. Effect sizes only give a reliable indication here if the methods you adopt to improve pass rates continue to be effective throughout your course, and are effective on students of low attainment. See 'Effect sizes and ability' in Chapter 6, p. 72. The figures in the table also assume large student numbers, so creating the 'bell shaped' curve mentioned earlier. However approximate these figures, it is inspiring to see what may be possible.

Effect size	Percentile gain or % improvement	Example change in pass rate
0.25	10	from 90% to 100%
0.52	20	from 80% to 100%
0.84	30	from 70% to 100%
1.28	40	from 60% to 100%
1.65	45	from 55% to 100%

An effect size of 1.0 is clearly enormous! So is this the answer for teachers, to read the effect-size studies for the common teaching methods? Think back to Chapter 1 on evidence-based practice and you will see why not.

This mind-map study is not much use on its own. It might have been a fluke result, however carefully it was carried out. To overcome this problem an expert statistician and researcher averages the results of all the effective experiments on mind maps over the last few decades. It will usually be found that these experiments have been carried out on students working at every academic level, and in every curriculum area, and in many different countries. The statistician creates an average effect size from hundreds, even thousands, of experiments. By combining experiments like this, the statistician is in effect creating one enormous experiment out of many smaller ones. His article might be called a 'research review' or a 'meta-study'. 'Meta-study' means a study of studies.

To write this review of research the expert, usually a university professor who has specialised in this area, uses all the effective experiments on mind maps, and other reviews and commentaries on the topic. The review will include an average effect size for student mind mapping as a means of summarising a topic. All poor experiments are eliminated from this review, firstly because poorly designed experiments are unlikely to be published in the first place, and secondly because the statistician and the mind-map expert will look very carefully at the experimental designs of the experiments reviewed and will abandon those that don't meet stated criteria. For example, if the method of assigning students to the control and experimental groups was not thorough enough, the study will be removed from the review. Academics carrying out such reviews set a very high standard indeed and often reject the vast majority of published research on their chosen topic as not being up to standard.

Unfortunately there are thousands of research reviews published every year, so we can't read them all. What are we to do?

Syntheses of effect-size study research

Luckily some academics have read these research reviews or meta-studies for us, and have integrated them in ways that enable us to compare teaching methods and find the most powerful, as shown in the figure below.

One of the great strengths of effect size is that it enables us to compare two strategies or variables and see which has the greatest effect on student achievement.

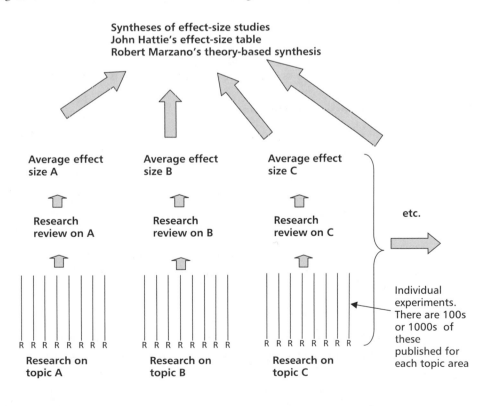

**Syntheses of effect-size studies
John Hattie's effect-size table
Robert Marzano's theory-based synthesis**

Average effect size A   **Average effect size B**   **Average effect size C**

Research review on A   **Research review on B**   **Research review on C**   etc.

R R R R R R R R   R R R R R R R R   R R R R R R R R

Research on topic A   **Research on topic B**   **Research on topic C**

Individual experiments. There are 100s or 1000s of these published for each topic area

What methods work best?

There are only two main syntheses of research reviews or meta-studies. Professor John Hattie has produced a table of average effect sizes. Robert Marzano has produced a theory-based synthesis that we will consider in the next chapter. We will look at both of these, following our strategy of always going to the top of the research 'feeding chain' to get expert overviews. But first we need to understand the limitations of effect-size studies.

Criticisms of the effect-size approach of Hattie and Marzano

Effect sizes allow us to combine research, and *compare* factors that influence student achievement. But remember that no one type of evidence can tell the whole story. Effect-size research has the following limitations:

- It assumes that all learners are the same, and have the same needs. In lumping students together important distinctions are overlooked.
- It ignores context. What works in one classroom might not work in another. In particular, most effect-size studies are done in schools: will the same strategies work in colleges or in higher education? (However, effect sizes would not be as stable as they are if this were true, and this type of evidence seems to show there are more similarities in how people learn than many educationalists give credit for.)

We can 'cover' these weaknesses by getting feedback on whether individual students are learning (as described in Chapters 2 and 15, for example), but mainly by reflecting on our teaching, and our students views of our teaching as described in Chapters 23 and 25. The second point above is not a strong one; we will see in Chapter 6 on Marzano that effect sizes are not very context dependent.

- It assumes that learning is brought about by gross external factors and ignores subjective factors, yet learning is a subjective process. That is, effect-size studies are too 'behaviouristic'.
- It does not tell us *why* the methods work.

We will cover these weaknesses by looking at the qualitative research considered in Chapter 2. The second point is not a strong one as meta-studies do consider this.

- Effect-size studies are usually short term, a matter of a few weeks. The tests used may measure very poor quality surface learning. So effect-size comparisons *may* not rate highly those methods that are designed specifically to create deeper learning and to develop thinking skills, as these take time and won't show up in simple tests.

Actually we find that study-skills teaching rates very highly, and deep-learning methods do too. But there may be *some* truth in this. We can cover this by taking Chapter 2 very seriously.

- Most of the research was done in schools.

Hattie and Marzano both find that effect sizes are remarkably stable and not much influenced by age, academic level, etc., as we see in the next two chapters.

. . . not much influenced by age . . .

Unsound criticisms of effect-size studies include:

- **The students can work out whether they are in the experimental or the control group, and those in the experimental group expect to do better, so they do.**

If this were so the effect sizes of all interventions would be about the same, yet they are nearly always remarkably stable for the same intervention, and very different for different interventions. However, Hattie argues that this effect, known as the 'Hawthorne effect', is a great thing, and we need more of it, so let's experiment!

Criticisms of the combining of effect sizes into meta-studies:

- **We may be combining apples with oranges. Just because researchers use the same name to describe their interventions is no reason to assume that the interventions were truly the same.**

The argument against this is that the stability of effect sizes would not occur if there were great differences between studies of the same intervention.

The main argument against all these criticisms is that effect-size studies have been subjected to two rigorous tests and passed them both. There are also two other ways to discover the best teaching methods, and both agree with effect-size study findings:

- **One way is the qualitative study of teaching methods we saw in Chapter 2. And the most constructivist teaching methods turn out to have high effect sizes.**
- **The other is to isolate the very best teachers, and observe what they do. We will look at this in Chapter 22. We will find remarkable agreement between effect-size studies and the methods used by the very best teachers.**

The success of this 'triangulation' should give us heart: a science of teaching is being born. Recent educational initiatives have concentrated on the differences between students, improving differentiation (coping with differences), and learning styles, for example. In doing so they have ignored their similarities. We should attend to these too.

Reference and further reading

A New Guide on Evidence-Based Practice: Identifying and Implementing Educational Practices Supported by Rigorous Evidence. This easy-to-read US government guide can be downloaded from: www.ed.gov/about/offices/list/ies/reports.html.

Marzano, R. J. (1998) *A Theory-Based Meta-Analysis of Research on Instruction*, Aurora, Colorado: Mid-Continent Research for Education and Learning. This can be downloaded from: www.mcrel.org/topics/productDetail.asp?topicsID=6andproductID=83.

5 John Hattie's table of effect sizes

John Hattie is Professor of Education at the University of Auckland in New Zealand, and is an educationalist of great international renown. He has analysed over 500,000 'effect sizes' from over 300,000 studies that represent experiments involving tens of millions of students and covering a truly vast range of strategies and innovations. See the references at the end of this chapter for how to download his paper – it's a stunning read.

In the last chapter we saw that we should not ask 'does it work?', but 'what works best?'

Hattie explains that effect sizes allow us to *compare* factors that affect achievement, such as teaching methods, teaching time, student motivation, and so on. In this way we can find what works best, that is, what has the greatest influence on student learning.

We know too much about learning and teaching; the handbooks that summarise research on education fill a substantial library that you could not hope to read in several lifetimes. What should we do with this embarrassment of riches? We need to synthesise it, summarise it, put it together into a coherent argument. In this project Hattie is a pioneer, and a world expert.

His method is startlingly bold and simple: it is to collect together effect sizes from the most reputable sources, ensuring they are statistically valid and comparable, and then place them on the same table. But he has not stopped there – he has also extracted some general principles from his table.

To help us interpret his table Hattie provides us with some comparators.

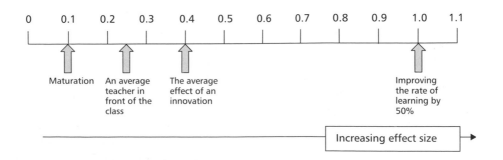

What methods work best?

An effect size of 1.0 standard deviation is enormous, and is typically associated with:

- advancing the learners' achievement by one year
- improving the rate of learning by 50 per cent
- average students receiving that treatment exceeding 84 per cent of the control-group students who do not receive that treatment
- a two-grade leap in GCSE, e.g. from a C to an A grade.

If you look at his table below you will notice that almost everything experimented with has a positive effect size. There is evidence for almost every hobby horse or bandwagon imaginable. Arguing that an initiative will have a positive result means next to nothing; we must compare initiative with initiative and implement the best.

Hattie's 300,000 studies have very varied effect sizes of course, creating the characteristic bell-shaped curve shown in the graph below. The mean effect size of all innovations is around 0.4. This then is the benchmark figure and provides a 'standard' from which to judge effects.

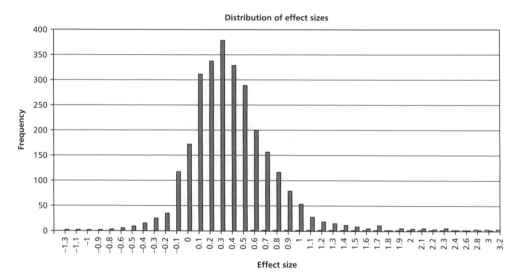

The average effect size for all 300,000 studies is 0.4.

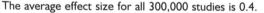

Sometimes the only difference between the experimental and the control groups is just one three-minute activity, yet it creates a substantial improvement in the performance of the experimental group, and so the strategy has a reasonable effect size. For example, 'advance organisers', which are summaries in advance of the teaching, has an effect size of 0.46, which is pretty average. But they only take about three minutes at the beginning of the lesson, and yet reward us with almost a grade improvement in students' achievement. This is clearly worth doing! Hattie's recent work stresses the importance of carefully communicating 'learning intentions' and the 'success criteria' for them. Such quick but powerful activities that take little or no class time I have marked with an asterisk in the table, as you might want to do them despite an unexceptional effect size.

Hattie's three principles

What has Hattie learned from reading 500 meta-analyses and from creating his table? He distils three principles from this vast enterprise, which summarise what works.

- Achievement is enhanced to the degree that students and teachers set and communicate appropriate, specific and *challenging* goals.
- Achievement is enhanced as a function of *feedback*.
- Increases in student learning involve . . . a *reconceptualisation* of learning.

So what works is setting a challenging goal, getting students to work towards this and then giving them feedback on the extent to which they have met the goal. The factors at the top of his table do this, the ones at the bottom don't, and that is why they are at the bottom.

The average effect of an innovation is 0.4 so Hattie points out that innovations work! This suggests the idea of 'Supported Experiments', which I describe in Chapter 25, where teachers deliberately carry out their own innovations for their team.

Issues arising from Hattie's research

Interpreting Hattie's effect-size table

If you have not already done so, have a quick look at Hattie's table (pages 65–68).

Notice that some effect sizes are 'Russian dolls' containing more than one strategy. For example, 'Feedback' requires that the student has been given a goal, and completed an activity for which the feedback is to be given; 'whole-class interactive teaching' is a strategy that includes 'advance organisers' and feedback and reviews. With so many sub-strategies it is perhaps not surprising it has a high effect size.

Are effect sizes additive?

Researchers tend to research teaching methods and other variables separately; if they used two variables at once they would not know which one had caused any improvement in achievement. But suppose you plan a lesson using a number of strategies with good effect sizes, then their effects may well be at least partly additive – that is, we may achieve more 'effect' with a number of methods together, than we could with any one alone.

Effect sizes are likely to be additive if they work on completely different aspects of learning, such as behaviour and feedback, but not if they focus on a similar aspect. For example, challenging goals and advanced organisers are both setting the agenda for a lesson and so their effect sizes are unlikely to be entirely additive.

Will I get the effect sizes quoted in my classroom?

The good news is that the effect sizes in Hattie's table are average, and we have learned a good deal from these very experiments about how to get a maximum effect size for each factor. For example, feedback has an average effect size of 0.81, but the effect sizes are much more variable here than for most factors. In the form of empty praise feedback has an effect size of only about 0.14. But informative feedback, or what I call 'medal and mission' feedback, has an effect size of over 1.0. We usually know what teachers did to get the highest effect sizes and this detail is given in the appropriate chapter.

The bad news is that we may not implement the strategies as well as the teachers in the research studies. Experts trained these teachers in preparation for the experiment in the best use of the strategies. You will not have that benefit, but you can read the detail in this book!

All in all it depends how effectively you implement the strategy, as you would expect.

Notice also who is in control of the variables in the table

It is the teacher who is in charge of almost all the variables towards the top of the table. This means that it is what good teachers do that creates achievement. Colleges or schools have relatively little impact except through their teachers.

Students' prior attainment is worth considering in this respect. The school can do little about this factor and it will certainly affect school achievement. However, in post-compulsory education the college's initial guidance and enrolment procedures decide the prior attainment of the students on each course, and can 'set the bar' for each student individually. This means it is the college that is in control of the prior attainment of the students in front of a given college teacher. We will consider this in more detail in Chapter 25.

If guidance and enrolment procedures are excepted, then the highest effect size which the college has any direct control over is 'aims and policies of the school' or college. This has an effect size of only 0.24; resources have even less effect. It is what good teachers do that makes the difference, so school management and resources should be focused on what goes on in the classroom if achievement is to be improved. Fascinatingly, Hattie's table shows strategies such as feedback that add more value than students' prior achievement.

Beware of comparing Hattie's and Marzano's effect sizes

For technical reasons Hattie's effect size for a given method or factor is usually smaller than Marzano's in the next chapter. This is because:

- Hattie has usually averaged *all* available effect sizes for each method. Marzano has only considered a subset of experiments.
- Marzano has reviewed research that uses *curriculum specific assessments*, which focus only on what was taught in the experiment. He thinks this gives the best indication of what is happening in the classroom. Hattie has reviewed research that uses *standardised tests*. These are the gold standard in research and are very reliable, but may not measure precisely what was taught in the experiment. Standardised tests are known to give effect sizes about a half or a third smaller than 'curriculum-specific tests'.

Rank order	Influence (The strategy or variable whose effect is being measured.) These 'influences' are explained in more detail elsewhere in this book. See the last column in the table. Strategies marked * take very little time and so are very worth doing.	The number of effects averaged to find the mean	Mean effect size	Who is in control of this strategy or variable? C = college T = teacher S = student H = home O = other	Read this chapter to find out more

The major influences

1	**reciprocal teaching** Strategy to help reading comprehension for students who find this difficult. It involves them in: questioning, summarising, clarifying and predicting what the text will say/cover next.	52	0.86	T	13
2	**feedback** Students getting feedback on their work from the teacher or from themselves (self-assessment) or from peers or some other source. This does *not* include the student doing remedial work as a result of the feedback; if this were included the effect size would be higher. Some feedback has much more effect than others; see Chapter 8.	3209	0.81	T	8
3	**whole-class interactive teaching ('direct instruction')** A specific approach to active learning in class, which is very teacher led, but very active for students. Students' work is marked in class and they may do corrective work. There are summaries at the beginning of the class, and reviews after one hour, five hours, and 20 hours of study. Highly teacher led, but very active.	925	0.81	T	9
4	**strategy training** Explicit teaching of subject-specific and general study and thinking skills, integrated into the curriculum	7649	0.80	T	21, 24
5	**classroom behaviour** The influence of appropriate student behaviour on achievement	361	0.71	T	26 (download)
6	**prior achievement** The prior achievement of students in the class. After 16 years this is dependent on the institution's guidance and selection procedures.	2094	0.71	C	25
7	**phonological awareness** In research on reading: teaching the awareness of the sounds of syllables and the sequence of these syllables in words. The National Literacy Hour now has systematic phonic training for learners.	429	0.66	T	
8	**early intervention** Preschoolers and younger children who are at risk of later learning difficulties or developmental problems. The term 'early intervention' covers programmes such as Head Start, Sesame Street, and other programmes which implement some kind of intervention or intensive treatment to prevent or minimise later difficulties.	30275	0.64	O	
9	**Piagetian programs** Programmes such as CASE designed to improve students' thinking and intelligence	786	0.63	T/C	21
10	**peer assessment** Students assessing each other's work	308	0.63	T	19
11	**cooperative learning** Specific teaching methods such as jigsaw that give	1153	0.59	T	12

	groups and individual students responsibility for learning, and for teaching each other relatively independently from the teacher				
12	**challenging goals** for students	959	**0.59**	T	2, 14, 16
13	**reading*** Students learning from reading, for example from a reading homework	14945	**0.58**	T	17
14	**mastery learning** A system of easy tests and retests with a high pass mark. If students do not pass they must do extra work and then take a retest on the material they were weak at.	933	**0.55**	T	19
15	**self-assessment*** Students assessing themselves	52	**0.54**	T	19

Worth having

16	**creativity programs** teaching creative thinking	2340	**0.52**	T	24
17	**interactive video**	1008	**0.52**	T	14
18	**psycho-linguistics** methods specific to learning languages	4404	**0.51**	T	
19	**peer influence**	366	**0.50**	T	19
20	**study skills** teaching students a group of useful study skills without integrating it into the curriculum.	3224	**0.49**	T	21, 24
21	**outdoor education**	294	**0.49**	C	
22	**in-service education** of teachers	18644	**0.48**	C	25
23	**socio-economic status**	1899	**0.48**	H	
24	**acceleration** putting an able student up a year.	371	**0.47**	C	
25	**motivation** students wanting to learn and to have mastery over their learning	2196	**0.47**	T	3
26	**peer tutoring** students tutoring their peers	2101	**0.47**	T	19

In the middle

27	**advance organisers*** giving students a summary in advance and a purpose for the learning	2106	**0.46**	T	16
28	**concept mapping**	18	**0.45**	T	10
29	**hypermedia instruction** integrated use of video, computer, etc.	317	**0.44**	T	14
30	**parent involvement**	2597	**0.43**	H/C	
31	**perceptual-motor skills**	7592	**0.42**	T	14
32	**home environment** issues such as social class, help with homework, extent to which the learner's education is thought important; etc.	25685	**0.42**	H	
33	**competitive learning**	144	**0.41**	T	12
34	**self-concept** learner's conception of themselves as a person not just a learner.	4925	**0.40**		
35	**individualised instruction** teaching a class with resource-based learning, each learner going at his or her own pace	4747	**0.39**	T	14

36	simulations	972	0.37	T	12
37	time on task	1680	0.37		
38	homework*	558	0.35		20

Almost there

39	activity-based programs hands-on practical activity as part of learning, e.g. in science	674	0.35	T	
40	remedial programs	1438	0.35	T	19
41	classroom climate	2726	0.35	T	19
42	social skills training	5472	0.35	T	26
43	computer-assisted teaching	16415	0.32	T	14
44	inquiry-based teaching students finding out for themselves	2740	0.32	T	17, 21
45	testing frequency increasing the frequency of tests improves learning	2346	0.32	T	19
46	acceleration putting able students forward a year	345	0.31	C	
47	within-class grouping	2359	0.31	T	
48	testing testing just measures, it does not improve	1463	0.31	T	19
49	problem solving	1141	0.30	T	21

The also rans

50	metacognitive interventions teaching students to take control of their own learning	921	0.29	T	21
51	audio-visual	2699	0.26	T	10
52	gifted programs effect on those who participate	47	0.25	C	
53	aims and policies of the school	542	0.24	C	
54	calculators	238	0.24	T	
55	mainstreaming	1635	0.19	C	
56	behavioural objectives* 'students should be able to . . .'	157	0.18	T	16
57	teacher questioning	476	0.17	T	15
58	play	129	0.16	T	
59	television	4337	0.15	H	

The disasters

60	programmed instruction students being taught by a computer or set of workbooks, by doing a series of prescribed tasks; if the student gets an answer wrong they are directed back to correct their misunderstanding.	801	0.14	T	
61	finances	1634	0.14	O/C	
62	ability grouping	5078	0.14	T/C	
63	teacher expectations of learners	912	0.14		
64	class size (little effect until size falls to below about 12 students, then a larger effect)	2559	0.13	C	5

65	diet	255	0.12	H	
66	gender (female-male)	9020	0.09	O	
67	**problem-based learning** giving students a problem that requires them to teach themselves	41	0.06	T	21
68	**inductive teaching**	570	0.06	T	2
69	**team teaching**	41	0.06	T	
70	**open versus traditional** 'alternative' student-directed learning versus traditional	3426	−0.01		
71	**summer vacation**	269	−0.07	O	
72	**retention** making weak students repeat a year	3626	−0.20	O	
73	**transfer of school**	354	−0.26	H	

Special education

	Area	No. of meta-analyses	No. of studies	Effect size	Who is in control?	Where to find out more
1	feedback	51	1095	**1.24**	T	8, 15
2	**Piagetian** Feuerstein's thinking skills programme, and similar	8	102	0.93	T	2, 21
3	**whole-class interactive teaching** (direct instruction)	10	100	0.90	T	9
4	**language intervention** programmes to enhance language skills	19	508	0.86	T	
5	**tutee** effect on the tutee of peer tutoring	17	134	0.59	T	
6	**psycho-linguistics** phonological awareness mainly	55	4846	0.55	T	
7	**social/behavioural** programmes that focus and motivate students to learn	7	294	0.55	T	26
8	**tutor** the effect on the tutor from peer tutoring	18	274	0.55	T	
9	**computer-aided instruction**	13	136	0.52	T	14
10	**parents** involvement of parents in their child's learning	9	427	0.51	H	
11	**early identification** discovering learners' needs early	71	8916	0.50	C	19
12	**cooperative learning**	1	4	0.48	T	12
13	**drugs** using drugs, e.g. for ADHD	23	2952	0.47	H	
14	**preschool** effect of attending pre-school on later achievement	5	266	0.45	H	
15	**student's attitude** to their disability	20	1866	0.42	T	
16	**mainstreaming** mainstreamed versus special classes	35	1347	0.21	O	
17	**diet** effects of various diets, e.g. Feingold diet	9	255	0.16	H	
18	**brain-familial**	19	678	0.11	T	
19	**perceptual motor**	25	2523	0.09	T	

Are we there yet?

So is this it? Is it true to say that all a teacher need do is to use methods high on Hattie's table, paying particular attention to setting challenging goals and ensuring students get feedback? It would be great if it were that simple, but it isn't.

Hattie only gives us 'quantitative evidence', though from a vast range of rigorously collated research. We need to consider the inherent limitations in this source of evidence mentioned at the end of Chapter 4, and we need to include evidence from elsewhere, especially from our own classroom. We need the 'whole truth' as outlined in earlier chapters.

Be careful interpreting the effect sizes of teaching strategies. They show what teachers have achieved, on average, with the strategy. We know more about how to use the strategies now, so we can do better than these averages in many cases. Low effect sizes may be due to poor implementation of the strategy. So more challenging goals and more feedback may make these strategies work better in future.

Feedback

Hattie has made it clear that 'feedback' includes telling students what they have done well (positive reinforcement) and what they need to do to improve (corrective work, targets, etc.), but it also includes clarifying goals. This means that giving students assessment criteria, for example, would be included in 'feedback'. This may seem odd, but high-quality feedback is always given against explicit criteria, and so these would be included in 'feedback' experiments. 'Feedback' does not include social or behavioural feedback.

As well as feedback on the task, Hattie believes that students can get feedback on the processes they have used to complete the task, and on their ability to self-regulate their own learning. All these strategies have the capacity to increase achievement. Feedback on the 'self' such as 'well done, you are good at this' is not helpful. The feedback must be informative rather than evaluative. See Chapter 8.

Other effect sizes

Other effect sizes in an earlier Hattie table included the following:

Instructional quantity
How many hours the student is taught for. Effect size 0.8 with 80 studies.

Class size
The relationship between class size and student achievement is complex. In his inaugural lecture Hattie explains that if class size is below 10–15 then there is increased achievement, attitude, teacher morale and student satisfaction, across all schools and all subjects and ability levels.

Cohen *et al.* (2000) has a useful consideration of the issue on page 224.

However Benjamin Bloom claims much higher effect sizes for one-to-one tuition, up to an astonishing effect size of 2.0. Small classes really do help, which explains

What methods work best?

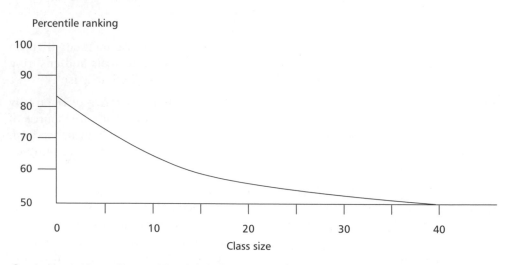

Percentile ranking

Class size

Graph adapted from Glass and Smith (1978).

the finding of the Basic Skills Agency that students on learning support are more likely to achieve than those who don't need that support.

There is little evidence that instruction methods change when class size changes, until the class sizes get very small.

Learning support . . . has a huge effect

References and further reading

Cohen, L., Manion, L. and Morrison, K. (2000) *Research Methods in Education* (5th edition), London: RoutledgeFalmer.

Glass, G. V. and Smith, M. L. (1978) Meta-Analysis of Research on the Relationship of Class-Size and Achievement, San Francisco: Farwest Laboratory.

Hattie, J. A., 'Influences on student learning'. This can be downloaded from Professor John Hattie's staff home page: www.arts.auckland.ac.nz/staff/index.cfm?P=5049.

Muijs, D. and Reynolds, D. (2001) *Effective Teaching: Evidence and Practice*, London: Paul Chapman.

Petty, G. (2004) *Teaching Today: A Practical Guide* (3rd edition), Cheltenham: Nelson Thornes.

Westwood, P. (2003) *Commonsense Methods for Children with Special Educational Needs: Strategies for the Regular Classroom* (4th edition), London: RoutledgeFalmer.

6 Marzano's theory-based meta-analysis

To my knowledge there have only been two modern attempts to summarise or synthesise metastudies across a broad range of educational fields: those by John Hattie and Robert Marzano. This is hardly surprising as it is clearly a daunting task to synthesise such a vast body of work.

Effect sizes put teaching methods and other factors that affect learning on the same scale, allowing us to compare their effectiveness. This is extremely useful! Even if you are not content to give effect sizes the last say in how you teach, you would be irrational not to take these summaries into account, and to see what you can learn from them.

We have already looked at Hattie's work. Now let's look at Robert Marzano's approach, or at least those aspects of it which deal with learning what he calls 'knowledge' defined at the bottom of the chart on page 74. This is the bulk of learning, and the bulk of his paper. His effect sizes for learning skills will be considered in Chapter 21.

Marzano (1998) only used effect sizes for factors that the teacher or students could change, typically classroom strategies. So, for example, studies of the impact of social class or home factors on achievement are not included and make his database much smaller than Hattie's.

He found 4000 effect sizes that met these criteria, but thought he would need at least three times as many to make firm statements. Nevertheless, this was all the evidence that he could find on alterable variables within the classroom.

Marzano did much more than just cherry-pick the strategies that worked best. He also classified all his 4000 effects in some very interesting ways. Let's see what he learned from doing this before looking at individual strategies.

What doesn't matter

He found that the academic level of the students in the studies did not influence the effect sizes of the strategies. What can work in a primary school can work just as well in university.

What does matter

Some interventions focus on what the teacher does, and some on what the student does. Those that affected what the student does had 20 per cent more effect (see table).

Intended user of the intervention	Effect size	Number of effect sizes
Teacher	0.61	2893
Student	0.73	1164

71

Marzano found some evidence that longer-term studies *may* have lower effect sizes, but there weren't enough of these to be sure (95 per cent of the studies were for just two weeks or less). This suggests that effect sizes *may* be in part due to enthusiasm for the novelty value of a new method. This is called the 'Hawthorne effect'. However, if the Hawthorne effect were the only cause of increased attainment, then the effect sizes of all strategies would be the same, which is clearly not the case. In any case we *want* this Hawthorne effect in our classrooms! If variety, and enthusiasm for experiments with new teaching approaches works, let's do it! But let's experiment with those methods that create the largest effects.

If there *is* a lower effect for longer studies, and there may not be, this is only an average effect. Some cognitive intervention studies go on for years, and yet end up amongst the top ten of Hattie's table, e.g. Piagetian programmes.

Effect sizes and ability

One disturbing finding was that strategies tended to have a greater effect on more able students.

This means the high-ability students in your classes will get about 40 per cent more advantage out of the methods in this book than your low-ability students. So improving your teaching tends to widen the gap between the advantaged and disadvantaged. This raises a serious issue. If we are to make use of effect-size research *without* disadvantaging the less able still further, then we must:

Student ability	Effect size	Number of effect sizes
High	0.91	942
Medium	0.70	1044
Low	0.64	824

- Concentrate on the few strategies that benefit the weakest *most*. This includes feedback, and the 'assessment for learning' methods described in Chapter 19. Fortunately these have very large effect sizes so are worth your extra attention anyway.
- Where able and less able students are taught in different classes or courses, for example in further education, we need to focus the improvement of our teaching on the least advantaged.
- We need to maximise our use of learning support, as this focuses the best teaching methods on the least advantaged. Again this has a huge effect, and so is worth our attention anyway.

To improve teaching in an institution without addressing this issue would be unethical.

I have tried to summarise Marzano's finding in the chart on p. 76, which also explains some of his technical terms. Marzano categorised teaching strategies and other 'interventions' depending on whether they activated in the student:

- *The self-system.* A set of beliefs the student holds about his or her capacities, the meaning and value of what they have been asked to do, along with the likelihood of success. I have called this 'The "Executive" and "Motivator"'.
- *The meta-cognitive system.* Students setting themselves goals, monitoring their progress towards these goals and adapting to difficulties. I have called this 'The Manager'.
- *The cognitive system.* This is the system that reasons, and thinks in other ways with the information at its disposal, to achieve the goals mentioned above.

Marzano classified all the experiments in his database as one of the above, and so obtained the average effect size for each. He found that activating the self-system had greatest effect, the meta-cognitive system the next most effect, and the cognitive system least, though it is still substantial. He argued that the self-system activates the meta-cognitive system, which activates the cognitive system, which creates learning! (No wonder teaching is so difficult!)

This is most helpful. Many teachers and educationalists, including myself, had thought the main object of teaching was to get learners to 'apply their learning': that is, to think with it, and to take responsibility for their own learning. These are indeed important. But prior to these, and more important still in terms of effect, is the teacher's role to motivate students by encouraging them to see the *value* of what they are about to learn, and to *believe* in their own capacity to learn it. We saw this in Chapter 3, and will see it again in Chapters 9 and 21.

A selection of Marzano's effect sizes

The effect sizes in the following tables are a selection only from Marzano's study. They are for strategies designed to improve students 'knowledge', which includes being able to recall information, use subject-specific mental processes or skills, and use psychomotor processes. Effect sizes for learning cognitive skills are given in Chapter 21.

For each strategy there is:

- An *average effect size*. This gives the average effect size of the N studies in standard deviation as described in Chapter 4. Remember, an effect size of 1.0 is roughly equivalent to a two-grade leap, an effect size of 0.5 is equivalent to a one-grade leap.
- The *number of research studies* or experiments averaged to get the effect size quoted (N). If N is large, that gives us more confidence in the average effect size.

The table (alongside) shows how effect size impacts on pass rates assuming that the intervention has an equal effect on all students, is used habitually, and is long lived in its effect. See also page 56.

Percentage of students who fail at present	Effect size required to achieve a 100% pass rate
40%	1.28
30%	0.84
20%	0.52
10%	0.25

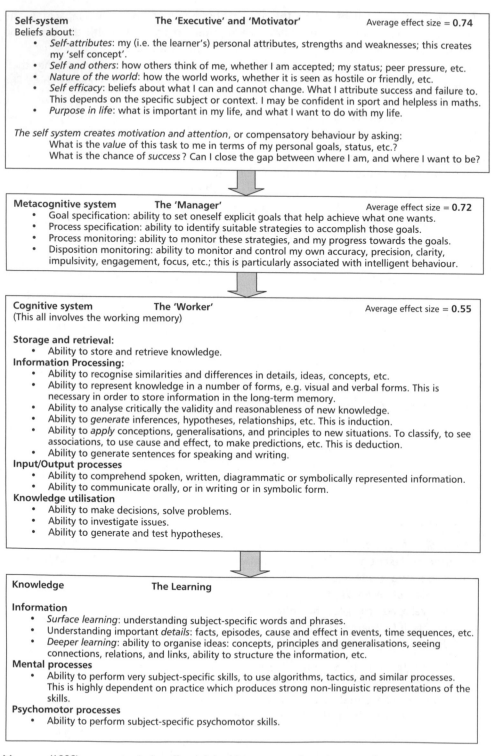

Self-system   **The 'Executive' and 'Motivator'**   Average effect size = **0.74**
Beliefs about:
- *Self-attributes*: my (i.e. the learner's) personal attributes, strengths and weaknesses; this creates my 'self concept'.
- *Self and others*: how others think of me, whether I am accepted; my status; peer pressure, etc.
- *Nature of the world*: how the world works, whether it is seen as hostile or friendly, etc.
- *Self efficacy*: beliefs about what I can and cannot change. What I attribute success and failure to. This depends on the specific subject or context. I may be confident in sport and helpless in maths.
- *Purpose in life*: what is important in my life, and what I want to do with my life.

The self system creates motivation and attention, or compensatory behaviour by asking:
What is the *value* of this task to me in terms of my personal goals, status, etc.?
What is the chance of *success*? Can I close the gap between where I am, and where I want to be?

Metacognitive system   **The 'Manager'**   Average effect size = **0.72**
- Goal specification: ability to set oneself explicit goals that help achieve what one wants.
- Process specification: ability to identify suitable strategies to accomplish those goals.
- Process monitoring: ability to monitor these strategies, and my progress towards the goals.
- Disposition monitoring: ability to monitor and control my own accuracy, precision, clarity, impulsivity, engagement, focus, etc.; this is particularly associated with intelligent behaviour.

Cognitive system   **The 'Worker'**   Average effect size = **0.55**
(This all involves the working memory)

Storage and retrieval:
- Ability to store and retrieve knowledge.
Information Processing:
- Ability to recognise similarities and differences in details, ideas, concepts, etc.
- Ability to represent knowledge in a number of forms, e.g. visual and verbal forms. This is necessary in order to store information in the long-term memory.
- Ability to analyse critically the validity and reasonableness of new knowledge.
- Ability to *generate* inferences, hypotheses, relationships, etc. This is induction.
- Ability to *apply* conceptions, generalisations, and principles to new situations. To classify, to see associations, to use cause and effect, to make predictions, etc. This is deduction.
- Ability to generate sentences for speaking and writing.
Input/Output processes
- Ability to comprehend spoken, written, diagrammatic or symbolically represented information.
- Ability to communicate orally, or in writing or in symbolic form.
Knowledge utilisation
- Ability to make decisions, solve problems.
- Ability to investigate issues.
- Ability to generate and test hypotheses.

Knowledge   **The Learning**

Information
- *Surface learning*: understanding subject-specific words and phrases.
- Understanding important *details*: facts, episodes, cause and effect in events, time sequences, etc.
- *Deeper learning*: ability to organise ideas: concepts, principles and generalisations, seeing connections, relations, and links, ability to structure the information, etc.
Mental processes
- Ability to perform very subject-specific skills, to use algorithms, tactics, and similar processes. This is highly dependent on practice which produces strong non-linguistic representations of the skills.
Psychomotor processes
- Ability to perform subject-specific psychomotor skills.

Marzano (1998) summarised: the effect of the 'three systems' on classroom learning.

If we concentrate on feedback, and the 'assessment *for* learning' strategies that help the weakest most, then the effect size required for a 100 per cent pass rate is lower than that in the table.

Effect sizes are a very crude measure and there is a danger of taking them too literally. But they are valuable 'ball park' measures of what works best. There are many strategies in the three tables below with effect sizes so large that if they were routinely adopted pass rates would soar. This is not an idle dream; Beacon schools and colleges routinely achieve pass rates well over 95 per cent on post-16 qualifications (where the student's prior attainment can be considered in guiding them to an appropriate course).

Sometimes there are different effect sizes for 'surface learning' (e.g. learning vocabulary and important details), and 'deeper learning'. In this case, both are quoted. If only one effect size is quoted there is little or no difference in the effect on surface or deeper learning.

In 'deduction', for example, the effect size is larger when students are acquiring knowledge of details than it is when they are learning about principles and theories. This may simply reflect that learning principles is harder than learning details.

Sometimes the average effect size was determined from a small number of studies; I have drawn attention to this in the table as this makes the average less reliable (e.g. '2 only!').

The headings in the tables signify the following:

- *Effect size:* average effect size in standard deviation (0.5 = one-grade leap; 1.0 = two-grade leap)
- *N:* the number of effect sizes averaged to get the average effect size
- *See ch:* refers to the chapter where you can find out more about the strategy in this book.

It is easy to get a bit lost in these tables unless you refer to the Marzano summary diagram on p. 76.

Methods that activate the cognitive system

These are instructional strategies that teach new 'knowledge' as defined in the Marzano summary diagram, by getting students to think with it, that is by getting them to use their cognitive system. The table below concentrates on methods with high effect sizes and large numbers of studies.

Instructional strategies that utilise the metacognitive system

Here the 'metacognitive system' is being used to develop 'knowledge' (see the Marzano summary diagram, p. 77 (top)).

Instructional strategies that utilise the self-system

Here the self-system is being used to develop knowledge and skills (see the Marzano summary diagram, p. 77 (middle)).

Strategy	Effect size	N	See ch.
Methods that activate the cognitive system to teach knowledge only (summary of all studies considered)	0.55	1772	18

Relevant recall questions: questions requiring students to recall what they already know about the topic or skill to be learned:
    Asked only *before* the lesson
    Asked *during and/or before* the lesson:
    • surface learning
    • deeper learning
	
	0.75
	
	0.93
	0.69
		
		83
		45
			16

Advance organisers: giving students special summaries in advance of what they are about to learn; they help students to structure the topic.
    All
    Surface learning only
    Deeper learning only
    'Mental processes' only, i.e. for subject-specific mental skills
	
	0.48
	0.56
	0.78
	0.60
		
		358
		36
		48
		15
			16

Note making: students create personal linguistic representations of the information being presented	0.99	36	20 10
'Same but different': tasks that require the learner to identify similarities and differences between two or more concepts, often one they are familiar with, and one they are presently studying. The best strategies involve students developing analogies that link new content with old. This would include 'compare and contrast' activities.	1.32	51	10
Graphic representations: students create their own diagrammatic representation of what they are learning, e.g. in a mind map.	1.24	43	10

Decisions, decisions: Students physically manipulate cards or objects or symbols which represent concepts or ideas they are learning about. Also called 'manipulatives'. This includes some computer simulation activities which can have an effect size of 1.45.
    Deeper learning only
    Mental processes only (see summary chart page 74)
	0.89
	
	0.82
	0.56
		236
		
		45
		24
			11

Induction: mainly deeper learning. The learner creates generalisations from information provided to them. (See the alternative 'deductive' methods below.)	0.11	237	21 2
Deduction: students learn a *principle or theory* by using it to make predictions or generate hypotheses. This is *deduction*. Some deductive methods did have high effect sizes, though; see below. Deeper learning only	0.38 0.45	242 212	18 2
Explicit instruction: direct teaching of deeper learning compared (I think) to methods that require students to work out deeper relations for themselves. Use of plenty of examples for more complex ideas.	2.55	2 only!	
Deductive strategies: students reason, and apply their learning of a topic in a way that requires deeper learning, e.g. evaluating a case study.	1.16	10	
Problem solving: students are given a problem that requires them to think about the topic or skill in a new way in order to overcome an obstacle. This deepens their understanding.	0.54	343	18
Experimental enquiry: students are required to generate a hypothesis about the knowledge or skill they are learning, and then test it.	1.14	6 only!	21

Strategy	Effect size	N	See ch.
Instructional strategies that utilise the metacognitive system to increase knowledge only (summary of all studies considered)	**0.72**	**556**	16
Specifying goals: students have specific written or verbal goals prior to a lesson. (This enables the learner to provide their own feedback.) Summary figures for learning knowledge: • highly specific behavioural objectives given by the teacher • less specific goals, some set by the student • psychomotor sports skills in gymnastics, track and field, etc. • psychomotor sports skills in ball games only	0.97 0.12 1.21 0.66 0.80	53 15 7	
Feedback: giving students feedback on the processes and strategies they were using to complete a specific task (medals) If the feedback was highly specific (medal and mission) feedback	0.74 1.13	488 139	8
Wait time: giving students more time to answer the teacher's verbal questions. (Marzano thinks this causes more use of metacognition.)	0.53	2 only!	15

Strategy	Effect size	N	See ch.
Instructional strategies that utilise the self-system to teach knowledge only (summary of all studies considered)	**0.74**	**147**	
Self attributes: 'medals': giving information about what was done well that is focused on the task, informative, and warranted, i.e. earned with a focus on the process (= the skill)	0.74	15	8
Cooperative learning: e.g. jigsaw. Marzano believes these methods work because of beliefs about self and others, e.g. peer pressure	0.73	122	12
Peer explaining: students explaining or narrating details to peers or the whole class. This does not include any corrective activity as there is in the method on page 247.	0.63	66	19 17
Self-efficacy: teachers persuading students that if they try they can succeed. This is most effective when students are actually working on the task, and when they are experiencing difficulty.	0.80	10	3

Conclusions regarding methods for teaching knowledge

The self-system (effect size 0.74) and the metacognitive system (effect size 0.72) have large effects. Although the overall effect size of strategies focused on the cognitive system is lower (effect size 0.55) some individual strategies are very effective:

– Same but different: 1.32
– Graphic or non-linguistic representation: 1.24
– Experimental enquiry (generating hypotheses): 1.14

For teaching vocabulary

- Give brief descriptions or definitions of new terms (effect size 1.53).
- Or get students to work out the meaning of terms from the content (effect size 1.59) or better do both (effect size 1.66).
- Get students to express the new terms and new content in their own words (effect size 1.27) and in non-linguistic ways such as mind-mapping (effect size 2.27).

For surface learning

For example teaching details, facts, meaning of terminology, etc.

- Get students to recall relevant prior learning (effect size 0.75) and questions (effect size 0.93). Present content in a narrative or in a story fashion or a richly descriptive context (effect size 0.63).
- Get students to represent the ideas in their own words in either oral or written form: notes (effect size 0.99), summaries or peer explaining (effect size 0.63). Also to represent ideas non-linguistically (effect size 1.24) in pictures, mind maps, charts, diagrams, etc.
- Same and different comparisons with new and already learned concepts (effect size 1.32). Get students to reason with the new information in games such as decisions, decisions (effect size 0.89).

For deeper learning

- Set clear goals, preferably involving the student (effect size 1.21). Teach abstract ideas, concepts, generalisations and principles fairly directly in concrete terms (effect size 2.55). For more complex ideas make sure you use plenty of examples.
- Pay particular attention to giving the structure of the information: advance organiser (effect size 0.78). Relations etc. are perhaps best given non-linguistically, for example in a graphic organiser (effect size 1.24).
- Get students to apply the concepts, generalisation, principles to new situations (effect size 1.16) (deduction). For example using decisions, decisions (effect size 0.89). Get students to use the ideas to generate and test hypotheses (effect size 1.14), or to solve problems (effect size 0.54).

For learning of any type

- Make sure students get detailed informative feedback on what they did well: medals (effect size 0.74). Better still give them medals *and* missions (effect size 1.13). Missions are specific targets for improvement, diagnosed from the work.

The diagram below puts some of Marzano's effect sizes on the 'PAR' model, which is explained in detail in Chapter 14.

This concludes our look at Hattie's and Marzano's work, being the two most comprehensive reviews of research on the effectiveness of teaching methods. We will now look at some of the most effective methods in detail.

Key: The figures are effect sizes, 0.5 being equivalent to a one grade leap. If two effect sizes are given, e.g. '0.93 → 0.69', then the first applies to easy learning, the second to more complex learning.

Review

Note taking 0.99
Graphic representations 1.24

(Formative teaching was not reviewed by Marzano but this could come in here.)

Apply (easy → difficult material)

Same but different (compare and contrast) 1.32
Note taking 0.99
Graphic representations 1.24
Decisions, decisions 0.89
Induction (creating generalisations) 0.11
Testing hypotheses: making predictions and then testing them 0.38 → 2.55
Deductive strategies 1.16
Deductive tasks using formal logic 0.98
Problem solving 0.54
Cooperative learning 0.73
Self-efficacy training 0.80
Peer explaining 0.63

Present (easy → difficult material)

Orientation

Relevant recall questions prior to and during learning 0.93 → 0.69
Advance organisers 0.48 → 0.60
Specifying general goals (but not behaviouristically) 0.97
Student and teacher specify goals 1.21
(Goals must be accompanied by stressing the *value* of the goal to the learner, and creating a *belief* in the learner that they can succeed with them)

Present

Explicit instruction of difficult material 2.55 (compared to finding out for themselves)
Explicit instruction is teacher directed but very active for the learner and includes feedback. See 'whole class interactive teaching'

Feedback

Medals (0.74) That is, informative praise that states what was done well
Medals *and* missions (1.13) Medal, plus a mission which is a specific target to improve that was diagnosed from the work.
This can be achieved in the present mode by by methods such as assertive questioning, pair checking, miniwhiteboards, etc.
In the 'apply' and 'review' modes feedback methods include self-assessment, peer assessment, teacher comments, etc.

Some effect sizes for teaching knowledge from Marzano (1998).

Reference and further reading

Marzano, R. J. (1998) *A Theory-Based Meta-Analysis of Research on Instruction*, Aurora, Colorado: Mid-Continent Research for Education and Learning. This paper is large and complex, but it can be downloaded from: www.mcrel.org/topics/productDetail. asp?topicsID=6andproductID=83.

This chapter only looked at the above meta-analysis, but see also:

Marzano, R., Pickering, D. and Pollock, J. (2001) *Classroom Instruction That Works*, Alexandria, Virginia: ASCD.

7 Extracting general principles from effect-size studies

So we have all these effect sizes summarised by the only two experts in summarising effect-size studies across a very wide educational spectrum. Now what? One obvious way forward is to isolate the top teaching methods and make use of them; we will do this in the next few chapters. We would be crazy not to try these methods given that the gold standard in educational research, the randomised control group study, has shown them repeatedly to be so exceptionally effective.

But should we stop there and just learn to implement these supercharged vehicles to student achievement? We would be missing a trick if we did. Firstly, if we used these methods over and over, our lessons might get repetitive and boring. But there are more telling reasons why we should not stop at the Top Ten.

Let's ask the question 'Why do these "top ten" methods work?' Then let's use our answers to this question to try to extract some general principles that explain their effectiveness. These principles will only be hypotheses (guesses), so we will need to test them by looking for evidence against them. But if our principles (hypotheses) hold up against these tests, we can use them to develop new methods and adapt our existing methods. This process is a form of 'bridging' which we look at in the form of a teaching strategy in Chapter 21. It is a powerful way to transfer learning and is the basis of scientific reasoning. It creates the deep understanding enjoyed by experts, and is high on the SOLO taxonomy.

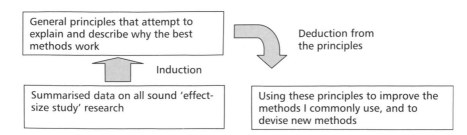

John Hattie has started us off. As we saw earlier he noticed three principles: the first two can be seen directly in the variables that populate the top of his table; the last is more conjectural.

- Achievement is enhanced to the degree that students and teachers set and communicate appropriate, specific and *challenging* goals.
- Achievement is enhanced as a function of *feedback*.
- Increases in student learning involve . . . a *reconceptualisation* of learning.

Secondly all of these top ten methods may not work well for you and your students. To be truly evidence based in your teaching you will need to use them before you refuse them, three or four times, preferably in supported experiments as described in Chapter 25. During this experimentation you will be bound to adapt the methods to your own subject and to your own context. But will your adaptations be as effective as the original tested in those effect-size studies? And will your use of the methods focus on the factors that really make the methods work? To use the methods effectively you must understand *why* they work in terms of general principles. Then you can often adapt and use them in ways that maximise their effectiveness.

So while I explain the top ten teaching methods, keep asking yourself the question 'Why does this work?' and see if you agree with the principles I try to extract at the end of this section. There is space for you to write your ideas down at the end of each chapter. By the way, I have just set you a challenging goal to reason with the information that I am presenting to you, which is one of the top ten methods, and one of Hattie's principles!

Part 3 The top teaching methods

8 Feedback or 'assessment *for* learning' (effect size 0.81)

If we think back to the idea of constructivism in Chapter 2 it is easy to see why good feedback has such a large effect on achievement. We saw that students don't construct meanings fully or accurately the first time, and so need to know their errors and omissions in order to improve their constructs.

The teacher also needs feedback on students' understandings to help improve them, and their teaching. Please look at the diagram below (p. 84).

- *Present.* Information is presented in the form of teacher talk, video, text, website, etc. This can be verbal, or can include a visual stimulus. Effective learners will create a weak construct of the meaning of this message. Weak learners may not do this well, or at all.
- *Apply.* The learner is required to carry out a task that requires the use of what was presented. This requires that even weak or demotivated learners form a construct linked to their prior learning and experience. Difficulties and learning points experienced during this activity will create feedback to the learner, which can be used to improve the construct, hence the two-way arrow.
- *Product and feedback.* Clearly the product made as a result of the 'apply' phase can be perused by the learner, teacher, and/or peers. This gives more feedback information to the learner, enabling their construct to be further improved. This also gives information to the *teacher*, enabling him or her to improve the instruction and so the construct. Then the improved product, and the learning, is reviewed.

Hattie shows that feedback has more impact on learning than any other general factor, but it requires an activity and a product. He also points out that too often teachers see feedback as giving information about their students, their home backgrounds and their grasp of the subject – 'and too rarely do they see such feedback as reflecting on their expertise as teachers'.

A highly influential and very comprehensive review of feedback or 'formative assessment' by Black and Wiliam (1998) concluded:

- Formative assessment methods have some of the highest effect sizes found in education.
- High-quality feedback has more effect on the weakest learners (so it reduces failure and drop-out rates).
- But common practice in formative assessment is not good practice.

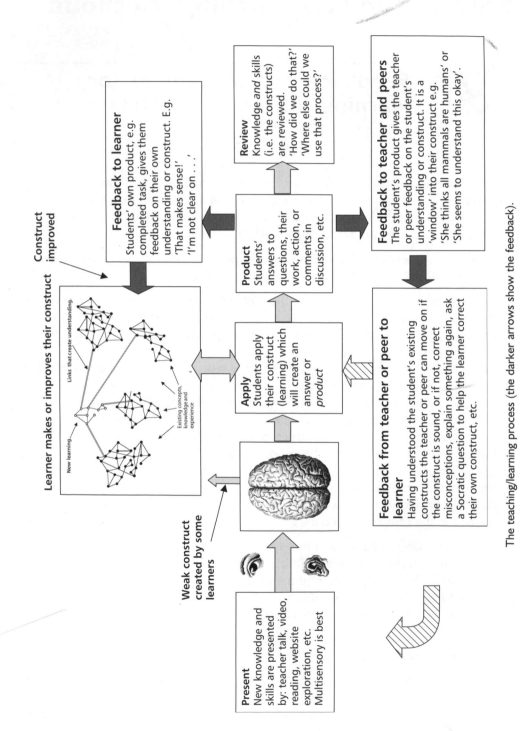

Learner makes or improves their construct

Construct improved

Weak construct created by some learners

Feedback to learner
Students' own product, e.g. completed task, gives them feedback on their own understanding or construct. E.g. 'That makes sense!' 'I'm not clear on . . .'

Review
Knowledge *and* skills (i.e. the constructs) are reviewed.
'How did we do that?'
'Where else could we use that process?'

Feedback to teacher and peers
The student's product gives the teacher or peer feedback on the student's understanding or construct. It is a 'window' into their construct e.g. 'She thinks all mammals are humans' or 'She seems to understand this okay'.

Product
Students' answers to questions, their work, action, or comments in discussion, etc.

Apply
Students apply their construct (learning) which will create an answer or *product*

Feedback from teacher or peer to learner
Having understood the student's existing constructs the teacher or peer can move on if the construct is sound, or if not, correct misconceptions, explain something again, ask a Socratic question to help the learner correct their own construct, etc.

Present
New knowledge and skills are presented by: teacher talk, video, reading, website exploration, etc. Multisensory is best

Links that create understanding.

New learning

Existing concepts, knowledge and experience

The teaching/learning process (the darker arrows show the feedback).

So one of the most powerful factors at our disposal is least well implemented.

Hattie's effect sizes	N	Effect size
Feedback: Students getting feedback of any kind on their work from the teacher or from themselves or from peers, etc. (excludes social and behavioural feedback)	13 209	0.81
Testing: Testing just measures a student's performance	1463	0.31

Marzano's effect sizes	N	Effect size
Feedback: Giving students feedback on the processes and strategies they were using to complete a specific task	488	0.74
If the feedback was highly specific (medal and mission)	139	1.13

Common and best practice compared

Let's compare two imaginary case studies to see why good-quality feedback for the students and teacher is so important. The first case study, 'Janet', describes *common* practice, and in the second, 'Tina', describes *good* practice. We will imagine that these two teachers have similar experience, and have parallel groups of students of the same ability. To begin with we will eavesdrop on the teachers' first lesson on drawing a graph; later we see how they teach a more complex topic.

Janet

1. Janet first explains how to draw a graph, showing how on the board.
2. She asks some questions to check understanding and the questions are answered well by volunteers.
3. Then she sets a task to complete some graphs in class.
4. Students complete the graphs while she circulates, giving help where necessary: e.g. 'You need to make sure you have a unit as part of your label.'
5. She collects the work in and takes it home for marking.
6. She marks the work by giving it a mark out of ten, and by writing comments on the work such as 'label axes', 'good' or 'neat work', etc. She records the marks in her markbook.
7. She gives the marked work back to her students the next lesson, and discusses weakness in the work with her class.

Janet's approach is so common that many teachers would be at a loss to know what was wrong with it, but compare it with Tina taking an exactly similar class. There are several differences: see if you can spot them and their purposes.

Tina

1. Tina asks her students what they already know about how to draw graphs. She writes up salient points they make on the board.
2. She discovers that they know a surprising amount already, but little about how to choose a scale, which she then describes. She shows some examples where the scales were badly chosen and asks what's wrong and how to fix it.
3. She asks students to devise criteria for a good graph. Students work in pairs, and make suggestions such as 'all axes labelled with a unit'. She writes agreed criteria on the board.
4. She sets students some graphs to draw and tells them they will be peer assessed.
5. Students complete their graphs while she circulates to give help where necessary. If she spots a weakness she says: 'Look at the criteria for axes – how have you done?' She uses the answer to diagnose any student difficulty and to help them.
6. While they work she reminds students to check their own work against the criteria before the peer assessment.
7. She collects the first graph from each student, and gives these out for peers to mark.
8. Students mark their peers' work against the criteria agreed in 3 above, writing comments in pencil. She circulates to help this process.
9. The work goes back to the rightful owner and she leaves a little time for them to read the comments on their work, to check the marking, and to improve the work. She asks two students whose work she was not happy with to redo it and to submit it to her at the start of the next class.
10. She asks what issues came up in the marking and clarifies a few points.

There are more steps in Tina's approach but some won't take long, for example 6, 7, and 10. Step 1 might actually save time. In *Assessment for Learning* Black *et al.* (2003) describe how teachers who made use of Tina's steps 1 and 2 found that on average these steps saved more time than they took.

Even if Janet does teach it quicker her students will learn it slower. They will be less clear of the goals, and will make more mistakes, and some will practise these mistakes many times before Janet has discovered and corrected them. Lots of class practice and homework will be required to correct misunderstandings; even so, the weaker students may never become competent.

What is the difference in their two approaches, and what beliefs about learning cause them?

Janet's approach

Janet's approach is to teach, test the learning, grade it, and then move on. She does give students some comments on how to improve, but her main aim when marking is to grade the work as accurately as possible.

A common assumption behind this approach is that learning quality and quantity depend on talent or *ability*, and that the role of assessment is to *measure* this ability. Poor learning is usually attributed to a lack of ability, flair or intelligence.

Tina's approach

Tina is a constructivist teacher, and believes that ability is not innate, but learned. She finds out what students already know, corrects any misconceptions, and then builds onto this. She wants students to understand the goals well enough to be able to give *themselves* good, continuous, informative feedback on their progress towards the goals.

Her approach to assessment is to make the goals clear, to diagnose errors and omissions in learning and then to correct these. In short she sees the purpose of assessment as improvement, not measurement. Weaknesses in learning are attributed to a misunderstanding of the goals or more likely, lack of practice.

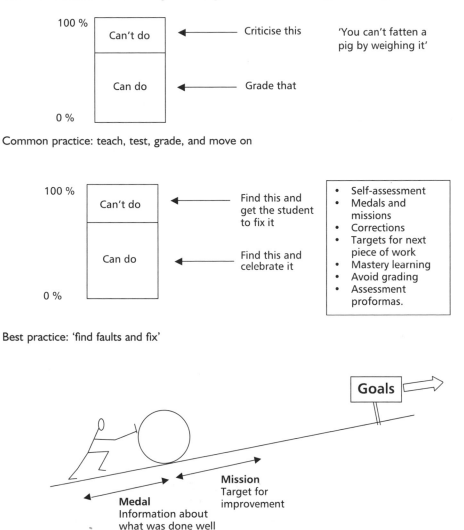

Common practice: teach, test, grade, and move on

Best practice: 'find faults and fix'

Mind the gap!

Medals, missions and goals

Sadler (1989) in a highly influential journal article showed that when completing a learning task students need feedback that gives them *information* about the quality of their work, not just generalised praise and encouragement.

He argued that whether you were teaching yourself, or being taught by another, there were just three things that you needed to know. I call these the goal, a medal, and a mission.

The goals

What you are aiming for, and the nature of good work – the objectives, the proper interpretation of the tasks you have been set – and of the assessment criteria; the nature of excellence for this task, etc.

A medal: where you are now in relation to these goals

- Task-centred information on what you did/do well, in terms of the goals (if this comes from another it needs to be in the form of informative comments, not grades or marks as we will see), e.g. 'Your axes are correctly labelled.'
- These 'medals' can be for 'process' (*how* you did it) as well as 'product' (*what* you did).
- Overall grades, marks, etc., are not medals as they don't give detailed enough information about *what* aspects of the task were done well.

A mission: how to close the gap between where you are now, and the goals

This is a specific target to improve performance. You might have process targets: 'check your work against the criteria before handing it in'; or product targets: 'Make sure your axes are labelled.' Missions could include:

- Corrective work or other improvements on past work, usually the last piece completed.
- Very short-term targets that are forward looking and positive for future work. (It is common for 'missions' to be backward looking and negative – 'There are too many spelling mistakes' – when they should be forward looking and positive – 'Next time check your spelling.'

Missions should be challenging but achievable. They can be for process and/or product

I have shown this diagrammatically above, imagining learning as like rolling a rock up a slope. Hopefully the rock is not quite as heavy as it looks! The idea of medal and mission is explored in more detail in Chapters 6 and 43 of *Teaching Today*.

Students can get this informative feedback from themselves (self-assessment), from others (peer assessment), and from the teacher, but eventually they must learn to provide it for themselves.

You need to give yourself feedback to improve your own work

Sadler explains that students need to be able to give *themselves* feedback *while they are working*. Otherwise they will be unable to succeed with tasks, or to improve. To do this they need to understand the goals, and to be able to evaluate their work in progress against these. See the diagram below.

For example, in Janet's class weak students may think the main goal is to work neatly and finish quickly, and they may believe they have drawn a good graph when they haven't. Until they understand the real goals, and can evaluate their methods, and their work in progress, and until they know how to fix any deficiency they find, then they cannot improve. In short, self-assessment skills are a prerequisite for learning. The cycle below shows why.

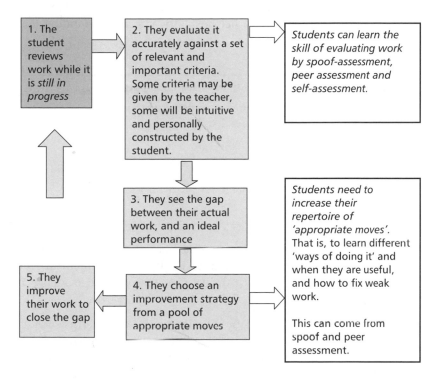

Students find it difficult to clarify goals

Many students suffer from 'failure of intent': that is, they are trying to do the wrong thing because they have misinterpreted the tasks and assessment criteria and other goals. Consequently they are striving in the wrong direction. They fail not because they are *unable* to produce good work, but because they don't know what it is. For example, if asked to 'give a graph a title' they might think that 'graph 1' will do when the goal is for a more informative title. Or when asked to 'evaluate your business plan' a student might believe that this means 'write down all its good points'.

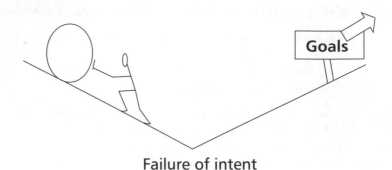

Failure of intent

Students are often unaware of their own difficulty here, believing they understand the goals when they don't. This may help explain why understanding your goals has such a high effect size.

Marzano's effect size	Effect size	N
Specifying goals: Students have specific written or verbal goals prior to a lesson where they are learning 'knowledge' (see the summary diagram on p. 74). (This enables the learner to provide their own feedback.)	0.97	53

Giving and explaining clear assessment criteria helps here, whether this is done formally or informally. Criteria can be specific to the task: 'Explain at least three causes for the war'; or more general: 'Always give reasons and evidence for your opinions.'

The criteria must *explain* the characteristics of good work. Avoid terms such as 'excellent' or 'thorough' and other qualitative descriptors. These beg the very question they are supposed to answer! What exactly *is* an 'excellent' error analysis, for example? It would be better to describe the contents and characteristics of such an error analysis directly and in concrete terms. Similarly, and more problematically, what is a 'coherent argument for improving the marketing plan' in a case study? What is a good critique of a poem?

Goals are often abstract, and abstract concepts are best learned by looking at concrete examples, as we saw in Chapter 2. Students will benefit from studying examples of good work (exemplars), perhaps by assessing these. This is spoof assessment as explained in Chapter 19. The tasks, assessment criteria and other goals that you give students also benefit from being expressed as *concretely* as possible. This is very hard to do, and even if you do it brilliantly many students will not understand them until they start to use them to assess or to guide their own work.

Here are a few examples of some assessment criteria for an assignment on an AVCE in business course. The students have to produce a business plan for a new product or service and evaluate this. The criteria are well written, but the student will still find the italicised words difficult to interpret until they have studied exemplars or worked towards them:

To achieve an E grade your work must show:
Justification of the approach taken to the construction of your plan.

To achieve a grade C your work must show:
An *accurate evaluation* of the business plan using appropriate *evaluation tools.*

To achieve an A grade your work must show:
Viable marketing, production and financial alternatives in your assessment of your business plan.

Students can find tasks just as difficult to interpret as assessment criteria. The task below is well written, but again many students will not understand the italicised phrase well.

'Make *effective use* of IT spreadsheets to present your financial projections.'

Students need concrete examples of the successful completion of these tasks, and the criteria being well met, in order to understand these goals, and so begin to meet them.

Meeting more complex goals

This problem of goals and criteria being opaque rather than 'transparent' requires even more attention when the tasks are complex. Suppose that our two teachers were teaching students how to critically appraise a poem, say, or a menu for a banquet. Here the criteria and goals are 'fuzzy', interconnected and vague, and much harder to define. They are also demanding.

As ever, these goals only take on a meaning when exemplified and illustrated by concrete examples. For instance, a student may wonder . . .

* What is a 'coherent argument'?
* What is a novel's 'theme' as distinct from its plot?
* What is an 'effective error analysis' in a lab report?

This is what Sadler calls 'guild knowledge', and we need to bring students 'into the know' about this. Students are not likely to score until they know where the goal-posts are. Spoof and peer assessment help students develop this 'feel' for good work and how to produce it. Often, the more complex the goal the harder it is to define, and the more likely a student's failure to meet the goal will be attributed to lack of talent, by both the student and their teacher. Actually the problem may be failure of intent, or a lack of understanding of the goal and how to meet it. It is not fair to leave students to pick up the 'rules of the game' by osmosis; we need to teach this. Some methods are shown in the 'bridging' diagram below.

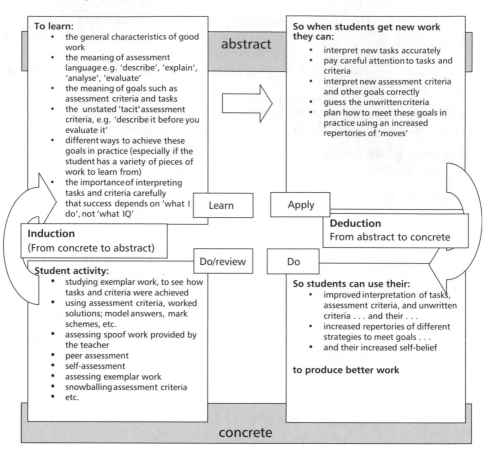

'Bridging' to clarify goals and learn how to meet them.

A big meta study by Kluger and DeNisi (1996) found that feedback only leads to learning gains when it includes guidance on how to improve. See Chapter 19 for methods that do that whilst also making goals and criteria clear.

Grading degrades learning

What sort of feedback maintains students' interest, and improves learning most? In a seminal experiment Ruth Butler gave students a series of three tasks each followed by feedback. Her experiment included both the most able 25 per cent of students, and the least able 25 per cent.

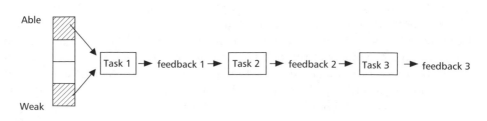

Butler gave her students one of three types of feedback:

* One-third received comment only.
* One-third received grades only.
* One-third received both comments and grades.

Butler found that the students' performance improved by 33 per cent if they received comments-only feedback, which was like medal and mission feedback. However, if they received a grade, or a grade and comments, their performance declined. Why? When graded, weak students despaired: 'I can't do this'; and the more able students became complacent: 'I got a B so why should I read the comments, let alone act on them?'

The interest of low achievers in the tasks was undermined by grading, but the interest of the more able was sustained at a high level throughout, though they were not interested in reading the teacher's helpful comments. Are you surprised!?

> *Black et al. (2003) thought much marking time is misguided.*

As students climb the attainment slope the 'better' students tend to stay in front and the 'weaker' ones behind. Black *et al.* (2003) argue that for this reason summative grading carries an unintended hidden message that ability is innate rather than learned: 'I always get good/bad grades so I must be good/bad at this subject.' This is a very disempowering message for at least half the learners, as Butler and others have shown.

This is a serious problem as students' work must often be graded to meet the needs of examining bodies. In any case students need to know how they are doing so they can plan for progression or careers. But how *often* do they need this summative information, which measures their learning, rather than formative information such as medals and missions?

This depends on the course, but on many full-time courses summative information once or twice a term may well be sufficient, in some cases less often. An exception might be if a student is failing. Other strategies for coping with the grading problem are given at the end of this chapter.

Do your students crave grades? Black *et el.* (2003) found that students prefer marking to be in pencil rather than red pen, and to be legible and understandable, but that they were very happy not to be graded. Their teachers were very surprised by this!

Medal and mission feedback is non-judgmental about attainment

To avoid the problem that grading can lead to despair or complacency, medal and mission feedback should *accept* the student's present position on the attainment slope in the diagram on page 87 without judgement. Whether the learner's attainment is high or low, they need to know what they did well, and what they need to do to improve. This creates a 'task focus' in contrast to an 'ego focus'.

Unconditional positive regard.

> *Carl Rogers stressed the importance of 'unconditional positive regard' in supporting learning over 40 years ago.*

Black and William's review (1998) included a close look at research on the feedback actually given to students by their teachers. They found that even when giving formative feedback teachers tended, consciously or not, to respond to the learner's class position.

• Able students tended to get medals but no mission – they weren't stretched.
• Weaker students tended to get a mission but no medal – their effort and learning was not acknowledged.

However, there was a disturbing exception. Students of very low attainment tended to get 'empty praise', that is, praise with no information about what was done well: 'Well done, Jo', or 'You've worked well today, Peter. I'm proud of you'. So they didn't get 'missions'.

The weakest learners got the least helpful feedback. These are the very learners who will find it difficult to work out for themselves what they have done well, and what they need to improve. In effect they were being prevented from learning by poor-quality feedback.

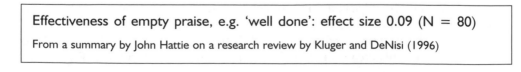

Effectiveness of empty praise, e.g. 'well done': effect size 0.09 (N = 80)

From a summary by John Hattie on a research review by Kluger and DeNisi (1996)

The psychological effects of judgemental and informative feedback are summarised in the diagram below.

Judgemental feedback
'Here is my measurement'

Informative feedback
'These are your goals, this is what you do well, and this is how to get better'

Characteristics of this feedback

The feedback compares students with each other, and encourages them to compete. It is 'norm referenced'.
The teacher gives grades, marks and comments that make conscious or unconscious comparisons with others.

There are clear assessment criteria and goals. Feedback consists of information about the extent to which these have been met. There are informative
medals: for what they have done well
missions : showing how to improve

Effect on self-esteem

Judgement creates a 'blame culture' making students nervous and protective of their self-esteem. They blame factors out of their control. They avoid risks and challenges. The self-esteem and complacency of high achieving students rises. *Disempowerment*

The student feels accepted, and that their efforts are being recognised and valued. Self-esteem and commitment tend to rise and there is increased emotional involvement in tasks. *Empowerment*

Consequent learning strategies

Maladaptive learning strategies
Extrinsic motivation, teacher driven, surface learning. Their eye is on the grade, not on understanding, learning or the task. The student memorises, seeks short cuts, copies, etc. They want the 'trick to get the tick'. Right-answer syndrome

Effective learning strategies
Intrinsic motivation, value driven, deep learning. Their eyes are on the goals, assessment criteria, tasks, and their 'missions'. High-quality learning aimed at understanding and improvement prevails. As esteem comes from effort, not comparative attainment, students are more likely to take risks and accept challenges.

Students' learning theory

Maladaptive and blaming learning theory
Ability is the key and it is inborn. 'It's in the genes'.
'Mistakes are shameful.'
'Effort shows you must be stupid.'
Extrinsic motivation: It's only worth working if you get something out of it.

Adaptive and blame-free learning theory
Ability is not inborn, it is learned from effort and practice which are all in my control. 'It's up to me.'
Mistakes are useful informative feedback.
Intrinsic motivation: learning is an end in itself.

Effect on low achievers

There is reduced interest, effort, persistence, self-esteem and self-belief, and less emotional investment in learning.

In some cases: 'learned helplessness':
'No matter what I do I'm bound to fail'.
The student withdraws and retires hurt, rejecting the teachers, college, etc.
Hostility towards learning

Learning is seen as something for others.

There is increased: interest, effort, persistence, self-esteem and self-belief.

In time: learned resourcefulness: 'There must be a way round my difficulties and if I find it I will succeed.'
'Learning depends on time, effort, corrected practice, and using the right strategies.'
Identification with the aims of the course.

Learning is seen as an end in itself.

Extremes of summative versus informative feedback: summarises some key ideas in Black and William (1998).

Some feedback strategies to try

How can we make sure all learners get clear goals and high-quality medal and mission feedback? Don't forget that *you* need feedback too, so that you can adjust your teaching. This approach to assessment has been called 'assessment *for* learning' to distinguish it from the summative, measurement-focused, assessment *of* learning.

Use interactive teaching methods
Chapter 15 deals with how to get feedback while students are beginning to learn new material.

Use feedback methods such as self-, peer and spoof assessment
Chapter 19 deals with these and other methods to ensure feedback after or possibly during an activity.

Give time for practice
Try to ensure that there is plenty of formatively assessed practice of similar tasks before work on such tasks is submitted for summative assessment.

Get students to show where they have met criteria
Ask students to mark in the margin where they have met criteria, for example writing '5' where criterion '5' is met. This makes them think about the goals (criteria), and saves you marking time!

Stress improvement
Give students time in class to read comments and to improve work, whether or not it is to be resubmitted. Get students to track their own progress up the attainment slope, for example by ticking off informal or formal competences such as 'Can draw graphs'. For long assignments get students to check their own and each other's work task by task, so it can be improved before submission.

Represent students' progress graphically
To ensure that students try to beat their own record rather than someone else's you can get them to record their progress on a graph. You can also give students stickers for progress made (not attainment); this is remarkably successful even with many 16–19 learners.

Withhold grades
Don't give grades or marks. If this cannot be done, record grades and marks in your markbook, passing them on: only during progress reviews; only when work has been corrected; only after the completion of the next assignment, etc. Whatever you do, stress progress over time, and downplay the importance of grades and marks. If grades are used get students to track their improvement with them rather than compare themselves with someone else.

Use group and pair work

Students naturally give feedback and help each other in groups, and you can encourage this by setting tasks to explain to teach other and to check each other's understanding.

Establish an 'assessment for learning' culture

For example establish ground rules that stress that learning is the result of effort, care, using the right strategy, getting help when you need it, time spent practising, and so on, rather than innate ability. The beginning of Chapter 19 considers this in more detail. But you need to adopt this culture in your own approach too. For example, treat mistakes as an interesting insight into misconceptions and an opportunity to learn, and prize effort and progress rather than attainment.

Align summative and formative assessment

Make sure classwork and other formative work involves similar tasks as summative assessment, and is assessed using the same criteria. In this way you will develop the skills required for assessment success. For example, mark students' practice essays using standard examining-body criteria. This is 'backward planning'.

Use assessment proformas

These have goals on them, and a space for medals and missions. See below and page 260 in Chapter 19 for examples. There are many more on www.geoffpetty.com. Assessment proformas are often used for formal assessments but they can be very informal and used for classwork, practical work and homework as well as for major assignments. Tina above used one. They are best presented before the task is started to make the goals clear.

Use learning loops
The target from one task or assignment is written in a target box at the beginning of the next. Students complete the new task trying to meet their target. Alternatively students can be given a minimum improvement target. See the diagram on p. 99.

There are many more informal ways to use 'learning loops'; for example, you can remind students before completing a task that they have done this before and ask: 'What did you learn about doing this last time, what do you need to look out for?'

References and further reading

Black, P. J. and Wiliam, D. (1998) 'Assessment and classroom learning', *Assessment in Education: Principles, Policy and Practice*, 5, 1: 7–74.

Black P. *et al.* (2003) *Assessment for Learning: Putting it into Practice*, Buckingham: Open University Press.

Clarke, S. (2001) *Unlocking Formative Assessment: Practical Strategies for Enhancing Pupils' Learning in the Primary Classroom*, London: Hodder and Stoughton.

Self-assessment			
Skill	**I didn't**	**I think I did**	**I did**	**Teacher assessment**
You planned the writing				
Used sentences well				
Used paragraphs well				
Used verbs well				
Proofread it				
Used capital letters well				
Used full stops and commas well				
Used apostrophes well				
Correct spelling				
Appropriate style				
Answered the question				
Good conclusion				
Strengths:				
Corrections needed for this piece of work:				
Targets for next written assignment:				

Example of an assessment proforma.

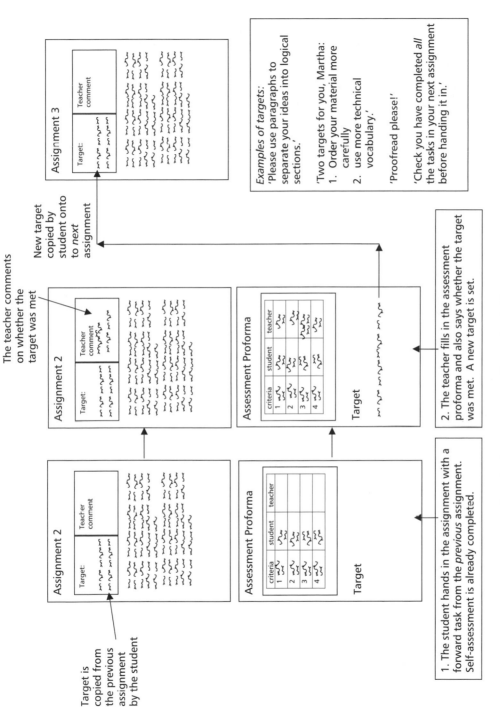

Learning loops: targets or 'forward tasks' for assignments.

Clarke, S., Timperley, H. and Hattie, J. (2003) *Unlocking Formative Assessment: Practical Strategies for Enhancing Pupils' Learning in the Primary and Intermediate Classroom* (New Zealand edition), Auckland: Hodder Moa Beckett.

Hattie, J. A., 'Influences on student learning'. Download from Professor John Hattie's staff home page: www.arts.auckland.ac.nz/staff/index.cfm?P=5049.

Kluger, A. N. and DeNisi, A. (1996) 'The effects of feedback interventions on performance: a historical review, a meta-analysis, and a preliminary feedback intervention theory', *Psychological Bulletin*, 119: 254–89.

Petty, G. (2004) *Teaching Today: A Practical Guide* (3rd edition), Cheltenham: Nelson Thornes.

Sadler, R. (1989) 'Formative assessment and the design of instructional systems', *Instructional Science*, 18, 119–44.

Torrance, H. and Pryor, J. (1998) *Investigating Formative Assessment: Teaching, Learning and Assessment in the Classroom*, Buckingham: Open University Press.

See also:

www.arg.educ.cam.ac.uk: website of the Assessment Reform Group, who developed the research and ideas in this chapter.

www.qca.org.uk/7659.html: Assessment for learning on the QCA website.

9 Whole-class interactive teaching (effect size 0.81)

'Whole-class interactive teaching' is not a single teaching method, but a family of highly structured methods. The methods are variously called direct instruction, explicit instruction, active teaching, or – more commonly now – whole-class interactive teaching. There is no agreed structure for any one of these methods, but they are all very similar, highly structured, teacher controlled, but active for the learner. I show some examples later in this chapter, and you might like to glance at these now to get the idea. Don't get too hung up on structure though; 'interactivity' is crucial too.

At the end of the chapter we will look at the principles that these methods share.

Whole-class interactive teaching tops John Hattie's effect-size table. This is the world champion and Olympic-gold-medal-winner of teaching methods, which has beaten thousands of other improvement factors with an impressive effect size of 0.81 (see Chapter 5). If all teachers used it whenever it was appropriate, all our students would do almost two grades better in their exams. Or would they? Despite this transcendent position in Hattie's table, many, perhaps most, education academics treat it with spitting contempt. This is rather like finding a sure cure for cancer that many doctors refuse to prescribe. What *is* going on?!

Whole-class interactive teaching has the misfortune to find itself slap bang in the middle of the disputed territory between two rival ways of looking at learning and teaching.

In the 1960s many researchers believed that a teacher's effectiveness could be predicted by their personality. But their research found there were some good extrovert teachers, and some bad ones; and there were some good introvert teachers, and some bad ones. And the same was true for any other personality factor they researched. More than a decade of scrupulous research drew an embarrassing blank. Now 'personality' hardly ever figures in the index of books on teaching.

So researchers began to turn to two other areas of study. Some focused on the learner, and asked 'What goes on in a student's head when they learn effectively?' and were often called 'constructivists' or 'cognitivists'. Chapter 2 was mainly dedicated to their findings. Others became teacher focused and asked 'What do effective teachers do in the classroom?' Chapters 4–7 considered their approach, and gave summaries of Hattie's and Marzano's findings.

These two research programmes amassed mountains of impressive evidence in favour of their respective ideas and theories. Many researchers and academics on each side became so impressed by the evidence in favour of their own 'side' that they often discounted the evidence for the other side. This resulted in 'methodological wars' where educationalists became progressively polarised into something like the two camps shown in the diagram below.

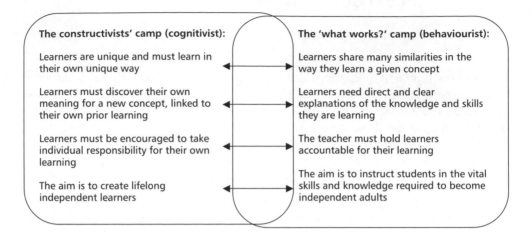

The more evidence each side amassed in its favour, the more they thought they were right and *so the other side was wrong*. Their mistake of course, was the conclusion in italics. If there is a lot of evidence for your point of view, that does not necessarily disprove another point of view, unless of course the points of view contradict each other. But have a look at the statements in this diagram. Are they contradictory? Couldn't we agree with them all?

The beef that constructivists have with whole-class interactive teaching is that it encourages rote learning without understanding, which leads to learning that cannot be applied to real problems; we looked at this issue in Chapter 2. The beef that whole-class interactive teaching advocates often have with constructivist methods is that students cannot discover everything for themselves. Sir Isaac Newton was a bright guy and even he took some considerable time to develop the laws of motion; will 'GCSE Physics 2b' manage it in an hour and a half on Friday afternoon?

These beefs make fair points, but all they are saying is that the 'other camp' advocates an approach to teaching that can be misused to the point that it creates very ineffective learning.

Of *course* constructivist methods such as guided discovery or 'teaching by asking' can be misused. And so can whole class interactive teaching. The trick is to use whole-class interactive teaching only when it is appropriate, and then in a constructivist way. And to use constructivist teaching only when *it* is appropriate, and then in a carefully structured (that is whole-class interactive teaching style) way.

This is not easy, but there is enough overlap between the two camps to make it possible. First you must refuse to buy the false dichotomy between the two camps, and you must accept that each approach is only appropriate in certain circumstances.

> *'Whole-class interactive teaching' owes its high effect size to being a 'Russian doll' that contains many any other strategies, such as explaining objectives, active learning, feedback, reviews, and homework. Many of these sub-strategies are extolled by constructivist teachers.*

A parable

Once upon a time there were two chefs working in the same kitchen. One thought that the quality of a dish depended on using the best available recipe, and the other that the best dishes depended on the quality and freshness of their ingredients. Each chef tried to persuade their customers with vivid arguments and experiments to prove their case. Everyone who ate in the restaurant was persuaded by one of the two chefs, and insisted that she prepared their food.

Then along came a little girl who listened attentively to both chefs, and then said she would like her dishes prepared with ingredients from the chef who believed in the importance of ingredients, but prepared with the recipe of the chef who believed in the importance of recipes. She ate very well.

Like many apparent dichotomies both sides see part of the truth, but the whole truth requires *both* points of view. Whenever I have observed excellent teachers they always seem to 'have it both ways', skipping blithely from camp to camp whenever it suits them, and Chapter 22 on excellent teachers shows that this is generally true. It is very likely that the teachers trained in whole-class interactive teaching before the experiments represented in Hattie's table were having it both ways too.

Whole-class interactive teaching and its variants and synonyms have been most commonly used in mathematics and literacy teaching, but if a topic or skill can be taught directly topic by topic, then it can usually be taught by whole-class interactive teaching . However, the teacher will use it differently to teach different topics.

The national literacy and numeracy strategies both use a form of direct instruction.

From BBC News 15 December, 2004*:

> England's Schools Minister, Stephen Twigg, said: 'The fact that our pupils have made bigger progress in maths than any other country highlights how our numeracy strategy has brought real dividends, and is testament to the hard work of teachers and pupils.'

It also shows that direct instruction works!

*news.bbc.co.uk/2/hi/uk_news/education/4092133.stm

There are several whole-class interactive teaching methods. You might like to adopt or adapt one of these to make it your own. Alternatively, you could read them all through, try some, and then combine the best of them with your own ideas to create your own approach. Or you could use the 'PAR' model, in which I have tried to distil the most effective aspects of this approach. This is described in detail in Chapter 14.

Model 1: Active teaching model

(See facing page.) This is an early method developed for the Missouri Mathematics Effectiveness Project (Primary Schools), but don't let that put you off; it could be adapted to any academic age or level, and to teach literacy, foreign languages, science – indeed any structured skill-based subject.

Note the built-in student practice and the weekly and monthly reviews. It assumes one lesson per day.

You see what I mean about being structured? There is never any doubt about the purpose of this lesson, and each part of it, and students will usually be very clear about what is being done and why.

Some teachers like this approach; others will say 'Hey, I teach English literature, I can't teach like that!' We will see later in this chapter, however, that this structure could work very well indeed in *some* English literature classes, for example for a lesson where a discrete interpretive skill is being taught.

It is not just the structure that defines this style of teaching, it is also the *interactivity* between teacher and learner. We will look at this in much more detail in Chapter 15. But let's look quickly at one way to get interactivity: 'assertive questioning'. Try to work out the value to teacher and student before I explain it below.

 ## Assertive questioning

1. Buzz groups work on a thought-provoking question or task, to produce a fully argued and justified answer:
   'Should the press be free to publish whatever it wants?'
   'Why do some animals create lots of eggs, and some very few?'
   'Sketch a graph for $3x^2 - 4x + 8$.'

2. The teacher monitors this work asking:
   'Does everyone have an answer? Ask me for a hint if not.'
   'Does anyone need more time?'
   If a group does not respond to this offer of help they are 'fair game' for the next stage. The teacher does *not* give the answer away until stage 6, even non-verbally, even if they help a group.

3. The teacher *nominates* individuals to give their group's answer, and to justify it:
   'Alice, what's your group's answer? . . . Why do you think that?' The teacher *thanks* the student for their answer, *but does not evaluate it*. When possible that teacher

1 Daily review (about 8 minutes, except on Mondays)

   a. Review of concepts and skills associated with yesterday's homework.
   b. Collect and deal with homework assignment.
   c. Ask several mental computation exercises.

2 Development (about 20 minutes) (introducing new concepts, developing understanding)

   a. Briefly focus on prerequisite skills and concepts.
   b. Focus on meaning and promoting student understanding by lively explanations, demonstrations, etc.
   c. Assess student competence:
      i. using process and product questions (active interaction)
      ii. using controlled practice.
     (Assertive questioning and other interactive methods are used here and elsewhere; see below and especially Chapter 15.)
   d. Repeat and elaborate on the meaning portion as necessary.

3 Seatwork (students working alone on exercises) (about 15 minutes)

   a. Provide uninterrupted successful practice.
   b. Momentum – keep the ball rolling – get everyone involved, then sustain involvement.
   c. Alerting – let students know their work will be checked at the end of each period.
   d. Accountability – check the students' work.

4 Homework assignment

   • Assign on a regular basis at the end of each maths class except Fridays.
   • Should involve about 15 minutes of work to be done at home.
   • Should include one or two problems that review earlier work.

5 Special reviews

Weekly review:
   • Conducted during the first 20 minutes on Mondays.
   • Focus on skills and concepts covered during the previous week. This is an active review in that students don't just listen again but 'do it again'.

Monthly review:
   • Conduct every fourth Monday.
   • Focus on skills and concepts covered since the last review; this includes 'doing it again'.

asks for part of the answer from each group and goes round the groups until all answers have been harvested. Answers may be written on the board by the student (this would work especially well in the case of the sketch graph), or the teacher.

4. The teacher gets a response from each group in this way, or at least a number of groups, and then points out any inconsistencies between the groups' answers.

5. The aim now is to get the *whole class to agree their 'class answer(s)'*. The teacher encourages the class to discuss and evaluate their various answers, and to agree, and to justify their 'class answer'. If there is no one right answer, then the class discuss the merits of the various answers. Minority views are allowed, but the aim is consensus.

6. Only when the class have agreed their answer does the teacher 'give away' the right answer, or evaluate and comment on the answers given.

7. The teacher praises students' efforts and achievements during the process above.

As we will see in Chapter 15, the aim of this questioning strategy is to get the students to participate, to give the teacher feedback on the extent of student under-standing, and to give the students time to think and to receive feedback on the quality of their answers. Hattie has found that feedback is crucial, with an effect size of 0.81, so it is no great surprise to find that high-quality feedback plays such an important role in whole-class interactive teaching. The method also teaches students to think.

When is it appropriate to use whole-class interactive teaching?

It is certainly true to say that this method was designed for teaching mathematics and basic literacy, and works best when teaching a discrete point or skill. (Look again at the example tasks in point 1 above.) But very many teachers do this, if not all the time, then some of the time.

Imagine for example an English literature class on imagery. It is a discrete technical skill to recognise imagery in a poem and realise its purpose, so this lesson could be structured in a very similar way.

TEACHING THE USE OF IMAGERY IN POETRY

1 Daily review

The teacher reviews the learning from the last session and she deals with homework queries.

2 Development

a. She *reminds* students of the meaning of the terms 'imagery', 'metaphor', 'simile' and 'personification', which have been briefly dealt with before and are all prerequisite knowledge for this class on imagery in Owen's poetry.

b. *Modelling.* She studies the first few verses of one of Owen's poems, and how to detect the types of imagery used, and why Owen used them. She then summarises the process of how to look for imagery.

c. *Controlled practice.* She then asks the students to work in pairs to look for imagery in another of Owen's poems. She visits pairs to see how they are doing, and to assess their competence at this task. Can they do this alone yet, and without help?
She chooses students at random to explain and justify the imagery they have found, and then asks the class whether they agree. Only then does she give her own ideas on the task, and in this way she 'eavesdrops' on the understanding of the students in her class.

d. She repeats 2a and 2b above with some other poems, until she finds that the students have developed the skill well enough to do some work on their own. This takes four cycles, but the last is quick.

3 Seatwork (students working alone on exercises) (about 15 minutes)

• She sets the class to work individually now on a new poem.
• She visits individuals as they work.
• She reminds students that their work will be checked very soon.

- She gets peers to check each other's work and to come to an agreement over any differences.
- She gives her model answers and allows the peers to check their own work against this model.

There is class discussion about some difficult points.

- She asks students to summarise the main points about imagery and uses these to compose a short note which students write down. This includes a reference to the section in their textbook on this topic.

4 Homework assignment

- She sets a homework on imagery, and a brief task on characterisation in *Romeo and Juliet*, which the students did last term. This last task is mainly a review exercise, but she sets a task on imagery in one of Romeo's speeches.

5 Special reviews

- She reviews the skills on imagery in Owen at the end of the week, by giving the students a task to find imagery in another poem.
- A month later there is a homework to look for imagery in another poet's work.

Is this a bad lesson? If skilfully implemented it could teach a discrete skill well. Note how carefully it checks the learning, and ensures that no student is left behind. It certainly isn't enough; there needs to be more discussion on interpreting poetry. But even here a variant of 'assertive questioning' could be used to explore interpretations of a poem and justify them using the text.

In Hungary mathematics teachers use whole-class interactive teaching, often following sequences like this:

1. The teacher states a problem.
2. Students debate how it could be tackled.
3. The teacher gives feedback on some of the students' strategies.
4. Class agreement on ways to solve the problem, facilitated by the teacher (there may be more than one way accepted).
5. Students solve the problem, and the teacher looks at their work.
6. The teacher gives feedback on the students' work, pointing out weaknesses.

7. Students self-correct their work after this feedback.
8. The teacher praises the students' effort, strategies, and skills.
9. The teacher and class evaluate the procedure(s) and review 'what we have learned'.
10. The teacher makes some extra comments, or sets an extension activity, and perhaps a homework which is often to prepare for the next class.

Throughout this sequence the teacher asks questions such as:

Why? . . . Who agrees or disagrees with that? . . . What's your reasoning there? . . . Where did you get that idea from? . . . How did you write the solution down? . . . How could you guess an approximation to the answer? . . . Who did it another way? . . . Who got a different result? . . . Is that answer correct or incorrect? . . . Why?

Why these methods work

You will gain a good deal by asking yourself why these methods work, and then checking your conceptualisation with what follows.

First of all the teaching is well structured. Goals are set, so students are clear what they have to learn, and they are more likely to stay on task. The teacher shows how to do it, step by step (this is called modelling), from known to unknown and from concrete to abstract. The teacher clearly indicates any transition in the lesson:

'OK, stop working on this exercise now, even if you haven't finished . . . John, Peter, you too. That's better. OK, I'm going to ask for answers now, and you are going to mark your own as we go through. Who has an answer for question 1?'

The method also involves moving from modelling to independent activity slowly; the teacher monitors students' understanding and explores misconceptions with the class. So students are much more likely to be successful in independent work.

During this modelling and monitoring the students get to know, as does their teacher, if learning is weak in any way. For example, a student might do a one-minute activity and then find they get poor answers. They can then do something about this: ask a peer, look at the task and answer more carefully, look at the modelled answers, listen to the teacher's explanation of why the good answers are good, or ask the teacher for help. In this way initial misconceptions are cleared up before causing problems in independent practice.

Once the teacher has discovered the mistakes and misconceptions made by the students, she can correct these before they get well learned.

Badly structured whole-class teaching often misses out modelling and controlled practice opportunities like this. Go back to the lesson on page 107 and imagine it without sections 2b, c and d. The lesson would not work nearly as well as teacher and student do not get feedback on their understanding.

Comparing whole-class teaching with students working alone

If students are learning mostly alone, for example in 'resource-based learning' approaches, they often miss out on the modelling and monitoring mentioned above, so both student and teacher are less clear if good learning is taking place before independent practice.

. . . she can correct these before they get well learned . . .

Ranking	Method	Effect size	Number of studies
1	Whole-class interactive teaching	0.93	1925
37	Individualised instruction	0.42	5948
48	Computer-aided instruction	0.32	18 231
71	Programmed instruction	0.14	801

It is instructive to compare whole-class interactive teaching with the above methods from Hattie's effect-size table (see Chapter 5), all of which involve students learning largely independently and at their own pace. Individualised instruction involves diagnosing the prior learning of a student and using this information to devise an individualised programme of study for them. The teacher then visits students in the class, usually one at a time. This is an almost unavoidable method if students arrive at the same class with very different prior learning. It is a similar method to what is often called 'resource-based learning'.

Programmed instruction was developed by the behaviourist psychologist B. F. Skinner in the 1960s, and also involves students working alone, but this time they interact with a teaching machine which takes them step by step through the topic responding appropriately to the answers the student gives to questions. Research showed that students would soon get bored with programmed instruction, even if they were learning successfully with it. Computer-aided instruction uses a similar strategy though with a much more powerful teaching machine, the computer. This is not simply students using computers, though; the students are being taught by specially designed software.

The difficulties that learners have with computer-aided instruction have been well documented. See the further reading section at the end of this chapter for references.

As Hattie's inaugural paper states, students usually get much less interaction with the teacher in these more solitary methods than with the more interactive whole-class method. Other difficulties with learning alone, compared to whole-class teaching, include poor feedback to teacher and student, poorer monitoring of student progress, lack of social contact, and lack of pace. Good quality whole-class teaching is sociable and enjoyable, and there is a real sense of momentum and progress for teacher and student.

Knowing these weaknesses, individualised and computer assisted learning is being improved; see for example the pilot and navigator approach in Chapter 19. There will always be times when whole-class teaching is not appropriate, and alternative methods must be used, for example when the starting point of students in a class is radically different.

Does this method work with students of very low attainment?

Yes. Peter Westwood is Associate Professor in Special Education at the University of Hong Kong and has reviewed research on teaching in his excellent book *Commonsense Methods for Children with Special Educational Needs* (2003). He looks at strategies for the regular classroom and says that students with low attainment learn just like the rest of us! He advocates whole-class interactive teaching methods for content and for skills and processes, but also more open methods for variety and for differentiation. Hattie's table of effect sizes for special education, which includes low attaining students, gives the method an effect size of 0.90. Maybe all teachers could take that advice, whoever they teach. Chapter 22 on expert teachers will explore this further.

As you get better at using whole-class interactive teaching:

- Use challenging and interesting questions and challenges, not just routine questions.
- Expect precision in the way that students use terminology.
- Expect full participation, nominating students who are not participating to answer questions.
- Expect students to present work to the rest of the class, justifying their thinking.
- Model respect for students' answers, however weak.
- Explore students' misconceptions and use them as teaching points.
- Use assertive questioning and student demonstration in the way described in Chapter 15.
- Get students to express their own understandings and use these as the basis for notes.
- Create an atmosphere of positive interaction in your classroom.
- Make sure you don't use this method all the time!

Hattie's table of effect sizes for special education has an average effect size of 0.90 for whole-class interactive teaching. There are 100 studies.

References and further reading

Good, T. L., Grouws, D. A. and Ebmeir, D. (1983) *Active Mathematics Teaching*, New York: Longman.

Muijs, D. and Reynolds, D. (2000) 'School effectiveness and teacher effectiveness in mathematics: some preliminary findings from the evaluation of the Mathematics Enhancement Programme (Primary)', *School Effectiveness and School Improvement*, 11, 3, 273–303.

Muijs, D. and Reynolds, D. (2001) *Effective Teaching: Evidence and Practice*, London: Paul Chapman.

Petty, G. (2004) *Teaching Today: A Practical Guide* (3rd edition), Cheltenham: Nelson Thornes. See Chapter 24 on whole-class interactive teaching.

Westwood, P. (2003) *Commonsense Methods for Children with Special Educational Needs: Strategies for the Regular Classroom* (4th edition), London: RoutledgeFalmer.

www.ericdigests.org/pre-922/role.htm gives an interesting account of the importance of review in teaching.

10 Visual representations and graphic organisers (effect size 1.2 to 1.3)

In this chapter we are going to have a look at one of the most powerful routes to understanding that research has uncovered, and see how you can make use of it in your own teaching. While you read about these methods, try to think how you could use them with topics that are hard to teach, or hard for students to learn. However, given the power of the methods, a case could be made for representing almost every topic in a visual manner, no matter how 'un-visual' and abstract the topic appears to be. Indeed the more abstract the topic, the more important it is to represent it visually. Few of us are practised at this, so expect the skill to take time, for you and for your students.

Before reading on, scan through some of the diagrammatic ways to represent information in this chapter, and ask yourself 'Why do they work?'

These are called 'graphic organisers' because they organise content graphically. They may contain text, but the position of the text *shows relationships within the information*: for example, this causes that, this is part of that, or this comes before that, and so on. Organisers are best at showing this relational information and can often show this best if there is a minimum of text to distract the student, at least to begin with. It works well to give students a diagram with a little text on it, and then ask them to add text detail as they learn about the topic.

Graphic organisers greatly help most dyslexic and very right-brain learners especially.

Once we have these modes of representation at our disposal, and as students become more practised at using them, we can use them in many ways. At the end of this chapter we will see that graphic or if you prefer visual representations can be used:

- By the *teacher* as a means to display information to the class on the board, hand-outs, etc., or to provide an advance organiser, summary or handout. This can help you explain and acts as a focus for your written or oral questions.
- By the *student* as an activity (creating or completing one), and as a means to plan writing, make notes, as a support to help them answer questions or discuss issues, and as a learning game.

Before we consider these uses, let's look at this 'visual vocabulary'. There are a number of tools at our disposal and few of us are practised at using them all.

Types of graphic organisers and other visual representations

The best form of visual representation to use depends on the information you want to display, especially its structure. Often it helps to represent the same concept in more than one visual way; for example, an economics teacher might use a causal flow diagram, a mind map and a graph to represent different aspects of the pricing of a manufactured product.

Because ideas can be represented in more than one way beware of leaping on the first representation that occurs to you. Scan through the possibilities a few times to decide on the best way(s). At the end of this chapter is an exercise to choose the best organiser for ten topics.

The examples I give below are very dull looking. Your own and your students' creations can be greatly enlivened by the addition of relevant images, symbols, icons, and so on. Metaphorical images are particularly powerful; for example, 'health and safety' represented as a shield, the conservation of energy represented as money changing hands, and so on.

The best visual representations are often free form, metaphorical, and involve a number of aspects of the methods shown below. I believe, though it is hard to prove, that every concept can be represented visually.

Simple illustrative methods

These hardly need explanation, but here are a few examples. Can you make use of them more? Bar and pie charts and pictograms are also helpful, but they are well known and I won't deal with them here.

Such diagrams on posters, leaflets and in notes can be expressive, but some diagrams show the *structure* of information and are particularly powerful. These are called 'graphic organisers'. I sometimes represent handwritten or typed text as just a squiggle in the diagrams that follow.

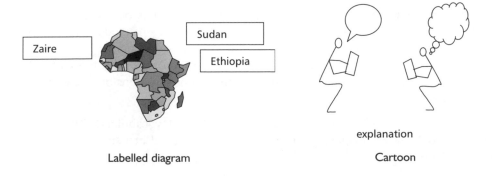

Labelled diagram

explanation

Cartoon

Graphic organisers

The atomistic mind map

This is the usual way to produce mind-maps, webs, semantic maps concept maps, spider diagrams, and bubble diagrams, etc., which all mean pretty much the same thing. The topic is cut up into a number of pieces, and these parts are then displayed separately as shown on the right. This cutting up makes the representation 'atomistic' rather than holistic. There are specific ways of mind mapping, for example that advocated by Tony Buzan, but I am not aware of any evidence that one way is better than another.

A topic can often be split up in more than one way, each capable of producing a different mind map. For example, transport in the UK could be atomised along the lines of land, sea and air as shown in the diagram above, but also England, Scotland and Wales and Northern Ireland; or as private, commercial and public, and so on.

Closely related diagrams include the tree diagram (see the example below), for example organisational charts that show the hierarchy of command in large organisations, family trees, and so on; and the target diagram.

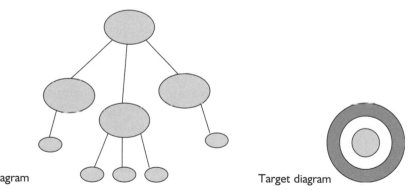

Tree diagram   Target diagram

The Venn diagram

As we saw in Chapter 2, a concept such as 'ball', 'empowerment' or 'feudalism' is best developed by seeing examples of this concept. The examples should be typical to begin with, but then less typical and more varied in their contexts. (If all the examples of 'empowerment' are in a business context, then the learner might mistakenly believe it is exclusively a business concept.)

Concept development with Venn diagrams

Suppose a biology teacher is trying to develop the concept of reflexes, such as pulling your hand away from a hot object. As part of this, she gets her students to create a Venn diagram. They put examples of reflexes inside the boundary and non-examples outside. A 'non-example' is one that shares some features with reflexes, such as a quick movement, but is not in fact a reflex. Marginal cases, if there are any, can be placed on the border. Students need to be clear of the justification for all of these placements.

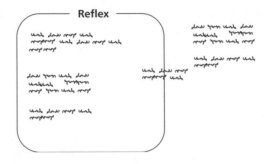

We can do more with Venn diagrams, however. Once examples and non-examples have been placed, then the students, teacher or class could place on the diagram:

- Statements about the characteristics of reflexes, e.g. 'It is done without thinking.' Statements are placed inside if they are true of osmosis, outside if they are not.
- Illustrations of reflexes: these can be placed inside; illustrations of non-examples, or incorrect diagrams, outside.
- Past-paper questions that involve reflexes (even if they don't mention it by name): these can be placed inside, others outside.

etc.

Venn diagrams are great to put in students' notes. They are also useful if displayed and created on boards or flip charts; or with Post-its, cards, magnetic boards; or with drag-and-drop text boxes on a computer or interactive whiteboard displays. Colour coding often helps; statements could be in blue, questions in red, and so on.

Venn diagrams can be used as the basis of a learning game, as we will see on page 000. Students are given cards, Post-its, or text boxes with the statements, diagrams and questions on, and have to work in pairs to move these inside or outside the boundary as appropriate. This then becomes a 'decisions, decisions' game as described later.

Classifying with Venn diagrams

Concept development can be aided by getting students to classify with Venn diagrams, or just in columns. Suppose a teacher wanted to develop the concepts of noun, verb and adjective; or capitalism, Marxism and post-Marxism. Students can be given statements that they must place in the correct column or position on a

Venn diagram. These statements can be simply written, or in the game form they can be supplied on cards and moved to the right place. Non-examples are most important for concept development or the student might include too much, or too little, in their construct, for example believing that 'red' is a noun 'because it is real – you can see it'.

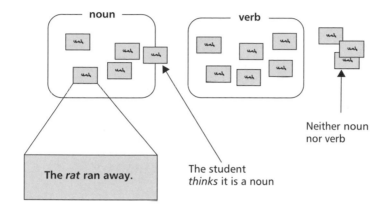

Same but different (effect size 1.3)

In some situations Venn diagrams overlap, as shown in the diagram below.

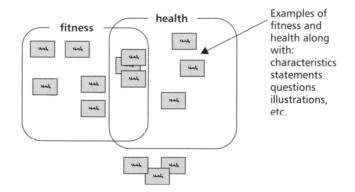

This then becomes a means of representing similarities and differences between fitness and health. This is sometimes called a 'compare and contrast' activity. A student activity in this form has an effect size of 1.3, one of the very largest average effect sizes in Marzano's database. If the concepts are difficult it is often best to compare and contrast a known concept with one that is being learned, for example learning fractions, and then comparing them to percentages. Two unfamiliar concepts may overload our poor students' working memories!

Another method of displaying similarities and differences graphically is to use a table or matrix. This hardly seems graphical at all until you realise that the placement of the text has meaning, just as it does in a mind map. Tables are more amenable to Bill Gates's word processors than Venn diagrams, and can hold a lot of textual detail.

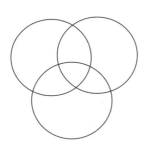

Compare and contrast osmosis and diffusion	different	same
fitness	• Students write here • Students write here	• Students write here
health	• Students write here • Students write here	

It is possible to compare and contrast more than two concepts on either a table or a Venn diagram, but this can get complicated.

Another way to represent similarities and differences in 'X' and 'Y' is to create a mind map for 'X' and one for 'Y', and then combine them as in the diagram below.

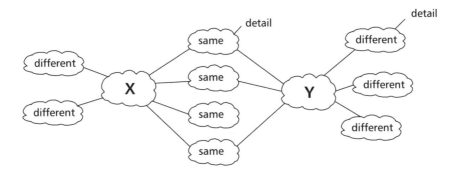

Some examples of concepts that could be given the 'same but different' treatment would be:

- Psychosis and neurosis
- French and traditional English cookery
- Rail and road transport
- Walking and swimming as heart exercise
- Voluntary and public sectors
- Fencing and hedging
- Christianity and Islam
- Momentum and energy.

The continuum or spectrum

The continuum is a well-known device to show the grey areas between two extremes: specific examples are usually placed at the appropriate place along the line. Like all visual representations, continua could be used much more often. For example, they could show the 'spectrum' between:

- top-down (controlling) and bottom-up (delegating) approaches to management (various strategies could then be placed along this continuum)
- left-wing and right-wing approaches to penal reform
- objective/subjective methods of assessment
- the electromagnetic spectrum from radio waves, through light to gamma radiation.

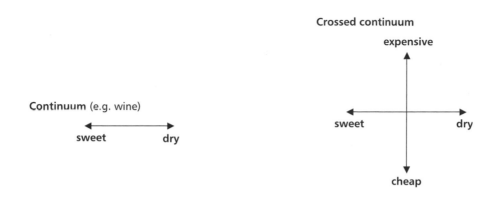

Continua can be 'crossed' to represent two independent criteria; for wine this might be sweet/dry and expensive/cheap. Every wine is now a dot on this graph, and similar wines are clustered together.

The principles diagram

This involves writing a general principle at the top, such as 'hot air rises' or 'delegation creates empowerment'. Examples that illustrate this principle are then shown below. A Venn diagram can also be used. (See p. 116.)

It is important to show non-examples so that students learn the extent of application of the principle. It also helps to put the reasons 'why' on the diagram. Students can state reasons why the principle is true, and reasons why each example is a genuine example. This can be done by adding relational links from the relevant part of the diagram in the style of a mind map.

A principle is a concept and is most 'naturally' learned like any other concept from concrete to abstract. This suggests the use of a Venn diagram.

Another approach to visually representing principles is to create an atomistic mind map with the principle written at its centre, and with examples round the outside.

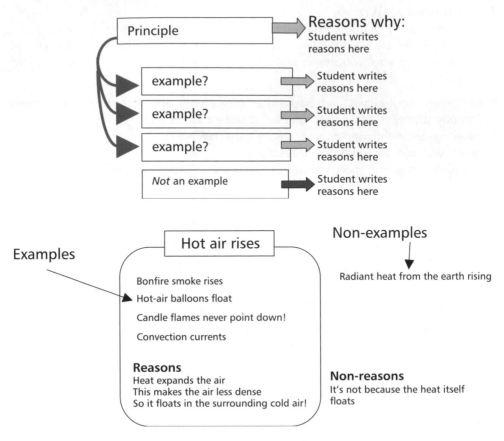

Principle	→	**Reasons why:** Student writes reasons here
example?	→	Student writes reasons here
example?	→	Student writes reasons here
example?	→	Student writes reasons here
Not an example	→	Student writes reasons here

Examples

Hot air rises

Bonfire smoke rises

Hot-air balloons float

Candle flames never point down!

Convection currents

Reasons
Heat expands the air
This makes the air less dense
So it floats in the surrounding cold air!

Non-examples

Radiant heat from the earth rising

Non-reasons
It's not because the heat itself floats

Two principles diagrams.

Methods to represent changes with time

The best-known methods to show changes with time are of course graphs, but there are many other ways.

The storyboard

You could explain, for example, an official complaints procedure using a comic-style cartoon story with speech bubbles and other text. This can be challenging to draw for you or your students, but thankfully the effectiveness of these methods does not depend on artistic ability! A good laugh at poor drawing can sometimes help a lesson.

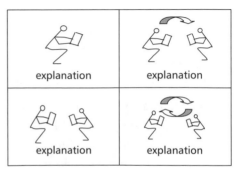

Storyboards can also portray the growth of a plant, the movement of troops on maps, the splitting of the atom, and so on.

The timeline

A timeline is a well-known way to show change, or development over time. It is commonly used to show evolution, geological change, foetal growth, childhood development, cell division, and so on. You can simply write the events or periods along the timeline, or represent them there diagrammatically. You can also use the vertical axis in some way to create a type of graph, or to show different themes as shown below.

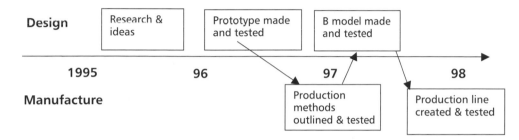

The flow diagram

Flow diagrams are very familiar but also underused. Look at the 'plot flow diagram' used to show the structure of a short story or even a poem. If the same graphic is used over and over with different stories, the student begins to look for the structure in new stories. Getting students to look for the wood rather than at the trees is one of the strengths of many graphic organisers.

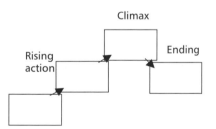

Plot flow diagram.

Flow diagrams can also be used to show mathematical procedures. They are especially useful where students tend to lose the logic of the whole process in the detail of the steps.

Vocational processes, such as drawing up a business plan, or planning a procedure or event, can also be shown in this way. There are bound to be many uses for flow diagrams in your own subject. Can you think of any?

A cause-and-effect diagram can be placed on a timeline. For example, when analysing a play or novel the causes of a central event can be shown in the acts or chapters in which they occur.

Reasoning diagrams

Reasoning can be shown on a flow diagram too, for example to show the causes and effects of a war, or the justification of a political policy. Such diagrams can also show changes over time and are particularly useful in subjects such as history and economics, and in plot analysis in English literature.

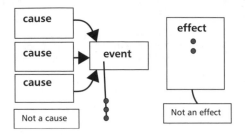

Decision trees

Decisions can also be shown as a flow diagram. They are often used by teachers of mathematics and computer programming, who also use flow diagrams, but their use could be much more widespread.

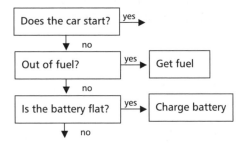

Cycles, systems and clocks

Flow diagrams can show anything from simple cycles to very complex feedback systems. Notice how graphic organisers cut the detail, but show the relationships of the parts. This helps the learner rise up the SOLO taxonomy we saw in Chapter 2.

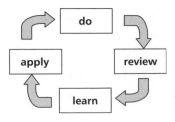

Human interaction outline

This is used for examining conflict and other interactions, for example in social studies, politics, history, literature, etc. It might be used to analyse such interactions as:

– Margaret Thatcher and the run-up to the miners' strike
– The Montague and Capulet families in *Romeo and Juliet*
– The relationship between the allies in the Second World War.

As with all these visual representations I show the basic shape only, and it could be simplified or expanded to suit you and your students. In practice outside influences may well need to be shown on the diagram, but these can be easily added in mind-map style.

As with all visual representations, the graphic suggests key questions; indeed this may be one of their greatest strengths: Who is involved? What are their goals? Did they conflict or cooperate? Why? What was the outcome for each group? And so on.

The structure below was suggested by Jones *et al.* (1988/9). It looks complicated and you might want to design something simpler, but Jones found that this graphic works well.

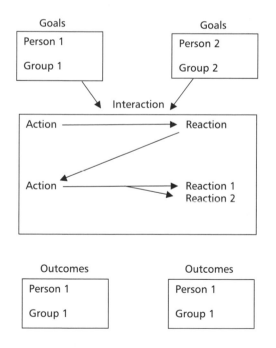

Making models

One of the best biology teachers I ever met used to get his students to make magnified models of complex biological structures such as blood, cells and DNA. The side benches of his lab were festooned with assemblies of painted lavatory rolls and drinking straws, photos of which often got into a biology teacher's journal. I secretly wondered if this was the best use of his students' time, but they were never in doubt. Neither was I when I saw their exam results.

Once the students have made a model, you can base questions on it:

'What would happen to blood if the body were fighting an infection?'

'Why do platelets have a rounded shape?'

These models do not need to be robust and neatly constructed. Once finished, take a photo of them, and put this on the intranet. There may be glass-fronted cases to display your students' models in the corridor.

Tables or matrices

In the holistic mind-map example on page 127, a table is used to hold text in a structured way. This may not look like a graphic organiser until you realise that the position of the text has meaning; it conveys a structure for the information.

Such tables are particularly useful for note making, displays such as posters, lesson activities to complete such tables, and to help students plan writing. We will look at their use in more detail in Chapter 21.

It is usual for students only to write summary notes of the key points in these tables. However, the addition of an 'introduction' and 'conclusion' box can help to encourage students to take a holistic view and to prepare for writing. Which structures are most useful in your own subject?

Some very well known structures can work well: simple columns of text to classify, or to give strengths and weaknesses etc.; or rows of text for lists or bullet points. These rows can be indented and numbered as they are in a business report. Let's look at some less well known structures.

Kipling table

This is for a simple description, for example 'What is a digital multimeter?' or 'Describe the job of a district nurse'.

Title	
Student writes in the rows below to explain:	
What	(what it is used for)
Why	(why it is used)
When and where	(when and where it is used)
How	(how it is used)
Who	(who uses it)

Criterion table

This works well with 'spectacles' as you can see in the diagram on page 127. A criterion is some important factor, issue, period of time or point of view which can act as 'spectacles' to view the whole. For example, if you observed a lesson your spectacles might be 'planning'; 'student activities'; 'resources'; and so on. Criterion tables can be used for simple descriptions or for:

- *Characteristics*. 'Describe the advantages of good dental care'
- *Development or change*. 'How does the introduction of regular exercise improve health?'

Criterion, factor, part, 'spectacle', etc.	Development, change, characteristic, etc.
Criterion 1	
Criterion 2	
Criterion 3	
etc.	

Comparison table

If you split the right-hand column of the criterion table above, you can compare two things using the same criteria. This is a remarkably adaptable and powerful table, and can be used to compare: with and without; before and after; for and against, etc. It actually teaches students to think in a comparative way. Most students compare without using the same criteria throughout, which is not rigorous or 'fair'.

Comparison tables can be used for topics such as:

'What is the advantage of crop rotation?' (with and without crop rotation)

'What was the effect of floating the company on the stock exchange?' (before and after)

'Which of these two marketing plans would you advocate and why?'

Criterion, factor, part, 'spectacle', etc.	Tsarist Russia	Soviet/Communist Russia
Criterion 1		
Criterion 2		

Like all these tables they can be developed into an essay-planning tool by adding an introduction and conclusions. Once students are used to these simple tables, it might help to add more columns, for example one for 'evidence, examples and illustrations'.

Table for 'compare and contrast' by criteria

Criterion, factor, part, 'spectacle', etc.	Tsarist Russia	Soviet/Communist Russia
Criterion 1	Same:	
	Different:	Different:
Criterion 2	Same:	
	Different:	Different:

There are more such tables for download from www.geoffpetty.com.

The above tables are a brilliant means to help students to structure their writing; see Chapter 21 on how to use them. However, they make excellent notes in their own right.

The holistic mind map

At the beginning of this chapter we considered the atomistic mind map (page 115). It cuts a topic such as 'transport' into parts such as land, sea and air transport. But there is another way of analysing a topic. We could look at the whole topic of transport from different points of view such as 'environmental damage', 'cost per mile' or 'passenger convenience', and many other factors or issues. We have already seen the use of criteria or 'spectacles' like this in Chapter 2. In Chapter 21 we will see that students tend not to do a holistic analysis unless taught to do so. But it is a very powerful aid to students' understanding, raising their game on the SOLO taxonomy.

This 'holistic' analysis leads to a holistic mind map, and/or to a holistic criterion or comparison table like those just considered.

The student can then go on to devise a plan for an essay or assignment using both an atomistic and a holistic analysis. This approach is shown in the diagram below, visually of course! The atomistic parts are labelled 1, 2, 3, etc., and the holistic spectacles are labelled A, B, C, etc. Have a look at this now.

General principles are very powerful 'spectacles' and can create a penetrating analysis and teach the principles concerned. For example, a management studies student could use general principles such as 'delegation increases empowerment' to help analyse a case study.

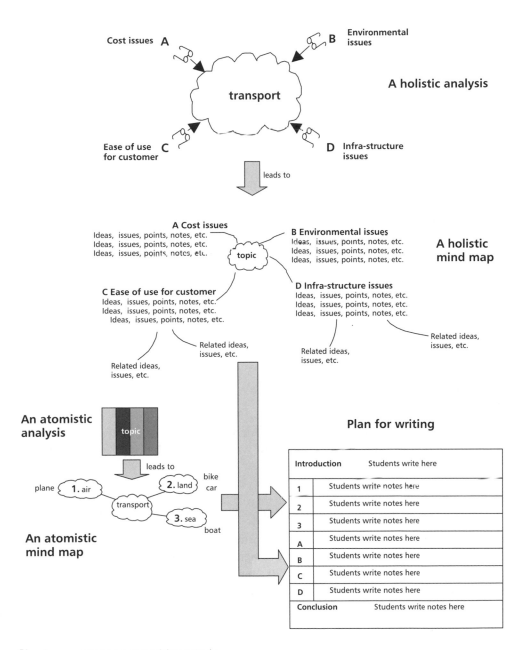

Planning an essay or summarising a topic.

To represent creativity, problem solving, and decision making

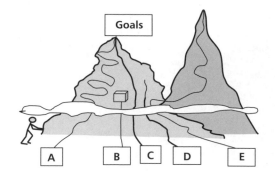

This mountain-climbing model looks simple, but it is remarkably powerful. In Chapter 24 we will see that it can be used to represent the following.

Creativity

This involves setting yourself a goal, or having one set for you, then devising some alternative routes to this goal, choosing the best route, and then working your way up that path, evaluating your progress as you go. Sometimes the only way to find whether a route leads to your goals is to try it. The cloud, obscuring from below whether the route achieves the summit, represents this uncertainty.

Decision making

Here the student is presented with some given alternatives routes and must choose which one.

Problem solving

Here the student is on the way to a goal but finds there is a problem blocking the way (route B). The student can now find a way round the block, or go back to take another route to the same goals.

Evaluation

Students evaluate a 'route' by seeing if it is the best way to get to the goals.

The aim of the model is to help students think holistically and strategically about creativity, etc. Students can use such a diagram to write in their goals, name the paths, and so on; then it can be used to make choices as described in Chapter 24. Alternatively you can just use it as a metaphor: 'OK, so that route is blocked, but are there any others that lead to the same goals?'

Opinion stool

Opinions should be supported by, and be consistent, with factual evidence, true beliefs and accepted values. A graphic organiser in the shape of a three-legged stool can represent this.

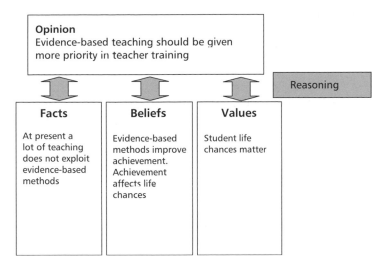

An opinion can fail if any of the 'legs' of the stool fail, or if the reasoning that connects the legs to the opinion fails. Chapter 24 considers this in more detail.

Visual essay planning

Students can create their own graphic organiser, by structuring information for themselves. This method is described in Chapter 18.

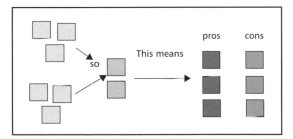

Visual essay planning or visual display of an argument with Post-its.

- Give students a question or essay title.
- Students work alone to write down three to five pertinent issues on separate Post-its, including some non-obvious points.
- Students share their Post-it ideas, placing those that make the same point on top of each other and discarding minor points.
- They then structure their major ideas by putting them in clusters.
- They name the clusters, and even cluster these clusters if it helps.
- They look for relations between the clusters; these are often logical relations.

This is an excellent way to summarise a topic or to plan writing. To prepare students for this method, if they need this, create cards with summary points for a topic, plus cards with less important points, and ask them to structure these as described above.

Analogies, metaphors, and similes (effect size up to 1.3)

Our understanding is fundamentally analogous. Time is not really a line that flows from left to right, but it helps to 'think of it that way'. As we saw in Chapter 2, mentalese is a fundamentally analogous language, turning abstract ideas into a form that our nomad's brain can recall and manipulate.

Why is water being pumped round a circular pipe a metaphor for electricity? Because they have many similarities at the abstract level. For example, if you pump water harder it flows faster; in the same way increasing the 'voltage' of a battery increases the electrical current in a simple circuit. The analogy allows learners to use their existing understanding of flow to understand electrical flow.

Analogies are rarely perfect, but if we know their limitations they can be most valuable.

For example, an accountancy teacher might represent cash flow by analogy with a bath being filled while the plug is left out. The relative rates of water in-flow and out-flow determine the changes in the level of the water in the bath. This 'models' how cash in-flow and out-flow changes the cash in a bank account. The model can be extended by imagining more than one tap and more than one plug hole. The most complex cash-flow situations can be 'modelled' in this way, and this can greatly aid understanding. Similarities between analogy and reality do some of the thinking for us.

If you don't give students analogies they will often invent their own. For example, students and teachers often hold the following analogies/theories about teaching and about intelligence:

- *The jug and mug analogy.* Teachers pour their knowledge into the student's mug.
- *The athletics coach analogy.* Students, like athletes, get better by training or practice, and the teacher's role is to direct this practice in ways that improve their performance.
- *Intelligence is like height:* it is a fixed physical attribute.
- *Intelligence is like muscle strength:* it grows with exercise.

Analogies are often unconscious, and can have profound influence on our beliefs, and so on our behaviour.

Using analogies in practice

Analogies work best if students *use* them; this encourages them to integrate the analogy into their representation of the concept. So:

- Get students to identify the similarities and differences between the analogy and reality, perhaps using a Venn diagram (page 116) or a comparison table.
- Get students to identify what in the analogy represents what in reality, for example the battery is represented by the water pump.
- Ask questions about the analogy and then ask them to translate this into reality:
  - 'What would happen if I half blocked the plughole?'
  - 'What would be the analogous cash flow situation?'
- Ask questions but ask students to use the analogy to answer them.
- Ask your students to create their own analogies; these can be great fun, and they don't forget them. Make sure they fit reality though.

Below is an analogy for learning that I will use in Chapter 8 on feedback.

Kinaesthetic representations

Information can sometimes be represented by bodily movement; for example, students can move their hands in the shape of an arc, a circle and an ellipse to show the meaning of these terms, or in the shape of a letter in the alphabet. They can also make static shapes to show understanding as shown in the diagram.

radius   diameter   circumference

'Decisions, decisions' games can involve bodily movement, as described in the next chapter.

Why do visual representations work?

These methods have very high effect sizes indeed, so there is probably more than one reason why they work. Consider a flow diagram as a typical example:

- The diagrams cannot contain all the detail, so the learner is forced to isolate the key points and their relations. To see the wood for the trees. This imposes a structure on the information.

- Only structured information can go into long-term memory, so this helps recall.
- Much teaching is left brain, sequential and linguistic, but we all have a right brain, which is holistic and visual. These methods create whole-brain learning.
- Recall is almost always visually triggered, and the visual representation acts as a 'cue' triggering the full memory.
- Related information is shown connected correctly so the representation is quite high up the SOLO taxonomy; that is, it represents a deep understanding of the topic rather than just surface detail.
- The visual language is probably very close to the brain's 'natural' language, 'mentalese'.

To explain that last point, we saw in Chapter 2 that our nomadic hunter-gatherer brain represents information in a number of ways simultaneously. Our senses and brain were built to perceive and represent concrete objects arranged in time and space; changes with time; simple cause and effect; a geographical map of our environment; and simple geometry. This understanding of our everyday world is *not* represented directly in language, as this was not available until very recently in evolutionary time. Instead, our understanding is represented directly in the software and even the hardware of our brain, in a wordless language of pure understanding called 'mentalese'. It might be that graphic organisers translate more readily into mentalese than does a pure language explanation.

Right-brain students may take to these modes of representation more readily than left-brain students, but all students have a right brain, and all represent information in neural networks using mentalese, so *all* students will find them helpful. However, it often takes time and practice to be able to make good use of them, and their benefits may not show themselves immediately.

Underlining and highlighting

So these methods work because they require students to pick out key points and to structure their understanding and so make meanings. This suggests other well-known but effective methods. Students are given a text and asked to underline the key points and/or to use a coloured highlighter to pick out key terms and passages. These can even be colour coded if it helps; for example, for and against arguments can be highlighted in green and red, or underlined in pencil and pen. See 'methods to help students analyse', page 328.

How to make use of non-linguistic representations in the classroom

The aim is to create non-linguistic representations *in the minds of the students*. This is why it is often best if the students create representations themselves, or add considerably to the outline 'graphic organisers' that you give them.

If you use complex organisers such as the tables above, consider getting students to use them first on topics they find familiar and interesting, for example comparing boyfriends or university courses! This is all explained in more detail in Chapter 21.

Organisers work best if there is a minimum of text to distract the student, at least to begin with. It works well to gradually add detail as they learn about the topic. They are more vivid and interesting if they also contain appropriate images.

To help learners to explore and structure information so as to create meaning, graphic organisers can be used as:

- A *student activity.* 'Study the website, and create a mind map to summarise it.' Students can create posters, leaflets, handouts, web pages, PowerPoint presentations, etc.
- A *learning game.* Graphic organisers can also be turned into a game where students must place information in the right place on the organiser. This was described under Venn diagrams above and is explored in more detail in Chapter 11.
- A *thinking tool and source of questions:*
  - 'Use your flow diagram to predict what controls the rate of spread of the disease in the population.'
  - Here's one for you! 'Draw a diagram to show the difference between a visual representation and a graphic organiser.'
- A *way to make notes:* preferably during, but also after study.
- A *summary.* Either the teacher or the learner can create this. The students' summaries can be corrected as explained in Chapter 19.
- A *means to plan:* to help structure material before writing.

To help teachers or students to teach, graphic organisers can be used as:

- An *advance organiser.* See page 195. This shows the structure, and a summary of new material before it is presented.

Which graphic organisers would be most appropriate for the following tasks?

1. Brainstorm the main advantages of stock taking.
2. Distinguish between a viral and a bacterial infection.
3. Describe the main events leading up to the Second World War.
4. Describe the procedures followed when an employee makes an official complaint.
5. How did the introduction of fast food in the late 20th century affect dietary health?
6. Consider common teaching methods from the point of view of whether the teacher or the student is most in control.
7. What reasoning is used to justify having a Department for Trade and Industry?
8. Describe the main types of computer printer, giving examples.
9. Consider the various strategies used by managers and their effects on worker morale.
10. Plan a foyer exhibition of your class's work this term for a parents evening.

- A *display of information*. For example, a graphic organiser can be displayed on the board, screen, or on a poster or leaflet, etc., while the topic is explained. This can then be added to during the explanation.
- As *a source for questions and activities*.

References and further reading

Hyerle, D. (1996) *Visual Tools for Constructing Knowledge*, Alexandria, Virginia: ASCD.

Jones, B. F., Pierce, J. and Hunter, B. (1988/9) 'Teaching students to construct graphic representations', *Educational Leadership*, 46, 4: 20–5.

Marzano, R. J. (1998) *A Theory-Based Meta-Analysis of Research on Instruction*, Aurora, Colorado: Mid-Continent Research for Education and Learning. Download from: www.mcrel.org/topics/productDetail.asp?topicsID=6andproductID=83.

Petty, G. (2004) *Teaching Today: A Practical Guide* (3rd edition), Cheltenham: Nelson Thornes. See Chapter 32 on visual methods.

Some useful links

www.mapthemind.com/research/research.html: research on thinking maps.

www.mindgenius.com: software that enables you to create mind maps. Integrated with Microsoft Word, PowerPoint, Project, Outlook.

www.mind-map.com: Tony Buzan's website.

www.thinkingmaps.com: website for thinkingmaps Inc in the US; whole districts have implemented the approach across schools and the improvements in results in all subjects are impressive.

Students can download copyright 'friendly' or free photographs and other images from:

www. pics.tech4learning.com and www.openphoto.net.

11   'Decisions, decisions' (effect size 0.89)

This is a series of highly adaptable learning games, sometimes called 'manipulatives', which Marzano finds has an average effect size of 0.89. Students are given sets of cards, which might contain text, diagrams, formulae, computer code, photographs, drawings, or some combination of these. They are then asked to sort, match, group, sequence or rank the cards in ways described below, or to place them appropriately on a graphic organiser or to label a diagram. Have a quick scan through the diagrams in this chapter to get the general idea.

Instead of cards, students can drag and drop text boxes or diagrams etc. on a computer screen, or on an interactive whiteboard. These games are best played in pairs or perhaps threes, so students can discuss, and correct each other. Some computer simulation activities of this sort have an effect size of 1.45.

It makes the game much more effective, demanding, and fun if there are spurious cards or 'distractors' that do not match or group etc. but must be rejected. This makes students think hard about each card and improves concept development.

Matching cards or text boxes

Students can match technical terms with their meanings; questions with their answers; parts of the heart with their function; tools with their uses; etc.

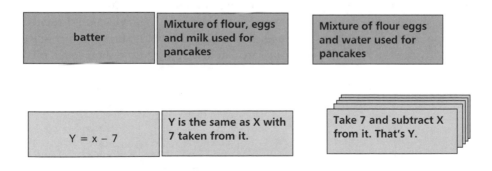

The second diagram shows mathematical statements being matched with ordinary English statements that mean the same thing. Spurious cards make this more thought provoking. There are many such mathematical games, and a supporting video, aimed at teaching elementary algebra in Swann and Green (2002).

Sorting cards or text boxes

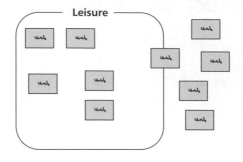

This is a great method to develop a difficult concept such as osmosis. It is almost identical to the graphic organiser shown on page 116. But rather than write on the diagram, students are given cards or text boxes to place on a diagram. The cards can contain:

* Examples and non-examples: examples are placed inside, non-examples outside.
* Statements about the characteristics of leisure, e.g. 'Leisure time is greater for middle class than for working class families.' Statements are placed 'inside' if they are true, 'outside' if they are not.
* Illustrations or diagrams, for some concepts such as gravity, osmosis, or blood circulation. These are placed inside if accurate and relevant, outside if not.
* Past-paper questions: those that involve the concept (even if they don't mention it by name) can be placed inside, others outside.

etc.

Grouping cards or text boxes

Concept development can be aided by getting students to classify cards into Venn diagrams, or just into columns. Suppose a teacher wanted to develop a related set of concepts such as *noun*, *verb* and *adjective*; or *capitalism*, *Marxism* and *post-Marxism*. Students can be given statements on cards or text boxes that they must place in

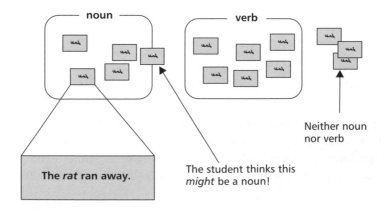

the correct column or in the correct Venn diagram. As we saw in Chapter 2, non-examples are most important for concept development, so do make spurious cards.

You can make a grouping game whenever a topic includes a classification, for example when there are different types of energy, diseases, tools, care plans, theories or models, etc.

Grouping games could be created to teach, for example:

- metaphor, simile and personification, etc.
- examples of conduction, convection and radiation
- igneous, sedimentary and metamorphic rocks
- valid and invalid arguments for the increased crime rate in cities
- categorising errors in punctuation under 'comma', 'full stop', etc.
- valid and invalid evidence for competences.

Students can also categorise verbal or mathematical statements into:

True; False; Depends; Doesn't mean anything

Sometimes true; Always true; Never true; Doesn't mean anything

This game can be played at absolutely any academic level. For example, students with learning difficulties could be given digital photographs or drawings of what they might or might not take on a trip. These they must group as: 'Everyone needs it'; 'No one needs it'; 'Our group only needs one of these.'

Grouping can be used to improve students' performance in assessment in the following two ways.

Question typing

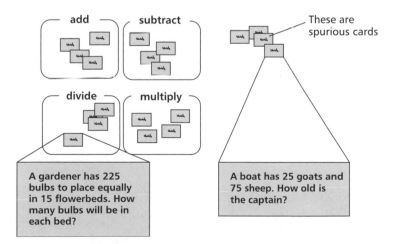

Students are given questions on cards but are told not to answer them. (They like that!) Instead they are asked to classify the question by what knowledge or method

they would use to answer it. Even able students sometimes don't know 'which chapter of my notes' to use to answer some questions. This can lead to poor examination performance. For example, a business studies student may not be sure whether to use motivation theory or quality system theory, or both, to solve a problem given as a case study.

Answer typing

This is similar to question typing but focuses on answers. Students are given two or three questions, along with about four made-up answers to each question. Some answers *describe*, some *explain*, some *analyse* and some *evaluate*. Students are asked to classify each answer under the terms in italics. The teacher, of course, chooses assessment terms that are often found in questions and tasks that students must complete in assessments.

Students often produce poor evaluations, for example, because they don't understand what an 'evaluation' is. When they can correctly classify some concrete examples of evaluations, they will have developed a better understanding of 'where the goalposts are'. Now they are in a better position to score!

Similarities and differences (effect size 1.3)

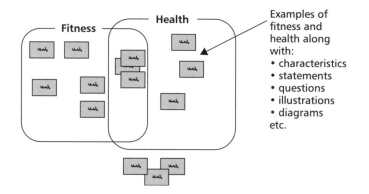

We saw in the previous chapter that in some situations Venn diagrams overlap, when they can represent similarities and differences between concepts. This 'compare and contrast' activity makes a great game to develop concepts. Read page 117 for some more pointers on this representation.

You could use this game with any pair of related concepts, especially if students tend to confuse them, or if their similarities or differences are important. For example:

- sine and cosines, or percentages and fractions
- parliamentary and presidential systems
- murder and manslaughter.

Sequencing cards or text boxes (rank by time)

I once saw students studying what to do if someone suffered a suspected electric shock. Instead of teaching by talking their teacher gave groups a set of cards, and asked them to reject those describing what they would *not* do, and put the others in time order.

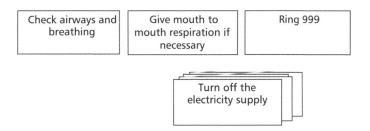

Two students I was watching went through the cards one by one; their teacher had placed them in a thoughtful order. They first picked up the 'Ring 999' card, and one student stated authoritatively that this must come first. Then they picked a card reading 'Give mouth-to-mouth respiration if necessary'. 'Hey,' said the other, 'when you're ringing 999 he could be dying!' They agreed to place respiration first! Later they picked up a card reading 'Turn off the electricity supply'. 'Hey,' said the one, 'when you're giving him mouth-to-mouth, he's still plugged in!'

There were also spurious cards. One read 'Wear rubber gloves and Wellingtons'. This the students solemnly placed in order until they encountered the card saying 'Turn off the electricity'. Then they both agreed they could do without rubber gloves and Wellingtons!

Here are some examples of where this sequencing approach could be used. In all these games spurious cards are helpful to develop the concepts concerned:

- English literature students place events in a novel or play in order.
- Business studies students sequence activities which prepare for the launch of a new product.
- Drugs education: placing drugs in order of danger to health or addictiveness
- Students with learning difficulties sequence digital photographs taken yesterday of them making tea.
- Plumbing students sequence the process of fitting a new central heating system.

Sequencing text

A very simple use of the above game is to take one of your existing handouts and cut it up into about a dozen or so pieces, about a paragraph or so for each piece. Students must now read the pieces and place them in order to create a meaningful handout. If this is done electronically students now print off the text as a handout. This is surprisingly effective, and at least makes sure that students have read and understood the handout!

Ranking cards or text boxes

Here students put cards in order of size, effectiveness, importance, cost, time taken, etc. For example, they might be given cards which describe the possible causes of a war they have been studying to place in order of importance, rejecting those that were not causes.

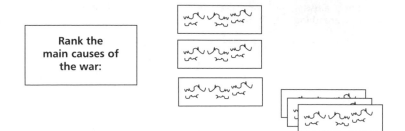

Or business studies students could be given cards that describe three different marketing policies, and be asked to place these in order of effectiveness. Then they could be asked to place the same policies in order of cost.

John's marketing policy	Liz's marketing policy	Ann's marketing policy
Brief description of the marketing policy here which the student has to evaluate compared with the others in the set	Brief description of another marketing policy here which the student has to evaluate compared with the others in the set	Brief description of yet another marketing policy here which the student has to evaluate compared with the others in the set

Most effective   Least effective

This game has very many applications in vocational education, especially where useful factors for ranking include effectiveness, importance, cost, ease of implementation, efficiency, etc.

Graphic organiser games

Any of the graphic organisers we saw in the last chapter can be the basis of a decisions, decisions game, not just the ones I have shown above. For example, rather than presenting students with a complete mind map, they can be given its elements on cards, and can then arrange these into a coherent structure. Students may create slightly different structures, but this is fine, and can be quite illuminating.

You could give students statements that describe a process, asking them to turn it into a flow diagram. Or give them statements to place in a decision tree.

References, further reading and research

Petty, G. (2004) *Teaching Today: A Practical Guide* (3rd edition), Cheltenham: Nelson Thornes.

Swann, M. and Green, M. (2002) 'Learning mathematics through discussion and reflection' (CD-ROM, video and print materials), London: LDSA.

www.loopcards.net: cards being used in mathematics.

Try searching the Internet with 'manipulatives geography' or some other subject to find ready-made games.

12 Cooperative learning

Cooperative learning	Effect size	Number of studies
Hattie	0.59	1153
Marzano	0.73	122

Giving students something to do and asking them to help each other is *not* cooperative learning. Neither is just using groups. 'Cooperative learning' is the name given to a clutch of special teaching methods that are structured to achieve specific characteristics thought to enhance learning. See if you can work out what these characteristics are as you read about the methods. Cooperative learning works for every subject, at every academic level from nursery to postgraduate, and with students of every class and social background.

Well used, these methods can improve students' achievement by at least a grade, but even if there were no improvement in achievement we should use them because they improve students' behaviour, self-esteem, and more crucial still, their attitudes to each other.

I feel uncomfortable raising this issue but it has to be faced. We live in a divided society. One day my wife Liz met me in the foyer of a college I had been visiting. She asked me why most of the students grouped themselves by their ethnic origin. I looked around. There was a clutch of Asian lads by the entrance, and in the foyer three Chinese girls on one side, and a group of White Caucasian students on the other. I have visited hundreds of colleges and schools and had become so used to seeing this I didn't notice it.

Many students, though of course not all, live their lives in an ethnic and cultural bubble, protected from the reality of their society, and perhaps even alienated from some of it.

Most teachers use friendship groups in class, which perpetuates these divisions, and unintentionally affirms and cements them. 'Multiculturalism' is often interpreted to mean that the teacher should respect different cultural groups. But ethnic and other groupings must also learn to respect each other, and themselves. There is a wonderful opportunity here for teachers. Research on cooperative learning shows that if we get mixed groups of students working together in a relaxed, friendly and cooperative manner this improves their understanding and acceptance of 'the other', raises their self-esteem, and so prepares them to make a positive contribution in the real world. It also raises their achievement!

'But the aftermath of 7/7 [London bombings] forces us to assess where we are. And here is where I think we are: we are sleepwalking our way to segregation. We are becoming strangers to each other, and we are leaving communities to be marooned outside the mainstream.'

Trevor Phillips, Chair of the Campaign for Racial
Equality (2005) (www.cre.gov.uk)

It is not only students from ethnic minorities who benefit socially from cooperative learning. Shy students can find very ordinary social relations difficult. They lack the confidence to present themselves as a potential collaborator, workmate or friend, even to students of their own ethnic grouping. Cooperative learning and other methods that use randomised grouping help these students to make contact even if they find this a bit painful at first.

The desire to be included, respected, accepted and enjoyed for what you are, and who you are, is vital for full psychological functioning. Maslow thought of this need to give and receive ordinary affection as a psychological 'vitamin', for which there was no substitute. Without it we are unhappy, and eventually malfunction, becoming withdrawn, or angry and antagonistic. The importance of meeting this need is hard to overstate.

Are the following unrelated to Maslow's findings on 'belongingness and love needs'? That the greatest harm you can do many youths, and indeed adults, is to disrespect or 'dis' them. That 'respect' is a catchword for Afro-Caribbean and other young people at present. That militant Islamic fundamentalists believe 'the West' disrespects their origins, and their religion. That suicide bombers rage against a society they believe has trampled on their identity. That 'loners' are more likely to contemplate suicide, or even to become psychopathic killers? The teacher may be powerless in these very extreme cases, but even here may have a preventative role. Perhaps if such people had been included and invited out of their bubble they would have functioned better in society.

And I find myself wondering whether the victims of racial murder such as Stephen Lawrence would be alive today if their murderers had always related to black classmates in a productive way in the classroom as a matter of routine.

Such thoughts are often criticised as 'social engineering', or as patronising, or even racist, but I am unrepentant. It is not disrespectful of a student, or of an ethnic group, to want to include them, and to want them both to understand others and be understood by others. It is not patronising or racist to want everyone in our society to flourish.

I believe we must have it all, multiculturalism *and* a less divided society. The identity that comes from difference *and* a shared set of values worked out in real-world encounters with each other. Classrooms may be the very best place to do this. And if we don't do it, who will? I certainly wonder how governments and the judicial system could do it. Teachers may have a vital, even the supreme, role here, to create a world we would all be proud to live in.

Martin Luther King Junior famously said: 'I have a dream that my four children will one day live in a nation where they will not be judged by the color of their skin, but by the content of their character. I have a dream today.' The research shows that cooperative learning, and other randomised grouping methods, could help make that dream walk on our streets.

The main cooperative learning methods are also amongst the most powerful and enjoyable methods for raising achievement; they are jigsaw, academic controversy, and learning together. These are all 'teaching without talking' methods, of which Chapter 17 has many more.

Jigsaw (effect size 0.75)

Try peer explaining (see Chapter 17) before using jigsaw to ensure your students can succeed with peer explaining. Do a small topic for your first jigsaw, so you and especially your students get the hang of the method.

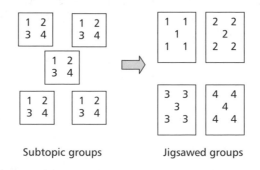

Subtopic groups   Jigsawed groups

In the diagram above, each number is a student, and each rectangle a table. I imagine in the diagram, and below, a class of 20 students being taught a topic with five subtopics. For example, a teacher might teach childhood diseases, and split this into the five subtopics of measles, mumps, meningitis, chickenpox and whooping cough. However, jigsaw does *not* need a specific number of students or subtopics.

Jigsaw

1. Divide a topic up into, say, five subtopics.

2. Divide students into five groups, each of which studies one subtopic for about ten minutes from resources, writing key points which are checked by you. These resources can obviously include information and learning technology (ILT) resources including video etc.

   The students in each group now number themselves '1', '2', '3', and so on. All the 1s go to one table, and all the 2s to another, and so on. The new groups now form a jigsaw of random social composition, which contains one student 'expert' on each of the five subtopics.

3. In these jigsaw groups, students:
   a. Teach each other their subtopic covering all the key points.
   b. Complete a 'combined task' together, which requires knowledge of *all* the subtopics. For example: 'Find three characteristics all the childhood diseases share, and two that are unique for each. Then place the diseases in order of severity, and prepare a justification for your ranking.'
   c. The groups present their ideas for the combined task and the teacher debriefs the whole class on this.
   d. Students, still in jigsaw groups, prepare for a quiz on the key points, led by a member of their group. They are given the challenge to ensure that each member of their group gets a minimum of, say, 7/10 in a quiz they must take as individuals.
   e. Students complete the very short quiz individually and mark their own papers. Great cheers all round if their group members all get 7/10 in the test. (A challenge like this is more motivating and more important educationally than a competition to get the best mark, as the effect sizes on competitions below show.)

4. Then each group asks itself these questions about how they operated as a group:
   a. In what two ways did our group work well together?
   b. In what way could we do better next time?

5. You debrief the class on the group goals above and remind them of these before the next cooperative learning activity.

You may need to split the activity between two lessons if you use jigsaw on a large topic. The obvious place to 'break' the activity is between 1 and 2 above.

Jigsaw can work with classes of any size

Above I described a 5 × 4 jigsaw with five groups of four becoming four groups of five. This requires 20 students, but suppose I have too many or too few?

Suppose you have 22 students, making two too many. Put the 'extra' students into two different groups to spread the problem. *Just before* breaking into the jigsaw groups, pair students up as shown and ask them to share the explaining but not the test. Little will be lost as these students prepare expecting to explain alone.

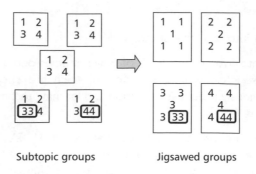

Subtopic groups   Jigsawed groups

Suppose you have 18 students but need 20 for a 5 × 4 jigsaw. Spread the problem by ensuring each group is a maximum of one student down. Number students yourself in these small groups to ensure that there is a different missing number in each group. This ensures that no jigsawed group gets two missing students. You then visit the jigsawed groups to explain any missing subtopic or spectacle. Again, little will be lost.

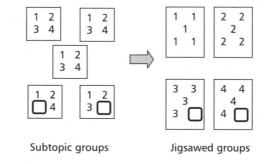

5 × 4 jigsaw with too
few students   Subtopic groups   Jigsawed groups

Any number can be accommodated with a jigsaw. Above we saw that five groups of four must become four groups of five just because of the jigsaw numbering system: 5 × 4 = 4 × 5 so it must work with no missing or lost students! In the same way the numbering system creates viable groupings, with no students lost or missing, with other combinations of groups:

3 × 4 = 4 × 3 Three groups of four becomes four groups of three.

3 × 3 = 3 × 3 Three groups of three becomes three (different) groups of three, etc.

Any combination works: 2 × 2, 2 × 3, 3 × 3, 3 × 4, 4 × 4, 5 × 4, etc. Download 'jigsaw arithmetic' from www.geoffpetty.com if you want more detail!

How to plan a jigsaw

First decide on the number of subtopics or spectacles you will use. Divide students into this number of groups. Then the jigsaw system usually just takes care of itself! It *has* to work because of the laws of arithmetic! The only things to look out for are having too few or too many students as described above, or having groups that are larger than about five, which can become unwieldy.

You can fix over-large groups by splitting your class into two. For example, suppose you have 24 students studying a topic with only three subtopics; this would make groups of eight. Split the class into two groups of 12 and then do a 3 × 4 jigsaw with each half. Make sure the two halves don't mix when they jigsaw; this can be done by asking one group of 12 to number themselves '1, 2, 3, 4' and the other 12 '5, 6, 7, 8'; but you could just remind them not to mix!

For the mathematically minded:

If you have N students and X subtopics then:

You must start with X groups.

These then jigsaw to N/X groups (with X students in each group).

Jigsaw with spectacles

This is an alternative 'holistic' approach that is easier to resource, and can create deeper learning.

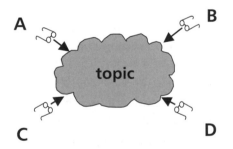

All students are given all the materials for a topic, but teach group is given a different perspective, or question to consider. For example, groups could be asked to look at childhood diseases from points of view such as symptoms, treatment or infectivity, etc. Or they could be given a story to analyse from the point of view of plot, characterisation or themes, etc.

Each group studies the same materials from a particular perspective, then students number themselves and get into jigsaw groups. The method now continues the same as above.

This is a good method to teach students' analysis skills.

Academic controversy

This method is for a topic where there are two or more conflicting points of view and one of them is not obviously much better than another.

Do prisons work?

Is this marketing policy effective for a small country hotel?

Is this mathematical procedure sound?

You can make almost any topic into a controversy by presenting an argument or policy, etc., and asking whether it is right or wrong, effective or ineffective, etc.

The method requires some emotional maturity in your learners. However, you can use it to teach conflict resolution as described in Chapter 24, telling students to seek a win-win or compromise point of view. You can use the method to teach them to listen well in conflict situations, without getting angry.

My description below assumes that there are just two points of view, but it is easily adapted for more.

1. Students are allocated one of two opposite points of view, and given materials that explain the topic, and, if really necessary, some hints about their point of view. They research and prepare their point of view, and its justification, preparing a persuasive 'best case possible' for their position. They could pair up with someone else who is preparing the same point of view to do this. They could also work in groups.

2. Random grouping is used to arrange students in pairs with *opposing* points of view, or put them in groups of four containing two students from each point of view. Sides take turns to present their position in as persuasive a manner as possible. No interruption from the other side is allowed at this stage.

3. Students engage in an open discussion in which they argue forcefully against the other side, and rebut the attacks given in 2 above.

4. Optionally, students swap positions and present the *other* position as accurately, completely, persuasively and forcefully as they can. It's best to tell students this is coming so that they listen to the opposing view! However, if you feel mischievous you can spring this on students and make a teaching point about how badly they listened earlier on!

5. (Optional.) Students check each other's arguments for the swapped positions.

6. Integration: students drop their advocacy roles. They try to reach a consensus on the issue by synthesising the two positions.

7. After the above is completed each group asks itself these questions about how they operated as a group:
   a. In what two ways did our group members work well together?
   b. In what way could we do better next time?

8. You debrief the class on the group goals above and remind them of these before the next cooperative learning activity.

This method works best if used in conjunction with 'peacemaking' approaches; see www.co-operation.org/pages/peace.html. It's great to teach the skills of evaluation and critical thinking skills, and issues around bias, etc.

Learning together

I will explain this method by an example in A-level business studies.

1. The teacher explains marketing strategies to students and they do some introductory activities. Students are then put into random groups of four by numbering round the class 1, 2, 3, 4, 1, 2, etc.

2. Each group is given the same scenario about a small business that is in trouble, and a copy of its marketing strategy. The teacher has carefully devised the scenario to bring out all the objectives for this topic. The task is to:
   a. answer some basic questions on the marketing strategy, making use of concepts already taught
   b. evaluate the marketing strategy
   c. improve the marketing strategy with a full justification for every improvement.

3. Each student is given a different short document to study that explains a particular aspect of the business. They are not allowed to show this to others, but they are allowed, and expected, to explain it.

4. Right at the start each group is asked to appoint a project manager, a learning checker, a vocabulary chief, and a scribe. This gives every group member a role that is carefully defined by 'role cards' (see page 228).

5. Right at the start it is also made clear that there will be a quiz which students will take individually, on some factual questions on the basic concepts. Students are also told that the activity will conclude by each student being asked to justify an aspect of his or her group's evaluation and their suggested improvements.

6. After the above is completed each group asks itself these questions about how they have operated as a group:
   a. In what two ways did our group work well together?
   b. In what way could we do better next time?

7. You debrief the class on the group goals above and remind them of these before the next cooperative learning activity.

The activity takes about an hour, including the quiz, which takes about five minutes, and the debrief on the group's evaluation and suggested improvements, which takes about 15 minutes. Every member of every group answers some questions.

What is different about cooperative learning?

Can you see the common characteristics in the cooperative learning methods above?

- *Groups sink or swim together.* Individual students are held accountable by their peers. Peer pressure is used constructively to motivate students to learn.
- *Students work interactively.* There is a good deal of peer teaching, discussion, etc., which is very 'constructivist'.
- *Students have a goal to learn, but also a goal to help others in their group to learn.* Groups soon find their weakest members and are motivated to support him or her so the group does better in the assessments.
- *Students are held accountable by the teacher* for both the above goals, for example with tests or quizzes.
- *Students learn how to cooperate effectively* by reviewing how well they worked as a group.

Research on cooperative learning

There are three ways to organise teaching:

- *Competitive.* Students compete with each other for grades and marks to see who is 'best'.
- *Individualistic.* Students work more or less independently, paying little attention to each other, for example students working alone through workbooks.
- *Cooperative.* Teaching methods are used which require students to cooperate with each other as they learn. The lesson is structured so that students have a vested interest in each other's learning as well as in their own, and are held accountable for what they have done and learned.

A synthesis of research on these three approaches, Roger and Johnson (1994), has found that cooperative learning is much the best, though most teachers use competitive and individualistic methods; see the tables below. Cooperative learning is very challenging for students, but is very popular with them, and creates a very positive classroom climate.

The following tables summarise the findings of the research review. In each case one approach is compared to one other; for example, cooperative methods are compared with individualistic methods. The 'effect size' is how much better the first method is than the second.

As can be seen, cooperative learning is much better than the alternatives in terms of academic performance, and 'classroom climate', that is, students liking each other, and liking themselves (self-esteem). Cooperative learning should be a main plank in any equal opportunities policy.

Academic performance of cooperative, competitive and individualistic teaching methods		
Academic performance	**Mean effect size**	**N**
Cooperative versus competitive	**0.66** For highest quality studies: **0.86**	**128**
Cooperative versus individualistic	**0.63** For highest quality studies: **0.59**	182
Competitive versus individualistic	0.30	39

Social performance of cooperative, competitive and individualistic teaching methods		
Interpersonal attraction **(students liking each other)**	**Mean effect size**	**N**
Cooperative versus competitve	0.65	88
Cooperative versus individualistic	0.62	59
Competitive versus individualistic	0.08	15

Effect on self-esteem of cooperative, competitive and individualistic teaching methods		
Interpersonal attraction **(students liking each other)**	**Mean effect size**	**N**
Cooperative versus competitve	0.60	55
Cooperative versus individualistic	0.44	37
Competitive versus individualistic	–0.19	18

From www.co-operation.org/pages/overviewpaper.html

Reference and further reading

Roger, T. and Johnson, D. W. (1994) 'An overview of cooperative learning'. This can be downloaded from: www.co-operation.org/pages/overviewpaper.html.

13 Reciprocal teaching (effect size 0.86)

Palincsar and Brown (1984) invented this method for students who could read, but who were on average 2.5 years behind their peers in reading comprehension. However, every teacher can make use of this extraordinarily powerful approach. It can be used on its own, or as part of peer explaining or 'jigsaw' methods described in Chapters 12 and 19. It is particularly useful for learning difficult material, and for helping weak students. Reciprocal teaching also provides a vivid insight into the nature of effective learning.

Palincsar and Brown's experiment has been repeated about 50 times in different contexts with similar results. Their students (who were not learning disabled) were taught specific comprehension techniques in groups of five or less. They practised on non-fiction texts that were appropriate for their age, not their ability – a really challenging goal for them, and their teacher! But in 20 days these learners had caught up with their peers in comprehension, and this gain remained long after the special teaching they received. It wasn't just the small groups that made the teaching so effective. The two control groups were also taught in small groups: one read the same texts, and answered questions on them, the other was in their normal reading group, but neither made the same gains. It was reciprocal teaching that added the value.

The effect size of this method is not just for improved understanding of the *content* they studied. It is for comprehension *skill* generally. This makes the very high effect size all the more remarkable. The students who received reciprocal teaching improved in their ability to comprehend, summarise, and ask pertinent questions. These gains also proved time stable, and, what is more, their improved skills transferred to situations where the learners were not required to use the specific comprehension techniques they had been taught. These improved comprehension skills seem to have been integrated into their everyday reading and listening practice.

The success of this method shows that comprehension is a teachable skill – something of a shock to those teachers who still believe that ability is a fixed characteristic of the student. And when the students in this study found that comprehension questions could be answered by careful study of the text, they were shocked too! This is an important finding that we return to in Chapter 21.

Why are some students poor comprehenders? Because they have not developed adequate strategies to:

- create understanding
- monitor understanding
- improve and clarify their understanding when comprehension fails.

Reciprocal teaching aims to teach these skills. The cycle of activities is not in the least arbitrary, but carefully designed after much research. It aims to model good comprehension strategies, to require students to practise them, and to provide learners with immediate feedback on their use of these strategies.

I will describe how the method was used in Palincsar and Brown's study, but the method is much more widely applicable as we will see. While I describe it, think how you could adapt the method for *your* students, even in whole-class teaching, then compare this with my ideas at the end of the chapter.

Students aged 12 or 13 years were put in groups of about five or less. They were on average 2.5 years behind their peers in reading comprehension. But soon to catch up! A non-fiction text was used with a length of around 1500 words, suitable for the students' age rather than their ability. To begin the process the teacher discussed any relevant background knowledge to the non-fiction text. This is similar to 'relevant recall questions' mentioned in Chapters 6 and 16. Then the cycle in the diagram below took place.

The reciprocal teaching process (effect size 0.86)

The first cycle is completed by the teacher taking the role of 'teacher' as you might expect. In later cycles a *student* takes the role of 'teacher'. Students take turns at leading a cycle in this way. For this reason the word 'teacher' is in quotes in the diagram.

The events shown on the diagram are not isolated activities; they occur as part of a meaningful discussion about real reading. In particular 'clarifying' and 'predicting' take place only when they are useful or necessary. The goal is to make a meaning of the text, and to check and correct this meaning as it is made. The other goal is, of course, to model and to develop the skill or process of reading for comprehension. For example, the teacher might discover poor comprehension and say:

Teacher   No that's not it. I don't think you've got it yet, what should we do?
Student   *(who is playing the teacher)* Read it again?
Teacher   Good idea! Let's all read it again, but more slowly this time, because this bit is hard.
(They all read it again more slowly.)

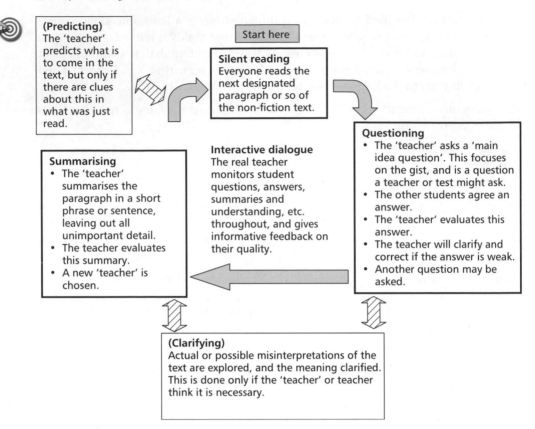

The reciprocal teaching process.

An interactive dialogue like this takes place between the teacher and the students throughout the whole process. It is unlikely to be a coincidence that we also saw interactive dialogue making whole-class interactive teaching work so well.

The teacher leads the first cycle, asking a question, getting an answer, and then summarising in order to 'model' the 'teacher' role in reciprocal teaching. The teacher also 'thinks aloud' so that the process of comprehending, which is usually private and hidden, is out in the open. For example: 'The main point here must be something about haemoglobin, so I suppose a good question would be . . .'

After this modelling the students take it in turns to lead the group round this same cycle.

Questioning

The student with the role of 'teacher' sets a new paragraph or so of the text for everyone to read silently. After reading, the 'teacher' asks a question that focuses on the main idea in the paragraph. This is a question that a teacher or test might ask of the passage. The aim is for the 'teacher' to begin to isolate a key point, to self-check an understanding of this by creating an answer to her own question, and to check the understanding of the others in the group.

'Teachers' have real difficulty asking questions at first! Here are some 'teacher' questions generated in the first half of training in reciprocal teaching. In brackets after each attempted question is what the pupil was trying to ask! All the extended dialogue in this chapter comes from Palincsar and Brown (1984).

'What were some of the people?' (Meaning to ask: 'What kinds of people can serve on a jury?')

'There's you know, like a few answers in here and one of my questions is, uh, anything that burns and explodes can be fast enough to . . . See, they got names in here. OK?' (Meaning to ask: 'Name some explosives.')

A few days later the same students ask questions such as:

'Where does lightning get its charge?'

'What does haemoglobin do?'

It is not easy for a teacher (meaning the real teacher) to take a weak question and to clarify it into a better one. Here is a teacher doing this with Charles, a minority student with an IQ of 70. He is about 12 years old but his comprehension is like that of an 8 year old. Here he is playing 'teacher' on his first day of reciprocal teaching. He is trying to ask a question on a passage about snakes:

Charles	What is found in the southeastern snakes, also the copperhead, rattle snakes, vipers – they have. I'm not doing this right.
Teacher	All right. Do you want to know about the pit vipers?
Charles	Yeah.
Teacher	What would be a good question about the pit vipers that starts with the word 'why?'
Charles	*(no response)*
Teacher	How about, 'Why are the snakes called pit vipers?'
Charles	Why do they want to know that they are called pit vipers?
Teacher	Try it again
Charles	Why do they, pit vipers in a pit?
Teacher	How about, 'Why do they call the snakes pit vipers?'
Charles	Why do they call the snakes pit vipers?
Teacher	There you go! Good for you.

Many teachers would give up on Charles after a few minutes of this! But here he is again on day 4 trying to ask questions on a text comparing a female spider with her mate which reads: 'Spinner's mate is much smaller than she, and his body is dull brown. He spends most of his time sitting at one side of her web.'

Charles	*(no question)*
Teacher	What's this paragraph about?
Charles	Spinner's mate. How do spinner's mate . . .
Teacher	That's good. Keep going.

Charles	How do spinner's mate is smaller than ... How am I going to say that?
Teacher	Take your time with it. You want to ask a question about spinner's mate and what he does, beginning with the word 'how'.
Charles	How do they spend most of his time sitting?
Teacher	You are very close. The question would be, 'How does spinner's mate spend most of his time?' Now you ask it.
Charles	How does spinner's mate spend most of his time?

Would you still be persisting with Charles? Would your dialogue challenge him this much? Here he is again on day 15 asking a question on the following text:

> Scientists also come to the South Pole to study the strange lights that glow overhead during the Antarctic night. (It's a cold and lonely world for the few hardy people who 'winter over' the polar night.) These 'southern lights' are caused by the Earth acting like a magnet on the electrical particles in the air. They are clues that may help us understand the Earth's core and the upper edges of its blanket of air.

| Charles | Why do scientists come to the south pole to study? |
| Teacher | Excellent question. |

Notice the teacher's skilful use of interactive dialogue to give students feedback and to provide just the degree of help necessary for the dialogues to remain on track. The students are left to take as much responsibility as they can. Because students are required to respond, the teacher can use the response to gauge their understanding and competence, and to provide them with precisely focused feedback. The teacher can carry out a real-time diagnosis, and finely tune her response to the trial-and-error approach of the learner. This is a very natural and powerful way to learn, and is characteristic of top methods such as reciprocal teaching and whole-class interactive teaching.

If students are unable to ask good 'main idea' question, or to give an adequate summary, this is not regarded as a failure to perform the skills but as important information that comprehension is not proceeding as it should. Remedial action is then taken, such as questioning, clarifying or rereading.

Summarising

This is not regarded as a failure.

The student playing 'teacher' now summarises the passage of text giving the main idea only, in a phrase or sentence that leaves out all the detail. The aim of summarising is to identify and integrate the main points in the text, and so to create a meaning.

Throughout questioning and summarising the teacher gives specific, accurate and informative feedback to the 'teacher'. Here is an example. Sarah is 12 years old and more able than Charles; it is her turn as 'teacher' on the following text.

The text: 'How can snakes be so flexible?'
The snake's skeleton and parts of its body are very flexible – something like a rubber hose with bones. A snake's backbone can have as many as 300 verte-brae, almost ten times as many as a human's. These vertebrae are connected by loose and rubbery tissues that allow easy movement. Because of this bend-able, twistable spinal construction, a snake can turn its body in almost any direction at almost any point.

Having asked a question on this text and accepted the answer she has a go at summarising it.

Sarah   *(as 'teacher')* Like if a snake is turning round, he wouldn't break any bones because he is flexible.
Teacher   And the reason he is so flexible is . . .
Sarah   If someone stepped on his tail, he wouldn't be able to move unless he was flexible.
Teacher   OK. That explains why it would be helpful to be so flexible, but what makes the snake so flexible? I think that is an important part of the summary.
Sarah   So he can move faster?
Teacher   That is another reason for being flexible. Let me do a summary for you. Sarah is right. The most important thing we have learned is that the snake is very flexible. The reason they can bend so easily is that they have so many little bones in their backbones and each of them can move separately, making the snake very flexible. Does that make sense?

After seven days of reciprocal teaching Sarah is typically able to read a passage of similar complexity on lava, and summarise it like this:

Sarah   My summary would be that this paragraph is about magma and magma is molten rock and I wouldn't add anything else.
Teacher   Good. Good.

To begin with, the dialogue between teacher and student tends to be a 'ping pong' between the teacher on one side and a student on the other. Eventually, however, the majority of the cycles are student controlled with the teacher providing informative feedback and encouragement. Student–student interaction becomes the norm.

Clarifying

The aim of clarifying is to improve understanding. But it is also to alert the *'teacher'*, and the others in the group, to the idea that comprehension can fail, but that there are strategies to deal with this. As ever with this method, teaching is at two levels, to both comprehend the text, and to teach the skill of comprehension.

The 'teacher' asks for any points that need clarifying, and may also provide some. Particular attention is given to any ambiguous or difficult text. The 'teacher' and class then resolve any difficulties through dialogue. See the example dialogue below.

Predicting

This is only attempted if there are clues about what the unread section of the text might be about. The 'teacher' guesses what the text might say next. This guess is tested later. The aim here is for the 'teacher' to use prior learning and common sense to make sense of the text, and to maintain a purpose for the reading. 'This is gonna tell us about what our blood does and why we have it.' 'Predicting' is always done after reading the title of the text.

When a cycle is completed the 'teacher' or teacher will appoint another student to take the role for the next paragraph, and so on. Alternatively the students can take turns. The students were shown progress charts that showed the improvement in the skills of comprehension, question asking, etc., on a weekly basis during reciprocal teaching, and their improvement was discussed with them.

Let's see the whole process in an example dialogue from early in a reciprocal teaching group.

> **The text: Can snakes sting with their tongues?**
> No – snakes' tongues are completely harmless. They're used for feeling things and for sharpening the snakes' sense of smell. Although snakes can smell in the usual way, the tongue flickering in the air picks up tiny particles of matter. These particles are deposited in two tiny cavities at the base of the nostrils to increase the snake's ability to smell.

1. **Anne**   Do snakes' tongues sting?

2. **Kevin**   Sometimes.

3. **Anne**   Correct.

> Kevin was wrong, but Anne says he is correct! But note that the teacher does not step in. She wants the students to develop this checking skill.

This paragraph is about do snakes sting with their tongue, and different ways that the tongue is for and the senses of smell.

4. **Teacher**   Are there any questions?

> The teacher wants the students to check this.

5. **Chris**   Snakes' tongues don't sting.

6. **Teacher**   Beautiful! I thought, boy, I must have been doing some fast reading there because I missed that point. Anne, could you ask your question again?

7. **Anne**   Do snakes' tongues really sting?

8. **Teacher**   Now, Anne, since you have asked the question, can you find in that paragraph where the question is answered?

9. **Anne**   *(reading from the text)* 'No – snakes' tongues are completely harmless.'

10. **Teacher** So we'll try it again. Can you generate another question that you think a teacher might ask?

11. **Anne**   What are the tongues used for?

> The teacher wants a better meaning, so asks for *another* question. (And gets a better one!)

12. **Teacher** Good!

13. **Louis**   The sense of smell.

14. **Teacher** Is that correct? Anne, do you disagree? Yes.

15. **Anne** That answer was right, but there are other things that the tongue can do.

16. **Louis** But she only said tell one, she didn't say tell all of them.

17. **Teacher** OK.

18. **Beth** It is used to pick up tiny particles.

19. **Teacher** OK, I think that this is an important point. You have the basic concept which is correct, OK, but what the question really is saying is, is it used for smell? OK?

20. **Beth** They are used for feeling things for sharpening snakes' sense of smell.

21. **Teacher** OK. They are used for sharpening the snakes' sense of smell. Are they used for smelling? That's the point we aren't clear on.

22. **Louis** In my answer I said it is for the sense of smell.

23. **Teacher** That is fine; this is what the technique is all about. What it means is not that you are right or wrong or good or bad. What it says is that we have just read something and have had a disagreement about what it says. We need to work it out.

24. **Anne** My prediction is that they will now talk about the different things about snakes. Where they live, and what they eat and stuff like that.

25. **Teacher** OK. Good. What do you think they eat?

26. **Anne** Animals.

27. **Louis** Deserts.

> Louis still thinks the point is to get praise and right answers. The teacher wants the goals of reciprocal teaching to be clear.

28. **Chris** I challenge. Snakes, all of them, don't live in the desert. They live in the woods and in swamp areas.

Look back over the above dialogue and see if you can see where the following take place: questioning, summarising; clarifying, and predicting. You will notice that these phases are not neatly separated. Note the quality of the dialogue, which while not perfect shows high-quality feedback to all students, and especially to the teacher.

Some teachers explicitly teach the four processes in reciprocal teaching first, using a whole-class interactive teaching approach. Only then do they use the process in small groups as described above. This is now recommended practice and Rosenshine and Meister (1993) give details. For example, students are taught that questions can start with 'who', 'what', 'when', 'where', 'why' and 'how'. They are then given practice at asking questions on text, discuss as a class how to devise questions, and compare good and bad questions.

The success of reciprocal questioning does not lie in questioning, summarising, and so on, but in the quality of the interactive dialogue during these activities. The activities must be used to teach the content, but also to lay bare the skill of comprehending, and to show students how to go about the process of making meaning from text.

What makes this method work is:

- the belief that students can make sense of the text being fulfilled (students in the study were astounded to discover that close reading can reveal the meaning of difficult text – presumably they attributed their difficulty to a fixed low ability)
- modelling the sense-making process by dialogue, especially thinking aloud
- the feedback to learners about how well they are doing at both comprehending the text and using the comprehension strategies such as checking, re-reading, etc.

The method requires the verbalisation of thoughts and so creates a window into how well students have made sense of the text, and the teacher uses this to instruct the learners, and to gauge how much more responsibility they can take during the cycle.

Dialogue is greatly helped by students leading the discussion. Peers are more likely to challenge each other than they are the teacher, and are less threatened by a challenge from a peer than from a teacher. Peers also understand each other's difficulties better than does the teacher. For teachers, comprehension is a much more automatic process. Dialogue also encourages help-seeking and help-giving behaviour.

> *Cognitive conflict is a useful strategy to create dialogue in reciprocal teaching. See page 182.*

The gains for reciprocal teaching

The success of reciprocal teaching shows that it is the strategies that students adopt that create comprehension, not their IQ. These strategies are as useful when listening as when reading and are entirely transferable. The teachers that took part in this study were without exception sceptical that their students would be able to participate in reciprocal teaching. But these teachers made the method work, and noted that their students' study skills and thinking skills had improved. They were better able to locate important information and organise their ideas.

Students very much enjoyed the method, especially being the 'teacher' (the most challenging role by far), and said that 'finding the good right question' was the hardest, and that summarising was the most helpful activity.

In order to measure the improvement of comprehension skills, Palincsar and Brown gave students *unassisted* comprehension exercises on a novel passage of text every day of the study. Before reciprocal teaching students scored 40 per cent correct; after, they scored 80 per cent correct, just like their peers. This dropped a little after six months, but rose again to 80 per cent after one extra day of reciprocal teaching. The control groups, who were in the same-sized groups, and answering questions on the same texts, did not make these gains.

How could you make use of reciprocal teaching?

Think how you could make use of this method before reading on. It is particularly useful for text, worked examples, or ILT resources that students find difficult.

- You could train some or all of your students in reciprocal teaching and get them to lead small groups round the cycle, to help them learn from text, worked examples, video, ILT resources, etc. See the 'Teaching without talking' methods in Chapter 17.
- You could use reciprocal teaching with 'jigsaw', requiring a group leader to use it to learn from the resources. See Chapter 12. Jigsaw has an effect size of about 0.75 even without reciprocal teaching, and may have more with it.
- You could use the cycle when students do peer explaining as described in Chapters 17 or 19.
- You could simply set students the task of devising questions for their peers to answer.
- You could set students the task of summarising, and improving each other's summaries.
- You could also use the cycle for whole-class study of a text with large classes, though this might not work as well as some of the above ideas. However, you might be able to teach the cycle in this way for later use by small groups.

This concludes our close look at the most effective teaching strategies; now we will consider what general principles we can learn from them and from Chapter 2.

References and further reading

Palincsar, A. S. and Brown, A. L. (1984) 'Reciprocal teaching of comprehension-fostering and comprehension-monitoring activities', *Cognition and Instruction*, 2, 117–75.

Rosenshine, B. V. and Meister, C. (1993) 'Reciprocal teaching: a review of 19 experimental studies', Technical Report No. 574. Available free on the Internet. Just type the title into Google to find it.

Part 4 Seven principles for evidence-based teaching

14 The seven general teaching principles and PAR

In Chapters 4–13 we looked at the teaching methods that create the highest achievement. I suggested in Chapter 7 that rather than just blindly using these methods we should try to learn from them. This is because:

- We will only use a method well if we know why it works.
- We can only adapt or improve a method well if we know why it works.
- If we understand general principles we can use these to evaluate our own and other teaching methods, and to design new ones.

I will combine what we learned in Chapters 4–13 with what we learned in Chapters 2 and 3 about high-quality learning. So we will try to put everything we have learned from all the research reviews into one set of principles. In the rest of the book you and I can use these principles to guide us.

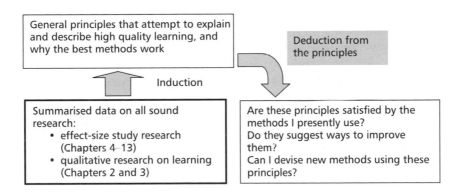

What evidence have we got? Look again at the summary at the very end of Chapter 2, and at the chart I used to summarise Marzano's theory-based meta-analysis of research on instruction (page 77). Remember also that Hattie noticed three principles underlying the effectiveness of all the teaching methods in his table, which is the most comprehensive synthesis of effect-size studies. His first two principles can be seen directly in the variables that populate the top of his table and in other methods too; the last is more conjectural but it links with Chapter 2.

- Achievement is enhanced to the degree that students and teachers set and communicate appropriate, specific and *challenging* goals.

- Achievement is enhanced as a function of *feedback*.
- Increases in student learning involve . . . a *reconceptualisation* of learning.

Putting all these summaries together I get what follows, though you might like to create your own synthesis particular to your own teaching context.

Seven principles common to high-quality learning and achievement

The following principles, which are highly interrelated, do not just apply in ideal circumstances. They also apply in the most difficult – when you have too much to teach in too little time. In Chapter 22 we see that teachers in this situation who get the best results apply these principles with rigour. To maximise learning all seven principles should operate, and to the maximum degree – a daunting prospect that leaves us all with a professional challenge!

In experiments in classrooms the control and experimental group are taught for the same length of time. The control group usually does less student activity, and so gets more teacher explanation and more detail, but often does a grade or two *worse* than the experimental group.

. . . too much to teach in too little time.

1 Students must see the value of the learning

Students need to be persuaded of the value and purpose of learning what they are about to learn. If students set themselves the goals this is done fairly automatically, but it cannot always be done. However goals are set, they must see them, and/or the journey to these goals, as useful and enjoyable. Maslow's theory of motivation shows that learning should provide for the following needs: self-actualisation, self-esteem, and belongingness and love needs.

Evidence
Marzano (see the summary diagram on p. 74) gives this top priority; so do 'value expectancy' theories of motivation. Maslow's theory of motivation in Chapter 3. Goals and advance organisers have very high effect sizes.

2 Students must believe they can do it

Students must expect some success, though not necessarily total success. It is not easy to strike the balance between challenge and students' expectation of success. Ladders of tasks that end in open reasoning tasks do this best (see page 74). There is an inescapable need for good teacher judgement here.

Evidence
Marzano (see the summary diagram on p. 74); attribution has a very high effect size indeed; see Chapters 3 and 21. Dweck's theory of motivation.

164

3 Challenging goals

This is one of Hattie's first principles, and a characteristic of factors with high average effect sizes. We can say more about the nature of the challenging goal; the first points below are about motivation.

The goal involves student activity on constructivist methods

This is required if the students are to make their own sense of the topic, and provide student and teacher with feedback.

Evidence
Nearly all the methods of high effect size involve such student activity. Chapter 2: constructivist methods require the student to make sense, and have high effect sizes; for example whole-class interactive teaching, reciprocal teaching, graphic organisers, note making as opposed to note taking, etc. (Chapters 4–13). Student activity gets the best results in high-stakes examinations, as seen in Chapter 22.

The goal involves reasoning not just reproduction

This is required for deep learning. The goals must be intellectually challenging for the student, even a student of very low attainment. A ladder of tasks involving reproduction tasks can be used to climb to this goal.

Evidence
Chapter 2; reasoning is a characteristic of challenging goals, and a characteristic of all the methods at the top of Hattie's table.

High participation rate

All students should work towards the goal and carry out the activity. This is usually achieved by a combination of using fun methods, and holding learners accountable for their own and perhaps each other's learning. See, for example, how cooperative learning does it. Strategies such as pair checking and assertive questioning can also ensure high participation rates.

Audience, variety and fun

It helps to create purpose and value for the student if the product produced by the active method has an audience that matters to the student. Peers often matter at least as much and often more than the teacher. For example, students might make a poster to show the rest of their class, to display in the corridor or for example in a health centre. It also helps if there is variety in the type of goal set.

4 Feedback and dialogue on progress towards the goal

Student activity provides feedback to the learner and teacher. It is a window into the quality of the students' 'constructs' or understanding. Constructivism shows us that constructs have errors and omissions. Students can provide much of this feedback and construct improvement for themselves. The following bullet points are described in detail in Chapter 8:

- *Students need 'medals'* that give information about the extent to which they have achieved the goals.
- *Students need 'missions'* that describe how to improve and progress.
- *Students need to develop a growing understanding of the goals.*

Evidence

Feedback tops Hattie's table. Constructivism predicts the importance of feedback; see Chapter 2. Methods that top Hattie's table involve feedback to the student and to the teacher, for example the interactive dialogue in reciprocal teaching and in whole-class interactive teaching. See Chapter 8 for the details on feedback.

5 Establish the structure of information and so its meaning

This involves relations between concepts, seeing the wood for the trees, and stressing the meaning of what is being learned. Students must be aware of the following: the key points, the key principles, the lesson's purpose, and how these relate to each other and to other topics.

- *From known to unknown.* See Chapter 2, especially the example of using relevant recall questions to teach division.
- *From concrete to abstract.* See Chapter 2, especially SOLO.
- *The structure first, then add the detail.* Understanding takes time and too much detail obscures meaning and structure. Learning details once the meaning is clear is easy, but hard or even impossible if the meaning is obscure. Many teachers violate this principle because of our overcrowded curriculum. This is not just a matter of summarising key points in advance, but of restricting the delivery of detail so that there is time to develop understanding of the substantive issues.

Evidence

Chapter 2 showed that deep learning comes from how constructs are structured in the student's mind. The SOLO taxonomy describes learning quality by examining the structure of students' work. Only structured information can go into permanent memory. Most very high effect-size methods found by Marzano make structure very clear to learners; for example advance organisers, graphic organisers, relevant recall questions, goals, note making rather than note taking.

6 Time and repetition

Students need familiarity with material to 'chunk' it into meaningful bits – six encounters at least. Students do not simply 'write' concepts and logical relations onto their hard disk. Much learning is intuitive and below consciousness, and to assist this we need to use:

- *Multiple contexts.* Students need to see examples and non-examples of concepts and ideas in many different contexts in order to 'get' them.

- *Multiple perspectives.* Students need to see what they are learning through different 'spectacles'. See SOLO, and Chapter 21 on analysis.
- *Multiple representations.* Students need right- and left-brain representations, that is 'whole-brain learning' to aid understanding. Note the very high effect sizes of graphic organisers and 'decisions, decisions', which are visual and 'right brain'.

Evidence

See Chapter 2. The main evidence for multiple representations is the Coffield report and the exceptionally high effect sizes of graphic organisers and decisions, decisions. Deep learning and high SOLO require multiple perspectives and familiarity. Whole-class interactive teaching involves repeated reviews.

7 Teach skills as well as content

If the teacher makes time to teach students important study skills and thinking skills and integrates this into their teaching, then students both learn these important skills *and* their achievement is improved with an average effect size of 0.77.

Evidence

See Chapter 21.

There is remarkable agreement here between the 'qualitative' view of learning in Chapter 2 and the 'quantitative' view of Chapters 3–7. But this is a book for teachers rather than researchers, so tempted as I am to look at this agreement in detail, I will restrain myself!

Notice that this means that high-quality learning and teaching is the best way to bring about high attainment. Many teachers suggest that they must teach badly to produce high attainment, for example teach to the test etc. This is not the case. We will see even more convincing evidence of this in Chapter 22.

These principles should not be read as meaning that we should not use conventional teaching strategies such as lectures, demonstrations, or students watching a video. However, conventional use of these methods can be greatly improved by application of the principles, as we will see in Chapters 15–20.

Anyone can invent general principles that claim to determine good quality learning and teaching, and many have. But the principles above are not based on my personal whim, or even on my expertise; I have tried to base them on the best evidence available. They are not a complete set, just a set that can be fully justified by evidence on quality learning. I worry that there is not enough emphasis on the humanistic and affective side of learning; you, however, can take such matters, and others, into account in your own work.

Introduction to the PAR model

One way of applying the principles above is to use them to outline a structure for teaching a short topic. I will do this by adapting the PAR model from *Teaching Today* (page 424), to create an evidence-based model of teaching. I have already hinted at this in Chapters 2–7.

The diagram on p. 169 describes how you might teach a short topic, not necessarily all in one lesson. It is explained in more detail below and especially in Chapters 15–20. The sequence of elements is not a necessary one, and in practice the teacher may visit each of these phases many times. They may do a bit of 'present', a bit of 'apply', then a bit more 'present, and a bit more 'apply', then do a 'review', and so on. Whatever the sequence, however, it is difficult to imagine a topic being taught well without visiting all three elements in the PAR model.

So we can characterise good teaching as being like a three-legged stool, and if a leg is missing the stool falls over! Are your lessons up to PAR?!

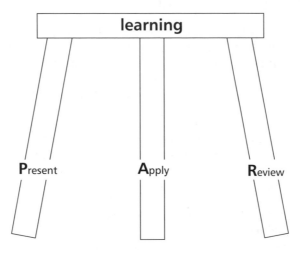

I do not mean to suggest of course that you should slavishly follow the structure suggested here. It just shows the components commonly, but not invariably, found in effective lessons. Usually it will benefit from being adapted or revised to suit the context on the day.

I hope I have shown that for the most part there is remarkable agreement between the qualitative (Chapters 2–3) and quantitative (Chapters 4–7) ways of looking at learning. If you are not convinced yet, I hope the rest of the book will persuade you (for example Chapters 21–23). However, we have left out at least two pairs of spectacles in the above analysis, and I leave to you the difficulty of addressing the issues they raise as I have no space here, though *Teaching Today* considers them.

- Firstly, the long-term view: what happens if you look at learning over a lifetime rather than over an hour or two?
- Secondly, humanistic psychology, as personified by Abraham Maslow, Carl Rogers, John Holt, Malcolm Knowles and others. This is present but not complete in these principles. The quote below invites us to use the principles and the PAR model with humanistic caution!

Present   Maximum 35%?

Orientation: the learners are prepared for learning.
- Recall learning of last lesson
- Recall other relevant prior learning
- Persuasive account of the relevance, importance and value of the learning
- Advance organiser to structure the new content
- **Challenging goals** are given or negotiated

New material is presented
Knowledge, reasoning, theories, etc. are explained to students or learned in some other way. Abstract ideas are illustrated with concrete examples

Practical and intellectual skills are demonstrated e.g. how to use a tool or formula, or punctuate a sentence. This stresses both process and product. Key points are emphasised. Showing how on the board. Students studying 'exemplars' (good work)

Typical learning strategies:
- Listen to teacher talk or watch a video
- Watch a demonstration
- Study exemplars, e.g. spoof assessment
- 'Teaching by asking' (rather than by telling)
- 'Teaching without talking' strategies such as learning from ILT and other resources

Feedback for learner and teacher:
Learning in progress is checked and corrected, e.g.:
- Interactive question and answer
- Other interactive dialogue, e.g. in group work
- Students demonstrating one on the board, followed by class discussion etc.

Apply   Minimum 60%?

Students work towards their challenging goal. The task(s) require them to apply the knowledge, theories, skills, etc. that have just been presented. This involves them in *reasoning* not just reproduction, e.g. *problem solving, making decisions, and creating things such as mind maps, etc.*

Typical learning strategies:
When learning a practical skill
- Practical task to carry out the skill

When learning cognitive skills
- Answering questions on a case study in groups
- Exercises, questions, worksheet, essay, etc.
- Class discussion to develop an argument or answer a question, etc.
- Decisions decisions game
- Student presentation
- Critical evaluation of exemplars, e.g. are these sentences correctly punctuated?

Feedback for learner and teacher
This may not be a separate activity and may involve the students more than the teacher. The aim is to:
- Inform learners of what is good, and what not! (medals and missions)
- Provide support for those who need it
- Check attention to task, quality of work, behaviour, etc.
Common strategies include: self-assessment, peer assessment, class discussion, teacher comments, etc.

Review   Minimum 5%?

Were the goals met? **Summary and clarification** of what was to be learned. Emphasis on the *key points* and *structure*, etc.

Learning strategies
- Note making
- Creating a mind map, poster or handout that summarises the key points.
- Class discussion
- Advance organisers revisited and more detail added
- Reviews at the beginning of a lesson with a short task
- Peer explaining of key objectives followed by check by the teacher
- Quiz, test, etc.

Feedback for learner and teacher: Learning is checked and corrected, e.g.:
- Question and answer in an interactive dialogue to discover and clarify weak learning
- Class discussion on difficult points, etc.
- Peer and self-assessment

Structure for teaching a topic: the PAR model. All elements are needed, and are often visited many times.

> *'When we've taught students in ways that enable them to score high on accountability tests, but in the process have made them scurry away from math or feel repelled by reading, have we educated those students properly?'*
>
> W. James Popham

How to teach in an evidence-based way

I am going to imagine that your students are about to embark on an hour or two of learning which might include some homework time. How could you structure and plan the learning and any teaching, using the evidence-based principles and

---

ART AND DESIGN PROJECT TO DESIGN A BOOK COVER USING PAR

Jason's common practice is to hand out the assignment, talk a little about it, and then set students to work. He then monitors and marks their work himself. Here, by contrast, is a PAR approach.

Present

Orientation. Jason sets the goal of designing a book cover which will be peer assessed. He asks the students what they know about book design already, and what designs have impressed them. There is a snowball activity on this, followed by class discussion. Jason makes a persuasive account for the import-ance of cover design commercially and aesthetically.

Practical and intellectual skills are demonstrated. Then students are asked to judge a book-cover competition after determining and agreeing criteria for good cover design. Jason improves and explains the criteria they will use.

Apply

The students then research and design their book covers, self-assessing against the criteria as they work. Jason monitors this and helps them to improve their designs.

Review

Students peer assess their designs using the criteria; Jason then surprises his class by showing them commercial designs for the same books they have just designed covers for. He leads a discussion on 'what we have learned about book cover design', then leads another discussion on 'what we have learned about the design process'.

Later, just before another design brief, Jason reminds learners of the book-cover activity and what they have learned from it about the design process, and they set themselves targets based on this and on self-assessment.

The above approach realises the seven principles better and uses more high-effect-size methods than Jason's usual practice.

---

high-effect-size methods that we have just established? What methods or student activities could you choose from, and how would you use them?

Throughout this book I write as if you are teaching a topic to a class in a classroom or workshop etc. However, the model works in almost any learning situation, including, for example:

1. A resource-based learning (RBL) situation where students are learning alone or in a classroom from resources such as a workbook. For example, learning how to use a spreadsheet from a workbook.

DESIGNING AN ILT RESOURCE USING PAR

Amarjit, a new ICT teacher, is writing ILT assignments for her students. One assignment she inherited on 'Health and safety for computer workers' has not worked well in the past. It has involved giving students links to websites on health and safety and requiring them to fill in a worksheet. She has decided to redesign the assignment using the PAR structure.

Present
Orientation. Her online assignment is designed so that the first screen sets a goal to design a leaflet on health and safety aspects of computer use in a call centre. It explains that their finished designs will be displayed on Open Day, and used to design a leaflet on health and safety for student use in the college.

The next screen is a diagrammatic advance organiser that picks out the key aspects of the topic in outline only. The leaflet must address all these aspects. A case study of a past student with repetitive strain injury makes a persuasive case for the importance of the topic.

New material is presented. The next screen presents web links on an interactive graphic version of the advance organiser. There are 'teaching without talking' activities for some of these links. On one, students must copy text from a screen and highlight the key points; they then compare their highlighting with a model.

Apply
Students design a desktop-published leaflet on health and safety and are asked to check that all the aspects on the advance organiser have been covered.

Students present their designs in a corridor exhibition and give each other advice on improvement. Students improve their work, then email it for assessment.

Review
Students take an online test on the topic which requires them to do remedial work on their weaker answers.

---

2. A project or design-brief situation, for example in art and design, where students are given a brief to create, say, a design for a ceramic brooch.
3. A practical unit where students are learning a practical skill, for example joinery, by stepping through a series of 'jobs'.
4. ILT/ICT students learning alone or in small groups using resources such as the Internet, video, etc. Indeed the PAR approach, and the methods in Chapters 15–20, constitute a complete pedagogy for ILT.
5. An educational visit and indeed almost any other learning situation.

In all these situations the PAR structure describes an effective approach, and the methods later in this chapter can be applied. Let's look at two examples.

There is no need to stick rigidly to the PAR approach for every topic you teach, of course, but it should be considered very seriously for difficult learning.

In Chapters 15–20 I will step through the PAR structure mentioned earlier, suggesting methods in each stage for you to choose from. We will start by looking at how you can monitor your students' understanding as you teach. This immediate or 'real time' feedback, *from* the learners and *to* the learners, is a crucial issue.

Part 5 Choosing and using teaching methods

15 Feedback through interactive dialogue: the self-correcting classroom

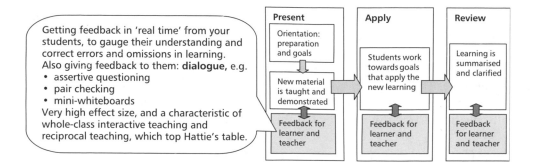

Getting feedback in 'real time' from your students, to gauge their understanding and correct errors and omissions in learning. Also giving feedback to them: **dialogue**, e.g.
- assertive questioning
- pair checking
- mini-whiteboards

Very high effect size, and a characteristic of whole-class interactive teaching and reciprocal teaching, which top Hattie's table.

Present

Orientation: preparation and goals

New material is taught and demonstrated

Feedback for learner and teacher

Apply

Students work towards goals that apply the new learning

Feedback for learner and teacher

Review

Learning is summarised and clarified

Feedback for learner and teacher

The diagram above shows where we are in the PAR process and gives an 'advance organiser'. I start describing the PAR process here because good dialogue is central to each part of PAR, including orientation.

Look at the diagram on the teaching/learning process on page 9. As described at the end of Chapter 2, students apply their construct (their learning) and so produce a product such as an answer to a question. This can be used by the learner to get feedback on their understanding ('I don't see how my answer can be right, I must have misunderstood something. Perhaps . . .'). And the teacher or a peer can use the product to get feedback on the learner's construct ('she thinks "mammals" means just "humans"'). This can lead to correction. Hattie says this 'feedback' is crucial to success; it also forms the basis of whole-class interactive teaching. How do you get answers from the questions and tasks you set students?

In terms of the seven principles in Chapter 14, the precise questioning strategy you adopt can make a big difference to the proportion of students who participate in your class, both mentally and verbally. It also affects the quality of feedback you and your students get on the depth of understanding, and the time students have to reason out their answer: their 'thinking time'. Feedback is crucial: students need it to correct their constructs; you need it to adjust your teaching to the pace at which your students are learning, and to discover and correct misconceptions. The most commonly used methods in classrooms are much less fun and far less effective than the best methods, as I hope to show, so most of us have some work to do here!

Below are six alternative question and answer strategies. They can be used in the teaching of any subject, whether there are clear 'right answers' to questions as there often are in mathematics and science, for example, or whether there are many acceptable answers though some unjustifiable ones, as there often are in English literature or art appreciation, personal social and health education, for example.

The methods are evaluated later against the seven principles from Chapter 14. What do you think of them?

Which questioning strategy?

Question and answer: volunteers answer

Students volunteer to answer questions posed verbally by the teacher. This is usually done with 'hands up' but sometimes students call out their answer. If more than one student volunteers, the teacher chooses who will answer. The 'thinking time' between asking a question and the answer being delivered is usually less than a second here. There is often a low 'participation' rate because students learn that if they keep their hands down they will not be asked to contribute. If some students call out the answer this reduces the thinking time of the others.

Question and answer: nominees answer

Students nominated by the teacher answer questions asked by the teacher. This is often called the 'pose, pause, pounce' strategy. The teacher 'poses' the question, 'pauses' for students to think, and then 'pounces' on an individual to answer. (Optionally, the teacher can choose a student who appears not to be attending to answer the questions.)

Buzz groups: volunteers answer

Students work in small groups, or pairs, to answer a thought-provoking question, or do a calculation or similar task. The teacher asks each group in turn to contribute part of the answer; for example: 'Can you give me *one* advantage of using a laser printer? . . . Can this group give me another?' A volunteer answers for the group. They are called 'buzz groups' because of the buzz of conversation created while they work.

Buzz groups: nominees answer

As above, but the teacher nominates the student in each group who will contribute that group's answer(s) and justify or explain it. The teacher only chooses which student will give the group's answer *after* the group discussion. All members of the group are then likely to attend, and to try to understand the group's answer, as any of them may be asked to give and explain it. (Optionally, the teacher can choose students who do not appear to be attending to explain their group's answer.)

Assertive questioning

1. Buzz groups work on a thought-provoking question.

2. The teacher monitors this work, asking:

   'Does everyone have an answer? Ask me for a hint if not.'
   'Does anyone need more time?'

   If a group does not respond to this offer of help they are 'fair game' for the next stage. The teacher does *not* give the answer away if they do help a group.

3. The teacher *nominates* individuals to give their group's answer, and to justify it: 'Why do you think that?' The teacher *thanks* the student for their answer, *but does not evaluate it*.

4. The teacher gets a response from each group in this way, or at least a number of groups, and then points out inconsistencies between the groups' answers, if any. (If there aren't any, perhaps the question could have been more challenging, though in early practice easy questions are helpful.)

5. The aim now is to get the *whole class to agree* their 'class answer(s)'. The teacher encourages the class to discuss and evaluate their various answers, and to agree, and to justify their 'class answer'. Minority views are allowed, but the aim is consensus.

6. Only when the class have agreed their answer does the teacher 'give away' the right answer, or evaluate and comment on the answers given.

This method works whether there are right answers or whether different interpretations and answers are likely, for example in a critical appraisal of a painting.

(See the diagram below (p. 176) and 'Whole-class interactive teaching', Chapter 24 in *Teaching Today*.)

Pair checking

The teacher asks a question, and students work alone to answer it. Pairs then compare their answers and each individual says something positive about his or her partner's answer and one thing that would improve it. The teacher now gives the correct answer. Pairs suggest another improvement to their partner's answer. This can be done with pairs combining into fours to compare their answers. The teacher listens to some student conversations throughout.

Which is the best questioning strategy?

Let's look at these six methods from the following points of view. These 'spectacles' are derived from the seven principles in Chapter 14. So this is an evidence-based evaluation.

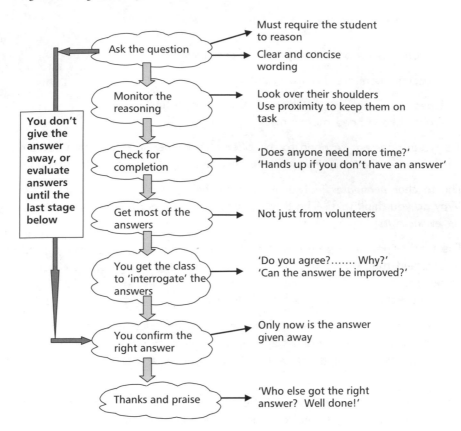

Assertive questioning works well whether or not there is a 'right answer'.

Participation rate

Participation is high if at any given time a very large proportion of students are engaged in trying to answer the question for themselves, that is if there are very few 'passengers'. (Principle 3: challenging goals.)

Student feedback and dialogue

Constructivism requires that all students receive feedback on the quality of their answer, and so on the quality of their constructs (see Chapter 2). Ideally this is in the form of a dialogue with peers and then you. This helps them correct their constructs: 'Oh! Why have I got that one wrong?' (Principle 4: feedback and dialogue.)

Teacher's feedback

This factor is high if you get *representative* feedback on the quality of all the students' reasoning and understanding. If only *one* student answers correctly this can fool you into believing that *all* your students are able to answer correctly. Representative feedback requires answers from many students, though perhaps not from all of them all the time.

If you discover that a number of your students are not getting the right answers you can obviously do something about this. If the classroom is very active and inter-active you can discover misconceptions very quickly and put them right before they prevent students keeping up. Hattie has shown that this is of paramount import-ance. Teacher's feedback is highest quality when there is dialogue between the teacher and the class. (Principle 4: feedback and dialogue.)

Student comfort

'John, what's your answer?' If you put students 'on the spot' they may feel humili-ated if they cannot answer well, however pleasant you are about their fumbling. This varies greatly from class to class, but it is clearly an issue. However, you may well be prepared to sacrifice *some* student comfort if it creates better learning. The ground rules on page 178 help make students comfortable. (Principles 1 and 2: valuing learning, and self-belief.)

. . . you may be prepared to sacrifice some student comfort . . .

Thinking time

This factor is high if a given student is able to spend a good deal of time thinking productively about the question or task. This will ensure that students use their constructs, establish links between them, and improve them where necessary. This is absolutely central to the learning process as constructivism shows, yet Rowe (1986) found that the average time between a teacher asking a question and a student answering it was 0.7 seconds! So weak students (the 'Roberts' of Chapter 2) will still be wondering what the question means when they hear the answer, especially if the question requires reasoning. We need the thinking time to be long enough for the weakest students to be able to attempt the question or task. Otherwise the weakest students are disadvantaged by our questioning strategy. (Principle 6: Time and repetition.)

I have asked many hundreds of teachers to evaluate the six methods, and the table below sets out a typical response.

Key: *** Excellent ** good *weak !! poor

Questioning strategy (Students anticipate these strategies in advance)	Participation rate	Students' feedback and dialogue	Teacher's feedback	Student comfort	Student comfort
Q&A: volunteers answer Students volunteer to answer questions.	!!	!!	!!	***	!!
Q&A: nominees answer Students nominated by the teacher answer questions (ratings depend on group size, who you ask, and pauses).	**(*)	*	*(*)	*/!!	!!/* Depends on wait time
Buzz groups: volunteers answer Students work in small groups to answer a thought-provoking question. Teacher asks each group in turn to contribute part of the answer. A volunteer answers for their group.	**	**	**	***	*(*)
Buzz groups: nominees answer As above, but the teacher nominates the student in each group who will contribute that group's answer(s) after the group discussion.	***	**	**(*)	*	***
Assertive questioning Groups work on a thought-provoking question. Teacher asks individuals to give their group's answer, and then asks the rest of the class to discuss and agree a 'class answer'. Only then does the teacher 'give away' the right answer.	***	***	***	*(*)	***
Pair checking Teacher asks a question, then students work alone to answer it. Pairs then compare their answers, giving their partner one good point and one way their answer could be improved. The teacher then gives the correct answer. Pairs suggest another improvement to their partner's answer.	***	**	**	***	***

High scores here create a 'self-correcting classroom'

The self-correcting classroom: why interactive dialogue works

If shepherds drove their sheep in the way that many teachers teach, they would be in deep trouble. They would drive them without noticing in which direction the sheep had decided to travel, and without doing anything about those who were running off at a tangent. The fact that our country is not populated by lost, bemused and aimless sheep is a testament to the quality of feedback to shepherds, and to sheep. If our students are more complex than sheep, and they certainly are, then this only underlines even more strongly the imperative of feedback. It may not be pushing the metaphor too far to say that the many ill-educated, lost and bemused and aimless *people* in this country are in that state at least in part because of poor-quality feedback.

> *There is said to be 0 per cent illiteracy in Japan, and about 12 per cent in this country. How much of this is due to feedback quality, and to how we act on that feedback?*

The classroom, indeed any teaching situation, involves two feedback loops shown in the diagram on the teaching/learning process on page 84, one to the learner and one to the teacher. Firstly, let's state a few truths that are obvious when stated, but are often breached in practice.

- You must know roughly how many of your students have 'got it' so far.
- Each individual student needs to know if they have 'got it' so far.
- If everyone has 'got it' there is of course no problem, and you can proceed, and may even increase the pace or challenge of your teaching if this seems appropriate.
- If some or all of your students have *not* 'got it', then you want those individuals to know about it so they can improve their constructs (Chapter 2).
- Also you need to know *which* students have not 'got it', so you can take some remedial action. You might, for example, use diagnostic questioning to discover and correct the misconception, or explain it again, or require the student to seek clarification from a peer, or some combination of these.

For your classroom to be self-correcting you need a very high participation rate with student feedback, and then very high quality (representative) teacher feedback. You must also of course ensure that good-quality remedial action takes place when misconceptions do occur. This requires high-quality dialogue (student–student, teacher–student, or teacher–class), checking that the misunderstandings have been fixed before proceeding too far.

A self-correcting classroom ensures that all your students learn, and that when one gets 'lost' something is done to get them back on track. Corrective procedures can often take only a few moments, but they are vital because the rest of the lesson may not make sense to a 'lost' student without it.

Choosing and using teaching methods

In order to achieve a self-correcting classroom your question and answer strategy must deliver a very *high participation rate*, and very *high student and teacher feedback scores*. Have a look at the table of scores above.

You will notice that the most common question-and-answer techniques have the lowest score for self-correction. Assertive questioning has a very high score. It forms a vital part of whole-class interactive teaching near the top of Hattie's table (see Chapter 5). It is commonly used in the countries that routinely top international performance tables, such as Japan, Singapore, Taiwan and Hong Kong. That could be a coincidence of course, or a function of their cultures, but Reynolds and Farrell (1996), experts on school effectiveness, don't think so.

Assertive questioning is great fun, and withholding the answer can create a genuine sense of suspense and curiosity in your students. If a teacher wrote a detective novel I reckon she might start it with: 'Well it was the butler that did it, in the pantry, with a rolling pin and this is how it all happened . . .' It is *not* knowing the answer that keeps us interested! Assertive questioning achieves two apparently contradictory benefits: it creates a genuine sense of curiosity and interest in the subject while giving clear instruction.

Assertive questioning is very constructivist (see Chapter 2). The learners are required to make their own sense of the topic and constructs are diagnostically checked and corrected. Again this gives the lie to the belief that whole-class interactive teaching style approaches must necessarily contradict constructivist ideas.

Some useful responses to students' answers: let's get a dialogue going (see *Teaching Today* p. 57).

Wait! Students will often say more if you remain silent but interested
'Thanks. Could you say why you think that?'
'What do you/we think of John's answer?'
'Can that be right, Josie?'
'Can anyone add anything to that?'
'Anyone disagree?'
'Anyone agree, and if so why?'
'Pete thought . . . Alice thought . . . Can anyone bring this together?'
'OK, work in pairs for one minute: what do you think is missing from our answers so far?'
Cognitive conflict: e.g. 'But if you are right, and light energy alone builds plants, then the biggest plants would all be in the desert!'

In Chapter 22 we will see that exceptionally expert teachers tend to ask a question, get an answer, and then ask for a justification for the answer, and create a relaxed, blame-free culture in their classrooms.

Getting the culture right for a self-correcting classroom

It is not easy to get students to give you answers, and especially to explain why they hold a misconception. Students, like teachers, squirm when they are shown up in front of their friends, and seethe if it is in front of their enemies. Yet the examination of misconceptions is vital for a constructivist, self-correcting classroom. How can you get the blame-free culture you need in your classroom?

You will need to develop a set of beliefs and values in your students, and hence a set of ground rules, that develops a blame-free culture if you are to maximise interactive dialogue, feedback, and the correction of weak constructs.

Recent research by Judith Harris (1995) has shown that children and young adults everywhere are socialised by their peer group, not by their parents or teachers. They establish their beliefs and values partly by adopting ideas from outside and partly by producing their own ideas. Being accepted by the group is very important to young people, so peer pressure is a very powerful means of developing the right culture in your classroom, but this requires that the students see the ground rules as being 'theirs' rather than 'yours'. So explain constructivism, then *ask* students for *their* ground rules and try to get them to agree what follows through class dialogue. Write down their finding using their own words where possible.

We will learn best if we all work towards a 'blame-free' classroom

- It's OK if you don't fully understand a concept first time; learning takes time.
- What counts is whether you *understand* the question or task, and its answer, *eventually*, not whether you get it right first time
- I ask challenging questions so it is *not* humiliating to make a mistake. We all make mistakes when we learn. Indeed that is part of *how* we learn. If we don't make mistakes the work is too easy for us to learn at our maximum rate.
- Mistakes are useful because they tell us where we can improve.
- If you make a mistake, bet your life half the class has made it too.
- It's good for learning to say 'I don't understand' and to ask for clarification.
- You should *never* ridicule another student for their mistakes, even in a joking way, because *you* wouldn't like it if you were ridiculed, and because it stops us learning.
- Peers should give 'medal and mission' feedback (see Chapter 8) which is forward looking and positive.
- You will only learn from mistakes if you find out how to do it without mistakes next time, and really understand this.
- Let's help each other! The helper learns at least as much as the helped.

Ground rules and understandings like these are best established very early on, and are best developed Socratically by asking students for *their* ideas for class ground rules. 'We all want to enjoy ourselves and we all want to learn well, so what should be your ground rules?' Note it is 'your' not 'my' ground rules!

You will need to keep these ground rules rigorously yourself, so no laughing at silly answers!

The ground rules need to be vigorously enforced for the first few lessons; do this by pointing out to offenders that 'you have broken one of your ground rules'. The blame-free culture can often establish itself quite quickly, especially if you stress why it helps – students are usually very grateful for it. Ground rules on bringing pens to class and turning up on time will also be suggested, and these can be enforced in the same way.

> *You could even ask the class whether a ground rule was in fact broken if you think you would get the class support.*

An example of blame-free interactive dialogue in the classroom

Imagine a weak GCSE science group. The teacher uses an approach called cognitive conflict to challenge misconceptions here. This is explained more fully in Chapter 2. We eavesdrop in the middle of a lesson:

Teacher   So how do mammals keep warm in winter? . . . Alice?

Alice   They wear cardigans and stuff.

> Diagnosis: the teacher realises she is not clear on the meaning of the word 'mammal' and the rest of the class may be no better.

Teacher   Well, that's certainly true for some of them. But does 'mammal' just mean 'human'? *(Bridget is looking puzzled)* . . . Bridget?

Bridget   No, a mammal is like any animal who looks after its young. Like a dog.

Peter   They have lungs.

> Diagnosis: they are interpreting 'mammal' too broadly.

Teacher   Well, mammals do look after their young, and they do have lungs. But so do birds and some reptiles.

Alice   Yes, but mammals have teeth and birds don't . . .

Peter   . . . and mammals have mammary glands.

Teacher   Well done. Yes, mammary glands are the key thing here as reptiles can have teeth too. But only mammals have mammary glands. So give us a few examples of a mammal . . . Jason?

Jason   Monkeys, dogs, rabbits. Even whales like in the video.

Teacher   Good, so how do mammals keep warm in winter?

Alice   *(anxious to correct her earlier weak answer)* They have fur.

Teacher   That's it! They have fur. There are a few exceptions because if you remember from the video, whales and dolphins are mammals too. How do they –

Peter   They have blubber, which is like fat and all over the outside.

Teacher   That's it. Like a cardigan of fat. OK. I want you all to work in pairs: tell me some things that are true of mammals, but are not true of fish or reptiles. You've got just one minute!

This is the 'interactive' bit in 'whole-class interactive teaching'. Notice how the teacher uses the answers formatively to diagnose and improve the students' conceptualisation of the word 'mammal'. The students here would benefit from a 'same-but-different' activity that addressed the characteristics of fish, amphibians, reptiles birds and mammals, as explained in Chapter 10. We also saw interactive dialogue in reciprocal teaching, which has a high effect size.

Although it is particularly important to use interactive discussion like this during this phase of the lesson while skills are being established before private practice of the skill, the general approach could be used at almost any stage in a lesson. Interactive dialogue and self-correcting classrooms are almost always helpful to learning. Let's look at some other ways of doing it.

Student demonstration

This is an excellent method to test and develop students' understanding of a simple skill such as mathematics problem solving, punctuation, scientific reasoning, detection of imagery in a poem, etc. It can also be used for a practical skill. It is very similar to assertive questioning and is used in eastern European countries and in Pacific Rim countries such as Taiwan and Singapore, which routinely achieve top ranking in international comparisons of student achievement in maths, science and language learning.

The method is used after a teacher demonstration of a practical or intellectual skill. The aim is to check and correct understanding of a skill before all students practise it. It is initially a bit daunting for students but they will greatly enjoy the method if you introduce them to it properly. Use peer explaining first (see Chapter 19) this prepares them for student demonstration very well. When they peer explain well, set them tasks to do in pairs followed by a student demonstration, perhaps asking for volunteers. Then move on to pair work followed by you nominating the student to demonstrate. Give them fair warning of any changes.

The basic procedure for student demonstration is very like assertive questioning above.

Student demonstration

1 You set a task

'Working in pairs, factorise $6x^2 + 9x + 2$.'

'OK, in pairs, punctuate this paragraph.'

'Working by yourself this time, can you see any personification or metaphors in the third or fourth verse of the poem?'

2 Students work on the task

This can be done in pairs initially, but after a bit of practice at the task students should work individually, perhaps checking each other's completed answers in pairs.

They strive to get the answer, with a justification. Pairs make sure that either of them can provide this justification.

3 You monitor the work

You check attention to task and occasionally ask:

'Can everyone do this one?'

'Can you all explain your answer?'

Students who can't answer the question are required to own up and get help at this stage, otherwise they are 'fair game' for the next stage.

During this stage you secretly identify some students with good answers, and some with weak answers. You might choose two good answers that differ in some way; for example, a maths teacher might notice two students who both have the correct answer, but by a different method.

4 You choose students to demonstrate their answer(s) to the rest of the class

If students are in pairs you choose one student from the pair at random to give the pair's answer. (To begin with you might just get one pair's answer but later get two or three, as described below.)

5 The student(s) gives their answer on the board

They explain each step and its justification to the class. You and the other students can ask questions to clarify, but do not yet evaluate the answer.

'Why didn't you use 6 and 1 as the factors of 6?'

'Why did you choose a full stop and not a comma?'

'So how did you choose between personification and metaphor?'

6 You ask for a 'class answer'

You ask the class if they agree with each student's answer and its justification, or whether either could be improved. The aim is not to criticise a student's answer, but for the class to agree a 'class answer'. The student who did the demonstration becomes the class scribe, writing up any changes the class agrees to. You again facilitate without evaluating the answers or the arguments.

'Why do you think it should be plus four and not minus?'

'How many think it should be a comma? Why?'

'So why exactly is it not a metaphor?'

7 *You comment on the class answer*
Praise any useful contributions and confirm any correct reasoning, and correct any weak reasoning.

8 *The process is repeated with another task*
After sufficient practice the students can do stage 2 as individuals rather than in pairs.

Students are often initially resistant to doing a demonstration if they are not used to it. So you could make use of volunteers to begin with, but try to move on to students nominated by you as soon as you can. They will be more confident of answers that they have produced in pairs than answers produced in isolation, so start the topic with pair work. Scrupulous attention to the ground rules for a blame-free classroom mentioned above is important here.

The student demonstration is not enough by itself, of course; students will need to do some individual work now to practise the skill, that is they need an 'apply' phase.

It is instructive to compare these two sequences, as in the diagram below, where you can see that whole-class interactive teaching adds a stage.

Conventional teaching	**Whole-class interactive teaching**
Teacher shows how to do some problems on the board	Teacher shows how to do some problems on the board
⬇	⬇
	Student demonstration on the board
	⬇
Students have a bash at doing similar problems alone	Students have a bash at doing similar problems alone

This added stage often means that students are more successful and quicker at the individual practice. So the extra stage can actually save time. See, for example, another way of providing the 'missing stage' called peer explaining of model answers in Chapter 19 (page 251).

All the arguments in favour of assertive questioning apply also to this method. You might like to compare student demonstrations with other methods you use in similar situations, using the criteria we used earlier in this chapter. The method is great fun for both you and your students when done well.

Class demonstration

This is usually done after one of the 'normal' demonstration methods described in Chapter 17, and might not be necessary for a simple skill.

Here the class tells the teacher 'how to do it'. The teacher asks for what to do, step by step, asking 'why?' for each step. Further questioning and explanation is used where necessary to get a fully persuasive justification for each step. This works for a practical or an intellectual skill.

Teacher	OK, you've decided on the paragraph breaks and full stops. Now what?
Jason	We need speech marks for what Annie says in the first paragraph.
Teacher	OK, where do you want them exactly?
Jason	Around what she says: 'I don't want to go to the party'.
	(The teacher puts the speech marks on the board as Jason suggests.)
Teacher	Why didn't you start them here, just before 'Annie said'?
Sally	Because Annie didn't say 'Annie said'.
	(Class laughter.)
Teacher	That's right. OK, now what?

You could use any of the methods we looked at in Chapter 15 during this class demonstration, but few teachers use the highest feedback methods towards the end of this list:

– Individual volunteers answer: Jason puts his hand up and you choose him.
– Teacher nominees answer: You pick Jason to answer.

- Buzz groups work on the task and a volunteer from the group answers.
- Buzz groups again but you choose the student in the group who answers.
- Assertive questioning.
- Pair checking.

As we saw in Chapter 15, the last two give the highest quality feedback to teacher and to student. As does the student demonstration, which is closely modelled on assertive questioning.

This comes from the Mathematics Enhancement Programme:
www.ex.ac.uk/cimt/mep/index.htm

From our observations and contact with schools, and more recently through the work of the MEP regional directors, Liz Henning and Rob Smith, we have found that successful implementation of MEP strategies in the classroom depends on:

- Effective implementation of the full range of recommended MEP strategies, including:

  - good lesson preparation
  - highly interactive teaching, with pupils demonstrating and explaining at the board
  - using a variety of activities in a lesson, some done with the whole class and some as individual work, which is closely monitored then reviewed with the whole class
  - individual pupil mistakes used as teaching points with the whole class
  - correct mathematical notation and vocabulary used at all times
  - homework seen as an integral part of the learning process
  - emphasis on mathematical logic, rather than trial and error, and encouragement of creative thinking
  - relating mathematics to real-life applications where appropriate.

Using mini-whiteboards

This is another brilliant way to get answers, and so feedback. It is possible to buy a class set of A3, A4 or A5 whiteboards, each complete with a dry-wipe pen and eraser in a sealable plastic wallet for just over a pound each. Or you can make your own sets by laminating card. Or you could use slates like your great-grandmother!

The idea was first invented in primary schools but they are used everywhere now, including university, though there is a hi-tech version described later: 'clickers'.

Seven mini-whiteboard methods

Question or task

This starts off very like student demonstration.

1 You set a task
It works well to start off with students working in pairs, but later working individually. Tell them if you are going to do this so that they work towards their own independence. You can give the question verbally or using the board:

> 'Working in pairs to begin with, factorise $6x^2 + 9x + 2$.'

> 'By yourself this time, punctuate this sentence: "Some people such as farmers work outside."'

> 'Working by yourself this time, write down any phrase from verses three or four that involves personification.'

2 Students work on the task and write their answer on their board
Once students have their answer:

3 You check what is on the boards
Ask students to hold up their boards all at the same time so that you can see their answers. Students will crane their necks to see everyone else's answers!

4 You ask students about their answers
Students need to know not just whether they have the right answer, but whether they arrived at the answer using the correct reasoning. So you can ask students 'why' they have the answer they have:

> 'That's right, Phil, why did you decide to put the comma where you did?'

> Alternatively you can withhold your evaluation of the answers to spark a class discussion:

> 'OK, some of you have a comma after "people", some after "farmers". What do we think?'

Clearly you can get students to call out their answers and so dispense with the board – 'OK, what is the first word in your sentence with a comma after it?' – but this will only work for very simple questions. It is not that easy to get everyone to call out at the same time and it can be noisy with some classes.

> For more on mini-whiteboard products:
> www.easyteach.co.uk/dry.html
>
> For more on high-tech interactivity:
> www.einstruction.com

Here are some more mini-whiteboard methods kindly supplied by Jim Judges of Sutton Coldfield College.

Quiz

Ask students to write their answer to multiple-choice questions, A, B, C, D, etc. – holding up their answers as you go along. (They can even keep a record of their score on the reverse.)

Recaps

These work well at the end of a lesson, or at the beginning of a lesson when the last lesson can be recapped.

- Ask students to work individually to write down three key things they can remember from the lesson.
- They hold their points up.
- You then give your three key points.

You can also ask student to compare their points with their neighbours before displaying their points. Or you can 'snowball' by asking students to compare with each other and revise their points before showing their boards, but this gives you less feedback.

Picture this

Ask students to explain something using pictures. For example, give each student a definition, or paragraph and ask students individually or in pairs to produce a pictorial representation. Take it further by numbering each board and passing them round asking each student or pair to deduce what each diagram represents, jotting their answers on a piece of paper for discussion later.

Mini-Pictionary™

This is a variant of a well-known board game. Students take turns to 'explain' a key concept to their partner – for example how sedimentary rocks are formed – simply by drawing (no talking and no letters or words). There are two ways to give them the concept:

- on sets of cards which they turn up one by one for each go
- 'flash' it to all those about to draw, using your own mini-whiteboard, while the other students look away. Watch out for reflections!

List

Ask students to write a number of items or bullet points (e.g. 'Give four properties of a metal' or 'List five reasons for producing a business plan', etc.). Then students look at each other's answers, tick any answers that are shared, and add any that they do not have.

Speed learning

This is useful for revision. Each student has some time to prepare a quick learning guide to a different section of the syllabus, using diagrams and key words. They write this on their board. Students then pair up and have a short time, say four minutes, to explain their brief nugget of knowledge to each other – that's about two minutes each. Students then swap boards and form a new pair and must explain their newly learned topic to the next person, and so on until everyone has learned everything!

'Clickers': high-tech methods to get participation and feedback

A number of companies make 'clickers', devices rather like television remote controls, where students log their answers to multiple-answer questions by pressing button A or B, etc. Software then indicates how many students thought the answer was A, B, etc. Such systems are sometimes fitted as standard in lecture theatres in higher education, but mini-whiteboards give you and students more detailed feedback on questions, as long as the answers are short enough to fit on the board.

Making 'interactive whiteboards' genuinely interactive

Often the interaction is only between the teacher and the board, and most of the class are soon bored despite the initial 'wow' factor. To use the board in a genuinely interactive manner requires that you use it with Socratic questioning, assertive questioning, or a student demonstration using an approach similar to those above.

Interactive dialogue

The term 'interactive' is used to describe teaching where there is high participation, high-quality feedback, Socratic dialogue, and so a 'self-correcting classroom'. However, 'interactive' is not really specific enough. One can have interactivity with only a few members of the class participating, and answers are not used to provide feedback or challenge and improve constructs. High-quality interactivity requires simultaneous *participation* and so *student feedback*, *teacher feedback*, *thinking time*; and so a *self-correcting classroom*. *Student comfort* may also be an issue.

You can adopt the best strategies, combine them, or devise your own, based on what you have learned by studying the approaches above. Whatever techniques you deploy, they can be used in every single phase of the PAR process and in almost every activity in the lesson. They can also be adapted for working with very small groups or even with individuals. They differentiate exceptionally well.

References and further reading

Black P. *et al.* (2003) *Assessment for Learning: Putting it into Practice*, Buckingham: Open University Press.

Harris, J. R. (1995) 'Where is the child's environment? A group socialization theory of development', *Psychological Review*, 102, 458–89.

Reynolds, D. and Farrell, S. (1996) *Worlds Apart? A Review of International Studies of Educational Achievement Involving England*, London: HMSO.

16 Teaching methods for the 'orientation' phase: setting the scene

The teaching methods in this book are arranged around the three phases in the PAR model shown in the diagram below and in Chapter 14 (page 169). We will look first at methods suitable for the 'Present' phase, which has two main parts: 'Orientation' and 'New material is taught'. This is not to say that you must cut your teaching up into the PAR phases; some activities combine the functions of its parts.

Orientation: the learners are prepared for learning

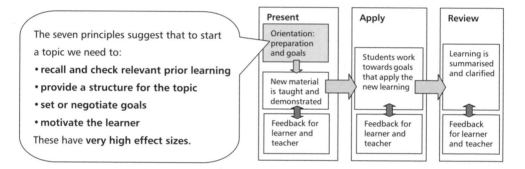

The seven principles suggest that to start a topic we need to:
- **recall and check relevant prior learning**
- **provide a structure for the topic**
- **set or negotiate goals**
- **motivate the learner**

These have **very high effect sizes**.

Present
- Orientation: preparation and goals
- New material is taught and demonstrated
- Feedback for learner and teacher

Apply
- Students work towards goals that apply the new learning
- Feedback for learner and teacher

Review
- Learning is summarised and clarified
- Feedback for learner and teacher

Conventional practice often involves giving behavioural objectives, such as telling students 'At the end of this lesson you will be able to multiply fractions' and immediately teaching the new material. This is a huge missed opportunity with a small effect size. What would constructivism predict we should do at the beginning of a lesson?

Imagine a weak student in your class, one who might latch on to relatively irrelevant points and miss the key issues and principles – 'Robert' in Chapter 2. This learner experiences difficulty in 'structuring' or 'organising' this new learning, and building it onto what he already knows. This structuring creates meaning and deep learning as we saw in Chapter 2, helps distinguish the important from the noticeable, and gives a holistic overview of the meaning and purpose of the topic. It also helps learners apply and transfer learning. Most students have trouble with this.

Constructivism predicts that it would help students to get them to recall the relevant prior learning and experiences onto which they will build the new learning, and then *give them a structure* for this new learning. Once the structure and its foundations are in place, you can then present the detail. The learner would then have 'pegs' to hang the new learning upon. These strategies do indeed have very high effect sizes.

192

The purposes of methods that orientate the learner

Before we look at some methods, let's just recall what we hope they will do. This involves much of the seven principles we established in Chapter 14. It also ensures differentiation.

- *To recall and check prior learning.* The learner recalls 'prerequisite' learning such as recalling how to use a voltmeter before using one for the second time; also relevant everyday experience that can help them understand the new material. It also includes recalling analogous experience, such as examples of how an unjust authority figure has made us feel angry, before studying the Peasants' Revolt.

  This enables you to improve weaknesses in prior learning, and it puts it in students' short-term memories, ready for use.
- *Provide a structure*, for the new learning, built on what is already known. This involves prioritising the content, stressing the vital principles, concepts and key points. But also showing how these are related, for example what causes what.
- *Set or negotiate goals.* To explain the challenging goal, usually in the form of an activity, that you will set the learners.
- *Motivate the learner*, for example by persuading students of the purpose and *value* of the learning and the goals, and giving them a sense of *belief* that they can tackle the goal.

Hattie found the following effect sizes for activities related to this orientation process. Marzano's effect sizes are shown under the methods below. All these methods take very little time.

Strategy	N	Effect size
Goals	959	0.51
Concept mapping (one way to do an advance organizer below)	18	0.45
Advance organisers	2106	0.44
Behavioural objectives	157	0.24

Methods for the orientation phase

Here are some methods to experiment with; hopefully you will ring the changes rather than get into a rut with just one method. Consider using the most powerful methods for the hardest topics, though.

Methods that recall and check prior learning

Asking questions that recall relevant prior learning (ES up to 0.93)

This simple but remarkably effective strategy puts the foundations in place before you build on them. The effect size is Marzano's, from Chapter 6.

See the diagram on page 16. You ask students questions requiring them to recall the prior learning necessary to understand the new material before it is taught. Most teachers check recall of the previous lesson, but this goes further to include any prerequisite or helpful prior learning or experience.

The method is not as easy to use as you might think. It may involve working at the 'Principles' level in the SOLO taxonomy:

> 'We are about to look at a conflict between Henry VIII and the church. Now we have already seen conflicts between king and church – can you give me some examples? . . . Can you see any common factors in those conflicts?'

Or:

> 'We are about to use ratios to solve triangles. Where else have we met ratios?'

> 'What can you tell me about them?'

> 'What is so useful about them?'

As well as preparing the learner, such introductions help your students see your subject as a coherent whole rather than a string of disconnected detail.

If they have very little experience or prior learning that might help them, then try analogies. For example, a teacher trying to teach students about power relations might ask them: 'What would you think if a neighbour came into your house and started telling you how to run your home?'

'Recalling the previous lesson.'

Marzano's effect sizes	N	Effect size
Relevant recall questions: questions requiring students to recall what they already know about the topic or skill to be learned:		
• asked only before the lesson	83	0.75
• asked during and before the lesson	45	0.93
For complex learning only, i.e. that involves abstract principles and relations and making connections		0.69

Writing down everything you know

Students are asked to write down everything they already know about a topic you are about to teach more about. Their prior knowledge could be presented in a non-linguistic form; for example, they could devise a flipchart poster or mind map to summarise the key points. They could present these to the class.

Black *et al.*, in *Assessment for Learning* (2003), describe this method being used by schoolteachers who were surprised to find that their students often knew far more than they expected. So the method saved much more time than it took! Obviously it helps to do this at the end of the *previous* lesson, so you can digest the findings before you teach the topic. (PAR shows the structure for teaching a *topic*, which is not necessarily all in one lesson.)

Teaching by asking students to review what they know

An alternative and similar approach is to use 'teaching by asking'. You ask a question that requires recall of what you intend to build on; students create an answer in small groups, and report back to the class in assertive questioning style. You correct misconceptions and top up with anything they missed. See Chapter 17 for the detail.

Methods that show the structure of what will be learned: the 'advance organiser'

Having recalled relevant prior learning you can now explain something of the structure of what students are about to learn. This is called an 'advance organiser' (Ausubel, 1968) because it shows the organisation of the content in advance. I have produced an advance organiser for this chapter (see page 192). Have a look at this again. It is in graphical form, which is the most effective, but advance organisers can also be entirely verbal. We saw many formats for graphic organisers in Chapter 10, any of which might do for one of your advance organisers.

The advance organiser, whether graphical or verbal:

1. Gives an overview of the topic, a short summary of the main sections, or subheadings in the content, stating how they are related.
2. It can also stress any general principles that will apply, so establishing a high SOLO structure; see page 22.
3. It can state any links with any related topics and show how it is related to the whole.
4. It can stress the importance, relevance, purpose and value of what is about to be learned. This is linked with motivation.

You could just give a summary in advance, and this works well. But you can also do 2, 3 and 4 above. For example, if I were teaching the present topic I would show the diagram on page 192 and talk about it for about a minute, summarising the key points I was about to cover. But after leaving the organiser to teach the first bullet point in the diagram, 'recall and check relevant prior learning', I would return to the diagram to introduce the *next* bullet point, and so on through the whole topic. I could use my advance organiser again to summarise at the end of the topic, and indeed to review it at the beginning of the next lesson.

Don't confuse an advance organiser with giving behavioural objectives. Advance organisers can include them, but do much more and have a much higher effect size.

Marzano's effect sizes	N	Effect size
Advance organisers: Giving students special summaries in advance of what they are about to learn; these help students to structure the topic.		
All	358	0.48
Surface learning only	36	0.56
Deeper learning only	48	0.78
Highly specific behavioural objectives given by the teacher	?	0.12

Let's look at some strategies that you could use as part of an advance organiser.

The parable approach (effect size 0.53, N = 12)

This involves telling students a story which helps them to make personal, real-world connections to what they are about to learn. Jesus used this technique in his parables and it is often used in sermons, and in school assemblies. The speaker tells a story, and then extracts a principle from it, or perhaps leaves the listener to do so. When a social studies teacher is about to introduce the idea of bias, for example, she might tell a personal story that showed bias from her family life, and then ask her pupils for other similar anecdotes.

The purpose of this technique in constructivist terms is, of course, to require the learners to recall relevant experiences on which to build the ideas in the lesson. It is sometimes called a 'narrative advance organiser'.

Skim reading (effect size 0.71, N = 15)

When students are learning from text then you can ask them to skim read as the first task; this only goes some way to providing an advance organiser. The idea is to skim read a few pages, get the gist about what the text is going to say, and then go back and read it in detail. The effect size comes from Marzano *et al.* (2001), not his metastudy.

Students adding to a graphic organiser (effect size 1.2, N = 43)

The graphic organiser is an advance organiser in visual form as described above, and in Chapter 10. If students make extended use of these themselves, for example by adding to them extensively, then the effect size is particularly high.

Below are two graphic organisers for a lesson on Impressionist painters. One is at a higher level of abstraction than the content of the lesson, the other just summarises the content. It is not entirely clear from experiments which creates the highest achievement, but it is clear that they both work well.

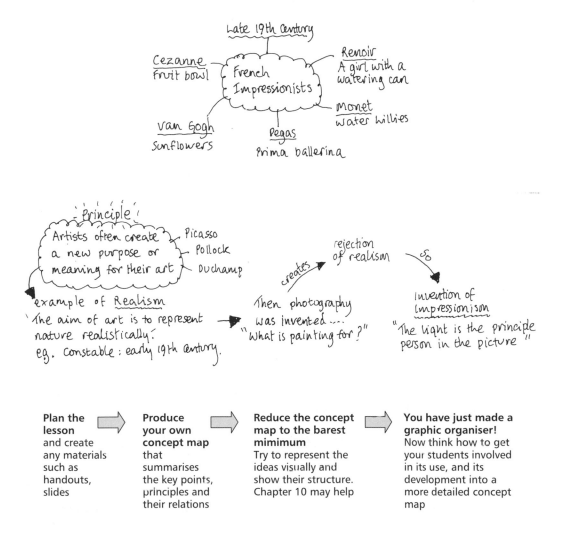

Plan the lesson and create any materials such as handouts, slides ⇒ **Produce your own concept map** that summarises the key points, principles and their relations ⇒ **Reduce the concept map to the barest mimimum** Try to represent the ideas visually and show their structure. Chapter 10 may help ⇒ **You have just made a graphic organiser!** Now think how to get your students involved in its use, and its development into a more detailed concept map

Using organisers in practice

Organisers seem to have more effect for difficult learning. They are also thought to be particularly useful when the learning experience is not well structured, for example when students are searching the Internet, on a field trip, or visiting an exhibition.

Refer to the organiser throughout the lesson, and ask students to use it to help them answer questions. This helps learners to see 'where they are' in the structure at any given time.

Consider using organisers on:

- handouts and workbooks
- notes copied from the board
- a flip chart left up for the whole lesson and at the beginning of the next one
- on the board or smartboard, and adding to it through the class.

Using graphic organisers in the next lesson

Recalling the last lesson will be covered in more detail later, but if the organiser is first presented in electronic form, on a smart-board say, or in a PowerPoint presentation, the detail added in the class can be covered

. . . adding to it through the class . . .

up with Post-it style text boxes, and the students asked to recall what is beneath. The Post-its could have clues on them if that helps. Similar follow-up activities could be used with other 'orientating' methods described in this chapter.

Curriculum maps and unit organisers

Another way of showing students 'where they are' in their learning is a curriculum map or unit organiser. These are advance organisers for larger chunks of learning and can be used in the same way.

Have a look at a few curriculum maps by typing 'curriculum map' in quotes into your favourite search engine. Or find some here:

www.ashburnham.kensington-chelsea.sch.uk/curriculummaps

Many teachers share their scheme of work with students in a very simplified form. This is sometimes called a 'curriculum map', which summarises a year's work in a subject on one or two sides of paper, showing the sequence of teaching, and perhaps how the units fit together.

If more detail is required then you might use a 'unit organiser', which shows how topics within a unit are sequenced (a unit is usually about 5–50 hours' teaching). Again this is usually so condensed that it appears on one or two sides of paper.

There is no accepted design, so create your own. Your map or organiser could also show:

- the types of thinking required: 'You will be required to analyse a care plan . . .'
- the tasks that will be set the students: 'You will design a poster to summarise . . .'

- assessments
- self-test questions: 'You should be able to explain . . .'

and so on.

Unit organisers should be used as well as, not instead of, advance organisers.

Unit organiser: The Industrial Revolution

Key concepts

Natural resources	Technology	Economic system
Waterways	Steam engine	Mass production
	Textile machines	Fair wage

Key questions
- What caused the Industrial Revolution and why did it begin in England?
- What impact did the Revolution have on the culture and society of England?
- How did the technology of the Industrial Revolution lead to a new Age of Imperialism?

Resources
Sadler Commission: Report on Child Labour
Engels: The Condition of the Working Class
Marx: The Communist Manifesto
Smith: The Wealth of Nations
Primary source photos (Internet)
Thompson: The Making of the English Working Class

Assessment
etc.

Setting goals (effect size 0.51–1.2)

Goal setting takes very little time, literally a minute or two in many cases, and yet it has a marked effect on achievement. As we have seen, Hattie believes that teaching methods work to the extent that they set students challenging goals, and provide feedback, so goal setting is central. Also, the positive effect of high expectations creating a self-fulfilling prophesy has been known for some time. You will set goals already, but given their potential you might be able to work out a better way of doing them.

From Hattie's effect-size table	**Effect size**	**N**
Goals	0.51	959
Behavioural objectives	0.24	157

Hattie finds that 'behavioural objectives' have an effect size of 0.24, and Marzano that 'highly specific behavioural objectives' get 0.12. The slight difference in the terms in quotes in the last sentence might explain the difference in their effect sizes. More important than the difference is that they are not as effective as other goal-setting strategies.

From Marzano's theory based metastudy	Effect size	N
Specifying goals: students have specific written or verbal goals prior to a lesson (summary figures)	0.97	53
If the goals are highly specific behavioural objectives given by the teacher	0.12	
If the goals are less specific, and if the student has some control over setting their own goals	1.21	

Most teachers don't set goals until they set the students an activity, which can be quite late into a lesson. Even then the goal is only implied by the activity, and does not usually involve the student setting themselves goals, which creates the highest effect size.

In all cases below, remind students of their goals from time to time in the lesson, and revisit the goals at the end of the lesson to see if they have been met.

One of the most persuasive and widely accepted theories of motivation we saw in Chapter 2 says that motivation requires two things, both related to goal setting:

– *Value.* Students must value the goal, they must see its usefulness, fun or relevance to them.
– *Expectation of success.* The student must expect to succeed in the task, at least partly.

Both value and expectation of success must exist for motivation to occur. So be as persuasive as possible, especially if learners lack motivation or self-belief.

 ## Setting goals at the start of the lesson (effect size 0.97)

Why not set students a goal *before* presenting them with information? If the goal is challenging and requires reasoning this will ensure that students learn better while they are listening to you or watching the video. See the 'Robert and Susan' graph in Chapter 2 (page 15).

You could set the goals very informally, for example by asking a rhetorical question:

'What was the effect on the people who used to weave these garments by hand, now that they could be made so quickly by machine?'

'How could we measure this atmospheric pressure? Let's find out.'

Rhetorical questions like these, if there is enough emphasis on them, can effectively set a goal, and can create curiosity and interest in your subject, as it begins to be seen not as an interminable list of important facts to memorise, but as a subject that asks interesting questions and answers them.

Keep reminding students of these rhetorical questions during the lesson. Consider displaying them on the board, or in running headers on presentations and on hand-outs.

Lenz *et al.* (1994) devised a method of questioning they call the Question Exploration Routine:

1. The teacher poses a guiding or 'critical' question to students that is central to the topic.

The students, with teacher help, then:

2. identify what information is needed to answer this guiding question, and so generate the sub-questions that can lead to its answer
3. answer the sub-questions and then the guiding question
4. transfer the learning, by seeing how it relates to earlier learning or other experience.

The last phase is called 'bridging', as explained in Chapter 8, and leads to particularly deep learning. Lenz found the achievement of his students with learning difficulties doubled. Free download at www.ku-crl.org/IAA%20Web/htmlfiles/research/reports/report11.doc.

Suppose, for example, a teacher is about to teach students about the role of the district nurse. She could give the students specific goals for the present phase, and for the main activity phase of the lesson.

'When I have told you a bit about district nurses, and we have seen the video, I will ask you in pairs to work out answers to the two questions here on the flip chart:

- What are the main roles of the district nurse?
- How does her role fit in to those of other health professionals?

So during the first part of the lesson listen carefully and begin to think through your answers to these questions.

Your other task today will be to work out what a district nurse would do in a few specific cases. The case studies are there in front of you. You will have to present your ideas to another group, so get really clear about how her role works in practice, not just in theory. Do we all understand these two goals?'

It is one thing to tell students that they '*should* be able to' do something – quite another to say they *will* be doing something. That is much more challenging and motivating.

Goals by exemplar

This involves showing students what they will be able to do at the end of the lesson. A computing teacher might show students a good example of a desktop-published document and say, or write in the workbook, 'At the end of this module you will be able to create documents like this.'

Teachers of any practical subject can use good-quality work in this way, and it can be very inspiring for students, as long as they believe they can do it! Teachers of academic subjects can use this too.

Goals by setting problems

'Here is a geometrical problem that we can't solve using any of the methods we have seen so far. But it *is* possible to solve! Let's see how we could do it.'

'Delegating to your staff empowers them, but as their manager you remain responsible for what they do. What if they begin to make a mess of it? Let's see how we can have it both ways: delegation, *and* control.'

Goals by cognitive dissonance

'The mass of the glycerine has increased overnight! Yet nobody has added anything to it! How can that be? It's your job today to find out!'

'Yesterday you all thought that if you tossed a coin and got a head, then tossing a tail next was the most likely. But look at the figures from your experiment. It just *isn't* the case. You found the chance of tossing a head was always fifty-fifty. What is going on?'

'Shakespeare wants to show that Romeo is really in love with Juliet. You might expect him to do this by describing his previous relationships as failures. In fact he does the exact opposite. Let's see.'

Goals by challenge

Challenges are much more motivating than competitions, as we saw in Chapter 12 on cooperative learning.

'Can you make a really persuasive case for this business plan? At the end of the lesson I am going to play the role of a speculative investor, and you will be the entrepreneurs with this plan. Will you be able to persuade me to invest?'

'I am going to explain a commonly used method of budgetary control which some managers are very critical of. I will explain it very positively, but I want you to think of its weaknesses. See if you can get all four of its main weaknesses!'

'Have a look at the marks you have had for exercises like this in the last month. What is your personal best mark? Well your challenge to day is to beat that!'

Goals that require visual representations (effect size 1.2)

This approach is considered in more detail in Chapter 10.

'I want you to design a poster that summarises all the key points in this topic and displays the main ideas as visually as possible.'

There are many other ways a teacher can set goals for a lesson, so vary your approach.

Students also set themselves personal goals (effect size 1.2)

Marzano found that studies on goals with the very highest effect sizes required that students set themselves goals *as well as* getting goals from the teacher.

Personal goals can be:

Very informal
Students can be asked at the end of a lesson to set themselves goals for the next lesson. Or at the beginning of the lesson you can say:

'Set yourself a goal now; write it on the top of your sheet. Think of something you want to improve about your work . . .'

Set by the teacher as well as, or instead of, the student

'Think back to the personal goal I set you at your last one-to-one tutorial. Find it in your file if you can't remember it. This can be your personal goal for this lesson.'

Goals can be diagnosed from a self-assessment. For example, a student might have self-assessed last week on a set of 'learning to learn' competencies like the example in the box in Chapter 24, p. 325, and decided that she would learn better if she asked for help in lessons more often. The teacher could remind the class of this self-assessment, and ask each student to set themselves a goal from it.

Group goals and explaining goals

You can pair students up and give each of them goals to explain to their partner the meaning of some key terms that you give them in advance. Cooperative learning (Chapter 12) and some feedback methods (Chapter 19) do this to some effect.

Negotiated goals (effect size 1.2)

You can negotiate a goal with a group, trying to find a goal that meets their needs. One way of doing this is to get the class to pose questions after the advance organiser; this works particularly well with adult or more able groups. Students can set themselves individual goals in the same way. For example, a business studies lecturer could give an advance organiser on decision making and then ask the class for a goal, or to choose a goal from some suggestions given by the teacher (e.g. to use the decision-making theory themselves with a decision that they must make in the near future).

Competency questionnaires like the one in Chapter 24, p. 325, can also be created for student behaviour. They are often best based on ground rules suggested by students at the beginning of the year, as described in Chapter 19. This provides personally set and personally diagnosed goals such as 'I'm not going to talk when Mr Petty is talking' (though it is hard for you to check them all individually).

However you set goals it is worth returning to them at the end of the lesson, to decide whether they have been met. This is dealt with in Chapter 20.

Are your goals challenging enough?

Hattie stresses that the goals should be challenging. They should involve reasoning, and ideally they should be open rather than closed so that every student is stretched but every student can respond (differentiation).

Once we have orientated our students we are ready for the 'New material is taught' phase in the PAR model.

The vital first five minutes

The effect sizes in this chapter are very high, yet they could all be achieved in the first five minutes of teaching a new topic:

- Recall prior learning using questions   0.91
- Give a structure for the new learning in graphic form   1.24
- Set a goal   0.51

- *Total effect size if all are done*   *2.66!*

That's five grades! And the lesson has hardly started yet! Well, effect sizes are not crudely additive like this, but it does show how important the first five minutes are, and how weak is conventional practice!

Feedback methods for the orientation phase

Feedback methods are teaching methods that enable either you or your students and preferably both to get feedback on the quality of students' understanding, that is the quality of their constructs as described in Chapter 2. Chapter 15 on feedback through dialogue has described some excellent interactive methods such as assertive questioning; there are more in Chapter 19.

References and further reading

Ausubel, D. P. (1968) *Education Psychology: A Cognitive View*, New York: Holt, Rinehart & Winston.

Black P. *et al.* (2003) *Assessment for Learning: Putting it into Practice*, Buckingham: Open University Press.

Lenz, B. K. *et al.* (1992) 'The effects of curriculum maps and guiding questions on the test performance of adolescents with learning disabilities', Institute of Academic Access, research report 11.

Marzano, R., Pickering, D. and Pollock, J. (2001) *Classroom Instruction That Works*, Alexandria, Virginia: ASCD.

17 Methods to present new material

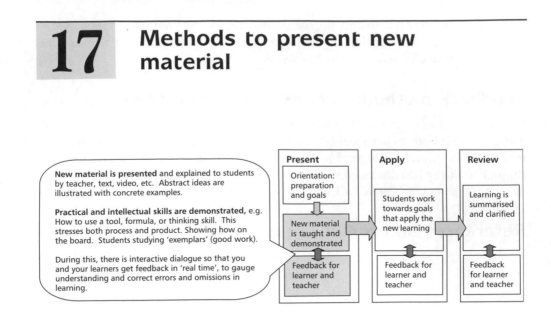

New material is presented and explained to students by teacher, text, video, etc. Abstract ideas are illustrated with concrete examples.

Practical and intellectual skills are demonstrated, e.g. How to use a tool, formula, or thinking skill. This stresses both process and product. Showing how on the board. Students studying 'exemplars' (good work).

During this, there is interactive dialogue so that you and your learners get feedback in 'real time', to gauge understanding and correct errors and omissions in learning.

Present
- Orientation: preparation and goals
- New material is taught and demonstrated
- Feedback for learner and teacher

Apply
- Students work towards goals that apply the new learning
- Feedback for learner and teacher

Review
- Learning is summarised and clarified
- Feedback for learner and teacher

The diagram above shows where we are in terms of teaching our imaginary topic. Orientation has already taken place, so learners have recalled relevant prior learning and had this checked, they understand the structure and outline of what they are about to learn, value its purpose, and have goals to work towards. Now it is time to present students with the new material.

Sadly this phase is often passive for learners. If no goal is set they sit back contentedly and just let it all flow over them as you work your socks off trying to make the material seem clear and interesting. Other students, freed from the distraction of actually having to do something, amuse themselves with what cognitive psychologists call 'compensatory activities'. You guessed it, that's 'mucking about'. Often the teacher fails to get sufficient feedback on whether students have understood; and students who seek feedback for themselves – 'Sir, am I right to think you're saying . . . ?' – were always a rare breed, but are now an endangered species. Botched teacher talk is a pedagogic calamity, yet it constitutes the majority of teaching time in many classes.

Many teachers believe that it is only in the 'apply' phase of the lesson that students can be working on a task, reasoning, meaning-making, doing, and getting feedback. To be frank I thought much the same myself during 28 years as a classroom teacher. But I was wrong.

Suppose we applied Hattie's three principles during the 'present' phase? You will remember that having read 500 metastudies and collected half a million effect sizes, Hattie concluded that teaching methods work to the extent that they set challenging goals, and provide the student with feedback after student activity towards those goals. What if the 'present' phase did this *too*?

There are three ways of doing this, which we will look at in order. We only have effect sizes for some of them, but these are high, sometimes stratospheric. Also, when I visit teaching teams that get outstanding examination results, I nearly always find these methods being extensively used.

1. *Hattifying conventional methods.* This involves using conventional methods such as teacher talk, demonstration, or watching a video, but ensuring they are done with goals and feedback. This is often the first stage of whole-class interactive teaching, the feedback being provided by interactive dialogue as in Chapter 15.

And two 'teaching without talking' methods. (These also meet Hattie's principles.)

2. *Teaching by asking* (instead of teaching by telling). Here the teacher does *not* provide resources that explain the topic, at least not during the present phase. Instead, students are asked a question that leads to what the teacher wants them to learn, and the students have to puzzle out the answer, reasoning from prior learning and common sense. Their answer is then improved by you. The topic must not be too conceptually challenging for this method.
3. *Teaching without talking using resources that explain the topic.* Here students use paper and/or electronic resources to learn the topic.

All three approaches involve the student in reasoning and so create transferable learning of important subject-specific thinking skills, as well as teaching the content. Let's look at them.

Hattifying conventional 'present' methods

The most common 'present' methods are:

− Students listen to a teacher explaining.
− Students watch and listen to a teacher demonstration.
− Students watch a video.
− Students use an ILT resource that explains the topic in a self contained way.

Methods like those above involve the teacher, or a video, explaining the new material. I look at how to use these methods in considerable depth in *Teaching Today*. An evidence-based, 'five principles' approach to these methods would be to fully orientate the students first with a check on relevant prior learning, an advance organiser and goals, and then:

• Explain the new material from known to unknown, and from concrete to abstract, asking questions on the way to create dialogue and check understanding.
• Check that the goal has been achieved, providing feedback to the learner on the quality of their constructs.

During orientation you will have given students a goal which may *only apply to a task* later in the lesson. But the present phase requires a goal for students to work towards *while they are being presented with the new material*.

'While I describe these three marketing strategies, I want you to work out the three most important differences between them.'

'While you watch the video listen out for the main functions of a health centre; you should find five. See if your group can get them all. I'll check you later.'

'While I explain how to find the unknown length in these triangles listen carefully, because you will have to explain a similar one to your partner straight after.'

Your goal could of course be less formal. For example, you could just ask a rhetorical question: 'What do you think Richard II would be thinking during this episode? I'll ask you this again after I have explained it.'

Setting such goals should ensure that students are cognitively engaged and making constructs *while they are being presented with the new material*. This means that even the Roberts of this world, (see Chapter 2), should be meaning-making, reasoning, and getting feedback on their constructs while they listen. In short 'Robert' will use the cognitive strategies that create good learning, even though these are not habitual to him.

During your explanation you remind students of their goals from time to time, check their understanding with question and answer, and at the end of the present phase you check that the goals have been achieved.

'OK, what were the three important differences between the three marketing strategies?'

'What were the five main functions of a health centre?'

'Now here are two worked examples where I have calculated the unknown side of a triangle. Take one each, study it, and then explain it fully to your partner. Explain not just what I did, but *why* I did it, for each line in the working.'

This gives both the learner and you feedback on student understanding, especially if you use methods such as 'buzz nominees' or 'assertive questioning' as described in Chapter 9. In the last example, feedback is best achieved in the way described under 'peer explaining' in Chapter 19, where this method is described in detail.

Twenty-eight methods for teaching without talking

Teaching without talking involves setting students a task that requires them to learn from resources, it is something of a misnomer as you *will* actually talk to students, you just won't teach them the content that way. These methods are a brilliant way for learners to learn from ILT or ICT resources such as Internet sites, CD-ROMs, etc.

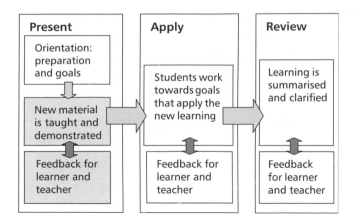

As these methods do not require a teacher and involve students inter-acting with resources, they are highly appropriate for tasks for students to undertake when using resources outside the classroom, for example independent learning (ILT). This is the pedagogy of ILT.

In order to improve your teaching, and that of your team, try out the likely methods as described under 'Supported experiments' in Chapter 10. You will need to try each method at least three times to decide whether it is likely to work for you and your students. It takes time for your students to get used to the method, and for you to adapt it to their needs. Share what works with your team; they will be most interested to learn what you have made work! Try the simple methods in small ways to begin with, and keep experimenting. Teaching is too difficult to get perfect, and the only way of improving teaching is to change it. Such experiments are great fun as well as improving the chances of your students.

Creating a Teaching Strategy Manual in your team

One way of using this book is to experiment with the methods that look likely:

1. Find methods which work best in your teaching.
2. Choose particular strategies for particular topics or lessons, etc.
3. Pool your team's best teaching strategies to add to the list.
4. Develop a Teaching Strategy Manual over a period of a year or more. Alternatively you could produce an Active Scheme of Work which suggests activities for each topic or subtopic on your scheme as described in Chapter 25. Share out the work amongst your team to develop the strategies and their resources in detail, as it is a lot of work.

The following 28 methods for teaching without talking are divided into three sections:

1. Methods requiring very little preparation or resources
2. Methods requiring resources such as handouts videos or Internet sites
3. Activities that require a bit more preparation; those requiring the least are given first.

Teaching without talking: without using resources

Convention has it that the only way to learn is 'teaching by telling'. Yet little weasels learn to be big weasels without formal schooling. Despite extensive observation of these little critters no blackboards have been found down their holes. How do they do it?

Weasels are born with some instinctual responses, but much of what an adult weasel knows was hard learned, like for example what hurts, what tastes bad and what is the way home. This is learned by trial and error, and by copying the grown-ups, that is by experiment and imitation. Arguably the animal brain has evolved to learn in this way. Nature's teacher is *curiosity*, and she does a damn good job. Why don't we make more use of it?

Animals learn this way, but as any teacher will testify, students are animals. Human babies learn in this animal way; they are great experimenters and imitators, which is why if anyone has a toddler there is chocolate all over their clothes and they can't find their remote. Animals (other than adult humans of course) use remarkably radical learning and teaching strategies!

Students will learn the animal way if you let them. It is a very natural way to learn, even if you think it an unnatural way to teach.

These are demanding ways to learn, and the topic must not be too conceptually challenging until students' learning skills have been developed by practice with these methods. They are greatly enjoyed if well managed, but they are not easy to use. *Teaching Today* has more detail on the use of these methods in Chapter 29 on guided discovery.

1 Teaching by asking

Rather than 'teaching by telling', start the topic by asking students a question that leads to what you want to teach. For example:

'What methods are used to market food products? Think of as many as you can.'

'Why do you think managers value staff training?'

'Who would have supported Cromwell, who would not, and why?'

'Here is a maths problem you can't solve with the methods we have seen so far – how would you solve it?'

Students work in pairs or small groups (buzz groups) to answer a question or series of questions using common sense, experience and prior learning. Students can all have the same questions, or they can be given different questions on the same topic. This group discussion can last for literally a minute or less, or for 20 minutes or longer.

Ensure that each group has a scribe, and check their attention to task, and the quality of their work, by checking what the scribes have written down. Ask them if they need more time, and if they have finished, ask each pair or group for one idea they have had, ensuring that each group offers something. Write the strong ideas on the board, saying a little in support of each idea if you wish. Allow the class to discuss any points of disagreement until it has agreed a common answer. (See 'Effective management of active learning strategies' below for more detail on this.)

When the class has its common answer, 'top up' the answer with any additional points the class has missed, and correct any misunderstandings. If students get half of the answer it saves half of the teacher talk, and generates interest and thinking skills. It works well with snowball (see 5 below), and can be assisted by resources if this helps, but these mustn't give the answer to your question away directly.

See 'Effective management of active learning strategies' below for more detail on how to manage this activity, and the activities, which follow.

(See also 'Interrogating the text' (12 below), where students are given a handout or other material to help them answer the 'teaching by asking' question you give them.)

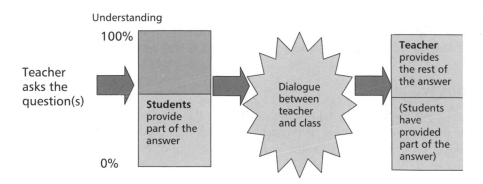

2 Class brainstorm

The teacher requests as many ideas as possible from the whole class, asking questions such as:

What are the advantages of prior booking?

What diseases are common in childhood?

Why might Hamlet not have taken revenge straight away?

The teacher or a student compiles the answers on the board, classifying them if necessary by writing them in groups. It is usual to be non-judgemental at this stage.

This method involves the whole group and can enliven a dull session. Optionally you could ask students to brainstorm in groups and the session then becomes like 'teaching by asking' above. (See also 5, snowball.)

Some people object to the term 'brainstorm', believing it offends people with epilepsy, and prefer the term 'thought shower'. However, all the people I know with epilepsy prefer the term 'brainstorm' and laugh when you ask if they are offended by it.

3 Thought experiment (or empathy)

This is a variation on the class brainstorm: students are asked to imagine themselves in a given situation, and are asked questions about the situation. For example, health studies students are asked to imagine that they are a child who has just been admitted to hospital. Students learning interviewing skills are asked what the interviewer would be looking for. (See also 5, snowball.)

4 Round

This method is useful for small groups if the experiences of the students are a particularly useful resource: for example managers on a part-time management course sharing experiences of how new staff are inducted into their organisation.

Each person has a minute, say, to describe their experiences on a given topic and to express their point of view while others listen. Students can 'pass' if they wish. This method is used to mine useful experience and elicit a range of viewpoints and build a sense of safe participation. (See also 5, snowball.)

5 Snowball

This is like 'teaching by asking' above but creates the best dialogue of all these methods and so is likely to work best. It involves an interesting way of collecting ideas from a brainstorm, thought experiment or round, ensuring full participation and more student discussion.

Like the methods above you don't *tell* them, but ask a question that leads to what you want students to learn, for example 'Why do you think we use stock taking? Think of as many reasons as you can.' Then:

ideas from other groups

1. Each *individual* writes down his or her thoughts without reference to others.
2. Students then share what they have written in pairs or threes.

3. Optionally the pairs or threes pair up to create larger groups, which again compare their answers, and then agree a group answer with its justification. Leave time for this dialogue.
4. The teacher asks individuals by name from each big group in turn for *one* idea their group has had; then asks for a justification, for example 'Why did your group think that?'; and then writes the useful ideas on the board, perhaps saying a little in support of each idea. Better, a full assertive questioning style can be used.

As in 'teaching by asking', the teacher then tops up and corrects the class answer, 'un-teaching' any misconceptions. Snowball involves more student interaction than brainstorm, round or thought experiment. The teacher can classify the ideas from the groups in groups or columns on the board, or as a concept map.

6 Teaching by asking with pair explaining

1. The teacher prepares two 'teaching by asking' style questions.
2. Students are split into fours, and these fours into pairs. Each pair is given one of the two questions and they work on it together for a set period of time; this could be from as little as one minute to 20 minutes or so.
3. Students stay within their 'foursome', but label themselves 'A' and 'B' within their pairs, and then the two As get together and the two Bs get together.
4. The students each explain the question they had, and the answer they produced during stage 2.
5. The students now try to improve their foursome's answers to both questions, or maybe stay in their pairs.

If students are grouped on the basis of proximity this can cause a minimum of movement in the class; it will even work in a lecture theatre if students turn round to work with those behind them. This is an excellent activity to get students used to explaining before doing a jigsaw (see Chapter 12).

7 Expert witness

You set your students the task of discovering something such as:

Is this the best method of purifying salt?

Would you recommend this management strategy?

Why did Hamlet procrastinate?

This diagram shows 'osmosis' taking place; can you explain osmosis and why it occurs?

This initial question should not have an obvious answer, but students should be able to reason most of it out in groups. Supporting text can help in some cases.

The class now plays a barrister or a judge, and you play the expert witness. Students ask you questions *but they are not allowed to ask you directly the question you have given them.* (Or a rewording of it!) Instead, your students must figure out the answer from your answers to *other* questions, a little like a barrister does with an expert witness. Groups of three or so can take turns to ask questions.

This can be great fun, especially if you are able to keep your answers short and a little unhelpful, so giving the students more to do.

Student   Surely the salt dissolves in the water?
Teacher   Not straight away.

It helps to review the process afterwards: what strategy did the students adopt? What were the most effective questions and why?

Teaching without talking: using resources that explain the topic

The aim of these 'teaching without talking' methods is to make the students active and goal orientated, with tasks that require them to reason and to form constructs *while* resources are presenting new material to them. This makes the methods ideal to use with computer-based resources (ILT) in or outside class time. But they work just as well in the classroom with paper-based materials.

The methods work best when you can find appropriate resources with a low reading age. As well as written material such as handouts, books and Internet site print-outs. etc., you can use videos, Internet sites themselves, CD-ROMs, photographs, posters and other images, tapes, real objects, etc. Some combination of these is ideal, and is what I mean by the 'resources' and 'materials' described below. Ask librarians to help you find materials; they are the world's experts at this, but do give them sufficient notice. Students may find materials on the Internet which can be kept for the next time you do the same lesson.

> *Consider keeping your materials in plastic document wallets or in cardboard envelope-style folders in a filing cabinet so they are available again next year. Photocopy back to back and keep them from year to year to save trees.*

So what is your role now that you are not going to be teaching by telling? Put your feet up and read the paper? I'm afraid the methods aren't that good! You will need to visit groups and listen as they work, see what they have written down, ask them questions, and where necessary give guidance. This gives that vital feedback by dialogue we saw in Chapter 15. Where work in progress is imperfect don't revert immediately to teaching! Give the students some time to try to sort it out for themselves. Your role during group work is very interesting, even more interesting than talking, as you get to know students individually, and get some revealing feedback on their difficulties. You listen, ask questions, especially questions that require students to justify their ideas, and when leaving the group you try to leave a challenge behind. 'See if you can think of some advantages that are from the customers' point of view.'

Calculating readability with the FOG index

The 'reading age' of text is the age at which the average person can read it. This means that many people of that age could *not* read it of course! So the reading age of your material may need to be lower than the chronological age of your students.

The procedure to find the readability is:

1. In a representative section of the text, select five to eight complete sentences. Find the total number of words (**n**) in the complete sentences (**s**).

2. Calculate the average number of words (**A**) per complete sentence: **A = n ÷ s**.

3. Select a passage of continuous text of exactly 100 words within your sample. Find the number of words of three or more syllables (**W**), in your 100-word sample. Don't count the -*ed* or -*es* endings of verbs, so that the word 'compounded' counts as only two syllables, despite being three syllables.

4. Calculate the reading age as follows:

   Add A to W, then multiply your answer by 0.4. Now add 5 years. This is the reading age of the material. For mathematicians:

   Reading age = 0.4 (A +W) + 5 years

For somewhat greater accuracy, select three or four passages from the book, and find the reading ages of these, and then average them. This is called the FOG index, which stands for 'frequency of gobbledegook'.

The average TV guide has a reading age of about 6 years; 17 years is very tough reading indeed, and only suitable for postgraduates.

To reduce the reading age simply shorten sentences, simplifying their grammar, and 'translate' difficult words into more common language, adding the formal word later if this helps, e.g. 'makes them feel they can make a difference, that is empowers them . . .'

Well-designed activities like these will usually produce better understanding and engagement than conventional 'teacher talk'. Again I assume that students have been through an 'orientation' phase.

All these methods can be used to model good study habits. For example, you could ask students to highlight and underline the text and then bridge this skill as described in Chapter 21.

8 Teaching by asking with resources

You use one of the 'teaching by asking' strategies described in methods 1 to 6 above, except that students have access to a video, handout, website or other resource before beginning their discussion of your question. As ever, snowball is the most useful method because of the quality of the dialogue; it is often worth the extra time and movement.

9 Cooperative learning: learning teams answer questions on resource material (effect size 0.75)

This is similar to teaching by asking with resources above, but more complex and structured. It is a useful preparation for 'learning together' and other cooperative learning methods.

Students are given a range of resources on a topic and they are asked to use them to answer a range of questions, from simple reproduction questions to ones requiring simple and then more complex reasoning. They are told of the quiz, test or exam-style question at the end of this method.

- These questions relate to the key points in the resources and to the key lesson objectives. They should be thought provoking, for example 'Who supported Cromwell and why?'
- The answer to the question(s) should *not* appear baldly and simply stated in one place in the resources. Students should need to construct their own understanding in order to answer the question, not just repeat the resources back to you.
- Consider having a range of materials of differing difficulty shared by the group. Or give each student in the group different resources, which may not be read by or to others, but can be explained to them by that student.
- It may help to give students individual roles in their group such as scribe, vocabulary chief, etc., as described on page 228.

Students work in groups, and when they have finished, feedback can be elicited from the groups one idea at a time, in assertive questioning style.

Finally learning is tested with a quick quiz or test or with an exam-style question on the subject, on which students work individually. This method is very similar to 'learning together', a cooperative learning method that has an effect size of 0.75. If you like it, do read Chapter 12 on cooperative learning.

10 Key points and questions

1. Students are put in groups and given unfamiliar Internet sites, handouts or other resources. They are asked to study their materials alone for a few minutes with an eye on the next task, and to underline and highlight key points.
2. The groups identify, say, five key points made by the text, and one question that the resources don't seem to answer.

3. The teacher then asks the groups to take it in turn to give *one* key point that has not already been mentioned. The class agrees or improves that point, and you write it on the board. (It helps if the number of key points requested in 2 above is the same or more than the number of groups, so all groups can contribute at least one key point.)
4. The groups now take it in turn to ask their questions of the class. If the class can't answer the question, the group gives their answer if they have one. If no one in the class has an answer, you answer it. If you can't answer it: set it as a Google homework!

After this activity, show how it models good study and independent learning habits, as shown in Chapter 6. 'Key points' can be adapted to become 'How does it work?' as shown below.

11 How does it work? and questions

Students are given some resources on an unfamiliar topic or procedure, a worked example, a labelled diagram, a set of accounts, a policy, a service provider, etc.

They are asked to study this and to summarise an explanation and justification of 'how it works' or 'how it could be used', etc., in, say, five key points. They are asked to frame one question for the class that the resources do not properly answer.

Now continue as from stage 3 in the method immediately above.

12 Interrogating the text

This may seem like a strange method, but it has been designed to model good study habits. Students are given an unfamiliar piece of text. In pairs or small groups they are asked to:

1. Skim read, and then formulate important questions the text should be able to answer, or they hope the text will answer.
2. Read the text, highlighting or underlining key points.
3. Discuss the key points and agree answers to the questions formulated in 1.

You stress that this approach can be adapted to study any source, including Internet sites and videos.

This method is modelled on 'reciprocal teaching' which has a very high effect size. It can be used to model good study habits as described in Chapter 21.

13 Transformation

Students are given an explanation in one format and are asked to present it in another. For example, a health leaflet could be turned into a newspaper report, or a set of instructions could be turned into a statement about how the device works and when it would be useful. A chronological account could be reformulated under given, non-chronological headings etc.

14 Peer explaining of subtopics

Students in pairs are given two sets of resources on related topics that have not been explained to them, for example one about measles and another about mumps. They each use the resources to study one of these topics alone for, say, five minutes. Alternatively they could use the same text/video etc., but look at different *aspects* of it. For example, students could watch a video or read a text on the marketing policy of a small company, and one student could look out for strengths in the policy and another for weaknesses.

Each student explains their subtopic to their partner, who asks questions until they understand.

Integrative task: The pair then works together at a task that requires them to work *together* on *both* subtopics. A useful task for this is to ask students to 'State what is the same and what is different about measles and mumps.' Or 'Considering both strengths and weaknesses, what do you think of the marketing policy? How could strengths be built upon, and weaknesses addressed?' This method is in effect a mini 'jigsaw' (see Chapter 12), and like jigsaw could finish with students preparing for (five minutes) and then taking a short test (up to five minutes).

15 Headings

Students are given a handout with no headings or subheadings, but with space for these. Students read the handout and decide headings *that summarise what follows in that section of text in the form of a statement*. This produces headings such as 'The heart is a blood pump'; 'The heart has four chambers'; 'Arteries take blood from the heart'; and so on. You could also ask them to formulate questions for the rest of the class to answer.

You can of course adapt an existing handout by removing existing headings, and/or by asking students to write a 'heading' for each paragraph in the margin.

You can do this activity the other way round, that is provide the headings and ask students to find out about each heading and then write a short section on it. This is a good way of structuring independent learning. For example, students studying the heart could be given the headings and asked to study and then write short notes under each heading.

16 Students create a given visual representations (effect size 1.2)

Note the exceptionally high effect size. Students are given resources on an unfamiliar topic, for example the quality system in a manufacturing company. They are asked to study the resources in pairs and then to produce a 'graphic organiser', such as a mind map, flow diagram or Venn diagram, comparison table, or same and different diagram, that summarises the topic, as described in Chapter 10. Alternatively they could be asked to place cards with text in the appropriate places on the graphic organiser as described in Chapter 11.

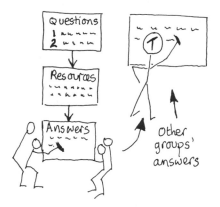

You can state the form of representation students will use – 'Make a flow diagram' – or you can let them choose which represen-tation(s) they use, in which case do teach students how to make such a choice using bridging, as described in Chapter 21.

It helps to motivate students if, after completing their representations, they show them to each other. They can leave theirs on their desk, walk about to see everyone else's, and then go back to improve their own. If they are working alone on computers they can email them to each other once everyone has finished.

If students create desktop-published diagrams they can email them to each other. If they create a flip-chart poster they can photograph it with a digital camera, and then insert it into a document in a word-processing application as a revision aid. It could also be put on the intranet, or Internet. Creating an audience for their work helps to motivate students.

17 Students create any visual representation (effect size 1.2)

In all the above cases the students were told what non-linguistic representation to create. When they have done a few of these, and you have taught them how to choose which representation to use as described in Chapter 21, then students can be asked to create their own representation of any style. It is particularly helpful if these are displayed to the class, as they will often be quite different. The pros and cons of the different formats can then be discussed. This helps learners use graphic organisers for themselves in the future, a critical study skill of great power.

18 Students transform graphic organisers (effect size 1.2)

Suppose you made use of a flow diagram to describe stock taking. You could ask students to use this organiser to create another, say a holistic mind map look-ing at stock taking from the points of view of customer, retail manager and retail worker.

Activities that require a bit more preparation: simplest first

19 'Decisions, decisions' teaching without talking style

Students working in pairs are given materials which, as ever, might include electronic or paper-based resources, along with:

'Summary' cards

These purport to summarise key points from the text, some of which are true and some of which are false; for example:

* The left ventricle delivers blood to the lung.
* Heart rate is measured in beats per minute, and if you are very fit your heart rate will probably be lower than average.

'Consequences' cards

These state consequences of the facts given in the text. The consequences are not actually stated in the text itself. Again some are true and some false; for example:

* If you blocked the left ventricle no blood would get to the head.
* Furring of the arteries would usually raise blood pressure.

The pairs of students must decide which cards are correct, and what is wrong with the incorrect ones. This is a greatly enjoyed activity with the atmosphere of a game; see Chapter 11 for a full account.

20 Student presentation

Students prepare a presentation on a topic in groups. It helps if the topic being studied can be divided up so that each group presents a different subtopic. Don't tell students which subtopic they will present until *after* they have studied the topic as a whole, to ensure that they do not overspecialise. Students could study the material using one of the other strategies described here.

21 Pairs work out 'how to' from exemplars

For example, a mathematics teacher could show students a correct worked example or two, which uses a method the students are not familiar with, and ask them to discover how the method works and why it is justified.

Many teachers assume that students must always be told how to do things, and cannot work it out for themselves from exemplars (examples of good practice). Actually, learning from example is a very natural way to learn, as we have seen, and as students must puzzle out an explanation that is meaningful to them from the exemplar it is very constructivist.

This strategy is useful for learning any simple or more complex skill, such as how to punctuate, design an experiment, critique a poem, write a business letter or memo, etc. The more complex the skill the more help students will need from you.

22 Peer teaching – for skills teaching

This is useful after methods involving exemplars have been used and the students already understand the basics of the skill quite well. Student pairs are given different tasks, such as different sentences to punctuate. Having completed this work they then explain to each other how they did their task, and why they did it that way. It has been found that students who explain their method to each other learn mathematics much faster than those who do not.

23 What's wrong here?

This works well after the methods above, which use exemplars to teach how to do something. Students who know roughly 'how to do it' are given examples of *bad* practice, including work with commonly made errors, and are asked to find these errors. It can be fun to slip in one piece of work that is OK, but don't leave them too long puzzling out its error!

Some teachers rail against showing students bad work, believing it will influence them to create bad work themselves. This is not the case. First of all students are very used to seeing errors: their own. Secondly students must develop the skill of detecting errors and weaknesses in work, and how to put these right. Peer assessment has a high effect size, as we will see in Chapter 19, and this makes explicit use of showing students imperfect work. As well as being highly instructive the method is great fun.

See also spoof assessment in Chapter 19.

24 Question pairs

Learners prepare for the activity by reading an agreed text, and generating questions and answers focused on the major points or issues raised. At the next class meeting, pairs are randomly assigned. Partners alternately ask their questions of each other, and provide corrective feedback on the answers.

If students have sufficient experience of reciprocal teaching (see Chapter 13) they could do this instead. This method helps to prepare students for reciprocal teaching – a demanding but exceptionally effective method.

25 Snowballing questions

1. Students are given resources explaining a topic, along with past-paper questions or multiple-choice tests. The questions should require more than just copying answers from the resources.
2. Students work on the resources and the questions individually or in pairs. It sometimes helps curiosity and the focus of their study if students read the questions *before* studying the resources.
3. Students who have been working individually combine into pairs, and those working in pairs into fours. They compare their answers to the questions and combine their work to produce a 'best answer' without further consultation of the reading unless really necessary. This promotes discussion, and requires students to justify their points of view, which encourages good learning.
4. Students are shown model answers with any reasoning or working made clear, and then asked to mark or score themselves.
5. It helps if students are given roles such as 'teacher' or 'questioner' as described later.

26 Independent learning (effect size 0.75)

1. Any easy section of the syllabus is identified and this is not taught.
2. Instead students are given an assignment which describes in detail what they must learn. More experienced independent learners might need less direction.
3. Students work on this task in pairs or small groups, usually outside of class contact time. The assignment activities are thought provoking, and are not entirely 'book and biro'. Visual representations and other methods above make good tasks. At least one task requires students to go beyond the simple reproduction of the ideas

in the materials, and to apply their learning. This is to encourage deep learning, otherwise students may simply collect information and write it down without really thinking about it or understanding it.

4. Students' work is monitored by a designated 'leader' in their group or by the teacher.

5. The students' notes are *not* marked (except perhaps in the first use of this method in order to check their ability to make effective notes). Instead their learning is assessed by a short test. One assignment task is to prepare for this. Optionally students can be required to retake tests, or do other remedial work if their test result is unsatisfactory.

6. After completing this independent learning assignment, or indeed before, students use an independent learning competences questionnaire to identify their weaknesses as an independent learner, and to set themselves targets for their next independent learning assignment.

This is not an easy teaching method to use but it is greatly enjoyed by students if it is managed well. See Chapter 33 of *Teaching Today* for a fuller description. See also Chapter 12 of this book, on cooperative learning, for similar methods.

27 Spectacles

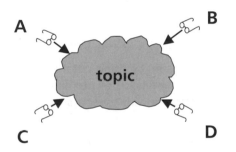

This method is best explained by examples. Suppose a teacher wants to teach the topic of 'saving'. Students need to know about building society accounts, bank accounts, shares and other ways of saving money. She asks her students to study materials on this topic, which describe all the relevant methods of saving, and asks them to consider each method of saving from a number of points of view: rate of interest, ease of withdrawal, can the value go down as well as up?, etc. She asks them to make notes on an A3-size table as shown (see p. 224). Alternatively they could produce a holistic mind map.

If the evaluation criteria are well chosen the students must study and understand the different methods of saving very well in order to make their judgements. The judgements the students make are a measure of how well they have understood the method of saving. Groups can compare their judgements by placing them on a class grid provided on a flip chart, board or OHT. They enjoy this, and the controversy it creates can help clarify misunderstandings.

How can we save?				
	Rate of interest Why high or low?	**Ease of withdrawal Why?**	**Can the value go down as well as up? Why?**	[etc.]
Building society account				
Bank account				
Shares				
etc.				

Like the other methods described in this chapter the aim is to get students to learn content (in this case, methods of saving) without direct explanation from the teacher. However, if the learning points are brought out with 'bridging' as described in Chapter 8 this method will also develop analysis and evaluation skills. Using a table in which to present ideas is not essential.

Other examples of the use of 'spectacles' include:

* learning about childhood diseases by using criteria such as 'method of immunisation', 'ease of immunisation', 'likelihood of permanent effects', etc.
* learning about computer printers with criteria such as print method, cost, speed, etc.

If the criteria are right the analysis can lead to a realistic evaluation. This method is greatly enjoyed, and is best done in groups. It can be used to develop analytical thinking skills and evaluation skills, as we will see in Chapter 21.

28 Marketplace

This method, which is from Paul Ginnis's excellent book *The Teacher's Toolkit* (2002), involves the following series of strictly timed stages:

Stage 1 (1 minute)
The test questions used at the end of this method (stage 6) are shown in advance, but students are not allowed to take notes.

Stage 2 (15 minutes)
Students are put in groups of three and are allocated one subdivision of the topic, or one 'spectacle' each. They study text on their subdivision only and create a visual representation or poster on large paper using coloured pens. They are only allowed,

say, ten words. Check that each student in each group has been involved by giving them different coloured pens.

Stage 3 (10 minutes)

The group designates one student to be the market stall-holder who stays with their poster. The other two go out into the 'marketplace' to visit the other 'stalls' and see their posters. They may divide up this labour. The stall-holders explain their poster to visitors, but they are only allowed to answer questions asked by visitors. They can answer with more than just 'yes' or 'no', but they must only answer the questions. The visitors take notes, preparing to explain this back to their group.

Stage 4 (10 minutes)

Everyone returns to their home base. Those who went to the marketplace to research information should now take turns to teach what they found out. Students can return to the posters and ask questions again if it helps. The aim is to prepare for the test; encourage students to write notes as this will help them.

During this stage you can distribute the test papers face down.

Stage 5 (10 minutes)

All notes and posters are put out of sight and the test is conducted under exam conditions, individually.

Stage 6 (5 minutes)

Either: Students mark their own papers using model answers and mark-scheme.

Or: the group check each other's papers and suggest improvements and then mark their own or each other's papers, but if you do this group-helping activity don't tell them about it at the beginning or some students will play the dumb passenger!

Finally the teacher goes through the test focusing on the tough questions, and asking for answers from the class. As a last resort teach what they haven't understood to fill in the gaps.

Effective management of active learning strategies to maximise participation

How do you implement these 'teaching without talking' methods, or indeed any active method in the classroom? This section summarises the process, but there is much more detail in *Teaching Today*.

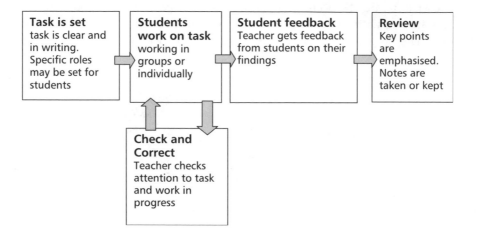

You may need to agree ground rules for student activities with your class, persuade them of the power and purpose of active learning, and ensure that seating arrangements are conducive to group work. Sitting round tables is better than sitting in auditorium style or at computers, for example. As ever, it helps to 'orientate' students as described in Chapter 16, and in particular to confirm any prior learning required for success at the task. Then:

Task is set

• The task is clear and in writing. There may be different tasks for each group.
• It often helps for a 'scribe' to be identified by the group or the teacher. There may be a task sheet to fill in.
• Time allowed for the task and subtasks is given in advance. Require *all* learners to be prepared to feed back for their group and justify their answer, as in assertive questioning (see Chapter 15).
• Ensure that at least some of the tasks involve reasoning rather than just reproduction of material or skills given the student. For example, make use of: analysis ('why' questions) synthesis ('how' questions) and evaluation ('which' or 'how good is this' questions).
• As well as the scribe consider giving some students roles such as teacher, checker, vocabulary checker, questioner, leader, etc. as described below.
• Challenging time constraints are given, i.e. the task doesn't go on too long.
• The scribe role rotates from time to time.

Students work on task

- Groups are formed, preferably random, for example by numbering round the room.
- A group scribe is appointed (by the group or teacher) to record ideas in progress. Avoid giving this role to slow writers or students with dyslexia unless they can work verbally. Rotate such roles from lesson to lesson.

Check and correct

This teacher's role is particularly important in teaching without talking.

- Check attention to task: are all students contributing?
- *Look* at the scribe's notes; are they on the right track?
- *Ask* and *listen*. Ask students to explain their ideas and listen carefully, asking 'Why do you think that?' and other clarifying questions. Try to get your students' trust; you must not appear threatening, which is difficult if students lack confidence. Do not over-help. If they are having trouble leave them with a clarifying question and say you will come back in a couple of minutes or so. Try to diagnose any misconceptions and to correct them with Socratic questioning.
- Also use Socratic questioning to move them on. For example, after each visit try to leave the group with a question or a task such as:
    'Look at this bit of the materials. Why do you think a sole trader would need to do this?'
    'What about the data? Does it fit your hypothesis?'
- Encourage and cajole. Feedback is 'medal and mission' at least some of the time: a 'medal' for progress made to date, effort, ideas, etc., and a 'mission' challenging them to go further.
- Challenge with support.

Feedback and review

For feedback:

- Every group is asked for their findings and no single group provides all the answers (for example, each group is asked to make one point only, one group at a time).
- Consider appointing a 'checker' and then picking anyone in a group at random to explain their findings.
- Key learning points are emphasised and written up on the board/OHT.
- 'Assertive questioning' style is used where the teacher gets a number of answers just saying 'thank you'. The 'correct' answer is not given away. The class are asked to agree a class answer. 'OK, some groups say . . . and others say . . . Who's right and why?' (see Chapter 15).
- You can make these activities 'double decker' by reviewing the skills the students used as well as the content, as described in Chapter 21.

For review:

- Students are asked to state their key learning points; these are improved by discussion.

- There is a tangible outcome: notes, mind map, summarising handouts given out, etc.
- Key points are reviewed by quiz, test or by question and answer at some later time.

Using roles to maximise participation

All the activities above are best done in pairs or small groups to promote dialogue. However, some can be adapted for individual students. It helps to give students in groups specific roles such as those which follow. It is unlikely that you would use all these roles at the same time. Useful combinations of roles are given later.

Role descriptors are given in a manner suitable for level 3, or adult learners. Please change these descriptors to suit your students. Students enjoy these roles and soon get used to them. However, don't expect students to use the roles effectively without practice. Just after the first time you use a role, ask students to reflect on how to make it work well, and then ask them for their ideas. Record any learning points for the next time you use such roles. If you give unmotivated students a role it prevents them becoming 'passengers'. Consider rotating the roles.

Role-card descriptors: usually only one or two of these roles are used at once.

Teacher

'Your role is to study an aspect or section of the materials that the teacher gives you, and to explain this to the other students in your group/pair.

You will be the only student in your group/pair to study your particular aspect of the topic, so make sure you understand it well and think out how to explain it! You can ask the teacher for help if you get stuck. You are not allowed to *show* any written materials to your group, but you can show any diagrams.'

Checker

'The teacher will choose students at random from your group to report back on what your group has learned and decided. The teacher may ask questions of more than one student from your group. They may also set a quiz or test on the material. Your role is to check that *all* the students in your group understand what your group has decided and why, and can report it to the rest of the class clearly. Do this by preparing and asking questions of your group. You are allowed a full five [?] minutes to do this. If one of your group can't answer the teacher's questions – guess whose fault this will be!'

Scribe

'Your role is to summarise the key points that your group is making, check that the whole group agrees with them, and then write them down. There is much more to being a scribe than just writing!'

Questioner

'Your role is to "skim" the resources and then decide on important questions that the resources should answer. For example, "Who supported Cromwell and why?" The aim is to focus the group's attention on the key points. You then give your questions to the group for it (including you!) to answer.

You can add to or change your questions as you get more familiar with the materials.

You may also ask supportive and clarifying questions to help the group complete its task(s).'

Vocabulary chief

'There is some technical vocabulary in this material. Your role is to research and explain the meaning of all the technical terms. You could devise a 'glossary' for your group if you think this would help. You will need to run a quiz with your group to check that *everyone* can explain each technical term.'

Leader

'Your role is to lead and manage your group in a democratic way, to ensure that the group completes all its tasks in the time available, and that every student participates, because each role is important. You can give other students in your group specific roles if you think this helps. You will need to share out the resources in a way that helps the group to work with maximum effectiveness.'

These roles work best if the teacher makes sure that she will test *every* student's learning after the activity. This can be done during feedback or with a quiz or test warned of in advance. If students know that any member of their group might be asked questions on the material, they will work with their checker to ensure that all members understand all the points.

The roles of questioner and checker etc. help to show students good practice in reading text. Do point this out to students. For example, good readers formulate important questions that the text might answer; ask themselves 'do I understand this?' and 'is this important?' as they read. They also check that they know the vocabulary and summarise key points etc. Hence the roles are not arbitrary or purely managerial, but model good study practice.

Students can be given 'role cards' with all the roles described until they get used to it. Roles can rotate from lesson to lesson.

Demonstrating and modelling skills

Here are some methods for showing students how to do something, whether the skill is

– *a practical skill*, such as how to serve at tennis, how to cut hair

– *an intellectual skill*, such as how to carry out a mathematical calculation, how to punctuate a piece of text
– *a high-order intellectual skill*, such as how analyse the use of imagery in a poem, how to write an essay, or how to evaluate a social policy. More details on how to teach these high-order skills are given in Chapter 21.

Many teachers will use a sequence of these demonstration methods, beginning with some of the earlier ones listed and then using some of the later ones to gradually hand over responsibility to the learner. Best practice concludes with student demonstrations, as in whole-class interactive teaching.

It clearly helps to establish that all or practically all learners know how to do it before the class practice which follows the demonstration. Otherwise you will find yourself in a forest of raised hands, if you are lucky, or if you are not, in a mire where all your students are doing it wrong. This requires the 'self-correcting classroom' created by the very interactive approaches described in Chapter 15, 'Student demonstration'.

Teacher demonstration

You do an example with students watching, thinking out loud in order to explain what you do, and why you do it that way, see Chapter 13 of *Teaching Today* for details, and for details on the following three variants:

Silent demonstration

You do it silently and then ask students why you did it that way and to justify the approach. This works best if the technique is a bit puzzling. This, and the previous approach, could be delivered by video or website etc.

Demonstration by exemplar

You show students examples of good practice already completed, for example business letters, critiques of poems, or trigonometry worked examples, and then ask the class.

'How has this been done? Why was it done that way? Could it have been done another way?' etc.

There is now a class discussion, preferably in assertive questioning style to maximise feedback and dialogue. The aim is to agree and understand general principles about what is good practice, and how this is done. I have no effect size for this, but I strongly believe it is an immensely powerful strategy that is tragically underused. One way to ensure that students examine the exemplar is to use 'spoof assessment' (see Chapter 19). For example, students could spoof-assess designs for CD covers before doing their own.

Feedback methods for the 'present' phase

You have just thrown some mud at the wall, but how much has stuck?

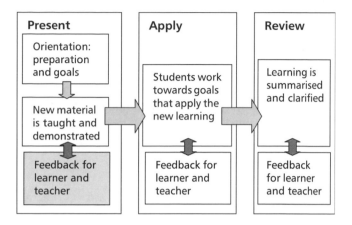

Feedback methods are teaching methods that give feedback on the quality of the students' understanding to you, or to your students, and preferably to both. These methods show the quality of students' constructs as described in Chapter 2. Ideally they also require that any weaknesses in the constructs are corrected. Many teachers just use question and answer as their feedback method. However, there are more powerful methods as described in Chapter 15 and in Chapter 19, 'Other methods that provide feedback'.

References and further reading

Carroll, W. M. (1994) 'Using worked examples as an instructional support in the algebra classroom', *Journal of Educational Psychology*, 83: 360–7.

Gibbs, G. (1992) *Improving the Quality of Student Learning*, Bristol: Technical & Educational Services.

Ginnis, Paul (2002) *The Teacher's Toolkit*, Carmarthen: Crown House Publishing.

Harris, J. R. (1995) 'Where is the child's environment? A group socialization theory of development', *Psychological Review*, 102, 458–89.

Petty, G. (2004) *Teaching Today: A Practical Guide* (3rd edition), Cheltenham: Nelson Thornes.

www.intermep.org: Mathematics Enhancement Programme. This has a special interest in whole-class interactive teaching.

www.clcrc.com: This is useful for cooperative learning.

On feedback methods

Chizmar, J. and Ostrosky, A. (1998) 'The one-minute paper: some empirical findings', *Research in Economic Education*, Winter 1998. This can be downloaded from: www.indiana.edu/~econed/pdffiles/winter98/chizmar.pdf.

Gunning, R. (1968) *The Techniques of Clear Writing*, New York: McGraw-Hill.

Mazur, E. (1997) *Peer Instruction: A User's Manual*, Upper Saddle River, New Jersey: Prentice Hall.

Savinainen, A. (2001) 'An evaluation of interactive teaching methods in mechanics: using the force concept inventory to monitor student learning'. Download from: kotisivu.mtv3.fi/physics/downloads.html. This paper deals with 'peer instruction' or peer checking.

tech-head.com/fog.htm: for the FOG index.

18 Methods for the 'apply' phase: deep meaning from hard thinking

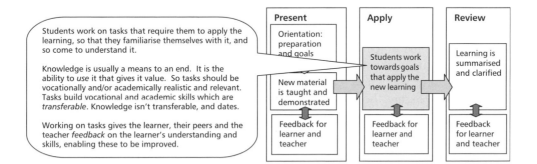

This chapter is about student activity being used to promote learning. Nearly all the high effect size methods described in Chapters 4–7 involve student activity, so this is the heart of evidence-based teaching. Remember that control and experimental groups are taught for the same length of time, so to make time for the student activity the experimental group usually gets taught less content, and has less detailed explanations. Yet they do more than a grade *better* than the control group. It is not teacher explanation but active learning that creates achievement.

We considered how to manage a student activity in the last chapter. There are many student activities considered in Chapters 3–20 that can be adapted to work well in the apply phase. (If you are not an experienced teacher you will find that my *Teaching Today* has detail on choosing and using teaching methods.)

The diagram above shows where we are in the PAR structure. Students have been 'orientated', so they have been persuaded of the purpose and value of what they are about to learn, had it summarised, had goals set, and recalled useful prior learning. Then they have been presented with the new material, skills have been demonstrated, and basic concepts have been developed. However, this has created a construct (understanding in memory) which is incomplete, contains errors, and is surface rather than deep. That is, it is not sufficiently integrated and related with other learning. Consequently it is not 'functional' as described in Chapter 2 (page 16) so the learner often won't be able to use it to complete real tasks.

We have seen in Chapter 2 that deep learning requires the learner to form constructs, and get feedback on their understanding, and that active methods do this best. We saw experimental confirmation of this in Chapter 5, from which Hattie concluded that challenging goals are vital even for low-level learning. We will see all this confirmed again in Chapter 22 when we look in the classrooms of the teachers who get the very best results nationally. All this evidence gives passive methods the most emphatic thumbs down, but many teachers are not convinced, and persist in three myths.

Myth 1: 'It is more important to cover all the content than to set an activity'

Half a million effect-size experiments (worldwide) say the exact opposite. Only active methods require students to make their own sense of the topic, so we are required to leave out detail to make space for this activity.

Teachers know too much. We must cut content to the very bone, get the skeleton (structure) of the topic understood, then add the flesh later. If you persist in telling them everything you know you will swamp short-term memories, confuse your students, and obscure the very key points and principles you are trying to explain.

If the detail is important you can get students to add this flesh to the skeleton later, by reading and researching homework, or assignment essay work, using the strategy outlined in Chapter 21 under 'Help! there's too much content' and the methods in Chapter 20.

'Can I be excused please? My brain is full.'

Our grotesquely overcrowded curricula perpetuate this myth, and paradoxically ensure that less is learned. What is learned is of little value, and soon forgotten. This is because the overcrowding means that surface learning drives out deep learning; specific knowledge, which often has a sell-by date, trumps transferable skills; quantity drives out quality; and so the dispensable drives out the indispensable, boring many students into the bargain, and perpetuating our 'tail' of underperformers.

Myth 2: 'Keep the task simple so they all succeed'

Many teachers argue that their students are not academically talented, and so should only practise straightforward 'reproduction' tasks. Others argue that there is only time to practice the reproduction-style 'set piece' tasks required by the test. To do more would be to compromise exam marks and league-table positions.

But Hattie's summary of research shows that it is challenging tasks and informative feedback that works, even for learning reproduction tasks. This is partly because the brain only retains what it has learned deeply and understands. Relational links are the glue that fixes learning in memory.

Our style of exams perpetuates this myth. Marks are awarded for points made, measuring surface learning of detail, so incoherent answers can get top marks if they tick the right boxes. Again quantity drives out quality. But even if you want to maximise simple recall, research shows that the best strategy is deep learning (see Chapter 2).

An impoverished diet of reproduction tasks does not work with students with learning difficulties either. Hattie's table for 'Special education' in Chapter 5, which includes such students, tells exactly the same story as his main table. Westwood (2003), a specialist in special education, agrees. Reciprocal teaching and Piagetian programmes such as Feuerstein's are pre-eminent for students with learning difficulties: they are both very active, both very demanding for the learner, and both in Hattie's top ten.

If you teach students of low academic attainment, set them tasks that make them make sense; like 'Robert' in Chapter 2 they are not in the habit of reasoning out meaning and vitally need tasks that require them to. Then they will learn.

We need to set, for students at absolutely every academic level, challenging tasks that require analysis, creativity, critical thinking and other reasoning. In any case, knowledge is a means to an end, and the end is to be able to think productively, to act, and to be able to judge. Knowledge can often be acquired by looking up information on the Internet or in a textbook.

Myth 3: 'Any activity will do, so long as it gives the little blighters some relief'

The activities must require the learner to study, reason and apply the key points and key principles and to express their own meanings so that these can be improved. The best methods require direct practice of the main lesson objectives. They also require students to use important subject-specific thinking skills, in 'double decker' lessons that review both content and skills, as described in Chapter 21.

Active learning on the learning flow diagram

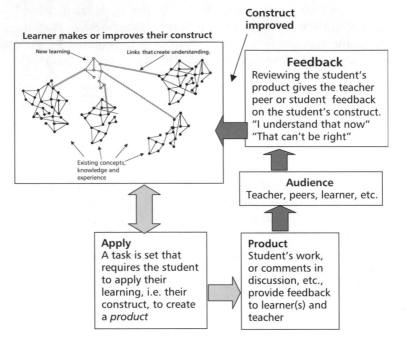

As the diagram above shows, the aim of the apply phase is for the learner to *use* the weak construct produced in the 'present' phase, and so produce a *product* which provides the *audience* (the learner, teacher or peers usually) with information on the quality of the learner's construct so that they can provide *feedback* to the learner. This will enable the learner to strengthen and improve their learning (construct). During the apply phase the learners are often the main 'audience'. They notice what they don't understand, or what they can't do, and endeavour to use this feedback to fix their construct. This process is often so natural that students hardly notice it. However, once the product is complete or nearly so, others may join the 'audience' and add their feedback. For example, the student may show their work to a peer or hand it in for marking.

This apply phase often requires a 'ladder' of tasks (see page 17) such as you might find on a worksheet, which begins with simple reproduction tasks that ensure basic familiarity and recall of what has been presented, moves on to simple closed reasoning tasks, but ends with open reasoning tasks that will challenge every student. Alternatively there might be just one open reasoning task, for example 'Design a series of illustrations to show the process of biodegradation of oil'.

Open reasoning tasks are vital for deep learning, but also for differentiation (ensuring that everyone learns maximally). A closed task has only one adequate response, identical for all learners. Consequently it is usually too easy for some students and too hard for others. It will also take weak students a long time, and keen or able students much less, perhaps leaving them in need of something else productive to do.

TASKS FOR THE APPLY PHASE

Reproduction tasks

- Stating information already given or using skills already demonstrated. This is a useful start but the reasoning tasks below are also needed.

Information gathering

- *Independent learning:* research skills, asking relevant questions, skim reading, using book index and contents, search skills on the Internet, etc.

Building understanding: analysis ('what' and 'why' questions)

- *Close reading/observation:* thoughtful attention to establish key points and key principles. Highlighting, interpreting, comparing, classifying, summarising. Distinguishing fact, belief and values.
- *Conceptualisation:* using examples and non-examples and similarities and differences between examples and concepts, e.g. percentages and fractions.
- *Analysis by section and spectacles* to describe the key points, empathy.
- *Explaining skills:* explaining why with multiple representations including diagrams, mind maps, posters, visualisations, etc., to summarise a topic. Relating ideas to general principles.

Productive thinking: synthesis, creativity, and evaluation ('how' questions and evaluative questions)

- *Writing* essays assignments and reports, and creative writing etc.
- *Responding to a design brief*, or creating an ordered plan of work in engineering, art, computer programming, carpentry, etc.
- *Problem solving*, including 'question typing', i.e. 'How should I do this question, by momentum, energy, or Newton's Laws?' How to proceed when the solution is not evident, e.g. in mathematics.
- *Particular assessment tasks:* giving a presentation; précis, comprehension questions, data analysis, critical appraisal of an experiment, etc. This includes responding appropriately to assessment language, e.g. distinguishing between, and being able to identify, describe, analyse, evaluate, etc.
- *Generating and testing hyptheses:* see box below.
- *Opinion forming*, connecting ideas into a meaningful whole. Generalising, inferring, predicting and then testing opinion by the *coherence* of the ideas, by checking the *evidence*, and by comparing the opinion with alternatives. Arguing from facts, beliefs and values.

Strategic and reflective thinking

- *Critical thinking skills:* the ability to evaluate or critically appraise an argument, policy, case study, poem, experiment, mathematical procedure or piece of creative writing. This includes dispositions or traits such as humility, fairness, courage, empathy, integrity, perseverance, etc.

- *Epistemological awareness:* i.e. to know how one approaches truth in a particular subject. For example: using appropriate methods of inquiry; testing hypotheses and other ideas by looking at the evidence, and by checking the coherence of the ideas. This is especially associated with the very best teaching, as we will see in Chapters 22 and 24.
- *Learning to learn*
- *Reflection:* annotating work in an art and design portfolio, Writing a reflective journal
- *Proofreading for errors, drafting and redrafting*

Affective and social skills

- *Practising mature behaviour:* role play, identifying features of mature behaviour
- *Interviewing* a new client, and devising suitable questions for an interview
- *Valuing and respecting others, even when they are not like you:* demonstrating respect during a discussion.

However, an open task (such as the design of the biodegradation poster) stretches or contracts like a concertina to accommodate each student in terms of time and difficulty. If an able or quick student appears to finish you can ask for more detail – 'What micro-organisms break oil down and how can they be encouraged?' – or more depth: 'Link your illustrations with what you already know about micro-organisms.' A weak student might just summarise all the key points.

The questions asked in devising activities for the apply phase

There follow five interrelated questions that we can ask to help us devise an activity. Because activity is the main source of learning it is worth considering the options carefully. These are summarised in the diagram at the end of this chapter. Take a look at this now.

1 What task(s) should I set?

This should be decided by the purpose of the lesson. Often a ladder of tasks from simple reproduction to simple closed reasoning and then on to an open task with real challenge works well (see page 17).

If the purpose of the lesson is to convey knowledge, ask yourself: *why* do students need this knowledge? This often suggests a task. For example, if they must know

GENERATING AND TESTING HYPOTHESES (effect size 0.79)

These all require the students to use high-order reasoning on material that has been presented to them, and they have a high effect size so it is worth considering the options:

Testing hypotheses directly

You give students some basic ideas and principles, for example about how photosynthesis in plants works (e.g. that it requires light), and students work out ways of testing these ideas. They devise an experiment and carry this test out. Students need to state their hypothesis clearly.

Once they get better at doing this they can begin to formulate their own hypotheses and test them. You may need to check their method of testing before they start on it.

Historical investigation

Students create a hypothesis and then collect evidence for and against it; for example: 'Criticisms of the Vietnam War in the USA were due to an increasing belief that it could not be won rather than economic cost, or a high rate of casualties.'

'What would happen if . . .?' questions

For example, you teach students about a government system to improve employment and then give them questions in a 'What would happen if . . . ?' format. Students must produce a reasoned response using their knowledge of the system, e.g. 'What would happen if inflation increased?'

Problem solving

Students suggest a solution and test it or get feedback on their ideas in some other way.

Literary critique

Students test a hypothesis such as 'D.H. Lawrence's *Sons and Lovers* is an indictment of the working-class males of his time' by using evidence from the text.

Invention

Students use their knowledge, e.g. of quality systems, in order to devise a new one for a particular novel context.

Decision making

Students use their knowledge to make a challenging decision.

about the biodegradation of oil to understand responses to oil spills, then maybe a case study on possible responses to oil spills will make a good series of tasks.

There is an infinity of tasks you could set; the more common are shown in the box on the next page.

2 How will students prepare their response to the task?

Students can work alone, in a pair or a group with neighbours or friends, or with a pair or group you have chosen. Groups of more than four should be avoided as 'passengers' become likely. Research comes down slightly in favour of teacher-chosen or random groups, perhaps because friendship groups sometimes gossip rather than complete your task. But use your judgement; some friendship groups are brilliant at helping each other.

Individual work may be your goal, but lower down the 'ladder' of tasks the support provided by groups may help students to that independence.

3 How will students express their response to the task?

By doing a practical task?
For example making a fat-free spread.

Verbally?
This is quick and spontaneous and requires a minimum effort to communicate the ideas, while allowing for dialogue and so easy improvement. But it is not permanent and so requires time for note making later, though that is no bad thing as note making has an effect size of 0.99.

In writing and/or calculations?
These have the obvious advantages of permanence, but they take time. They should not be the only method of communication, though. Written communication can be in bullet-point or summary form or can be written in full.

Computer files allow for revision, display on interactive whiteboards, and can be emailed as notes, and stored on the intranet or shared with memory sticks. But many individuals don't have enough hardware to hand.

Materials designed to explain to the class may not work as notes.

By graphic organisers?
These are concise and have an effect size of about 1.2, but how will they be improved and stored? Larger-sized paper helps with graphic organisers and with their display to groups; careful folding allows A3 to fit into an A4 folder, or you can photocopy A3 as A4.

By role play or drama?

This works best to illustrate an idea, especially in affective learning, for example the dangers of smoking; or when demonstrating a social skill, such as interviewing a client before a hair treatment or avoiding an argument or confrontation. It is a useful method to encourage students to empathise with someone, or with a character in a play etc. It also gives actual practice in putting words and phrases together ready for a real encounter.

Groups can do role plays simultaneously or one at a time to the class. See Chapter 20 of *Teaching Today* for more detail.

Role play or drama.

4 What medium will they use to display their ideas to their audience?

Realistically

Will they present practical work, a role play, video, example object, etc.?

Paper

A4 is usual but A3 is better for graphic organisers and to show ideas to a small group; pencils allow for easy revision.

Presentation

They can use flip-chart paper, OHTs, board, mini-whiteboards, interactive whiteboards or presentation software such as PowerPoint, but only the latter two will create a note for the class. Will you leave time for note making, get them to work on A3 and photo-reduce A4, or even take digital photographs/video of flip charts or practical work and put these online?

Especially with graphic organisers, students can leave their notes at their places and wander round to see everyone else's, then revise their own. See pages 271–2 for a structured approach.

Can you leave work on permanent display on the noticeboard? This is motivating, especially if it is anticipated, and can be a useful resource in later lessons. I have been to some extremely effective classrooms where flip-chart notes are three deep all round the classroom!

Graphic organisers in electronic form can be shared with intranet, memory sticks, CD-ROM, etc., giving students access to other students' work, which is often beneficial, especially if it is good! Graphic representations make great posters for permanent display in classrooms and corridors and other public spaces. Exhibitions can be created for foyers, or for relevant venues such as a local fitness club.

Combination

Students can present their graphic organiser or can write their ideas on the board and then explain them. These have obvious advantages.

5 What audience will students present to?

This could involve presenting ideas to a neighbour, another peer, your own group, another group, to the whole class, or to another class, etc. Students learn from each other's ideas, especially if these are critically appraised and discussed.

Students are more motivated when peers are the audience rather than the teacher. (Sorry, we just don't count!) They are also more motivated when they are not presenting to close friends or their own group. Friendly neighbours can conspire not to participate, or to do the absolute minimum. This is not possible when you don't know who you are about to present to, or you can't talk to them. There are profound social as well as learning benefits from peers explaining to peers who are not their closest friends.

If the group members are well acquainted ask them to give points of agreement but also of disagreement and points for improvement. The three-legged stool may help here (see page 345).

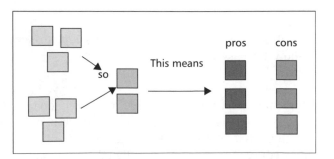

Visual essay planning or visual display of an argument with Post-its.

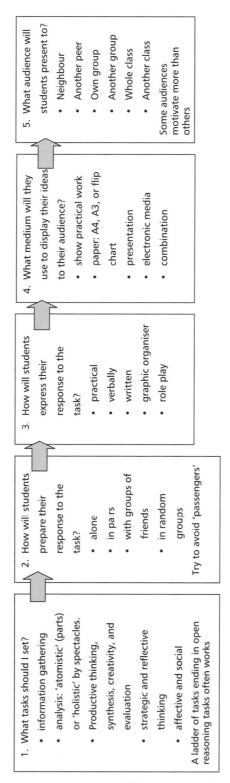

1. What tasks should I set?
   - information gathering
   - analysis: 'atomistic' (parts) or 'holistic' by spectacles.
   - Productive thinking, synthesis, creativity, and evaluation
   - strategic and reflective thinking
   - affective and social

   A ladder of tasks ending in open reasoning tasks often works

2. How will students prepare their response to the task?
   - alone
   - in pairs
   - with groups of friends
   - in random groups

   Try to avoid 'passengers'

3. How will students express their response to the task?
   - practical
   - verbally
   - written
   - graphic organiser
   - role play

4. What medium will they use to display their ideas to their audience?
   - show practical work
   - paper: A4, A3, or flip chart
   - presentation
   - electronic media
   - combination

5. What audience will students present to?
   - Neighbour
   - Another peer
   - Own group
   - Another group
   - Whole class
   - Another class

   Some audiences motivate more than others

Planning a student activity.

243

Choosing and using teaching methods

There are some good structured ways to do this: cooperative learning methods such as jigsaw; or debates, which can be formal where for and against arguments are produced and presented to the class for discussion and deliberation. Academic controversy gets more participation (see Chapter 12).

Writing

Students write handouts, academic papers, articles, newspaper articles. This can be followed by peer review or peer editing or peer assessment.

Visual essay planning

Students can create their own graphic organiser with sticky message pads, by structuring information for themselves. This method is described in Chapter 10.

References and further reading

Harris, J. R. (1995) 'Where is the child's environment? A group socialization theory of development', *Psychological Review*, 102, 458–89.

Moseley, D. *et al.* (2004) 'Thinking skill frameworks for post-16 learners: an evaluation'. This can be downloaded from: www.lsrc.ac.uk/publications.

Westwood, P. (2003) *Commonsense Methods for Children with Special Educational Needs: Strategies for the Regular Classroom* (4th edition), London: RoutledgeFalmer.

19 Feedback methods: assessment for learning

When to use feedback methods

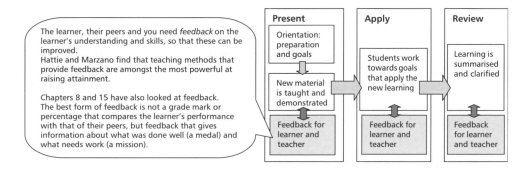

The learner, their peers and you need *feedback* on the learner's understanding and skills, so that these can be improved.
Hattie and Marzano find that teaching methods that provide feedback are amongst the most powerful at raising attainment.

Chapters 8 and 15 have also looked at feedback. The best form of feedback is not a grade mark or percentage that compares the learner's performance with that of their peers, but feedback that gives information about what was done well (a medal) and what needs work (a mission).

Present	Apply	Review
Orientation: preparation and goals	Students work towards goals that apply the new learning	Learning is summarised and clarified
New material is taught and demonstrated		
Feedback for learner and teacher	Feedback for learner and teacher	Feedback for learner and teacher

As we saw in Chapter 8, feedback methods are designed to explore, check and improve learning; they are often used after, and sometimes during the learning of a topic or subtopic. We also encountered some assessment for learning strategies in the 'orientation' phase, such as 'relevant recall questions' (Chapter 16). The diagram below (p. 246) shows our strategy for the methods in this chapter, and the diagram above when they are commonly used.

It is easy to see how to use the strategies below when setting tasks or questions where there is a clear right answer (convergent learning). Try such tasks first:

- mastering content: understanding basic knowledge, concepts and skills
- calculations in mathematics, science, accounts or similar
- punctuation, grammar, translation, recognising figures of speech, etc.

The methods can be adapted to teach practical skills or social skills such as rolling pastry, or dealing with a customer complaint.

However, all the methods can also be used when some tasks have many different appropriate responses (divergent learning), for example open tasks in subjects such as English literature, art and design or political science, as we will see.

Ground rules for self- and peer assessment

In Chapter 15 we considered the ground rules for a blame-free classroom. These same ground rules are important for all these methods.

We will learn best if we all work towards a 'blame-free' classroom

- It's OK if you don't fully understand a concept first time; learning takes time.
- What counts is whether you *understand* the question or task, and its answer, *eventually*, not whether you get it right first time
- I ask challenging questions so it is *not* humiliating to make a mistake. We all make mistakes when we learn. Indeed that is part of *how* we learn. If we don't make mistakes the work is too easy for us to learn at our maximum rate.
- Mistakes are useful because they tell us where we can improve.
- If you make a mistake, bet your life half the class has made it too.
- It's good for learning to say 'I don't understand' and to ask for clarification.
- You should *never* ridicule other students for their mistakes, even in a joking way, because *you* wouldn't like it if you were ridiculed, and because it stops us learning.
- Peers should give 'medal and mission' feedback (see Chapter 8) which is forward looking and positive.
- You will only learn from mistakes if you find out how to do it without mistakes next time, and really understand this.
- Let's help each other! The helper learns at least as much as the helped.

Assessment for learning

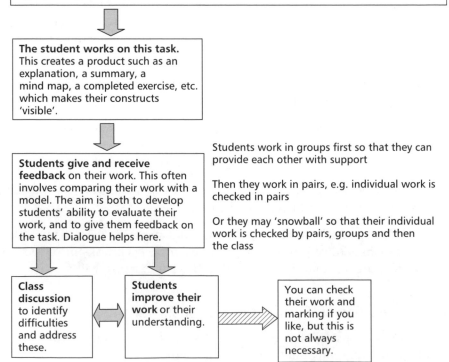

A review or practice task is set. This is meaningful, open, challenging, and eventually involves reasoning as well as reproduction. Its aim is to explore the students' understandings and misunderstandings (constructs) and to get these improved, perhaps by improving their response to the task.

The student works on this task. This creates a product such as an explanation, a summary, a mind map, a completed exercise, etc. which makes their constructs 'visible'.

Students give and receive feedback on their work. This often involves comparing their work with a model. The aim is both to develop students' ability to evaluate their work, and to give them feedback on the task. Dialogue helps here.

Students work in groups first so that they can provide each other with support

Then they work in pairs, e.g. individual work is checked in pairs

Or they may 'snowball' so that their individual work is checked by pairs, groups and then the class

Class discussion to identify difficulties and address these.

Students improve their work or their understanding.

You can check their work and marking if you like, but this is not always necessary.

When to use formative teaching strategies

These methods are designed to improve learning, and can be used in class or out. They are of less use after a learning unit has been completed; however, they can be used to improve work in progress towards a summative assignment.

You can of course mark students' work yourself after self- or peer assessment, though this will not always be productive or necessary.

Some of the strategies that follow are very demanding. If students find them difficult or tiring you might like to reduce the time spent on them, but don't give them up. They are too powerful to abandon.

Do listen in to the peer explaining and peer assessing conversations. They will give you valuable, if depressing, insight into the level of your students' understanding, but avoid the temptation to butt in too much.

If students are not much good at peer explaining, self-assessment or peer assessment this is no reason to abandon them: they are too powerful. It is a reason to give your students more practice. However, you might want to teach students how to use them. It helps to discuss the activity during or immediately after completing it. 'What are/were the difficulties?' 'How should we respond to them?' 'What would you do if . . . ?'

The methods fall into the following rough and overlapping categories: methods that get students to:

- express and improve their understanding
- assess work: this could be anonymous work (spoof assessment), peer assessment or self-assessment
- correct weak understandings or weak work.

The latter can often follow on from one of the former.

Feedback methods for the 'present' phase

Methods that get students to express and improve their understanding

Warn students that these methods are coming – in effect they give them goals for the 'present' phase.

Peer tutoring: pairs improve their answers to questions (effect size 1.0+)

This is done *during* the presentation of new material, rather than only at the end of a presentation. The method was devised to assist the learning of difficult conceptual material and is often used in university physics lectures, but it can be used at any level. It is sometimes called 'peer instruction'. See Mazur (1997) and Savinainen (2001).

Ideally you go through the procedure below every five minutes or so, after each subtopic has been presented, but do warn students that this will happen, or you might be disappointed by their poor answers! This method is very constructivist and a great way to break up the teaching of a long or difficult topic, as well as to check the learning. It can be used with the largest of classes.

1. Ask a conceptually demanding question that requires reasoning, not just reproduction, of what you have presented. Obviously the question should be answerable using only the material that has been presented so far. It can be quite hard to devise such questions on the hoof until you are used to it, so try to think them out in advance. The questions should be focused on the most important concepts in the material. Similarities and differences and graphical representations can sometimes be used as the basis of your questions.
   • 'Which of these graphs best describes the velocity of the falling object, and which its acceleration?'
   • 'What are the main *differences* between the terms "shareholder" and "stakeholder?" . . . What are the main *similarities*?'
   • 'In this first scene, what is Shakespeare trying to establish concerning the characters of Antonio, Salarino and Salanio?'
   • 'Watch this demonstration, then I want you to explain what you see.'

2. Students work on the answer individually, writing this down.

3. Students pair up and give each other their answers. They explain what their answer is, and how they arrived at it. This happens even if they are not sure of their answer.

4. Students try to improve their answers, and arrive at a best answer.

5. You give a model answer fully explained. A verbal answer may suffice.

6. Students work in pairs again to clear up any misunderstandings. Now students know the errors and omissions in their answer the aim is to understand why, and so improve the students' constructs. Students can of course ask questions of you to help this process, or you can start a class discussion.

7. Repeat later. You continue with the presentation and after a few minutes another question is given and the process repeats.

It clearly helps if you look at students' work during this activity; usually you will only have enough time to see a small proportion of it, so try to make this a representative sample.

If you use this method habitually students attend well during the 'present' phase, as they don't want to be found wanting when they work with their peer. The method is greatly enjoyed, and breaks up long or difficult presentations in a very constructive way. The effect size comes from Savinainen (2001) and is only an estimate. If you teach physics or mechanics you can get materials to help you from Mazur (1997).

You could do this in groups of three or four if you prefer.

Peer explaining topics: pairs improve their summary of key points

This is similar to the above. Before you teach a topic you give students prior warning that you will want them to summarise the topic in pairs by explaining the answer to two questions to each other. The questions are designed so that, together, they summarise the key points of the topic you are about to teach. For example, a maths teacher might give the following advance questions, putting them on the board:

'What is Pythagoras' Theorem, and when does it apply or not apply?'

'How can the theorem be used to find an unknown side of a triangle?'

A history teacher might ask:

'Who supported Cromwell and why?'

'What were Cromwell's key goals, and how do we know these?'

You then teach your lesson/topic in the usual way, while students try to work out the answers to both these two questions. Then:

1. Students are put into pairs and given one question each: 'Those nearest the window please answer the first question.'

2. Students prepare for a minute or so what they will say to each other. They work individually to write down a list of key points that they will mention in their explanation.

3. Students answer their questions by explaining their key points to each other.

4. The pairs improve their key points, their own first, then their partners'.

5. The teacher then gives model answers to the two questions, and asks the pair 'What did you miss out or get wrong?' Pairs then discuss this, correcting themselves first, and *then* each other.

6. Class discussion on what issues came up and what judgements were hard to make.

7. Optionally you can then ask students to prepare to repeat this peer explaining next lesson. This is a good review activity and gives the students the challenge to fix any weaknesses found in the first peer-explaining session.

There is a danger that you or your students will see this method as a 'cramming' technique to force rote memory. To minimise this, ask questions that require students to give details and reasons or that stress the meaning and structure of the information.

The one-minute paper: individuals improve their summary of a lesson

This method is very popular indeed in universities where there is a lot of evidence that it works (Chizmar and Otrosky, 1998). However it can be used at any academic level. Again this method works best when set as a goal at the beginning of the class.

Some examples of explaining tasks

'How can you tell whether to use a sine or a cosine to find the unknown side of a triangle? Draw some diagrams to help you explain. One of you take sine, the other cosine.'

'Explain in your own words where you would use a *comma*, and where you would use a *semi-colon* in a sentence. One of you take the full stop, the other the comma.'

'The one nearest the window explain what is meant by a care plan, and the other explain the main criteria for evaluating a care plan.'

Explaining tasks make great homeworks!

---

1. Students write a one-minute paper, just before the end of the class, writing a paragraph or two on these two questions:
   What is the most important thing you have learned in this class?
   What is the muddiest point still remaining at the conclusion of this class?

2. Students hand in their answers or post them in a box.

3. You read the responses and address the muddiest points in the next class.

If the papers are anonymous you get a very honest response; if not you can respond to personal difficulties. Some computing teachers use email for this, and can then respond individually to students who have any particularly muddy points.

The one-minute summary

This is a useful variation of the previous method.

1. Students write a one- or two-minute summary of what has just been presented. This could be in response to a question that summarises the key points to the lesson as in the previous method. Again, the one minute is timed accurately.

2. You give a model, for example your own key points.

3. Students improve their own or each other's summaries using these key points.

4. (Optional) You collect in the papers and comment during the next class.

Alternatively it could proceed rather like 'peer explaining-exemplars' below, with pairs checking each other's summaries before seeing the model.

Feedback methods for demonstrating skills

We have already seen other feedback methods for demonstrating skills in Chapter 5.

Peer-explaining exemplars: peers explain models to teach other

This method was devised and researched by Carroll (1994) for use in teaching mathematics but can be used for any paper-based 'how to' skill, for example teaching how to punctuate, recognise figures of speech, plan how to manufacture something, etc. Carroll found that this method enabled students to learn the skill faster, and make fewer errors, even though more stages are involved than the usual method (which is to use only 1 and 7 below).

1. You demonstrate 'how to do it' on the board, explaining and 'thinking out loud' in the usual way. For example, how to use tangents to determine an unknown angle, how to use apostrophes, how to write a care plan from a scenario, etc.
2. Students are arranged in pairs, preferably not with friends.
3. You have prepared two different sets of questions/tasks, A and B, with their model answers fully worked . Each contains a variety of tasks or questions very similar to the ones you demonstrated. One student has set A, and the other set B.
4. Students study their model questions and answers alone, preparing for the next stage (say five minutes).
5. Each student explains their set of model answers to their partner, pointing out what was done *and why*, and why the method and working is sound. 'This has an apostrophe because . . .'; 'He uses sine here because . . .'
6. Pairs discuss any differences or difficulties. You could start a class discussion based on these.
7. Students then practise doing some by themselves in the usual way.

The students, and you, will need feedback during this activity. Students can be asked to improve each other's explanations after they have been given. You can listen to some representative explanations; don't be too discouraged if they are weak. Students can only build good constructs by first erecting poor ones. Their understanding will improve when they do some on their own.

You can also give model explanations for some of the worked examples if you think this is necessary. Don't promise this, though, or students may wait for your explanation rather than participate.

The idea behind this method is that if teachers go straight from 1 to 7 this is too big a leap for many students. Weak students are trying to comprehend the method at the same time as trying to apply it, which is too much for them.

Weak students often report that they understand the teacher demonstration, yet are unable to 'do one by myself'. This strategy provides an 'extra rung on the ladder', requiring students to comprehend the skill before they apply it. Once students are used to peer explaining they can be encouraged to explain to small groups, or to the class as a whole. 'John, can you explain your solution to question 8 on the board?'

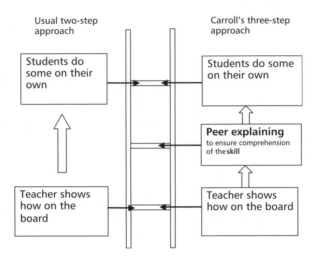

Models, exemplars or worked examples reduce cognitive demand, freeing cognitive capacity for *understanding* the method. They also reduce the time that students spend practising errors.

Another way to use worked examples is to produce a stepped sequence of worked examples. For example, if worked example A uses sines to calculate the length of the adjacent, and B uses sines to calculate the length of the hypotenuse, then a handout can be produced with this structure:

– a problem of type A
– the worked solution of this problem
– a problem of type A for the student to do, and a space for them to do it in
– a problem of type B
(etc. in the same sequence as for type A)

Carroll found that resources structured like this help students in situations where they cannot access help, such as when doing homework.

Pilot and navigator: students instruct/teach other to do a task

This works well for students working on computers in pairs, but it can be used in other contexts. Students are paired up; one takes the role of 'navigator', and the other is the 'pilot'. The 'navigator' tells the 'pilot' what to do *and why*. For example, 'OK, we need to insert the diagram now, so choose "insert" from the menu.' The pilot does this, and is corrected by the navigator if necessary. The navigator is not allowed to 'take the controls'. Students take turns in the roles. It's harder to explain clearly than it is to do it, so navigators often learn more than their pilots.

This method can be used for maths problems, punctuation, and for practicals, etc. Pilots are allowed to argue, but must explain why they disagree.

Study buddies and learning teams

Students can be paired or grouped for a term or a whole course to help each other with their learning. They can be asked to take some responsibility for each other's performance on the course, for example handing in work. They can hold structured meetings in class, and out of class time, with the aim of giving each other support. 'Is everyone up to date with assignment 4?' It is better if they are not friends to begin with. Download 'learning teams' from www.geoffpetty.com for details.

The advantages of peer explaining

'Explaining tasks' require students to clarify and check their understanding. There may also be corrective work done on these understandings. There is a focus on key points and structure as explanations are usually short. This requires students to structure their understanding, a prerequisite for it to pass into the long-term memory. Peer explaining methods can take minimal time and are very constructivist, as explained in Chapter 2.

Getting students involved in assessment

Why students must learn to assess

Students must understand the nature and qualities of good work if they are to create it themselves. In particular they need to know:

- The meaning of task language: for example, they may need to know what 'evaluate' and 'describe' mean. 'Do I need to justify my views in an evaluation?'
- The meaning of formal and informal assessment criteria. For example: 'What does "give evidence" or "show your working" mean? Do I need to give obvious evidence?'
- How the above tasks and criteria can be realised in practice: for example:
  - 'Can I evaluate by just giving a bulleted list of pros and cons with reasons?'
  - 'Is just writing "using Pythagoras" enough to show my working?'

Only when students know where the goalposts are, and know how to kick in that general direction, will they be able to score. This applies in all learning situations; for example it applies just as well when an amateur painter is learning to use watercolours. The best way of learning all this, as ever, is from concrete to abstract. So students learn this 'doing detail' best by careful study of their own work, and that of others. This is why students learn so much from assessment tasks.

While students work they are assessing all the time. When they say 'that's good enough', or 'no, I need to improve that', they are self-assessing. Self-assessment skills are a prerequisite for improvement (Sadler, 1989; or download 'Sadler' from www.geoffpetty.com).

To begin with students need to discuss meanings and judgements in small groups, and then to have their group decisions checked in class discussion. This support will help them to develop the independent self-assessment skills they need when they assess alone. They will benefit from assessing a number of examples of reasonably good work, which show criteria being successfully met in a number of different ways and contexts.

Once they have learned the nature of good work from 'spoof assessment' (see below) they will do a better job of peer or self-assessment. It is worth using the ground rules even for spoof assessment so as to practise using them before they are needed, for example in peer assessment.

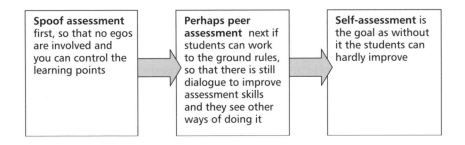

Spoof assessment first, so that no egos are involved and you can control the learning points

Perhaps peer assessment next if students can work to the ground rules, so that there is still dialogue to improve assessment skills and they see other ways of doing it

Self-assessment is the goal as without it the students can hardly improve

Using model answers

Many of these feedback methods require a 'model answer' provided by you. For example, when students mark their own work or check their notes they may do this by comparing it with:

- *An exemplar answer or response* – i.e. a very good answer. In mathematics etc. this could be just the numerical answer, or it could be a fully worked solution showing the working and reasoning as well as the answer. If there is no single right answer students may be shown two or more contrasting but effective answers. In other cases just a verbal statement from you will suffice; for example, you could set a question and then just give a verbal answer to it.
- *A mark scheme*, which can be very informal, or exactly as used by examiners.
- *Assessment criteria*. Again these can be formal or informal. Criteria can be specific to the task, or they can be more general, for example 'evidence is given for your opinion'. See Chapter 15 on feedback.

- *Alternative responses*. Where there is no one right answer, alternative responses can be given. For example, with a question such as 'Describe Hamlet's reaction to seeing the ghost of his father' you might provide some alternative responses, each of which would be acceptable, each with some key points.

Students will usually want a copy of these, so they are best given on handouts or put on the intranet to save paper.

To begin with you may ask students to devise their own criteria, or just to mark work using gut feelings. This can be a useful way to challenge your students' concept of 'good work' (see for example spoof assessment below).

Spoof assessment (in groups, pairs or individually)

A 'spoof' piece of work is one created by the teacher to give students practice at assessing work. It could be a piece of work done by a student in a previous year, with their name removed, though the student's permission is still required to meet copyright law. If students present work electronically it is not too difficult to save work for this purpose.

The advantage of spoof assessment is that all students are marking exactly the same piece of work, which makes class discussion easier. Also, you can put 'deliberate errors' into the work to make the teaching points you think most important.

Spoof assessment is best done in small groups first so that students can provide each other with support. Then snowballing is useful to develop independence, while still providing support. Then students should be able to spoof assess – alone, checking their judgements during class discussion.

Assessment criteria may or may not be given. If they are *not* given, students are often asked to come up with their own criteria before using these to assess the work.

A useful strategy is to give students two pieces of work; one is good and looks bad, and one is bad but looks good! (Gibbs 1981). Here are some examples.

Example 1
A mathematics teacher gives her students two pieces of work on trignometrical calculations, along with the worked solutions and answers to these questions. Students are asked to mark two pieces of work using their own criteria.

- One piece of work has all the right answers, but the methods are not explained or justified, some are overlong, and any working or reasoning is not clear.
- The other piece of work has some wrong answers, but the methods are good, fully explained and justified, and the working is well laid out and easy to follow.

If they are not given criteria most students will give the worst work the best mark, because they believe the goal is to get the right answer, and do not consider methods and working. Students can experience serious 'cognitive conflict' (Chapter 2) when they learn that the work they thought worst gets the best marks! Class discussion can then be very productive: 'Why do you think this work got such low marks despite getting the answers right?'

Example 2

Students of economics are given two essays. One is well presented, long, has many technical terms and impressive diagrams and is written in long sentences with quite complex grammar. But this student does not answer the question. The other spoof piece of work is short, only uses technical terms where necessary, but answers the question very well and very concisely. Again without criteria students usually give the worst work the best grade. Some will do this even *with* criteria, especially if they do not understand them well enough.

In both cases there is class discussion after students have given their judgements. 'Look at work X – did they justify their answer as question 3 required? What does it mean to justify an answer? Let's look at how Y did this. . . .'

> *The first time you use spoof assessment it is fun to tell students that one piece of work is an A grade and one is a D grade and ask them which is which. When they get them the wrong way round, as they usually do, ask them as homework to go away and work out why.*

If no assessment criteria are given to students, it helps to conclude discussions on spoof work by stressing what the criteria are. However, students will benefit greatly from being given criteria for later attempts, so that they can practise interpreting them and so learn what they mean.

> *Many students believe that 'describe', 'explain', 'analyse' and 'evaluate' all mean pretty much the same thing: 'write about'. Spoof assessment can really help them to understand assessment language and assessment criteria. And how to meet these criteria. Another useful method is to use 'decisions, decisions'. Students are given phrases or short paragraphs of text to classify as descriptions, explanations, analyses and evaluations.*

To begin with students may copy surface features of good work and may take much longer to emulate the deep qualities. This is often not as worrisome as some teachers believe. Copying is a way of learning, as art teachers know well, and once the student has gained from copying strategies they can often learn to do things in their own way. Varied exemplars will help, as they will show alternative 'ways of doing it'.

Spoof assessment with one piece of work

It is not always possible to have two pieces of work as described above, or the time to discuss them. An excellent homework activity is to give students one good piece of work from last year to assess against clear criteria immediately after they have completed an identical or similar task. Or indeed before attempting a similar task. They can mark in the margin where different criteria are being met by the work.

Students learn a great deal from examples of good practice like this. It is a very natural way to learn; animals learn this way – and we are animals after all! Well, students are, anyway.

Snowballing spoof assessment

This is a variant of the above and helps students to develop their ability to make assessment decisions independently.

- Students work *alone* to mark the same piece(s) of spoof work.
- They get into pairs and compare their findings.
- The pairs get into fours to agree how to mark the work.
- You ask each group of four to give justified decisions bit by bit – say one spoof question at a time without evaluating their answers (assertive questioning as in Chapter 15). Each group responds, then you ask the class to resolve any differences, then you give your own decisions fully explained.
- You ask the class to resolve any disagreements.
- You confirm and explain the learning points.

The first time students evaluate a certain type of work you can use snowballing in a similar way to get them to devise the criteria they will use to evaluate the work.

Individual spoof assessment checked in pairs

This is a variant of peer explaining topics described above, and is often done immediately after it.

- Students are put in pairs
- They are given a spoof piece of work with deliberate errors in it, for example three paragraphs of text with deliberate punctuation errors. The two students are given different pieces of work (though the first time they do this they could use the same piece).
- Students work on their own to find:
  – what's wrong
  – why it's wrong
  – how to do it right.
- Each student explains the errors in their spoof work to their partner.
- Pairs discuss any disagreements over their assessment decisions.
- You then ask students for the errors they have found, and discuss these – 'Why do you think that's wrong?' – and clarify misconceptions through class discussion.

This is a fun activity and a useful exercise to 'inoculate' students against common errors and misunderstandings. Some teachers object to showing students work with errors in it, but if students don't learn error-spotting skills they will not be able to proofread their own work.

Peer assessment

Students will do this better if they have spoof assessed first. It is most important that students keep to the ground rules, and if they are not mature enough to do this it is probably best to use only spoof and self-assessment. If some students find it humiliating to have their work marked by another, you can let some students self-assess instead. It would be worth checking their judgements.

Peer assessment has the advantage that students can help each other develop the skills they need for independence.

It helps to have a class discussion after any peer or self-assessment activity, though without blaming or shaming students. Ask them:

What issues came up?

What judgements were hard to make?

Peer assessment has a marginally higher effect size if it takes place a day or so after the work was completed so as to effectively review the work as well as to assess it. However, students may prefer to peer assess immediately.

Peer assessment in groups

- Students complete a piece of work individually and then get into a group of three or four.
- They pass their work around silently for a few minutes until everyone has seen everyone else's work
- They discuss any differences.
- They mark each piece of work, perhaps starting with a better one.
- You ask what decisions were hard to make and hold a class discussion.

This is a very simple and greatly enjoyed method, and is most powerful as peer pressure is strong and the groups create high-quality discussion. Do listen in to these discussions!

To make this method more effective use random grouping by numbering students off 1, 2, 3, 4, 1, 2, etc., and putting all the 1s etc. together.

Listen to these
discussions.

Snowballing peer assessment to a best answer

This is similar to the above method but involves students collaborating to produce a group answer.

- Students are arranged in groups of three or four; it's best if they are not friendship groups. It can be done in pairs, but the more learners in the group the more their answers are likely to differ in ways that help students to learn.
- Students are given questions or calculations to do, which they work on alone in the first instance (say five minutes).
- Students get into random groups of about three or four, and compare their answers, reasoning, methods, working, etc., noting differences. They discuss and try to agree:
  - which are the correct or best methods, workings, reasoning, answers, etc., and *why*
  - the group's idea of the 'best answer'
  - what errors were made by group members, and *why* (this is done in a supportive and constructive manner).
- The students are then given model answers and compare their group answer with your model answer.
- Class discussion. What issues came up? What judgements were hard to make?

Peer assessment with model answers

This is a strategy which Gibbs found almost doubled attainment on a university engineering course (quoted in Biggs 2003). This strategy is particularly useful if you are setting less work for students than you would like because you can't keep up with marking.

- Students do a worksheet of questions and put their name on it.
- They hand these in, and you give them out to other students to mark. Students do not know who is marking their work. Codes or pseudonyms can be used to make work anonymous, but there is more peer pressure if the student's name is on his or her work.
- Students mark their peers' work using 'model answers' or 'worked solutions' including a mark scheme provided by you. If you worry that students might not mark responsibly you could ask markers to initial their marking.
- You collect all the marked work and then hand it back to the student who did it. Students each keep the model, for example the worked solutions. Most students will probably check the quality of the peer's marking, but you needn't.
- You ask them what issues came up? What judgements were hard to make?

In the case Gibbs reports, the teacher did not even take down the marks that the students obtained. The average mark on the unit rose from around 45% to around 75% as a result of this strategy! (You could of course collect marks at this stage if you prefer.)

An alternative pair strategy is for the pair to work together to mark their own scripts, again using a model.

Using an assessment proforma to assist peer or self-assessment

Here is an assessment proforma for marking calculation in mathematics or science etc. It helps to focus students' efforts on the most important skills, rather than just on getting the right answer. See www.geoffpetty.com for many more examples of assessment proformas.

Assessment criteria	Teacher, peer or self-assessment
Methods: aim to make these appropriate, and as simple or elegant as possible.	
Methods justified: the principles or formulae used are made clear.	
Working: aim to make working clear, complete, easy to follow, stating principles or formulae used where necessary.	
Care taken: aim to check your work for errors, and present work neatly.	
Main focus needed for improvement	
Main strengths	

Peer assessment by swapping work with your neighbour

This is the simplest form of peer assessment. Students work alone on an exercise for five minutes or so, and then swap their work with their partner and assess each other's work. Feedback is usually verbal rather than in writing. It needs to be given in a supportive way. As ever it helps to have a class discussion about difficult issues or judgements.

Peer editing in pairs

* Students comment on or 'edit' each other's work while it is still in first-draft phase, before it is handed in. Students can mark against the task – 'Did she evaluate?' and against assessment criteria provided by you, or required by the examination board: 'Did she give evidence for her evaluation?'
* Class discussion about difficult decisions or other issues. For example: 'What does it mean by "justify your decision?"'
* Students are given time to improve their work.

- Students submit their work to you, or for peer assessment (preferably not by the student who edited the work).

Students need to recognise that even more than in peer assessment, the goals of peer editing are to improve the work and the student's understanding, and not to judge the work. You might even strengthen your ground rules for this.

Absolutely any sort of work at any level can benefit from peer editing: from sums to PhDs. The editor gains at least as much as the edited.

Peer assessment of peer explaining

In *Assessment for Learning* by Black *et al.* (2003) the following activity is described. As a review of recent learning each student took responsibility for part of the topic and explained it to a small group of their peers. The other students assessed whether the explanation was better than, equal to, or not as good as the explanation they could themselves have given. These assessments were given anonymously to the student after their explanation. Feedback from students indicated the value of this activity in encouraging them to analyse their own reasoning: 'Explaining to other people and listening to their explanations really helps me to understand it much faster than just reading it at home.'

The advantages of peer assessment

- Students come to understand the nature of good work more deeply, as they must use this understanding to judge a peer's work. This helps them understand their goals as learner, for example how marks are gained and lost. These goals are learned from concrete to abstract; this is the most powerful way to learn.
- They learn other ways of approaching a task than the approach they used.
- They become more reflective about their own learning and gain understanding by discussing disagreements. For example, if students realise they did one calculation wrong because they confused a sine with a tangent that is very helpful.
- Students can do more work than you can mark.
- Students tend to take pride in work that will be peer assessed: they are more likely to complete it, and to write more neatly than if you assess it (Black et al., 2003)!
- Students accept criticisms from each other that they would ignore if given by you! For example 'Your writing is really hard to read.'
- Students greatly enjoy this method, and both 'helpers' and 'helped' learn if they support each other constructively. (The standard of discussion is commonly higher than you expect!)
- It helps to develop the skills required for self-assessment.

However, the main advantage of peer assessment is its hidden message. It teaches students how to avoid mistakes, and how to improve, but more than this it teaches them that mistakes are avoidable, and that improvement is possible. It shows students that achievement is not dependent on innate talent, but on doing the job well. Students look at their own work marked by a peer, and at the model which they now understand well as they have used it to mark by, and they say: 'This isn't rocket science, I could have got a better grade if only I . . .'

In short it encourages students to attribute success to factors in their control. This is very empowering, as Dweck has shown (see Chapter 2). In Chapter 21 we will see that it can have an effect size of up to 1.4.

Self-assessment

There is a lot to be said for students having their assessment skills developed with spoof and peer assessment before they try self-assessment.

Self-assessment is marginally better if it takes place a day or so after the work was completed so as to effectively review the work as well as to assess it. However, students may prefer to do it immediately.

Self-assessment using detailed model answers

- You explain that students will mark their own work, and that you will *not* mark it. (If students know you will mark it eventually, they may put little effort into their self-assessment.)
- Students do an exercise, which might be a series of questions. When they have finished they proofread their own work before the next stage. This is marginally better if it takes place a day or so later so as to effectively review the work as well as assess it.
- Students are given model answers, assessment criteria, key points, or exemplars etc. These might include a mark scheme.
- The students mark their own work against these model answers. If they do not understand the model, or why their answer is wrong, they try to puzzle this out for themselves rather than ask immediately for help. You offer help only where needed.
- If students are working at about the same speed there can be class discussions about issues raised.
- Students can then do the next few questions, and so on. The self-assessment using model answers can be done in stages through a worksheet, for example every two questions.
- Optionally the students could correct their work as well as assess it. However, it is best if they do not offer this work for marking, as they will probably just copy the right answers from the model without trying to understand them! If you will not mark their work they are motivated to work out for themselves how they have done.
- An optional activity is for students to explain to a peer a correction they have made and why it improves their original answer. This will help them make sense of the correction.

Some students find marking their own work preferable to a peer or teacher marking it. Self-assessment develops understanding and confidence. It makes more demands of the learner and less of the teacher, a characteristic of effective learning method generally. This method is related to peer assessment methods. Indeed the same resources could be used to do both or either depending on student choice.

Students enjoy this method *much* more than you would think. The feedback is almost immediate so it is very motivating; some teachers arrange for it after about every five minutes of student work. You must then make sure that students only see the model answers for the questions that they have *completed*, of course!

Some students will need help concluding what they have learned from comparing their answers with the model answers. You could ask them to write this down or relate it to you before proceeding further. Ask them 'What are the key points to remember when answering questions like these?' As they relate these, acknowledge correct responses and then ask 'Why?'

Self-assessment in pairs or groups using detailed model answers

This is the same as the method described immediately above, but students are put in pairs or possibly small groups. They take turns to mark their own work watched by the group, and discuss any issues. Then you ask them for issues, difficulties or judgements that were hard to make. This helps students prepare for self-assessing alone.

Self-assessment using answers but without the working or reasoning

This is used mainly in quantitative work. For example, a maths or science teacher gives students some calculations to do telling them that he will give them the answers to enable them to check their own work.

When the students have answers for the first few questions they are allowed sight of the teacher's answers. Don't give them answers from the beginning, as they might work backwards from them instead of doing the calculations properly. When they have the answers students go back over any wrong calculations and try to work out where they have gone wrong.

If students work out where they went wrong it creates better understanding than if you tell them where they have gone wrong. It also teaches them proofreading and error-detection skills, and their importance. Self-checking like this can also produce a culture of care with work. If answers are released for every five minutes work or so, then students' misconceptions will be quickly corrected, and won't be reinforced by repeating the same errors in later questions. As ever, class discussion of difficulties can be helpful. You can support this activity by teaching students error-detection skills such as estimating.

Self-assessment against learning goals

- At the end of a task, topic or lesson students are reminded of the goals, objectives, or assessment criteria. Students are then asked to take, say, five minutes to look over their work and self-assess:
  - what they have learned, know, and can do
  - what they still need to learn or practice to achieve the goal or objectives.
- Students use this to set themselves an individual action plan, perhaps after a class discussion.
- The action plan is implemented in the next lesson, perhaps in peer tutoring groups.

A useful approach is to ask students to claim where they have met criteria, for example putting '5' in the margin of their work where they have met criterion 5.

Examples

- Students have just completed drawing a graph; they use assessment criteria developed and explained during the lesson to assess their own work.

- Students have completed a lesson on hair colouring, which had three objectives given in advance. The objectives are presented on the OHP, and students reflect on whether they believe they have met them.

- Students have completed three lessons on the rift valley. The teacher writes up a checklist of statements in the form 'I can now identify a rift valley on a map' etc. Students work alone to decide whether they can meet these goals.

- Students have just completed the first of two presentations. They self-assess against criteria that were determined in advance, and then set themselves goals for their next presentation.

Self-assessment using a video model

This is used to teach physical skills, especially in sports, and is routine in professional coaching. Students are given a model performance on video (exemplar), for example a tennis player serving, a good bowling action in cricket, or a defender attacking a forward in a real football game.

Students examine the exemplar performance on video, then have a go themselves. Their efforts are videoed using a similar camera shot if possible. Ideally, the exemplar and the student's video are now edited together to be on the same screen, side by side and synchronous. The student can now compare their performance with the exemplar, and set themselves learning targets. This can be adapted to involve peer assessment.

Self-assessment as a workshop review

Carol Nyssen of Oxford and Cherwell Valley College uses this strategy with her hairdressing and beauty students. She uses the strategy with her whole teaching team but you could do it alone.

- Objectives are stated at the beginning of each lesson by every teacher in the team and are written by students in an exercise book specifically for this purpose.
- Students review their learning against the objectives at the end of each session.
- There are weekly skills workshops where students review the objectives for the whole week, picking out those where they lack confidence.
- The workshop teacher deals with any objectives that everyone finds troublesome.
- Students are supported in individual work towards personally troublesome objectives, perhaps with peer support.

This workshop requires a teacher who can think on her feet and who has an excellent grasp of the whole curriculum, as any topic from any class may cause a difficulty. It also requires the availability of suitable books and other learning materials.

Reflective journals and personal targets

This method is widely used in developing professionals, for example in nursing, management, and of course teaching. There is more detail on this in Chapter 23, but below I describe how a journal could be used on any school or college course.

You may or may not provide a book for students to do this in.

- Students write a few lines at the end of each lesson or week, describing what they have learned and what they are unclear about, along with personal observations. You might give them some questions to ensure that they focus on important factors:
  - Did you bring everything you needed for this lesson?
  - Did you follow the class ground-rules?
  - What have you learned?
  - What did you find most difficult or unclear?
  - How are you getting on with your latest personal target?
  - Set yourself another personal target.

Whether or not you use questions like those above, make sure that your students complete their journal entry by setting themselves a personal target for the next class meeting or the next week or so. This encourages students to act on what they have learned from completing the journal.

A research study employing a similar method to the above *doubled* attainment in numeracy (see the Black and Wiliam Research Review 1998).

Self-assessment with traffic lights

- Students complete a quiz or test on the work they have done over the last few weeks.
- They self-mark their paper using a 'model' provided by you.

- They are provided with a list of concepts, skills and subtopics that appeared in the test, and are asked to mark each with ticks or coloured blobs as:
  - green if they can understand how to do them (ignoring careless slips)
  - red if they do not understand how to do them
  - amber if they are not sure.

How did you do on:	Name:		
	Red It's holding me up	**Amber** Not sure	**Green** It's not holding me up
sine			
cosine			
tangent			
Pythagoras			

- The teacher looks through these self-assessments. If there are lots of red blobs next to a particular topic, then this topic is reviewed.
- There is a class discussion to get more detail on the difficulties.
- Optionally, the greens help the ambers while you help the reds for some or all of the topics in turn.
- Students write action plans to respond to their individual weaknesses. For example: 'I need to remember to square root my answer when I use Pythagoras' theorem.'

This action plan could be checked by the teacher or by a peer (preferably not a close friend). For example, students could be asked to explain how to do the questions they have been working on to their peer in the next lesson. (See peer explaining above.)

Self-assessing against goals learned from an exemplar

This is based on a method in *Assessment for Learning* by Black *et al.* (2003) and combines spoof and self-assessment. It mimics real-life learning in a very natural and engaging way.

Students analyse a good piece of work for desirable characteristics. For example, English students could analyse a piece of writing and find good use of metaphor. Or mathematics students could find a well laid out mathematical argument. History students could find a good use of primary evidence.

Students set themselves goals or determine assessment criteria, based on what they have learned from the exemplar. For example: 'I want to think up and use a really good metaphor.'

Students create their own work, trying to achieve their goals.

Students self-assess using their self-set goals. Alternatively peers could assess.

Self-assessing to improve a summative assignment

The aim here is to use self-assessment to improve work in progress towards a summative assignment, coursework, investigation, project or dissertation or similar, so it can be improved before it is submitted. Check first that this procedure is acceptable to your examining body!

- Students produce draft work towards the summative piece of work which has assessment criteria.
- Students self-assess their draft against the assessment criteria.
- Students ask questions about the meaning of the criteria and how to meet them in practice as they work.
- Class discussion to clarify difficult points.
- Students go away and improve their work before submitting it. They may be asked to draw up targets during the class to help them with this.

This, of course, is what good students do without being asked! However, even they will benefit from the discussion. Weaker students will notice that they can improve their work if they attend to criteria carefully, which is very empowering. It may only be necessary to do this once with students and then remind them to do it for themselves in future. However, it might well be worth class time to do it habitually.

The advantages of self-assessment

- It makes students aware of the goals, and familiarises them with the characteristics of good work.
- It helps them work out how to improve, that is to identify the gap between their present skills and the learning goals.
- It encourages students to take responsibility for their own learning.

What should I do if my students are bad at self- or peer assessment?

Don't give up. Teach them to do it better. They cannot produce good work until they know what it is. It helps students if you do spoof assessment first, then peer, and lastly self-assessment. Start each by letting them do it in small groups, so they help each other. Have class discussion on any difficulties or issues that arise.

It does not matter if students do not make perfect judgements, and you need not correct them all. As in all other areas of human endeavour students learn to make good decisions by discovering when they have made bad ones. The desired outcome is that learners *slowly clarify their understanding of what is good work*, and set themselves goals for improvement. If *that* outcome is achieved, you and they are doing well, however bad their assessment decisions!

Your expert marking is needed too, of course!

- Students reflect on themselves as learners and so learn to learn; this 'metacognition' (thinking about thinking and self-regulating their own learning) has been shown in many studies to greatly improve learning.
- The most important advantage of self-assessment and peer assessment is that it makes students realise that success or failure depends not on talent, luck or ability, but on practice, effort and using the right strategies. This is motivating and empowering. See Chapters 3 and 21 on 'attribution'.

Find faults and fix methods

The following methods require that the learners really address the weaknesses discovered by self- or peer assessment. These methods can often be tagged onto the end of the methods described above.

Doing corrections and correcting draft work

This doesn't sound much fun, does it! However, getting questions right that you initially got wrong ensures that you improve understanding and unlearn misconceptions. It can also make students feel more positive about their performance if they eventually 'get it right'. These methods also make students more careful in their first attempts as they often wish to avoid corrective work. However, errors due to simple slips can usually be ignored; it's fundamental errors that require correction.

- Students complete an exercise, worksheet, quiz, test, etc. This method can also sometimes be used on a summative assignment, or for coursework in draft form, etc.
- Students' work is marked using self- or peer assessment if you can. (You can check this later if necessary.)
- Students work in small groups to help each other with what they got wrong. You can help with this, of course. Encourage learners to use any errors to diagnose and correct misconceptions. 'Why do you think you/he got that wrong?' (You could try choosing the groups yourself, arranging for one relatively strong student in each group.)
- Students correct or improve their work. One way of checking this is to give students the exercise or quiz etc. again the next lesson, and ask them to do only those questions they got wrong last time. Another is to ask students to explain the right answer to a question they got wrong last time to a peer.

This strategy, like most teaching strategies, can be overused. Students may find it too dispiriting if you ask them to correct all their work, and they may well not be able to keep up! However, the method can also be underused. Students sometimes need to have another go at something if they are really to understand how to do it properly. If groups are supportive this can be greatly enjoyed.

Peer helping

This method acts as a filter to discover what students find most difficult and to fix the rest.

- Students mark their own and a peer's work together, using model answers or assessment criteria.
- Where they both have difficulty the pair tries to work out why, and to put this right. Where they can't do this they ask help from other pairs or from you. Where they can't do this they write the problem on the board.
- You discuss the problems on the board with the class.
- The students then improve their own work with help from their partner.

Mastery test (effect size 0.5)

This method is suitable for checking the learning of vital knowledge and skills; it can be used in resource-based learning to assess whether a student is ready to progress to the next unit.

- After teaching a topic and after class practice and homework, etc., you confirm learning with a *simple* three- to five-minute quiz or test, requiring the reproduction of vital key points and skills:
  - recall questions on key facts
  - a number of simple calculations to do
  - a practical activity
  - some simple past-paper questions etc.
- Students mark their own papers against a model you give them. The questions need to be easy enough for students to understand the model answers, and to be able to mark their own paper.
- Students note the questions they got wrong, and why. In maths it may help if they do these questions again, covering the answers while they do so.
- There is a minimum acceptable mark of say 70–80% (it was an easy test on vital material). Students who get less than this take a retest when they are ready, perhaps a few days later; however, they only do the questions like those they got wrong the first time. Students also mark this retest themselves and the cycle repeats.

Lai and Biggs (1994) found that this method tended to encourage surface learning. Arguably this could be overcome if other tasks and assessments required a deep approach. It might also help if questions ask 'why' not just 'what'. Watch out for surface approaches even so. See Chapter 43 of *Teaching Today* for a fuller account of these pitfalls.

Students assess each other by writing their own questions

- Students work in small groups to write questions and answers or questions with a mark scheme. Each group may be given their own subtopic to write questions for.
- You check these and get groups to swap or circulate their questions and answers.
- Each group passes its questions for another group to answer, working as individuals. They may then swap papers or put their heads together to agree the best answers after doing the questions individually. You could set this last task without warning.

- The work is handed back to the question writers to mark, and to point out how the work could be improved
- The work is handed back to those that answered the questions to be improved.

The backwards test

Why should the marking come last?

- Students are given questions for a test they are about to take.
- They work in groups to devise a mark scheme for each question.
- They compare their mark schemes and agree a class mark scheme.
- Students take the test.*
- Peers mark each other's papers against the agreed mark scheme, and return them.
- Students discuss disagreements and improve their answers.

*If generalised criteria are devised, for example 'Label the axes of your graph: 3 marks', or 'Use quotes from the text to give evidence for and examples of your points of view', then the questions in the test they actually take can be different from those they used to devise the criteria.

Student questioning and 'mountain climbing'

This is less rigorous than mastery testing, but much more fun. I will describe a version of this game for level 2 learners, but it can easily be adapted for more advanced learners.

You appoint teams, and give each team a subtopic from the last few weeks of teaching. For their subtopic each team writes three or four reproduction questions (low on Bloom's taxonomy) with answers. You check these questions and answers, making sure they are on vital material, are truly reproduction questions, and have good answers. Groups make enough copies of their cards for what follows.

Research on asking students to generate questions and answers for each other has shown that the approach produces marked improvements in achievement. See Chapter 13 on reciprocal teaching.

The questions can be typed into a table in a word-processing application. (If you set 'autofit' to 'distribute rows and columns evenly' all the cards become the same size.) You can then print on thin card with a different colour for each subtopic if necessary, and cut them into question cards. Alternatively they can be handwritten, or an electronic version can be made.

Question: Give two key characteristics that make a question suitable for a mastery test **Answer:** accept two from: It should test *vital* knowledge, and be *low on Bloom's taxonomy*. The material must have been *practised*	**Question:** Give two key differences between a mastery test and a conventional test **Answer:** accept two from: The students must do *remedial* work. *Everyone* passes eventually. There is no mark, just pass or not yet passed. Questions are low on Bloom's taxonomy.

Students work in pairs, preferably with question cards on every subtopic. Alternatively card sets can be shared. In their pairs they take it in turn to ask each other a question. If the other student gets it right, they move their counter up one square on a game board with a mountain drawn on it. There are almost as many squares up the mountain as there are question cards. If students do not get their question right, they keep their 'wrong card' and can study the correct answer during the game. One square before the summit of the mountain is a 'base camp' where students must take a second attempt at all their 'wrong cards'. The object of the game is not to get to the summit first, but for the *team* of two 'climbers' to both get to the top of the mountain.

This is about twice as much fun as it sounds yet it has a very serious purpose. Mastery games can be used by themselves, or can of course be used to prepare for mastery tests.

Comparing notes: checking notes, mind maps or graphic organisers

Chapter 10 explains that graphic organisers have very high effect sizes. This has the advantage that it focuses on deep SOLO levels of understanding as described in Chapter 2 and improves it, structuring learning well so that it can be accommodated by permanent memory. It makes most sense as a review exercise at the end of a lesson or topic.

- Students create their own notes, concept map or other graphic organiser.
- Students compare their notes or graphic in groups of about three. They suggest improvements to their own work, and then to each other's.
- The teacher shows a model note or graphic, or perhaps two. (You could save some from this activity last year.)
- The groups notice differences between their work and the model, discuss these, and then suggest improvements to their own work, and then to each other's.
- These improvements are made.

This activity can be repeated later for the same topic as a recall test. 'Write notes from memory on the difference between tabloids and broadsheets.'

Black *et al.* (2003) contains an interesting variant of this, rather like 'marketplace' in Chapter 17. Groups of four create one concept map or other graphic organiser, then split into two pairs.

- Two go off and look at the other groups' maps; the other two stay to explain theirs.
- The pairs swap so that everyone has seen the other groups' maps.
- The fours get together and discuss improvements to their map.
- This could conclude in the same was as above with you showing a model map.

Other methods that provide feedback

This chapter misses out more common methods; in particular I have not mentioned methods that involve feedback from you, for example comments-only marking, leaving time for students to read and act on comments in class, and 'learning loops'. These are powerful methods, but I deal with them in Chapter 43 of *Teaching Today*.

What is so special about the feedback methods in this chapter?

- They give *learner feedback* on goals and gaps. Learners discover what they have done well, and clarify where and how to improve. They do this for themselves.
- Many of the methods give *teacher feedback* too, showing the teacher what students can do well and what they are having difficulty with. This gives teachers the information they need to respond to learner need.
- Learners *clarify goals*. Learners discover how they are supposed to answer questions, what is expected of them exactly, and where marks are gained and lost. They also learn assessment language; for example, humanities students might learn the difference between 'state', 'analyse' and 'evaluate'. Some of the methods require students to scrutinise exemplary work, which also helps them to clarify goals such as what tasks or assessment criteria mean.
- They increase the learner's *repertoire of moves*. That is, learners learn other and better 'ways of doing it', for example by looking at peer work and at exemplars. This helps them to meet similar goals in the future. Sadler thought this very important.

- They encourage *metacognition*. That is, they encourage learners to think about their own learning and their own thinking. They develop the skills and habits of self-critical reflection in the learner. This encourages learners to take charge and responsibility for their own learning. (It also encourages the teacher to take responsibility for their own teaching, as they get feedback too!)
- They create *internal attributions*. That is, they help the student to attribute success and failure to something the student can do something about, for example to using the right methods and reasoning, etc. About half of students attribute their weaknesses to a low IQ or a lack of innate talent – 'I can't do maths.' Then the learner will withdraw effort in the face of difficulty, instead of increasing it. Self- and peer assessment both show the student the *reasons* for weaknesses, and so make it clear that improvement is possible. (See the handout on Dweck's theory of motivation on my website.)
- They create *cognitive conflict*. That is, they often create a puzzle for students. 'Why did I get that wrong?' 'What's wrong with my answer?' Students are confronted with their own lack of understanding and with their misconceptions, and they feel powerfully motivated to puzzle out where they went wrong, and to restructure their understanding.

References and further reading

Black, P. J. and Wiliam, D. (1998) 'Assessment and classroom learning', *Assessment in Education: Principles, Policy and Practice*, 5, 1: 7–74. See also QCA (2001). A very readable summary and a full reference is given at www.pdkintl.org/kappan/kbla9810.htm and www.qca.org.uk/ca/5–14/afl.

Black P. *et al.* (2003) *Assessment for Learning: Putting it into Practice*, Buckingham: Open University Press.

Carroll, W. M. (1994) 'Using worked examples as an instructional support in the algebra classroom', *Journal of Educational Psychology*, 83: 360–7.

Chizmar, J. and Ostrosky, A. (1998) 'The one-minute paper: some empirical findings', *Research in Economic Education*, Winter 1998. Download from: www.indiana.edu/~econed/pdffiles/winter98/chizmar.pdf.

Lai, P. and Biggs, J. B. (1994) 'Who benefits from mastery learning?' *Contemporary Educational Psychology*, 19: 13–23.

Mazur, E. (1997) *Peer Instruction: A User's Manual*, Upper Saddle River, New Jersey: Prentice Hall.

Petty, G. (2004) *Teaching Today: A Practical Guide* (3rd edition), Cheltenham: Nelson Thornes. See also www.geoffpetty.com.

QCA (2001) 'Assessment for learning: using assessment to raise achievement in mathematics: a research report'. Download from: www.qca.org.uk/6311.html.

Sadler, R. (1989) 'Formative assessment and the design of instructional systems', *Instructional Science*, 18, 119–44.

Savinainen, A. (2001) 'An evaluation of interactive teaching methods in mechanics: using the force concept inventory to monitor student learning'. Download from: kotisivu.mtv3.fi/physics/downloads.html. This paper deals with 'peer instruction' or peer checking.

Any material you can find on assessment for learning, for example:

www.qca.org.uk/ca/5-14/afl
www.qca.org.uk/pdf.asp?/ca/5-14/afl/afl_maths.pdf
www.pdkintl.org/kappan/kbla9810.htm
www.qca.org.uk/ca/5-14/afl

20 Methods for the 'review' and homework phases

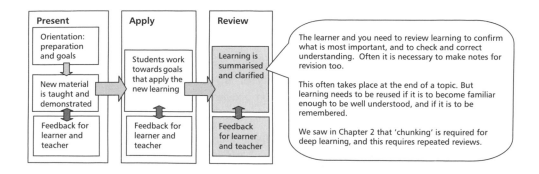

Present	Apply	Review
Orientation: preparation and goals		
	Students work towards goals that apply the new learning	Learning is summarised and clarified
New material is taught and demonstrated		
Feedback for learner and teacher	Feedback for learner and teacher	Feedback for learner and teacher

The learner and you need to review learning to confirm what is most important, and to check and correct understanding. Often it is necessary to make notes for revision too.

This often takes place at the end of a topic. But learning needs to be reused if it is to become familiar enough to be well understood, and if it is to be remembered.

We saw in Chapter 2 that 'chunking' is required for deep learning, and this requires repeated reviews.

At the end of a topic students are often confused about what is vital and what is detail. They can't see the wood for the trees. We need to ensure that their understanding is structured for it to go into permanent memory; this is one of the seven principles in Chapter 14.

It has been chilling for me in researching and writing this book to discover that in my 25 years teaching I did so many things wrong. Most teachers don't adopt the practice in this chapter, and nor did I.

Our examination of learning quality and the SOLO taxonomy has shown that students need many encounters with material in different contexts, and to use different 'spectacles' to gain the familiarity required for relational let alone for extended abstract representations.

Also, the permanent memory has an automatic mechanism for ensuring that only vital material is stored permanently. It is called forgetting. Every time something is recalled we forget it more slowly; there is no short cut to recall other than this repetition – if there were we would certainly all know about it!

It is no great surprise then that everything is reviewed six times in whole-class interactive teaching, the method that gets to the top of Hattie's table. And this does not count repetitions in revising for exams. There are reviews at the end of the lesson, at the beginning of the next lesson, after about five hours' tuition, after about 20 hours' tuition. (The obvious place for these later reviews is at the end of topics or subtopics.) Two more reviews are effected by homework, one while the topic is current, and another about a term or more later where a current homework or classwork question is contrived to review material learned very much earlier. Reviews should involve students doing it again, not you saying it again.

The aim of the methods in this chapter is to ring the changes during these six reviews and to ensure:

- *Structure:* to require students to identify the key points and key principles, and structure their understanding around these. That is, to 'see the wood for the trees' and climb the SOLO taxonomy.
- *Understanding:* to encourage students to express their understanding in their own words, and so require them to create a personal meaning.
- *Repetition.* Permanent memory usually requires at least six separate encounters with a topic. So does the familiarity with the material required for deep learning, and climbing the SOLO taxonomy.
- *Feedback:* to provide feedback, that is, a 'check and correct' for students, and you, on student understanding, and the quality of any notes students have made. This last is helped if students leave space for improvements between paragraphs and in margins.

In these days of photocopiers and intranets students writing their own notes may seem quaintly old fashioned, but it has an effect size of nearly 1.0. This is no surprise, as it is so constructivist, especially if there is a 'check and correct'. Yet teachers rarely leave time for note making in class; instead they often use the following less effective review methods.

- *You summarise.* This is useful as it shows the key points and structure of the topic, but it is not sufficient in itself. As the bullets above show, it is the *students* who must review their understanding, not you!
- *You give notes or handouts.* Both these are usually effortless for students so we should expect them not to work, and they don't. A 'good set of notes' can create an entirely illusory sense of security in both teacher and student. It is note *making* not note *taking* that works. (Your handouts have great value if an *activity* is based on them, though (see Chapter 17), and there are constructivist ways to give notes as we will see.)

If students have a good textbook, or you have some good handouts, use the 'teaching without talking' methods we saw in Chapter 17 for class activities or homeworks. These are constructivist, fun, and require little effort from you. Highlighting or underlining key points in handouts or personal copies of books is an excellent activity, for example.

Many teachers complain that their students can't make notes. However, the solution to this problem is not for students to file unread handouts or dictation, but to *teach* note making as described in Chapter 21 and under 'Building understanding: analysis' in Chapter 24.

So leave time for note making; it is central to understanding, to learning and to work, and while they are doing it, look over their shoulders to get feedback for yourself. Don't be put off by the bad notes you will certainly see; just get students to improve them with feedback methods as described below. Students only get to make good notes by first creating bad ones; constructivism tells us so, and so does the SOLO taxonomy. This is true of notes in particular, and notes in general.

The methods that follow can be used for any of the six reviews mentioned above, but the first ones are especially useful in lessons.

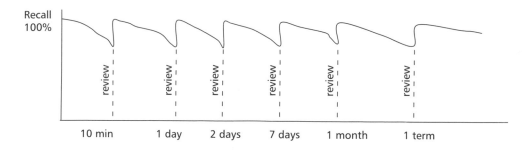

Note the irregular time scale on this graph, which shows how we forget over time.

Students making notes (effect size 0.99)

The effect size is from Marzano *et al.* (2001), and it is one of the highest he reports. In Chapter 22 we will look at Paul Ayres' research into the classroom practice of teachers whose students are in the top 1 per cent of attainment in 'value added' terms. Many of these teachers were found to use 'question-based note making', and 'note making as homework' described below. They ensure that points made by students in discussions or presentations are noted on the board as the ideas occur. Then they start student note making by turning to these and probing any deficiencies: 'What's missing . . . ?' After this discussion students create their own notes.

Marzano does not give separate effect sizes for different note-making strategies, but here are some to try; most include feedback to learner and teacher, which has a high effect size and is vital for such a difficult skill.

Mathematics teachers can ask students to write at least some notes in the form of worked examples with the students' own annotations. These can explain how the example was done, and why the method is mathematically valid. Most teachers require more than this, though; mathematics is more than a set of calculation tricks.

Reviewing and making notes in class time

Question-based note making and other structured note-making methods

Ask a key question or two at the beginning of the lesson or topic, as described in 'Setting goals at the start of the lesson' in Chapter 16. Focus your teaching on these questions, discuss them in class, and ensure that useful ideas are written on the board as they occur, by you or by your students. You can now discuss the board notes, ask questions to improve them, and students can use the questions and the board notes as a basis to write their own notes. Remember it is not the notes that are effective so much as the *process of making them*, so it is worth leaving class time for this. You can always cover the detail you had to miss out with 'Reading review as a homework: adding the detail' which is described below.

> *You could use past-paper questions or questions in exam style as a basis for this method.*

Rather than use questions you can structure notes around key points, advance organisers or graphic organisers if you prefer. However, it often helps to give students a structure of some kind to avoid omissions. You can use snowballing as described below with any of these structured note-making methods.

Teacher makes notes with class participation

This works well after snowballing, but with a good group can be done by itself.

You ask students for a key point or a first sentence for a note, and ask questions until this is well formulated and explained, assertive questioning style (Chapter 15). Then you write it up on the board in the students' words as far as possible. Students copy this. Then you ask for the next point, and so on. Use nominees rather than volunteers.

Creating graphic organisers and other visual notes (effect size 1.2)

Graphic organisers (Chapter 10) are a powerful note-making device, and may suffice for many topics, or students can add a bit of text to explain them. You can provide an 'empty' graphic as an advance organiser for students to complete; you can ask them to turn the lesson into a specific graphic such as a flow diagram or decision tree.

Eventually you should be able to ask them to produce their own visual representation so that they learn to choose the most appropriate sort.

Students really enjoy looking at each other's visual notes, so if you set it for homework, ask students to leave their graphic on their desk and to wander round the class to see everyone else's. Or they can present them to the class more formally. Anticipating this makes students more motivated to complete homework. After they have seen each other's ask them to improve their own.

They can also be asked to create posters, leaflets and graphics for Powerpoint or websites, etc., the advantage of which is that they can be shared online.

Snowballing

- You ask individuals to write key points with explanatory notes for each one, leaving plenty of space for improvement between paragraphs and in margins. If students find this difficult then *give* them key points or key questions, and ask them to write a note for each.
- Students get together in pairs to compare their notes and to improve them.
- Pairs get into fours and again notes are compared and improved.

- You ask the groups of four for their key points one point at a time, and for their explanation of each one. Nominate group members rather than asking for volunteers. You can then comment on what was missed, leave time for the class to improve their notes on this point, then move to the next point, and so on.

Reading review in class

You provide students with a handout which summarises the lesson, and students highlight or underline the key points, and then you check what they have highlighted and discuss. See the 'teaching without talking' method described on page 216. This could be snowballed as above.

Reviewing with a graphic organiser

You give students an advance organiser in graphic form (see Chapters 10 and 16), and at the end of the lesson you go back to this and ask students what they can recall about each part. After discussion you leave students a few minutes to write about it in their own words, or to add detail to their version of the organiser. You then do the same with the next part of the organiser, and so on.

Students then improve their notes by some method described below.

Reviewing and bridging skills

As we will see in Chapter 21, a good lesson will have involved students using a skill as well as learning content. This skill needs to be reviewed, preferably with the killer questions 'How did you do that?' and 'Where else could you use that skill?'

Glossary sheets and principle sheets

You give students a handout, or perhaps a poster in class, which lists the main technical terms, or the main (subject) principles you are teaching. This is for the whole course or unit, not just the class. Space is left for students to write explanations for each. These are best done in pencil as students will often be able to improve on these as they progress.

It is useful to have occasional tests or quizzes where students must recall the vocabulary and principles and give examples.

Reviews of practical lessons

I expect you use this already. After the practical activity students gather round one student's piece of work. The class uses this to go over what they did and why. Students learning practical skills will benefit from making notes after such a discussion, and recalling the lesson in a question and answer session at the beginning of the next.

Reviewing and note making out of class

The methods that follow are additional to reviewing and note making in class, rather than a substitute for it. They are great ways to help achieve six separate encounters with the material.

	Effect size of homework	
Students aged 9–11	0.15	Effect sizes from Marzano
Students aged 12–14	0.31	
Students aged 15–17	0.64	
Homework (all ages) with no comment or grade	0.28	
Homework (all ages) with teacher's comments as feedback	0.83	
Reading (all ages) (average of 14,945 studies)	0.58	Effect sizes from Hattie
Homework (all ages) (average of 568 studies)	0.41	

Marzano states that homework should have a clear purpose, be meaningful, be related to course aims, and should not involve parents! I expect the high effect size for the teacher's comments as feedback on homework might also apply to self- and peer assessment.

Note-making as a homework

You give students a homework along the lines of 'Read X and highlight all the evidence about Y, then develop your own set of notes.' Handouts or books can be used for this activity, which improves literacy and study skills as well as content learning. Before using this method for homework you could use it in class, as described in Chapter 17 (page 216), and develop students' 'analysis' skills as described in Chapters 24 and 21.

Reading review as a homework: adding the detail

You give students a handout that includes the detail you didn't have time to cover in class. The students are asked to read and highlight the most important points in the text; these should have come out in the lesson. However, they will also learn the detail, and how this relates to the key points. I know it is used on many courses that get some of the best results in their subject nationally.

Back-page summary
This is a variant that I use myself all the time. Ask students to print off a specific file or web page from the Internet or intranet, read it, and highlight/underline it. Then ask them to write a summary of the key points in their own words on the back.

You ask the class what they have highlighted at the beginning of the next lesson and correct. You can put your own highlighted/annotated handout version online, and they can compare this with their own. They can also print your version off and use it as an authoritative note for revision.

If you have too much content and too little time, like most of us, this approach solves many problems, and makes time for active learning in class time.

Studying worked examples

In mathematics or similar subjects ask students to study and annotate a few worked examples provided by you, explaining each step, and to prepare to peer explain them at the beginning of the next class. They could annotate a textbook example if the book is their own, or if they use sticky message pads.

Teaching without talking methods as homework

You can't talk to students when they are at home, so many of the teaching without talking methods we considered in Chapter 17 make excellent homeworks. For example, students could be asked to produce a graphic organiser from a text file or a website. This is an excellent opportunity to add detail to students' understanding, and to get students to make use of your ILT resources, and to learn their way round your intranet site. If you like this, see 'Independent learning' in Chapter 17.

Feedback: making your reviews and homeworks formative

Some of the methods above are at least partly formative (focused on improvement). Below are some more deliberately formative methods. Ask students to leave two or three lines at the end of each paragraph, and a wide margin for amendments to handwritten notes. Graphic organisers and laptop notes are easier to add to and amend.

You need feedback too! Note making is a most effective and productive class activity, which most students value, and it gives you a chance to look over shoulders and see what people are taking down, or not.

Students compare their notes with criteria, or with a model

After students have made notes, give them model notes, or a graphic organiser, or some criteria provided by you, such as key points, or questions that their notes should answer. Then leave students some time to use this to review and improve their notes. This is self-assessment, and it makes a great homework.

You could also use peer assessment; this works well if you are trying to improve note-making skills. Preferably after the self-assessment process above, ask students to peer assess each other's notes using your key points, questions or model. Useful criteria to help peer assessment are: does it give 'the truth, the whole truth and nothing but the truth?' That is, are the notes accurate, complete, and without error?

If you provide model notes or a graphic your students will want to keep them. So make sure you don't use this method all the time, as students will often make poor notes, knowing yours are coming.

Other feedback review methods

Chapter 19 has many active feedback methods that can easily be used for review and for homework, for example 'Formative tests and quizzes', 'Peer assessment with model answers' and 'Student questioning and mountain climbing'. See also 'Study-cover-recall-check' in *Teaching Today*, page 260.

Don't forget homework tasks that require students to use learning done a term or more ago.

References and further reading

Marzano, R., Pickering, D. and Pollock, J. (2001) *Classroom Instruction That Works*, Alexandria, Virginia: ASCD.

Petty, G. (2004) *Teaching Today: A Practical Guide* (3rd edition), Cheltenham: Nelson Thornes.

Part 6 Teaching intelligence

21 Teaching thinking skills and intelligence

The content trap

Weak teachers spend almost all their time teaching content; thinking skills are relatively ignored. They teach the easy stuff and ignore the hard. Teaching both skills *and* content gets much better results!

Have a look at the diagram on the next page. Some teachers have an exclusively 'content focused' approach. They determine what content needs to be taught and cram their teaching time with this. But the assessment requires thinking skills, such as the ability to present a coherent and justified argument, as well as knowledge of the content. Their students have not been taught how to do this directly, and so some do badly. Teachers then attribute the poor performance of their students to low intelligence. But the real problem is that they taught the easy stuff, and ignored the hard.

Compare this with best practice. The teacher determines the content, but also the subject-specific thinking and writing skills required for assessment success: 'generic skills'. Much teaching time is spent on content, but at least 20 per cent of the time is dedicated to teaching subject-specific thinking skills.

By 'thinking skills' I mean, for example, analysis, problem solving, critical thinking, creative thinking, study skills, and the ability to create and express a coherent and well-justified argument. These skills are partly subject specific and so include, for

---

It is not knowledge but these skills that are the true legacy of any education. They are priceless because they are 'transferable'. Whether a student ends up as an MP, a nurse, a garage manager, or hiring out paddle-boats in a holiday camp, he or she will need all or most of these skills to some extent. Knowledge, by comparison, is only useful if relevant to the task. Aged 10 I was taught the chief exports of Peru; I have never needed to use this knowledge, and I am now out of date. But the skills listed in the above para-graph I have used practically every day of my life. Now the thinking skills that enable us to adapt and to learn are even more vital than they ever were – because most people change jobs many times in their lifetime, and even if they don't, their job changes around them.

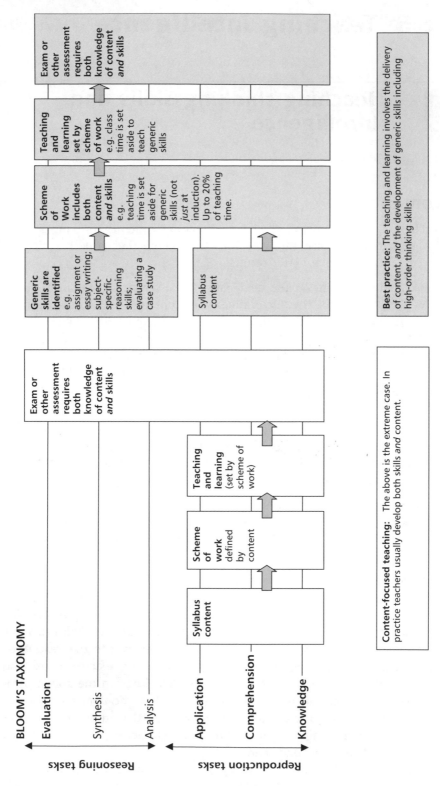

The content trap.

example, the ability to use the scientific method, or to critically appraise a poem. I will include the ability to write in this chapter too.

Knowledge is nearly always a means to an end; it is only helpful when relevant to our thinking. But is thinking teachable? Doesn't it just depend on intelligence?

Let me warn you that recent research on this challenges many of our culture's most deeply held assumptions about learning and ability. Most people, in the West, at least, believe that ability, whether this is academic, practical or artistic, for example, is mainly due to an inherited fixed attribute such as IQ, talent, or a gift such as musicality.

Our popular culture is steeped in tales of the effortless triumph of gifted individuals. When David Beckham was told by an interviewer that he was born with an astonishing gift for taking free kicks, he was most affronted. No, Beckham explained, his skill was due to intense practice. He had spent many hours a day trying to hit distant poles by kicking footballs at them. Patiently he explained that if you do this for three hours a day, after ten years you get quite good at it.

There is a well-known anecdote, true according to my father who was a keen fan, that the famous golfer Lee Travino holed a very long putt and a spectator muttered within his hearing 'You lucky sod!' 'That's right,' replied Travino. 'And it's a funny thing – the more I practise the luckier I get.'

There probably *are* genetic factors affecting performance; many psychologists believe that intelligence is partly heritable, for example. If so there is *some* truth to the talent myth, but we will see that genetic factors are dwarfed by the effect of practice. Let's look at the evidence; this is rigorous evidence with control groups and so on. I only have space to sketch this out; you can get more detail on each source of evidence below from my website (see 'References and further reading' below).

Evidence that ability is learned not inherited

Twin studies

Steven Pinker is a strong advocate of the influence of genes upon psychology. In 'Why nature and nurture won't go away' (2004) he considers the research on identical twins reared together. These share both 'nature' (genes) and nurture (very similar upbringing, friends, etc.). He explains that the correlation between the characteristics of such twins is about 0.5. Statistically, this means that nature and nurture *together* only explain about 25 per cent of why each twin turned out as they did. Pinker says it's anybody's guess what the other 75 per cent is due to, but he suggests accidental factors, and hints at individuals following their own interests and learning. For example, one twin might hear someone playing the guitar, like it, and learn. Later that twin may have

nature + nurture	learning?
learning?	learning?

What makes you what you are

become more 'musical' than the 'identical' twin. Remember that constructivism shows that characteristics will often be in the form of neural connections made by the individuals themselves.

Feuerstein's instrumental enrichment

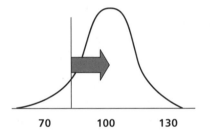

Reuven Feuerstein's methods are used in over 30 countries. Children with moderate learning difficulties, about three years behind their peers and with an IQ of about 70 to 80, are individually taught a specially devised two-year programme for one hour a day. After four years they have caught up with their peers and have a normal intelligence. They no longer have learning difficulties, of course, and can live a normal life. One student came to Feuerstein aged 14 unable to give him the days of the week and with behaviour difficulties. He is now a professor. How can intelligence be innate if about 80 hours' individual tuition can add 20 or 30 points to it? The control group also had individual tuition, of course, and did not show the same improvement, so it was what Feuerstein *did* that made the difference, and he taught thinking skills.

Cognitive acceleration

Professors Philip Adey and Michael Shayer have set up 'cognitive acceleration' programmes in schools to improve thinking skills, based in part on Feuerstein's methods. A thinking skills programme in science increased students' GCSE scores in mathematics and even in English by about a grade (Adey and Shayer 1994). The students were learning intelligence. It used to be thought that thinking skills were pretty much fixed by early adolescence, but neural physiologists now believe that thinking ability continues to develop well into early adolescence.

Research review on excellence

K. Anders Ericsson reviewed research on people with exceptional ability in academia, athletics, music, chess, typing and in many other domains. He found that innate ability played little part in such excellence; for example, he concluded that intelligence only accounted for 5 per cent of an academic's career attainment. Why is this?

When most of us learn a skill we begin on a steep learning curve; think for example, of when you learned to teach. But after a period of time we get reasonably competent: there is no blood on the walls after the lessons, and students seem to learn something. 'Great', many of us think, 'next lesson I'll do it the same way', and we continue to use the same strategies. But this makes a skill 'plateau', as the graph shows, because we don't learn as much in familiar territory as we do in unfamiliar territory.

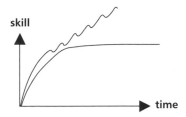

Ericsson looked at all the good research into people who had developed exceptional skills, and found that their secret was that they didn't plateau like this. They were always experimenting, always curious about what lay in unfamiliar territory, and were always getting out of their 'comfort zone' and doing it a different way. If this meant that they did a worse job because they were using unfamiliar methods, they didn't mind. They kept practising this method until they made it work, or until they knew that it wouldn't. Then they experimented with another improvement, and so on.

He summed up this finding by saying that in all fields, exceptional ability was learned through *deliberate practice*, by which he meant not just 'doing it again', but learners getting out of their 'comfort zone' and taking on a challenging goal to improve. Exceptional ability is learned. (See Ericsson *et al.* 1993.)

Let's look at an example from music, a domain where many believe talent plays a crucial part. Researchers studied 40 violinists at the internationally renowned Berlin Music Academy. The violinists were put into three categories, based on the opinion of their professors: the *best*, the *good*, and those studying to become violin *teachers* (!). They were all the same age, and they all spent about 50 hours a week on music.

When the researchers interviewed the violinists they found that *deliberate practice* was considered paramount by all, but despite this ranged from 24 hours per week for the best violinists to nine hours a week for those training to be teachers. The researchers then found the lifetime accumulated hours spent on deliberate practice for the violinists, which were:

- For future violin *teachers*   4000 hours
- For the *good* violinists   8000 hours
- For the *best* violinists   10 000 hours

It is not possible for the violin teachers to catch up because deliberate practice is so exhausting that one can only do about four to five hours a day, and the best violinists continue to practice at the maximum rate.

The 'talented' violinists had practised harder for longer. There were no examples of people so talented that they needed less practice to excel, which is what the idea of inherited talent suggests.

Of course this capacity to learn so intently, and the interest to do so, *might* be genetically endowed, but then it might not! Maslow (1971) thought that the exceptionally able have met all their other psychological needs, and so have more psychological energy to spare for 'self-actualising', that is pursuing their passions and interests.

This is not to say that genes play no part, but pitch a chess player with an IQ of 130 against another with an IQ of 100 and the brighter player may lose if he or she is less practised. Expert children often beat adults at chess, and at computer games!

Ability and talent surely exist, but they are largely learned, and this puts a huge responsibility on us as teachers. But *how* can we teach the thinking skills listed at the beginning of this chapter?

Skills are learned by corrected practice

Skills are a process that has been learned, often as a set of practised sub-skills. For example, Palinscar and Brown (1984) found that 10–12-year-olds who make spontaneous use of skills such as underlining, taking notes of important points, and drafting and redrafting while studying, perform as well as 16–17 year olds. Conversely, 16–17 year olds who fail to make use of such strategies produce work that looks like that of a 10-year-old. It is strategy that creates quality. However, these strategies will not be used effectively until they have been practised, with feedback: like everything else they are learned by corrected practice.

Some skills, such as creative or critical thinking, involve strategies that are not as simple as underlining, but strategies are used nonetheless. If these are made explicit, and taught directly, anyone can improve their performance. We will consider how in the next chapter.

Sports coaches know well that skill comes from using the right strategy or *process*. When teaching skills such as swimming, or serving at tennis, they concentrate almost exclusively on process: 'Bend your knees more'; 'Watch the ball'. They pay much *less* attention to the *product* – whether the ball was hit hard, or was in or out. That comes, once the process is right.

In contrast, poor teachers of academic skills often concentrate on *product*, what the student wrote, for example, rather than *process*, how it was planned and drafted. This is a mistake. Such teachers often fail to teach the processes involved in thinking and writing, and then attribute their students' poor performance to low intelligence.

Describe the **PROCESS** you expect students to use on a one-page handout if this will help them e.g. write a handout on how to plan an essay	Describe the **PRODUCT** you expect students to produce, i.e. the qualities and characteristics of good work
Use: • flow diagrams and/or mind maps of the process planning proformas, e.g. 'writing frames' to assist students (see examples on www.geoffpetty.com) student self assessment on how they use this process • write assignment tasks in terms of this process, e.g. set proofreading etc. as an assignment task teach the process explicitly, giving yourself time to check work in progress and give feedback induction activities	Use: • assessment criteria • self-assessment, teacher assessment (or both) against the assessment criteria • assessment proformas or competences • use the above to develop targets for improvement, feed-forward tasks, action plans, etc. • examples of good practice • examples of bad practice • activities to evaluate examples of moderate performance, e.g. students criticise an essay

Skills need a good deal of corrected practice. Look at the graph on page 288 again. Marzano (2001) quotes research from cognitive psychology showing that a skill that can be mastered might take five practice attempts to get to 50 per cent attainment, and 24 attempts to get to 80 per cent attainment. Skills take time.

...at skills do I need to teach?

This of course depends on the subject and level you teach, it helps to study examining body documents, syllabuses, past papers, examiner's reports, and marking schemes, but the box below gives a few examples from a vast field.

SKILLS YOU MAY NEED TO TEACH

Information gathering

- *Independent learning:* research skills, asking relevant questions, skim reading, using book index and contents, search skills on the Internet, etc.

Building understanding: analysis ('what' and 'why' questions)

- *Close reading/observation:* thoughtful attention to establish key points and key principles. Highlighting, interpreting, comparing, classifying, summarising. Distinguishing fact, belief and values.
- *Conceptualisation:* using examples and non-examples and similarities and differences between examples and concepts, e.g. percentages and fractions.
- *Analysis by section and spectacles* to describe the key points, empathy.
- *Explaining skills:* explaining why with multiple representations including diagrams, mind maps, posters, visualisations, etc., to summarise a topic. Relating ideas to general principles.

Productive thinking: synthesis, creativity, and evaluation ('how' questions and evaluative questions)

- *Writing* essays assignments and reports, and creative writing, etc.
- *Responding to a design brief,* or creating an ordered plan of work in engineering, art, computer programming, carpentry, etc.
- *Problem solving,* including 'question typing', i.e. 'How should I do this question, by momentum, energy, or Newton's Laws?' How to proceed when the solution is not evident, e.g. in mathematics.
- *Particular assessment tasks:* giving a presentation; précis, comprehension questions, data analysis, critical appraisal of an experiment, etc. This includes responding appropriately to assessment language, e.g. distinguishing between, and being able to identify, describe, analyse, evaluate, etc.
- *Generating and testing hypotheses:* see box below.
- *Opinion forming,* connecting ideas into a meaningful whole. Generalising, inferring, predicting and then testing opinion by the *coherence* of the ideas, by checking the *evidence,* and by comparing the opinion with alternatives. Arguing from facts, beliefs and values.

Strategic and reflective thinking
- *Critical thinking skills:* the ability to evaluate or critically appraise an argument, policy, case study, poem, experiment, mathematical procedure or piece of creative writing. This includes dispositions or traits such as humility, fairness, courage, empathy, integrity, perseverance, etc.
- *Epistemological awareness:* i.e. to know how one approaches truth in a particular subject. For example: using appropriate methods of inquiry; testing hypotheses and other ideas by looking at the evidence, and by checking the coherence of the ideas. This is especially associated with the very best teaching, as we will see in Chapters 22 and 24.
- *Learning to learn*
- *Reflection:* annotating work in an art and design portfolio, writing a reflective journal
- *Proofreading for errors, drafting and redrafting*

Affective and social skills
- *Practising mature behaviour:* role play, identifying features of mature behaviour
- *Interviewing* a new client, and devising suitable questions for an interview
- *Valuing and respecting others, even when they are not like you:* demonstrating respect during a discussion.

This is not a comprehensive list; if you are always complaining that students can't/won't/never do something . . . then this is probably a skill that needs more teaching.

Skills are even stored in a different part of the brain. Procedural 'skills' are stored in the neostiatum, whereas declarative 'knowledge' is stored in the hippocampus. Biggs argues that declarative knowledge (knowledge 'that' and 'why') is no use if you don't have procedural knowledge of when and how to use it.

See also the box on 'Generating and testing hypotheses' in Chapter 18 (page 239).

Research reviews on study skills

Hattie, Biggs and Purdie (1996) carried out a very thorough metastudy (study of studies) into the effectiveness of study skills programmes. These programmes interpret 'study skills' widely, to include how to plan writing in ways that encourage

WHAT SKILLS DO I NEED TO TEACH?

These all require the students to use high-order reasoning on material that has been presented to them, and they have a high effect size so it is worth considering the options:

Testing hypotheses directly

You give students some basic ideas and principles, for example about how photosynthesis in plants works (e.g. that it requires light), and students work out ways of testing these ideas. They devise an experiment and carry this test out. Students need to state their hypothesis clearly.

Once they get better at doing this they can begin to formulate their own hypotheses and test them. You may need to check their method of testing before they start on it.

Historical investigation

Students create a hypothesis and then collect evidence for and against it; for example: 'Criticisms of the Vietnam War in the USA were due to an increasing belief that it could not be won rather than economic cost, or a high rate of casualties.'

'What would happen if . . .?' questions

For example, you teach students about a government system to improve employment and then give them questions in a 'What would happen if . . . ?' format. Students must produce a reasoned response using their knowledge of the system, e.g. 'What would happen if inflation increased?'

Problem solving

Students suggest a solution and test it or get feedback on their ideas in some other way.

Literary critique

Students test a hypothesis such as 'D.H. Lawrence's *Sons and Lovers* is an indictment of the working-class males of his time' by using evidence from the text.

Invention

Students use their knowledge, e.g. of quality systems, in order to devise a new one for a particular novel context.

Decision making

Students use their knowledge to make a challenging decision.

critical thinking. An analysis of the study skills programmes that most increased student achievement led to these conclusions:

- Study skills are best taught by integrating them into the programme rather than as a separate module taught at the start.
- Students learn skills best by using them to complete real tasks.
- Students should be taught not just *what* to do, but also *how* and *why*. The *purpose* of the skills should be stressed so that students also know *when* to use the skill.
- They should be taught to use all the skills together, in a combined way rather than only separately.
- Students should *reflect* (self assess) on how well they use the skills, what gains they were getting, etc., then *action plan for improvement*. (This 'metacognition' was a marked characteristic of the study skills programmes that worked best.)

The mean effect size of this integrated approach was 0.77, while teaching study skills 'up front' gave an average of 0.45. These effect sizes don't describe how well the study skills themselves were learned, but how much the study skills programme had increased the students' attainment.

Which study skills increased achievement most?

The research review managed to isolate the effectiveness of different topics on study skills programmes. The following two topics had the greatest effect.

Attribution training (effect size 0.96 to 1.42!)

'Positive attribution training' is teaching students to attribute their success to effort, time, practice, using the right strategy, asking for help, and other factors *in* their control, and not to ability, luck, or other factors *outside* their control. Dweck's theory of motivation considered this (see Chapter 2). 'Positive attribution' can be taught directly, as it was on these study skills programmes, but it can also be learned indirectly through self-, peer and spoof assessment. See Chapters 15 and 19 on feedback and feedback methods.

The 1.42 effect size is the 'within programme' effect. That is, if you teach students to attribute success to effort etc. on a geography course, then the effect on their geography results is 1.42 – almost three grades. However, this benefit transfers to other subjects as well, with an effect size of 0.96, nearly two grades. These are very large effects indeed, and suggest that learners don't believe they can improve their skills, and that they can nevertheless be taught otherwise. In short, Dweck's theory of motivation, which deals with attribution directly, needs to be taken very seriously indeed, in skills learning especially.

Attribute their success to effort.

Structural aids (effect size 0.58)

Another strategy that had a large effect was 'structural aids'; these are strategies that show the *structure* and *meaning* of what is being learned. Students need to be taught how to use these, along with when and why they are used. Structural aids include skills such as:

- extracting the key points from the content being studied; this includes physically highlighting, underlining, or otherwise annotating text
- 'concept mapping' (or mind mapping, spider diagrams, etc.) (i.e. the graphic organisers described in Chapter 10)
- 'advance organisers', where students are told in advance what they will learn in a lesson or unit (see Chapter 16)
- note-making skills (see Chapter 20)
- summary writing, etc. (see Chapter 20).

Marzano also finds very high effect sizes for these methods.

How were study skills taught on the most effective programmes?

First you need to identify the study and thinking skills required for success in your subject (see the examples on page 290). Hattie, Biggs and Purdie (1996) found that the most effective strategy for teaching these skills was:

- Students are taught the importance of these skills and how to use them.

- Students self-assess how effectively they use these study skills; teacher assessment may also help. The students then work on the aspect of a study skill they find most difficult. This self-assessment can take place before, during or after the main instruction on study skills.

- Students learn the skills actively. They actually do it, they don't just hear about how it should be done.

- The different skills such as skim reading, note taking, highlighting, mind mapping, etc., are 'orchestrated' to the demands of the particular task and context. They are not just taught and used independently.

- The student takes control and chooses which technique to use when and why, while maintaining a clear sense of purpose. The use of skills is directed towards the subject-specific task(s), for example studying a handout or writing an assignment or essay.

- Students are required to self-monitor, self-assess and self-regulate their use of these skills, setting themselves targets for experimentation and improvement. This is called 'metacognition' and is given a heavy emphasis in this review. The effect sizes of strategies that require metacognition are nearly twice as high as those that do not. Metacognition in the *study skill*, say note making, is of course quite separate from the content the student is learning (what is in the notes).

- The very best programmes use bridging (see below) to encourage transfer of what students have learned to other aspects of their study. For example, students taught to improve their note making in biology might be asked to consider their note making in other subjects, and the importance of isolating key points and principles in study generally.

The constructivist approach to teaching skills

We have seen that metacognition and learning general principles are important in the learning of study skills. There follow two great ways to do this.

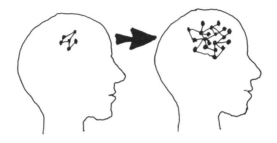

The basic idea behind these approaches is constructivist. The aim is to improve each student's present ideas about how to perform the study skill, rather than simply to teach them a new way to do it. The trouble with teaching students new strategies alongside their existing weak strategies is that they will often revert to their better-practised bad habits when they forget, or are under stress in exams. So we need to teach good habits, but also to 'unteach' the bad habits, to improve present constructs rather than simply develop new ones. Snowballing and bridging are great ways to do this, and both also develop the 'metacognition' that the review of research on study skills found so vital.

Snowballing

We have looked at this in Chapter 17, and it is advocated by Graham Gibbs in his seminal *Teaching Students to Learn* (1981) to teach such study skills as note making, writing, reading, preparing for examinations, and 'organising yourself'.

Suppose you were teaching note making. The snowball approach would be to get students to do some note making in a real lesson. Then:

1. In pairs, students look at each other's notes to find 'good' and 'bad' points.
2. Pairs combine into fours, and each student explains the good and bad points of his or her original partner.
3. The teacher hears feedback from each group of four on what is best practice.
4. The teacher corrects any misconceptions or bad practice and summarises best practice.
5. Students as individuals use this model of best practice to set themselves action plans for improvement.
6. Students do some more note making in the next lesson, implementing the action plan. They review their notes against best practice and set themselves another target, and so on.

If you are teaching a challenging study skill such as 'organising yourself' Gibbs suggests that you can begin the snowballing by asking individual students to tick off which statements they agree or disagree with from a list including such views as:

- I often seem to leave things like essays till the last minute.
- I find it hard to get down to work.
- I don't seem to be able to stick at a task (like reading through a chapter) for very long.
- I don't find it easy to talk to others openly about how much work I'm doing.
- I'm never quite sure what I've got to do next.
- I'm generally behind, sometimes several weeks behind schedule.
- I'm not sure I always do the most important things first.

'Bridging': a powerful way to teach skills

'Bridging' is a central plank in Feuerstein's teaching methodology, and of 'cognitive acceleration' programmes. A case could be made for this being one of the most powerful teaching strategies known.

Feuerstein thought that the main reason students didn't learn skills was that their brains are so swamped by the immediacy of the concrete experience that they fail to abstract general principles from the experience. So if students have just completed an essay on magnetism, for example, their focus both during the writing process and in reviewing it afterwards is the detailed facts about magnetism. Often the teacher's feedback is similarly concrete and 'product focused'. This focus on the detail of immediate experience, and on the product rather than the process, obscures the general principles of how to write a good essay. We need to shift the focus from product to process.

Student focus while learning:		The focus required to learn skills:
The product they make		Which skills and strategies they used
The topic/subject/content	⟹	The process they used for each skill
Their immediate concrete experience		The general principles in using skills
		How to improve

How to use bridging

Bridging takes place *after* the student has completed a task successfully, no matter how much help was given. Then the working memory is not flooded with product detail.

Bridging involves asking what I call Feuerstein's two 'killer questions'.

The first question, 'How did you do that?', is used to focus the learner's attention on the process used to get success. That is the strategies, skills, and general principles they used ('review' and 'learn' in the Kolb cycle shown).

The second killer question is 'Where else could you use this process?' Subsequent discussion encourages the learner to see the *widest possible* application of these skills. The session ends with the learner committing to improve their use of the skills in a future task ('apply' and 'do' in the cycle).

> *Joanne Miles, a teacher trainer in London, tells me that when she sets a demanding assignment she asks the class to plan what they will do to complete it, giving times for each stage. This has meant that most early assignments on her course are completed in time. Later she withdraws this support, expecting students to plan independently.*

Stepping through the process and bridging: a case study

A natural way to teach a skill, and unteach bad habits, is by 'stepping' through the process for that skill. Then bridging can be used to show how and where that process can be used.

Let's look at an example of stepping and bridging being used to improve students' report writing on a level 2 health and social care course.

First the students are given an assignment or brief to write a report. This is a real assignment. It requires them to write about the activities that take place in a local health centre. First the teacher uses Socratic questioning to get the students to *step through* the process of writing a report.

Teacher   What shall we do first?
Student 1   Get some information, we need to visit and . . .

Teacher   Hang on, is that the *first* thing we need to do?

Student 2   No, we need to read the assignment brief first.

Teacher   Well done, Cindy. *Read the brief.* Why do you think that is important?

Student 2   Because we need to think it all through, what we have to do. Think out what we want before we get the information.

Teacher   Good. We need to know what we have to do before we start doing it. What would happen if we *didn't* read the brief before we started?

Student 3   We might do the wrong thing. Like not do task 4 about the diagram.

Teacher   Good. So let's look at the brief we are given. What does this report need to include?

Later:

Teacher   OK, so we've read and understood the brief. What should we do next?

Student 4   Go on the Internet.

Student 3   No, not yet . . .

In this way the teacher steps the students through the whole process of researching and writing the report. If the students are stronger you can of course step through the whole process before starting work on any of it. Alternatively you can do as described above and complete each part of the process, then ask 'What should we do next?'

Eventually the students have written their report. They will have done a reasonable job because they used the right process. You give the work back marked and students read their comments. Most teachers would think it was all over, but this is where Feuerstein tells us to roll our sleeves up and get on with the real work to transfer the skills. The bridging begins:

Teacher   So we have just completed our first report, and everyone at least passed, some even got merits. We are going to have to write quite a few reports like this. So let's see what we can learn from the experience. How did we go about writing that report?

Student 3   We visited the centre and . . .

Teacher   Hang on. Was that the first thing we did?

Student 4   No. We did our plan.

Teacher   How did we write the plan, Michael?

Student 4   We read the brief and decided what we needed to know then we like, did our plan.

Teacher   What shall we call this process? I'll give you a minute in pairs to think of a title for it.

The class agrees to call it 'Read, think and plan'.

Teacher   What would have happened if we *hadn't* done a 'read think and plan'?

Student 5   We wouldn't have done tasks 3 and 4 and we would have done some stuff we didn't have to, like write about how many rooms it had and things.

Teacher   Right. So it saves us time, and makes sure we don't have to resubmit. And what did we do after 'Read think and plan'?

(etc.)

The teacher encourages the students to justify and write up the process in the most general way possible. This results in a process help sheet like that shown below.

Once a process is understood and agreed then it can be used for self-assessment, as well as for target setting: 'I need to take more care with proof reading'. See www.geoffpetty.com/genericskills.html, where there is a proforma for this, and help sheets, writing frames, self-assessment proformas, etc., on page 6 of 'Approaches to generic skills teaching'. These are mainly focused on writing, *but any process can be taught this way*.

The next chapter describes processes for analysis, creativity and problem solving, and evaluation.

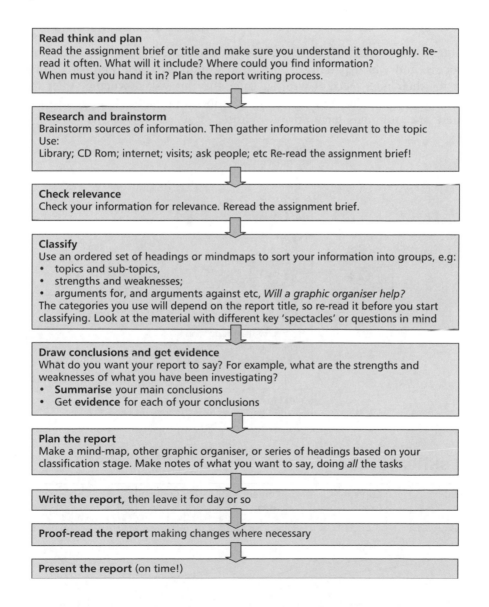

Read think and plan
Read the assignment brief or title and make sure you understand it thoroughly. Re-read it often. What will it include? Where could you find information? When must you hand it in? Plan the report writing process.

Research and brainstorm
Brainstorm sources of information. Then gather information relevant to the topic Use:
Library; CD Rom; internet; visits; ask people; etc Re-read the assignment brief!

Check relevance
Check your information for relevance. Reread the assignment brief.

Classify
Use an ordered set of headings or mindmaps to sort your information into groups, e.g:
• topics and sub-topics,
• strengths and weaknesses;
• arguments for, and arguments against etc, *Will a graphic organiser help?*
The categories you use will depend on the report title, so re-read it before you start classifying. Look at the material with different key 'spectacles' or questions in mind

Draw conclusions and get evidence
What do you want your report to say? For example, what are the strengths and weaknesses of what you have been investigating?
• **Summarise** your main conclusions
• Get **evidence** for each of your conclusions

Plan the report
Make a mind-map, other graphic organiser, or series of headings based on your classification stage. Make notes of what you want to say, doing *all* the tasks

Write the report, then leave it for day or so

Proof-read the report making changes where necessary

Present the report (on time!)

Teaching intelligence

Weaker students may think that this process works well for writing reports on health centres only! So to complete the bridging the teacher asks the last killer question:

Teacher Where else could we use this process?
Student 1 For writing the other module 3 reports?
Teacher Certainly. Anywhere else?
Student 2 It's a bit like essay writing isn't it?
Student 3 And key skills what we do with Mrs Singh on Friday . . .

The teacher leads the discussion to get as general a use of the process as possible, including use of parts of the process such as 'clarify the brief', which is as relevant in practical work as it is in written. We have stepped up the SOLO hierarchy to 'extended abstract', and the lesson has become almost infinitely transferable.

The bridging could finish with self-assessment and target setting. Students consider the process, and which parts of it they need to improve most, and set themselves targets for their next piece of writing. Later they are asked whether their targets were achieved. These 'learning loops' are described in Chapter 43 of *Teaching Today*, and there are proformas for it on my website.

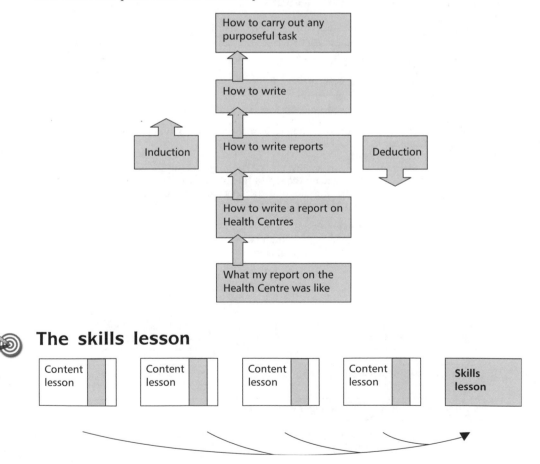

The skills lesson

This method was used by two colleges which, before using skills lessons, had amongst the best results in the country. Yet they greatly improved from this excellent position, a very difficult trick to pull off.

Solihull Sixth Form College:
History GCE A level with about 350 students a year

Before this strategy:	1995 pass rate: 81% with 46% A–C grades
After:	1998 pass rate: 94% with 67% A–C grades

Brockenhurst College:
Sociology GCE A level with about 40 students a year

Before this strategy:	1997 pass rate: 84% with 51% A–C grades
After:	1999 pass rate: 100% with 90% A–C grades

In both cases there was no change to the average GCSE score of the intake. Skills lessons could be used at any academic level, but it takes courage to reduce the time spent delivering content, so as to make room for the skills teaching. Let's explain it by example.

Suppose a history teacher teaches a string of 'content lessons' on Oliver Cromwell. These involve student activity, but the main purpose is delivering the content. Then the teacher runs a skills lesson where the students have to use a graphic organiser to plan an essay entitled 'Was Cromwell a dictator?' and present their plan to the rest of the class. This is a pure skills lesson, with *no new content*, though the content in the last four lessons is in effect reviewed.

While students plan their essay the teacher visits the groups in turn and coaches them in choice of graphic organiser, historical thinking and essay planning. 'When do you use primary, and when secondary evidence?' 'Have you considered arguments both for *and* against?' Then students present their plans and discuss their differences.

At the end of the lesson the *skill* of planning an essay is reviewed rather than the 'content' such as the details about Cromwell that came up in the lesson.

The improvement in results this strategy created at Solihull and Brockenhurst may in part be due to 'medal and mission' feedback which both colleges also employed. For more detail see www.geoffpetty.com/genericskills.html.

Both colleges created a skills curriculum and put this on their scheme of work.

Using graphic organisers as 'scaffolding' to assist writing and thinking

In Chapter 10 we saw many tables and frameworks to structure arguments and to assist thinking, note taking and extended writing. They have an effect size of about 1.2. How should you use them?

You could introduce the comparison table on page 125, for example by asking students to use it on very familiar material first. It's fun to get students to analyse their relationship with their parents, evaluate their town centre, and do a comparison table for two boyfriends or girlfriends. Don't ask them to hand this in! Alternatively they could use the table on a topic they already understand as a revision exercise.

Bruner (1977) uses the term 'scaffolding the task' to describe tables or help sheets like these being used to help writing. See www.geoffpetty.com/genericskills.html for more examples. Having used a few tables on familiar material:

- Begin by devising these tables yourself for specific tasks on new material. But explain why the design works. Make sure that crucial assessment criteria are reflected in the framework. For example, if there are marks for justifying arguments put a 'justification' column in the table.
- When you have used a few different tables, review them all focusing on their design. Give students an exercise to decide when to use which graphic organiser, help sheet or framework, etc., and how to devise these structures themselves.
- Then give them writing tasks with *no* framework or table, but require them to devise their own.
- Then give them a writing task without asking them to devise a table or other framework first. Shoot those who don't!

Eventually we need to *remove* scaffolding if students are to become independently skilful.

The double-decker lesson

When a government requirement cut the teaching time per A level, I thought that Solihull history department might drop their skills lessons. I rang Janice Evans, their head of department, but despite the cut they hadn't dropped the skills lesson; indeed she said 'all our lessons are skills lessons now'. Their 350 students a year now enjoyed a pass rate of 99 per cent with over 70 per cent of them getting A and B grades.

Their strategy is to retain the skills lesson, and in the content lessons to use 'teaching without talking' (see Chapter 17). This is an advanced approach, but any teacher could use it sometimes. Again let's see how it works by example.

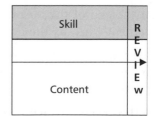

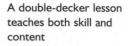

A double-decker lesson teaches both skill and content

Suppose the topic was the Nazi Party in 1930s Germany. The teacher could use many 'teaching without talking' methods, but suppose she chooses 'spectacles' as described on page 223. She introduces the Nazi Party for ten minutes at most, and then gives every student a copy of its manifesto. She puts students into groups and allocates one spectacle to each group: the church, women, middle class, working class, economic factors, and so on. Students study the manifesto using their 'spectacles' for about half an hour. During this the teacher circulates, looking at each group's ideas and challenging them to justify and improve them. Then the groups report back to the class.

All the students have studied the same document, so they can challenge each other's conclusions. The teacher uses an assertive questioning approach (See Chapter 15) where she does not give the 'answer' away if there is one, but requires the class to use historical arguments to come to an agreement if they can and to clarify their differences if they can't.

Towards the end of the lesson the class agrees key points about the Nazi Party based on the evidence in the manifesto. So far this looks like a very active content lesson. But the teacher can now review and bridge the skills used during the lesson, using Feuerstein's killer questions:

'We have just analysed a historical document: how did we do that?' (answer: we used spectacles). The teacher can then go on to explore issues such as: 'What other spectacles could we have used?' 'Which ones were most important?' 'What did we do when different spectacles created conflicting points of view?' Many other skills, for example justifying an argument, were used in the lesson and could be reviewed in this way.

This method effectively uses skills to teach content, and content to teach skills. Hattie's research shows that this is the best strategy for both!

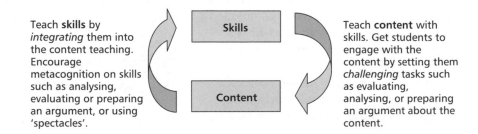

Teach **skills** by *integrating* them into the content teaching. Encourage metacognition on skills such as analysing, evaluating or preparing an argument, or using 'spectacles'.

Teach **content** with skills. Get students to engage with the content by setting them *challenging* tasks such as evaluating, analysing, or preparing an argument about the content.

Students are engaged with the content at a high cognitive level, from almost their first meeting with it. They are also learning the skill of close reading.

This method also works well for students with poor literacy skills who find it difficult to extract meaning from text. They need the practice, and as long as the text is at the right level, then this method, and other 'teaching without talking' methods, can work exceptionally well, not only to teach content and skills, but also to improve reading and literacy more generally. Experts on literacy in children, adolescents and adults all stress that literacy is improved by reading.

Help! There's too much content to teach skills as well

Teachers feel secure if they have said everything their students need to know, but this sense of security is a self-deceit if students don't understand this content, and don't know when and how to make use of it. It is not our job to 'cover' the content, but to enable students to learn it.

As we saw in Chapters 2 and 14 knowledge must be *structured* by the learner to get into permanent memory. This requires both an appreciation of what are the key facts and principles and why, as well as some experience in reasoning with the material. Reasoning is required for deep familiarity with the material, and to create relational links within the content, and between it and earlier learning. These links create a 'structure' which gives both meaning and functional learning. See the diagram in Chapter 2, page 22.

A student may be able to recite all the relevant facts about Cromwell or dental hygiene, but still be unable to harness these properly to answer an exam question, or to complete an assignment task.

If you have too much content to teach in too little time then the ideal strategy, tested in real classrooms and found to work, is to establish the structure, meaning and understanding *first* using only vital content. *Then* add the detail to this structure in a form which students can do alone. If you insist on delivering too much detail the structure is lost and the detail quickly forgotten. You have covered the material, but only in the sense of obscuring it.

 So:

- *Show the structure first*. Use advance organisers and graphic organisers, relevant recall questions, and metaphors that link the topic to what is already understood. Remind students of this throughout.
- *Deliver the content stressing the key points and key principles*. Do not overload with detail at this stage as you are developing structure and meaning first.

. . . too much detail, the structure is lost . . .

- *Check that students' understand why*. These 'why' links are the relational links that create meaning. Check also that they understand 'how' and 'when' to use this knowledge. (If there is not a use for it, why are you teaching it?)

- *Get students to reason with this content*, not just reproduce it. Then they have deep exposure to the material, and make their own meanings and relational links. (Just telling students about links doesn't work.)
- *Review the key points and key principles.*
- *Set tasks to fill in the detail.* Once students have the structure and understanding, give them assignments, essays, and especially reading and note-making homeworks to fill in the detail, and to fit this into their existing structure. Detail is learned quickly and enjoyably if students already understand the basics, not at all if they don't. See Chapter 20 and the teaching without talking methods in 17.
- *Check recall and understanding of the 'the structure'.* More than five separate encounters as a minimum are usually required for information to go into permanent memory.

The above sequence is the PAR structure mentioned throughout this book. Even if students don't fill in the detail well, or at all, they will at least have the key points and *understanding* of the topic, and so will be able to make use of what they know. If you 'cover' too much detail they will forget it, fail to understand it, and be unable to make use of it.

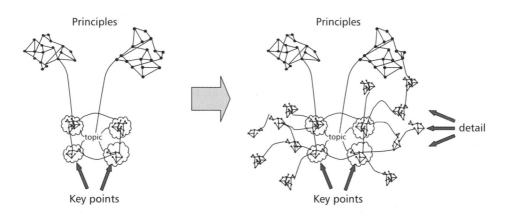

This 'fill in the detail later' strategy requires real teacher skill. What *is* the detail and what the key content? What relations are most important? What are the key principles? How are all these to be explained? What activities create understanding? This is a challenge to any teacher. However, the research in Chapters 2 and 23 points emphatically to this strategy.

Teaching skills by attention to the students' work

So far we have considered process; what about product? In Chapter 8 we looked at how assessment proformas can be used to create 'learning loops'. This is a vital aspect to skills learning with a very high effect size. If skills can be broken down into criteria such as 'gives evidence both for and against', and covers process as well as product – 'I produced a plan' – then this can improve skills greatly. Have a look a the assessment proforma download on www.geoffpetty.com/feedback.html.

Other methods to teach study and thinking skills

Backwards design

This is the most rigorous way to create a scheme of work. Look at the skills students must have at the end of their course by examining the literature from examining bodies, the assessments, by considering the 'rational curriculum' explained in Chapter 24, and/or by carefully considering the vital skills your course will develop.

Now find ways of teaching the content of the course by using and developing these skills. For example, suppose a science teacher must develop in students the ability to design an experiment. She looks over the content and considers which experiments she will 'cover', and for each one asks, 'Could they design this themselves, or at least have a stab at it?' Eventually she plans homeworks where students design an experiment the week before they do it in class. After doing their experiments the students write notes, correcting their original design where necessary. After designing four experiments students get quite good at it, and they really enjoy the task.

There is a comprehension question on every exam, so she devises comprehension activities to teach four topics. She also devises a set of comprehension competences so that students can self-assess after each activity and set themselves targets for next time.

She examines the verbs used in examinations and rewrites her classwork tasks to make use of those they might find difficult: 'annotate the diagram . . .', 'critically appraise . . .' She also changes some of her homework questions to mirror the style of questions in the exam.

Principles sheet

An important skill is to be able to use general principles in your subject such as:

'Delegation is empowering.'

'What are the rules for determining historical significance?'

'You need evidence for you point of view.'

You create the simplest handout imaginable. At the top of each sheet, a subject principle or a key question leading to such principles is stated, and the students must explain the principle and give examples, or answer the key question with examples. You can also add non-examples – situations where the principles don't apply. Students can add to each 'principle sheet' or 'key question sheet' each time an example of the principle is encountered on their course. You could make this principle sheet a poster on continuous display, which is added to through the course.

Marzano's summary on teaching thinking skills

When it comes to teaching thinking skills, most of Marzano's evidence is from the teaching of the experimental enquiry process in science. This is learning the enquiry process itself, not the knowledge gained from the experiments. This is very limited evidence, but it ties in with what we already know, so may generalise to other skills. Look at the table below and ask yourself why the 'algorithmic' approach is only about half as good as the 'heuristics' approach before reading on. An algorithm is a sequence of tasks; an example, for writing a report, is shown on page 299.

Algorithms can be devised for any complex task, such as writing a computer programme.

They are easy to teach and learn, but may not be understood deeply, and are too rigid to cope with every context. Also, they require very little metacognition, known to greatly assist skills learning. They may be followed blindly and so ineffectively in some contexts. It is a surface approach. Despite this, being simple it may be a good place to start if the skill is demanding.

We need more evidence, but in the meantime perhaps we should add metacognition such as self-assessment and target setting to algorithmic approaches, along with careful teaching of the *purpose* of each step. Having taught students an algorithm, perhaps we should move towards a more heuristic approach, as this is more adaptable and transferable than a rigid approach. An example of a heuristic approach is the diagram on page 329 'How to analyse'.

Strategy for skills teaching only	Effect size	N
Teaching algorithms: Teaching the process as a series of rigid steps	0.67	151
Teaching heuristics: This is teaching the general rules and allowing the student some trial-and-error learning of the experimental enquiry process, rather than teaching a very specific set of steps	1.17	45
Self system and processes: Teaching students how the skill (experimental enquiry process in this case) might be useful in their own lives	0.92	22
Providing feedback on the learner's use of the experimental enquiry process	0.94	43
Providing feedback when taught experimental enquiry using a heuristic approach, summary:	1.20	17
If feedback is immediate:	0.86	5
If feedback is delayed (this gives feedback *and* a review of the skill):	1.39	6

Marzano's findings also show the importance of setting clear goals; showing how the skill is important in our lives; and providing feedback. Delayed feedback works better than immediate feedback because the delay effectively means that the skill is reviewed. Delaying the reflection might also be more productive and accurate. However, it is not always easy to arrange delayed feedback.

References and further reading

Adey, P. and Shayer, M. (1994) *Really Raising Standards*, London: Routledge.

Bruner, J. (1977) *The Process of Education*, Cambridge, Massachusetts: Harvard University Press.

Ericsson, K., Krampe, R. and Tesch-Romer, C. (1993) 'The role of deliberate practice in the acquisition of expert performance', *Psychological Review*, 100, 3: 363–406. For a shorter summary of this see Ericsson's 'Attaining excellence through deliberate practice: insights from the study of expert performance' in Desforges, C. and Fox, R. (2002) *Teaching and Learning: The Essential Readings*, Oxford: Blackwell. See also my paper at www.geoffpetty.com.

Gibbs, G. (1981) *Teaching Students To Learn*, Milton Keynes: Open University Press.

Hall, J. (2005) 'Neuroscience and education: a review of the contribution of brain science to teaching and learning', Glasgow: SCRE. Download from: www.scre.ac.uk/resreport, and in summary form from: www.scre.ac.uk/spotlight/spotlight92.html.

Hattie, J., Biggs, J. and Purdie, N. (1996) Effects of learning skills interventions on student learning: a meta analysis', *Review of Educational Research*, 66, 2: 99–136.

Marzano, R., Pickering, D. and Pollock, J. (2001) *Classroom Instruction That Works*, Alexandria, Virginia: ASCD

Maslow, A. (1971) *The Farther Reaches of Human Nature*, London: Penguin Arkana.

Moseley, D. *et al.* (2005) *Frameworks for Thinking: A Handbook for Teaching and Learning*, Cambridge: Cambridge University Press.

OECD (2002) *Understanding the Brain: Towards a New Learning Science*, Paris: OECD. See www.sourceoecd.org.

Palinscar, A. S. and Brown, A. L. (1984) 'Reciprocal teaching of comprehension-fostering and comprehension-monitoring activities', *Cognition and Instruction*, 2, 117–75.

Pinker, S. (2004) 'Why nature and nurture won't go away', *Daedalus*, 133, 4: 5–17.

For Feuerstein see www.geoffpetty.com and Sharron, H. and Coulter, M. (1996) *Changing Children's Minds: Feuerstein's Revolution in the Teaching of Intelligence*, Birmingham: Imaginative Minds.

For sources of evidence that ability is learned, not inherited, download 'Ericsson' from the www.geoffpetty.com downloads page.

Part 7 What do the best teachers, schools and colleges do?

22 What do the best teachers, schools and colleges do?

In Chapters 2–7 we looked at evidence for what constitutes excellent teaching. Then in Chapters 8–13 we looked at the methods in detail and in Chapter 14 extracted from this seven general principles for excellent teaching. But how confident can we be of these findings?

One way to test them is to 'triangulate', that is, to look at teaching from very different points of view, using very different research questions and methods, and see if we get disagreements.

In this chapter we will look at expert reviews of research that asked the following questions:

- *What do the very best teachers do?* If they use the high effect size methods we saw in Chapters 4–7, and the deep-learning, high-SOLO approaches outlined in Chapter 2, then this confirms both these methods and the approaches outlined in Chapter 2.
- *What do effective schools do?* Do they concentrate on issues high on Hattie's table?
- *What do improving schools do?* Did their improvement result from concentrating on teaching and learning as Hattie's table suggests?

These questions test the ideas in earlier chapters, but we will find remarkable agreement with them which gives us some confidence.

Research on expert teachers

There have been very many attempts to describe teaching excellence, some of which governments have paid millions of pounds for. Most have not been very rigorous. They have stated hunches, perhaps well founded, but instead of testing them their authors have set off in search of evidence in their favour. The problem with this strategy, as Hattie finds, is that almost any factor you might expect to improve attainment usually does so (i.e. has a positive effect size). This leaves untested whether the suggested ideas, strategies and criteria are the most critical.

Hattie (2003) assembled the best criteria he could, and then subjected them to a severe test, and in so doing tested his own effect-size table too. He studied the literature on teaching excellence, consulted experts including teachers, and used this to devise 16 critical attributes of excellent teachers on which there was wide agreement.

He then determined the criteria that best distinguished excellent teachers, from experienced but less effective ones. He did this by measuring the degree to which known expert teachers met his 16 criteria, compared to the degree to which experienced teachers met them.

He worked in the USA, where there was already a highly respected, rigorous and multifaceted assessment system being used to identify the quality of teachers. He used this to identify expert teachers, and for comparison, experienced teachers who had taught for the same length of time as the experts, but who lacked their skill as measured by this teacher-assessment system.

Hattie then used trained researchers, observers and markers to score each teacher and their classes against his 16 criteria, using lesson observations, interviews with teachers and students, surveys and the like. For example, he used independent trained observers to code students' work on the SOLO taxonomy to measure the depth of their learning. Like all the researchers on this project they worked 'blind', not knowing whether any teacher was classified as 'expert' or 'experienced'.

Expert teachers scored higher than experienced teachers on all of Hattie's 16 criteria. He then determined which of these 16 criteria best distinguished expert from experienced teachers by using objective statistical methods (discriminant analysis and logistic regression analysis).

He used statistical methods to show that three of his 16 criteria explained 80 per cent of what it means to be expert as distinct from experienced. These three criteria show some remarkable agreement with the teaching principles he extracted from his effect-size table (see page 65) and were: challenging goals, the quality of feedback, and the teachers' high SOLO, deep understanding of both their subject and the teaching process. Let's look at these in more detail.

Expert teachers set challenging goals

The expert teachers realised that it was not enough to set tasks that required reproduction: they set challenging goals. This included surface learning and deep learning goals. Hattie found that 74 per cent of the work produced by students in the experts' classes was relational or extended abstract, i.e. deep, while only 29 per cent of the work from the experienced teachers' classes was deep. (See 'Learning quality and the SOLO taxonomy' in Chapter 2.)

Expert teachers had very deep understanding of teaching and learning

Hattie found that his experienced and expert teachers did not differ in the *amount* of knowledge of their subject, or knowledge about teaching. But they did differ in the *depth* (SOLO level) of their *understanding*. (See 'How experts structure their understanding' in Chapter 2.)

Their subject knowledge was more integrated, interrelated and built around general principles. For example, they related what they taught to prior learning and to other subjects. This deep learning enabled them to 'make lessons uniquely their own by changing, combining, and adding to them according to their students' needs and their own goals'.

The expert teachers' knowledge of the learning process was similarly deeper than that of experienced teachers. This enabled them to predict and avoid difficulties that students might have, and to see what was happening in their classrooms in terms of a deeper set of principles relating to how students learn.

This meant that expert teachers were better able to diagnose what was happening in their classrooms, and to adapt. They were more responsive to their students as a result. The teaching and learning principles they used were probably something like those outlined in Chapter 14.

Expert teachers monitor learning and provide feedback

Expert teachers seek feedback to test their own understanding of what is happening in their classrooms, and to determine their effectiveness. They also give more feedback to their students.

They anticipate and so prevent disturbances, where the experienced teacher only responds to the disruption.

Expert teachers are very selective about the information they gather, and are able to detect when students are uncomprehending, or becoming bored or inattentive.

When students are uncomprehending.

For the full 16 criteria, download Hattie's paper (see the references at the end of this chapter for details). The other criteria mostly confirm both common professional assumptions and the research, and will not surprise you greatly. For example, experts had a high respect for their students, developed a 'blame free' culture in their classroom, and 'saw' individual students rather than classes. Experienced teachers by contrast distanced themselves from students both physically and psychologically.

Expert teachers saw students' work as a reflection on their teaching, rather than on the student's characteristics. They were flexible and spontaneous, and none of them wrote lesson plans! However, they had complex mental plans enabling them to adapt to circumstances. They aimed at deep learning, and for their students' self-efficacy and self-concept.

Effective teaching in high-stakes exams

Ayres *et al.* (2004) carried out a study in Australia that was similar to Hattie's, though not as large or rigorous. Its focus was expert teachers of students on 'high stakes' courses equivalent to our 16–19 A-level examinations. Many teachers argue that the best strategy here is to strictly limit your teaching to the required curriculum, to focus on what is needed for the exam, to choose the easiest options, and not to be afraid to spoon-feed if it saves students time and effort. Ayres found that the most successful teachers in terms of exam success did *not* use this strategy. Indeed they often did the opposite, focusing instead on student interest and deep understanding.

Ayres found a cohort of 25 exceptional teachers; his criteria were that their exam results should be in the top 1 per cent nationally for over six years, and that their students should do much *worse* in other subjects. Teachers who met these criteria were chosen from a representative sample of schools from every socio-economic status. These superlative teachers turned out to be mature, with an average age of 44, working in a close team that shared ideas and resources in very stable faculties. This strongly suggests that it is not just what teachers do but what faculties do that makes the difference.

Ayres's team observed and interviewed these teachers in a structured and standardised way. (Where his findings confirm earlier findings mentioned in this book I sometimes put a note in brackets.) He thought one of the clearest messages from the research was that these teachers were *not* exam driven. They often deliberately chose the most difficult options (challenge) and thought nothing of going beyond the syllabus if it was interesting or relevant to deep understanding.

They had a passion for their subject, regarded class time as precious, and their teaching was highly structured and teacher led, with the teacher constantly involved. They made extensive use of whole-class question and answer (whole-class interactive teaching).

They expected students to be on task and there was high focus and energy. They were constantly experimental in what they did in classrooms (Ericsson).

Their lessons were structured in a ladder of gradually increasing challenge (PAR), as shown in the diagram below (top facing page).

Throughout the lesson there was a stress on the interrelationships in the knowledge, and a holistic understanding of the big picture (deep learning, high SOLO). There was no spoon-feeding, students in difficulties were not given answers during a task, and they had to write their own notes (constructivism). Handouts were given, but there was little reliance on them (see Chapter 20.) There was a non-threatening atmosphere with plenty of discussion, which was seen as preparatory for writing.

There needs to be much more research on expert teachers, but both Hattie's and Ayres's studies confirm many of the findings in Chapters 2–7. Expert teachers have

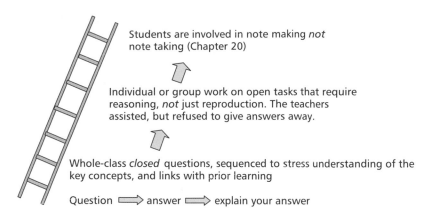

Students are involved in note making *not* note taking (Chapter 20)

Individual or group work on open tasks that require reasoning, *not* just reproduction. The teachers assisted, but refused to give answers away.

Whole-class *closed* questions, sequenced to stress understanding of the key concepts, and links with prior learning

Question ⟹ answer ⟹ explain your answer

knowingly or intuitively adopted a constructivist approach, using high effect size approaches such as challenging goals, interactive dialogue and students writing their own notes.

Research on school improvement and school effectiveness

As mentioned on the first page of this chapter, another test of our findings is to ask

- What do effective schools do? and
- What do improving schools do?

There have been decades of research, costing many millions of pounds, in Europe, North America, Australia, New Zealand and elsewhere to try to answer the above questions. There is much agreement in the findings of these two areas of research so I will consider them together in the main.

If schools had more effect than teachers then we would expect that variation in achievement *between schools* would be great, and that variation *between teachers* in the same school would be relatively small. Actually we find the exact opposite. Two teachers in the same school can have *very* different pass rates. This confirms an aspect of Hattie's table: that teacher effects are greater than school effects.

Muijis and Reynolds (2000) found that variation between teachers in a school dwarfs variation between schools, by a factor of three or four times. Other reviews of school effectiveness and school improvement also conclude that teaching quality in comparable schools has three to four times the effect on student achievement than whole-school factors such as resources, management systems, or the aims and policies of the school. Again, this confirms the relative effect sizes of school and teacher effects in Hattie's table (see Chapter 25.).

Gray *et al.* (1999) summarised the findings of school improvement and school effectiveness research. The authors found a strong concentration on learning and teaching in both effective and improving schools. Download 'school improvement' from www.geoffpetty.com if you want to know more detail, or better still read their book! It is unlikely that colleges develop in different ways.

School improvement research: 'How do schools improve?'

The main findings according to Gray *et al.* (1999) are that improving schools exhibit:

- *Collegiality:* the development of collaborative and professional relations within a school staff and among their surrounding communities.
- *Research.* School staff study research findings about, for example, effective schools and teaching practices or the processes of change.
- *Action research.* Teachers collect and analyse information and data about their class-rooms and schools and (sometimes and more recently) their students' progress.
- *Curriculum initiatives.* Changes are introduced within subject areas or, as in the case of ILT/ICT, across all curriculum areas.
- *Teaching strategies.* Teachers discuss, observe and acquire a range of new teaching skills and strategies.

School effectiveness research: 'What are the characteristics of effective schools?'

The main findings of this research movement are that effective schools exhibit:

- *Leadership.* The school's leaders focus on mission, but involve staff in planning to meet it. A democratic and participative approach is used.
- *Academic push.* There are high expectations and a tendency to increase learning time.
- *Strategies for parental involvement.*
- *Strategies to secure pupil involvement* in the classroom and outside in clubs and societies.
- *Fostering organisational cohesion.* Staff ownership and involvement are fostered through planning and coordination and an effective flow of information. Expert staff are used to develop other staff, and lessons are consistently good across the school.

Hattie has used his table of effect sizes to produce the following analysis of the effect of key agents on student achievement in schools. This would surprise many parents and politicians, who assume it is headteachers and secretaries of state who have most effect on achievement. In fact the evidence is overwhelming that your effect on achievement is inversely related to the size of your office and your salary! Unless, of course, your position in the hierarchy is to improve teaching.

In further education, where the college can guide students onto a course at any level to suit the learner, the impact of students' prior learning is much less than it is in schools. An entry level 1 a student might fail in a school, but can pass in a college. This would reduce the influence of 'students' in the list below very dramatically.

This is perhaps why the best FE colleges get an average pass rate well over 90 per cent while schools, stuck with the same-level qualification for almost all their students, get nearer 50 per cent.

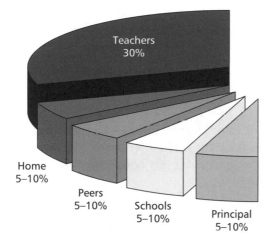
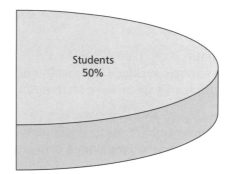

Percentage of achievement variance.

- Students   50 per cent
- Teachers   30 per cent
- Peer effects   5–10 per cent
- Homes   5–10 per cent
- Schools including principles   5–10 per cent

Conclusions

We have tested the findings in earlier chapters in this book by looking at teaching with entirely different questions in mind, and have found that good schools and improving schools both concentrate on learning and teaching. We have also seen two studies that show that expert teachers who get very exceptional results use methods suggested by the research. We can take great heart from this confirmation, though it is far from complete. There is plenty more evidence that also confirms earlier chapters, such as Gibbs' (1992) study on improving student learning in higher education. But space is limited, so let's move on.

References and further reading

Ayres, P. *et al.* (2004) 'Effective teaching in the context of a Grade 12 high-stakes external examination in New South Wales, Australia', *British Educational Research Journal*, 30, 1 (February).

Biggs J. and Collis, K. (1982) *Evaluating the Quality of Learning*, New York: Academic Press.

Brown, G. and Atkins, M. (1988) *Effective Teaching in Higher Education*, London: Routledge.

Gibbs, G. (1992) *Improving the Quality of Student Learning*, Bristol: Technical and Educational Services.

Gray, J. *et al.* (1999) *Improving Schools: Performance and Potential*, Buckingham: Open University Press.

Hattie, J, A. (2003) 'Teachers make a difference'. Download from Hattie's website: www.arts.auckland.ac.nz/staff/index.cfm?P=8650 and follow the download links to 'Influences on student learning'. You can also get it from www.geoffpetty.com.

Muijs, D. and Reynolds, D. (2000) 'School effectiveness and teacher effectiveness in mathematics: some preliminary findings from the evaluation of the Mathematics Enhancement Programme (Primary)', *School Effectiveness and School Improvement*, 11, 3, 273–303.

Ramsden, P. (1992) *Learning and Teaching in Higher Education*, London: Routledge.

Part 8 Your own evidence

23 Your own evidence: reflection and experimentation

At the end of Chapter 4 we noted a problem with effect size, and much other research. It does not consider the differences between individuals, or between groups of students, or other contextual factors. For this reason the best evidence is not what happens in *other* classrooms, but what happens in your own!

This may seem a strange statement after such a detailed look at what works in general, and at what science tells us about the nature of learning. But that can only be a guide. In the end it is your teaching, your students and your context that counts. In this matter your experience and judgement is the supreme court, and you are the supreme court judge.

Circumstances are always changing in education and we must adapt to survive. But even if everything were stable, teaching is just too damned difficult to get right. We can always improve, however skilled we are. It is the easiest thing in the world to keep teaching in the same old way, but then we can end up boring ourselves, as well as our students. In any case it is only in the last few years that evidence for what works has come in a form that really helps.

So let's experiment! It's great fun, it can revive our flagging spirits, and it can improve the learning and life chances of our students.

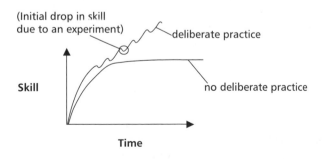

I hope you will experiment with some of the many methods in this book, and that you will adapt your usual methods, and devise new ones. But don't expect these experiments to work first time – and please forgive yourself when they don't! You will need to adapt them, and adapt *to* them, and so will your students. You would not be human if you didn't feel like giving up on some methods when they don't work, but try them two or three times even if they have obviously failed. Set your students the challenging goal to make the method work, tell them they can do it, and see what happens. Teachers touch students' lives for ever – so it's worth the effort to make powerful methods work.

> *'Champions keep playing until they get it right.'*
> Billie Jean King

Aim for evolution rather than revolution. Trying new methods one at a time is usually best, or your students will get unsettled even if you don't! Most methods only take a small proportion of a lesson, so if a method doesn't work well you can usually retrieve the situation. Your successes will greatly outweigh these failures in the long run.

Graham Gibbs (1992) is very experienced in encouraging this 'action research' approach, and I adapt his advice below:

- *Involve others.* Innovation can be a lonely and risky business and you will learn more if others are involved. Whatever you do, don't do it alone.
- *Identify the problem clearly.* Collect evidence to identify where you can make useful change.
- *Use research evidence* to convince others and to find promising strategies.
- *Start where you can.* It is always possible to start tomorrow with some level of innovation, even if it is very small.
- *Start small.* The smaller the change the easier it is to implement, monitor, and adapt.
- *Don't reinvent the wheel.* It is not necessary or helpful to act as if you were the first person to think of these methods.
- *Involve the students.* If students are on your side they can be very useful allies. It helps students to think about how they learn, so they benefit from collaborating with you.
- *Change as you go along.* You won't get it right first time, so evaluate as you go, and make changes where necessary.

The ideal is for a whole teaching team to experiment separately and then share the outcomes as described in Chapter 25. There are some ready-made experiments to try at www.geoffpetty.com/experiments.html.

The power of reflective practice

You may well be familiar with Kolb, who showed that most if not all our learning is due to experience, and involves the cycle below. The cycle helps us learn from experiments, and from our teaching generally.

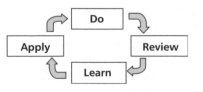

Review

We review our teaching in a particular lesson or sequence of lessons, and look for evidence for what worked and what didn't.

Difficulties: Being brave enough to collect evidence that might be uncomfortable, and honest enough to face up to problems without blaming ourselves or our students.

Learn

We try to learn from this review, not just what worked or didn't, but *why*. This creates general principles that we can apply elsewhere.

Difficulties: Asking 'why' persistently enough to enable us to learn the root cause of success or failure. Being able to 'bridge' this learning to other contexts by asking 'Where else in my teaching could I use what I have just learned?'

Apply

We plan an experiment, perhaps adapting what we did in an earlier 'Do' phase.

Difficulties: Finding the courage, time and inclination to do things differently.

Do

We carry out our experiment. The cycle repeats.

This is not an easy cycle to use as the difficulties show. It is so much easier to repeat our old methods, even if they don't work well; at least we know what will happen!

Theory in use

You have beliefs about what creates good learning, and what doesn't. This is called your 'theory in use'. It is your own personal construct, and is almost certainly not exactly the same as that of the very best expert teachers – yet! Your 'theory in use' decides pretty much everything you do in the classroom, so it is worth improving!

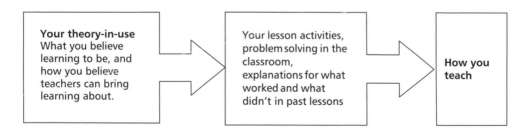

If your theory in use truly reflects reality, then it will be a faithful guide in the classroom, suggesting strategies that will work, and effective ways to solve your problems. But if it doesn't reflect reality truthfully you will be badly advised, and your students' learning will not be optimal. If you are not familiar with this idea, download 'reflective journal' from www.geoffpetty.com/selfassess.html.

Your own evidence

You can improve both your theory in use and your teaching strategies by using the reflective cycle well. Here are some things to try.

Collect feedback on your teaching

This is not as scary as it sounds. Hattie has shown that feedback to you as well as to your students is a first principle. You need a reality check, then you need to think about this and learn from it. So how can you get feedback?

Use methods that give you feedback in 'real time'

We have considered such methods in Chapter 15, for example assertive questioning and pair checking. This is a very natural and powerful way to collect evidence, and being in 'real time' you can fix any weaknesses you discover straight away.

Look at students' work as evidence of a teaching weakness

We often use work to give feedback to students, but *we* can learn from it too. You might do this already but it is worth doing it very deliberately, especially for hard topics.

Use questionnaires and class discussions

You can ask students questions about their learning or the lesson, or ask them to complete feedback questionnaires. This is usually done at the end of a course of lessons, but that is too late for those who have completed the questionnaire! There are some questions and questionnaires to download and adapt at www.geoffpetty. com/selfassess.html. One of these asks students about what teaching methods they learn best from. Another asks them to reflect on the quality of feedback they get. You can also evaluate whether you 'teach to each' by using a whole-brain approach as described on page 32.

Peer observation and other lesson observations

You can ask a peer to observe your teaching and perhaps reciprocate. There may be a scheme in your institution, or people with a role to improve teaching who would give you constructive feedback. Teachers are the same as their students in that graded feedback doesn't help as much as 'medal and mission' feedback.

Do a seven-principles check: Hattification of your common methods

In Chapter 14 we determined the seven principles that underlie excellent teaching, informed by the best qualitative and quantitative research. These are very powerful ideas, and we can use them to evaluate our teaching methods. We have already done this in Chapter 15 to evaluate different questioning methods.

Here we use the same approach to evaluate your most commonly used methods, and to improve them. Remember that the methods in this book are only a means to an end; if you can satisfy the seven principles in some better way, do it!

If you are evaluating a whole lesson or course then you can use all seven principles in Chapter 14. However, to evaluate a specific strategy or teaching method the seven principles usually reduce to the headings in the columns of the table below.

Don't ignore your own principles! I hope you have a keen sense of what you are trying to achieve in your teaching. So make an extra column or two in the evaluation table below for your own ideas about what you are trying to achieve. For example, we have only indirectly considered affective aspects of teaching, but these are important. There is overwhelming agreement that students need to be respected and included, as Chapter 12 on cooperative learning explained, so you could add 'inclusion and respect' as a column in your table.

Evaluation grid	Excellent*** good*** weak* poor !!			
Teaching strategy (Students anticipate these strategies in advance)	Challenging goal	Participation rate	Teacher's feedback	Student's feedback and dialogue
Practical demonstrations	!!	*	*	!
Student practical	***	***	**	** but only from me!

High scores here create a 'self-correcting classroom'

The example above shows a hairdressing lecturer using the grid to do an evidence-based evaluation of the way she usually does a practical demonstration followed by a practical. Up to now she has demonstrated in a pretty teacher-directed way, gathering the students around her, explaining what she was about to do, how and why she would do it that way, pointing out any health and safety issues, and so on. After the demonstration she would summarise. After doing the evaluations described in Chapter 15 to get the idea, she scored the table above and produced these notes on her demonstrations.

Challenge: They only have to watch and listen really.
Participation rate: They know they will have to do it themselves after the demo, but quite a few don't listen well, and make a mess of it. I do ask if there are any questions but I don't get many.
Teacher's feedback: Whoops! I ask a few questions but it is volunteers who answer.
Student's feedback and dialogue: Quite a few walk away with misconceptions that they don't know they have got, so there certainly isn't enough feedback to

them. The main reason I think is because they don't have a challenging goal and they work alone and silently.

Jeanette then thought how she could improve her demonstration and practical by improving each of the factors in the table. It took her some time to work out how to increase the challenge of her demonstrations, but taking a hint from an advanced practitioner attached to her department she used strategies like peer explaining as described in Chapter 19.

She established some new ways to demonstrate similar to those in Chapter 15. One involved checking any vital prior learning by question and answer, then setting a goal to peer explain what was done and why. Then she carried out the demonstration, stopping every now and then to ask questions. Students were given a few moments to write key points before explaining. After peer explaining they checked these points against Jeanette's summary.

An alternative strategy she used was 'teaching by asking'. This required her students to watch the demonstration silently (Chapter 16). They then worked in pairs to agree what she was doing, why she had done it that way, and when the technique would and would not be used. Then she used assertive questioning to get ideas back from the class, nominating students rather than using volunteers to explain their pairs' answers.

Another approach she developed for more complex demonstrations was to give students challenging questions to discuss in pairs, if necessary on a worksheet. She nominated students to give their pair's answer, and to justify it. Again she collected ideas in assertive questioning style.

She found these methods hard to use to begin with, though students soon began to enjoy them very much, and there were often heated discussions and much laughter as students expressed and improved their views. The main advantage of these methods was that the subsequent practicals went much better, as students had a better understanding of what they were doing and why. Jeanette is now considering how to use self-assessment to improve student feedback during practicals.

References and further reading

Gibbs, G. (1992) *Improving the Quality of Student Learning*, Bristol: Technical & Educational Services.

Hillier, Y. (2002) *Reflective Teaching in Further and Adult Education*, London: Continuum.

Pollard, A. (2002) *Reflective Teaching*, London: Continuum.

www.geoffpetty.com/selfassess.html: for questionnaires and standards for excellence.

Part 9 The rational curriculum

24 The rational curriculum

In Chapter 2 we saw that the best way to teach is to get students to reason, not just to reproduce what they must learn. This requires thinking skills, and Chapter 21 showed us that these were teachable, especially if we integrate skills teaching with content teaching. This can be done by snowballing; by 'stepping through' skills in dedicated skills lessons; by backward design; and by 'double decker lessons' where skills and content are taught in parallel. We also saw the power of metacognition such as bridging to ensure the transfer of these skills. *Making* time to teach skills raises achievement, improving not just the skills but understanding of the *content*.

The importance of thinking skills such as problem solving, critical thinking and ethical thinking is inestimable for the individual not just in learning but at work, at home and as a citizen. They are the means to personal goals and ambitions whatever these might be, and to corporate goals such as a fully functioning family, community, business or democracy.

The government and examining bodies have created a meticulously detailed curriculum for the content we must teach, but in comparison, and by a striking oversight, they have nearly ignored thinking skills. This puts the most vital part of the curriculum in your hands. You must decide what thinking skills should be taught, work out how this thinking is best done, and how it can be transferred. I call this the 'rational curriculum', the jewel in the crown of education, and it is almost entirely in your control.

> *Education is what remains when you have forgotten what you were taught.*
>
> B. F. Skinner

This is an enormous responsibility – and opportunity. It is no exaggeration to say that almost every aspect of private and public life is driven by our ability (or inability) to use these thinking skills effectively, and to 'think straight'.

Most of us were not taught thinking skills ourselves and know them intuitively rather than explicitly. This chapter gets explicit about these skills, looking at ways to explain them to others, along with the common oversights and biases that lurk ominously in the many dark corners of these skills.

There is a remarkable commonality in these skills across subjects, and I will take a generalist approach here. You, however, will need to establish a subject-specific approach, thinking out much of the detail for yourself, to create your own resources.

The rational curriculum

The ideal is to do this school or college wide, but don't be afraid to work alone. This is hugely important to student success and to life and society, and is most rewarding work. To start you off you might like to download and then edit files on www.geoffpetty.com/genericskills.html. I hope to expand this in coming years, making it more subject specific; if you can help me with this, perhaps by devising student materials, don't be shy – please contact me from my website. I will of course acknowledge sources.

David Moseley *et al.* (2005) produced an integrated framework for understanding thinking and learning, and I find this more comprehensive and useful than Bloom's taxonomy or other alternatives. This chapter, like the last, will follow their model by first looking at cognitive skills in order of difficulty, and then looking at 'strategic and reflective thinking'.

Strategic and reflective thinking
Engagement with and management of thinking/learning, supported by value-grounded thinking (including critically reflective thinking)

COGNITIVE SKILLS		
Information gathering	**Building understanding**	**Productive Thinking**
• Experiencing, recognising and recalling • Comprehending messages and recorded information	• Development of meaning (e.g. by elaborating, representing or sharing ideas) • Working with patterns and rules • Concept formation • Organising ideas	• Reasoning Understanding causal relationships • Systematic enquiry • Problem solving • Creative thinking

From Moseley et al. (2005)

Remember when reading what follows that these skills can be taught directly, but need to be integrated into your teaching and need to be reviewed in a 'double-decker lesson' manner as described in the last chapter. Teaching them up front in induction is useful, but by itself is only half as effective – and a tenth the fun!

Information gathering

This includes research skills, asking relevant questions, skim reading, using a book index and contents, search skills on the Internet, etc. See Chapter 33 on 'Independent learning' in *Teaching Today*.

Like other skills this can be taught with competencies. You develop a set of competencies appropriate for your course; see the extract below (the full version is on pages 18 and 19 of 'Approaches to generic skills teaching' at www.geoffpetty.com/genericskills.html).

INDEPENDENT LEARNING COMPETENCIES Name: Phil Evans	Can't or don't do	I do this sometimes	I can do this well
Books I can find suitable books in the library	1		
I can find the relevant sections using contents,	1		1
and index			
Internet I can do a logical search using Google, etc.		1	
Coping strategies If I can't understand I try harder	1		
or change resources	1		
I recognise when I am stuck and change strategy		1	
I have the courage to ask: a fellow student for help		1	
a lecturer for help	1		
etc.			
Set yourself a target for your next independent learning or research assignment:	*I'm not going to give up if I don't understand straight away, I'm going to look for easier resources*		

You can now use the metacognitive approach from Chapter 21: students self-assess against these competencies, and then set themselves skills targets to work towards during their next information-gathering task. This is then repeated to develop skills further. If students continue to use the same competency sheet, and mark the competencies with a '1' for the first task and a '2' for the second, etc., then their progress is made clear, which can be motivating.

Building understanding: analysis

The aim of analysis is to 'understand'. In practice this means asking 'why' and explaining rather than simply describing. Explanation in terms of general subject principles is the deepest, and highest on the SOLO taxonomy.

Atomistic and holistic analysis

We considered this briefly in Chapter 10 on non-linguistic representations, where you can find some examples of its use to plan a piece of writing, and used it to look at the SOLO taxonomy in Chapter 2.

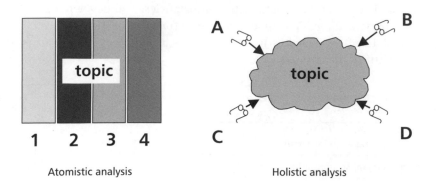

Atomistic analysis

Holistic analysis

There are two ways to analyse a topic: atomistic and holistic; *both* are needed for a full understanding.

Atomistic analysis or analysis by parts

You can cut the topic up into discrete *bits* and look at these one at a time. For example:

- splitting the story in a novel, or an historical event, into a series of events to describe 'what happened'
- looking at childhood diseases by splitting them into measles, mumps, whooping cough, etc.
- splitting a scientific experiment up into a sequence of tasks.

There is often more than one way of analysing something by parts; for example, a play can be analysed into a *sequence of events* (plot), and/or into a *list of characters*.

Holistic analysis: analysis by spectacles

You can look at the *whole* from *different points of view*, including different people's points of view or different criteria, reasons, factors, issues, themes, etc.

For example:

- using different themes or issues raised in a play, novel or poem to consider the work as a whole
- looking at a historical event from the political, economic, religious and social points of view
- looking at all childhood diseases from the points of view of infection process, immunisation, symptoms, etc.
- looking at scientific experiment from the points of view of criteria such as reliability, validity or methods of improvement, etc.

Atomistic analysis by parts often produces what teachers disparagingly call a 'descriptive' piece of work. When students have 'covered' all the parts, they often think they have 'finished' and so stop work. If they are taught to analyse using spectacles as well as by parts, the quality of their work can improve greatly. Biggs's SOLO taxonomy considered in Chapter 2 shows that students' work is graded higher if they make effective use of spectacles, and even more highly if they look for relations between elements in the whole. To begin with you can give them the spectacles to use, but eventually they should be given practice in deciding their own.

Analysis by parts and by spectacles can help a learner structure both their understanding and their written work; see the diagram on page 127. Atomistic and holistic mind maps are useful ways to carry out the analysis and to show the findings.

Elephant traps

The danger of using analysis by parts *only* (a common fault) is that the learner won't see the meaning and purpose of the topic, that is they can't 'see the wood for the trees'.

Weaknesses in using spectacles are very common and include:

- Failure to use the most useful and revealing spectacles.
- Using one (or more rarely two) spectacles only. For example, a school or college can be seen through many spectacles: funding; planning; quality and other systems; from student or teacher point of view, etc. No single spectacle gives a complete account, and when using one spectacle we are ignoring the others. Fundamentalism is a consequence of this fault.
- Believing that if spectacles contradict each other, one of them must be right and the other wrong.

Cognitively the aim of building understanding and analysis is to create a structure for the information, and to 'hang' (relate) the detail to this structure. See the diagram in Chapter 21, page 305. This enormously helps understanding, transfer and recall of this information. The process takes time, and results in the learner climbing the SOLO taxonomy considered in Chapter 2. To get to the top of the SOLO hierarchy students need to identify which general principles apply in the situation and relate the material to this. For example, when looking at a case study where staff failed to comply with quality and safety procedures, the student may go beyond the procedures themselves to see the problem as essentially one of motivation, and use motivation 'spectacles' to problem solve. Done well this would be a high SOLO response, and allows the study to be related to other situations where motivation counts.

Methods to help students analyse

Whether they are analysing a text, a case study, or perhaps even a mathematical procedure, students can be taught to use the following procedures. You will have to teach these methods overtly as described in Chapter 21.

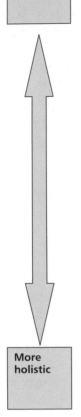

More atomistic

More holistic

- Underlining; highlighting; annotating; marking important paragraphs by a pencil line in the margin, the more important the more lines, etc.

- Extracting key points, using your own words to make notes, verbal explanations, summaries, etc.

- Analysing by parts: finding a way of cutting the whole into parts and looking at these in turn – an 'atomistic analysis'.

- Using 'spectacles' to look at the whole. Finding useful ways to look a the whole – an 'holistic analysis'.

- Creating 'graphic organisers' such as mind maps or comparison tables. These are enormously powerful methods with an effect size of 1.2 or more; see Chapter 10.

- Looking for relations within the whole, especially by asking 'why?'

- Looking at the whole through the 'spectacles' of general principles. Relating the topic to what has already been studied. This is necessary to climb to the top of the SOLO taxonomy and get top grades. See Chapter 2, and jigsaw with spectacles in Chapter 12.

Two approaches to teaching analysis

Students need to learn to use the separate skills described above in a combined and meaningful way. The diagram below (top facing page) outlines this process for students. You will need to adapt it to make it more subject specific. The diagram gives a heuristic (holistic) process as this works better than an algorithmic approach (a rigid sequence of steps), as we saw in Chapter 21. However, your students might find an algorithm easier to start with; for example: (1) read for the gist, (2) read again and mark key points, etc., as in page 7 of 'Approaches to generic skills teaching', which you can download from www.geoffpetty.com/genericskills.html.

Analysis is not peculiar to the arts and humanities. When teaching mathematics, students can analyse a mathematical process by parts, and explain each step holistically by appealing to general mathematical principles. This can be displayed graphically to stress the holistic meaning. Here is an example created by students to explain the percentages calculation in the middle.

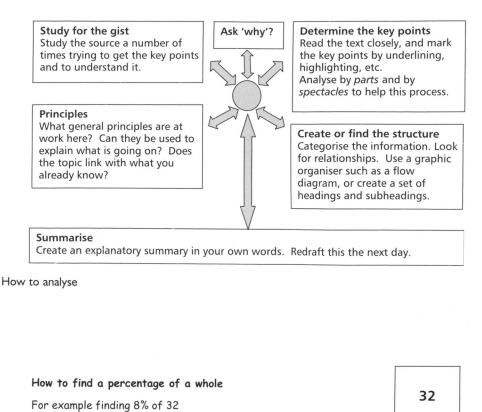

Study for the gist
Study the source a number of times trying to get the key points and to understand it.

Ask 'why'?

Determine the key points
Read the text closely, and mark the key points by underlining, highlighting, etc.
Analyse by *parts* and by *spectacles* to help this process.

Principles
What general principles are at work here? Can they be used to explain what is going on? Does the topic link with what you already know?

Create or find the structure
Categorise the information. Look for relationships. Use a graphic organiser such as a flow diagram, or create a set of headings and subheadings.

Summarise
Create an explanatory summary in your own words. Redraft this the next day.

How to analyse

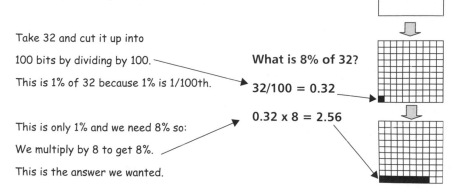

How to find a percentage of a whole

For example finding 8% of 32

Take 32 and cut it up into 100 bits by dividing by 100.
This is 1% of 32 because 1% is 1/100th.

What is 8% of 32?

32/100 = 0.32

0.32 x 8 = 2.56

This is only 1% and we need 8% so:
We multiply by 8 to get 8%.
This is the answer we wanted.

32

The approach shown above has made use of 'multiple representations' as considered in Chapter 2. The mathematical procedure is represented in everyday language on the left, in graphic form on the right, and in mathematical language in the centre. The different representations are related to each other by arrows. This aids comprehension and meets the needs of different learning styles.

Teaching students to conceptualise and to distinguish concepts

When building understanding, students come across new concepts; for example, a trainee teacher may come across 'formative' and 'summative' assessment. Graphic organisers such as Venn diagrams (Chapter 10) can help them to:

- clarify a concept by careful consideration of examples and non-examples: 'Is a class quiz summative or formative?'
- ask what some examples of a concept have in common to get the overlying principle
- distinguish two similar concepts by exploring their overlap (page 117): 'Could a quiz be both formative and summative?'

To begin with it helps to draw the Venn diagram, but after a bit one can often manage without.

Teaching analysis by 'teaching without talking' methods

The 'teaching without talking' methods described in Chapter 17 all require the learner to study resources and make sense of them; they are suitable for any subject. After using these methods, do a 'double decker lesson' style review of the analysis methods students used to create meaning: 'Did you underline key points?' . . . 'Did it help?' If the students who used 'building understanding' strategies most thoroughly do better in the task, point this out. Students need to see 'ability' as a set of learnable strategies.

Productive thinking: creativity and problem solving

Creativity takes place in every curriculum area: extended writing, problem solving, design, invention, projects, entrepreneurial initiatives, writing computer programmes, fault finding, experimentation, or any other productive thinking. I have written about this extensively in *How to Be Better at Creativity* (1997), and there is a chapter on it in *Teaching Today*; what follows is a bare outline.

Like all skills, creativity is misattributed to talent, but is really the effective use of a *process* that can be improved by practice. To help your understanding of what follows keep in mind an example of creativity in your own subject, an extended piece of writing, say, or a practical problem. Here is an example of the latter which doesn't require specialist knowledge to answer.

We will look at three versions of the creative processes that could be used on this problem.

The creative process model 1: early closure

1. Read the brief or problem once.
2. Get an idea that is not obviously inadequate.
3. Work this idea to a rough completion.
4. Stop.

The lift problem

A large company in London is housed in an eight-storey office building with only two lift shafts. For some time the managing director has had a nagging problem: his employees keep complaining about the length of time they have to wait for a lift. Consequently he has asked for quotes from engineering companies for the installation of a new lift shaft.

Two quotes have arrived, one for around £7m for an extra lift shaft, three for about £1m for faster lifts in the existing shafts. But one quote has arrived from an engineer who says he could solve the problem for £60,000.

This cheap solution still works well today. What is it?

If the brief is to find somewhere safe to put down your tea mug, this strategy works fine. If the brief is complex like the lift problem, expect very weak work however clever you are.

Many people use this 'model 1' strategy, and wonder why they are not 'creative'. Yet even the most able creative people, who might be able to get away with it because of their great experience, almost never use it. It is a myth that exceptional creativity comes in a 'lightening flash' insight; it is the product of deep exploratory thinking and trial and error. So what process *should* be used?

'All rising to a great place is by a winding stair.'

Sir Francis Bacon, philosopher (1561–1626)

The creative process model 2: the algorithmic approach

1. Read the brief or consider the problem. Ask yourself 'What exactly does this mean/require?'
2. Get lots of ideas about *where* to get lots of ideas.
3. Research in the places you identified in 2 above and brainstorm your own ideas.
4. Work your best ideas to a rough completion.
5. Evaluate your work asking whether it does what you decided in 1 above.
6. Improve the draft to produce a second draft.
7. Repeat 5 and 6 until you have quality work.

This is much better, but it is not ideal, as we will see. We saw such an algorithmic approach being used to teach report writing skills on page 299. This is a good start if students have never written a report before.

The creative process model 3: 'icedip', the heuristic approach

So far the approaches have been fairly linear or 'algorithmic'. This can work well for a task the student finds fairly straightforward, and where originality or quality are not prime concerns. Let's look at a more flexible, and demanding, process: 'icedip', consisting of six working phases, *inspiration, clarification, distillation, perspiration, evaluation and incubation*. During a particular piece of creative work each phase should be experienced many times, in no definite order, sometimes for a very short time. At any given time the student considers the strategic decision of which of the six phases is most useful at that time. This can be asked about the work as a whole, but also about each part. For example, you can use 'clarification' on a word, sentence, paragraph or the whole piece of writing.

A given piece of creative work involves a long chain of the 'icedip' phases, each phase being revisited many times. But a chain is only as strong as its weakest link. You need to know your weakest phases, and the techniques and mind-sets which will help you make them stronger. There is a student handout and a competency questionnaire for 'icedip' on www.geoffpetty.com to explore this further, and to aid self-assessment and target setting for the process.

As ever, self-assessment and target setting can greatly help the development of this skill; there are proformas for student use on the creativity page of my website.

Creativity involves the six phases described above, each of which will be visited many times when doing a single piece of work.

- The phases will not be visited in any particular order.
- You many visit a phase for hours or for just a few seconds.
- Each phase has its own mind-set given in bold above.
- Creative people are good at each phase, and know which one to use when.
- They also know the right mind-set to use for each phase.
- For more detail on how to use each phase appropriately see *How to Be Better at Creativity* by Geoff Petty (1997) (see www.greenfields.u-net.com).
- Notice that creativity is 'whole brain', not just right-brain as sometimes characterised.

The Creative Process

Inspiration.
In which you research and generate a large number of ideas

deeply engrossed, fearless and free

Clarification
In which you focus on your goals or brief

strategic, unhurried and free thinking

Distillation
In which you look through the ideas you have generated and try to determine which ones to work on

positive, strategic and intrepid

Perspiration
In which you work determindedly on your best ideas

uncritical, enthusiastic, and responsive to your evaluations

Draft and redraft

Incubation
In which you leave the work alone, though you still ponder about it occasionally, leaving it 'on the surface of your mind'.

unhurried, trusting and forgetful

Evaluation
This is a review phase in which you look back over your work in progress

critical, positive and willing to learn

Creativity involves the six phases described above, each of which will be visited many times when doing a single piece of work.

- The phases will not be visited in any particular order.
- You many visit a phase for hours or for just a few seconds.
- Each phase has its own mind-set given in bold above.
- Creative people are good at each phase, and know which one to use when. They also know the right mind-set to use for each phase.
- For more detail on how to use each phase appropriately see How to be Better at Creativity by Geoffrey Petty (Kogan Page) (1996) www.greenfields.u-net.com
- Notice that creativity is 'whole brain', not just right-brain as sometimes characterised

The mountain model of creativity

A useful analogy for the 'strategic and reflective' thinking involved in 'icedip' and other creative thinking is this mountain-climbing diagram. Take a look at this now.

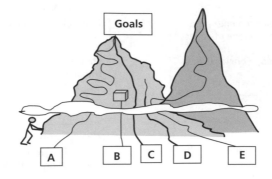

Introduce this model to your students as a story without mentioning that it is an analogy of productive thinking, and establish that the hiker must explore all the paths and choose the one that best gets where she wants to go (path C). And there is a danger she might not notice the following (please ignore the analogous points in italics on first reading):

1. She might struggle up the first path she finds (A), though it is not the best.
   (The first idea that comes to you might not be the best.)

2. She might take a path up the wrong mountain (E) if she's not careful.
   (You need to be sure of your goals before you decide which idea to work on.)

3. Some paths are much easier than others. An apparently difficult climb (path A or B) is made easy by choosing the best path (C).
   (Don't give up if a task is hard; try alternative approaches and ideas.)
   (Decision making requires that all alternatives are explored.)
   (Exploring ideas is not a waste of time; more haste can mean less speed and less effectiveness.)

4. If a block to progress is found (path B) you have a choice: find a way round it, or go down and choose an easier path.
   (This is 'problem solving', and many people use the 'wasp at the window' strategy of battling with the problem rather than finding an alternative route to their goals.)

5. Even if the hiker has no clear destination in mind, and she is just exploring, many of the arguments above apply.

We return to the mountain model on page 339, where it helps us with evaluation. To relate the mountain model to the icedip phases:

– *Inspiration* is exploring all possible paths.
– *Clarification* is deciding what peak to climb (the goals).
– *Distillation* is choosing the best path.

- *Perspiration* is climbing up the chosen path.
- *Evaluation* is checking you are still heading for your goals and are on the best path.
- *Incubation* is a short rest!

The lift problem

If you read the brief on page 331 again, you will find that the real goal is to overcome the boredom of the employees, not to fit a lift. Clarification can prevent you from scaling the wrong mountain! The solution adopted was to supply soft furnishings, newspapers, mirrors and fish tanks close to the lift button. You can use the lift problem and other examples to improve your students' understanding of the creative process.

> *Arguably the models 1 to 3 above are all useful, but need to be chosen on the basis of 'fitness for purpose', depending on whether one is putting down tea mugs or writing a poem.*

Evaluation and critical thinking

The main problem with evaluation or critical thinking, etc., is that students often don't know what it *means*, let alone how to do it. This is no surprise; accomplished politicians have trouble, and if we are honest, so do we all.

> *'Everyone thinks; it is our nature to do so. But much of our thinking, left to itself, is biased, distorted, partial, uninformed or down-right prejudiced. Yet the quality of our life and that of what we produce, make, or build depends precisely on the quality of our thought. Shoddy thinking is costly, both in money and in quality of life. Excellence in thought, however, must be systematically cultivated.'*
>
> www.criticalthinking.org

Students should evaluate on any course whatever its academic level; it improves their understanding of content, and so their grades, and it prepares a vital thinking skill for educational progression, and life. Students need to be taught all the terms in your subject that may require this sort of thinking, such as 'to what extent' or 'appraise', and any differences between these. I will use the term 'evaluate' below, but the ideas apply to any critical thinking or reflection. What do your students need to evaluate?

- an argument, point of view or theory, e.g. in history or sociology
- an action, procedure, proposal, policy, etc., e.g. on a vocational course from the pragmatic and/or the ethical point of view
- a poem, novel, painting or sculpture, characterisation, etc.
- the solution to a design problem, e.g. in engineering, computer programming
- their own work or practice

etc.

There are four models, but the early ones are weak. Very weak students often think evaluation means 'Do I like it?', or 'What's wrong with it?' and give answers like 'I think it's very good' with no justification and with no prior analysis of what they are evaluating. This is model zero and is never satisfactory. Students should be taught to use one of the following models of evaluation, *after* analysing what they are to evaluate. Encourage students to climb towards more sophisticated models as they progress. An approach as in Chapter 21 is best, integrating the use of this skill into their content learning.

Model 1: Using specific evaluation criteria

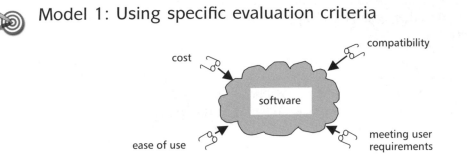

Evaluating with criteria

Evaluation frame	Strengths	Weaknesses
User requirements		
Ease of use		
Costs		
Compatibility		
Conclusion		

You can teach students to evaluate something specific, for example care plans, software, a piece of literature, or menus, using appropriate criteria. They use criteria as 'spectacles' to look at what they are evaluating, and to decide to what extent each has been achieved; they then draw a balanced conclusion. This requires students to memorise many sets of criteria even for one subject, for example one set for poems, another for novels, characterisation, etc.

You will not be starting from scratch, so the aim is to improve students' existing use of criteria, as described in Chapter 21. So:

- Snowball the criteria themselves, and make sure students understand them.
- Snowball the students' use of these criteria, perhaps after spoof, peer or self-assessment.
- Use bridging to ensure transfer.

Students can rough out their evaluations on graphic organisers like that above, either drawn up in rough or duplicated (see Chapter 10). These have an effect size of 1.2 and are called evaluation frames. Once criteria and frames are established, ask them to do an evaluation *without* reminding them of the process, leave them for a minute or two, then praise those using the criteria, and shoot those who aren't! Discuss how one knows when to use the criteria, and why they help.

The main problem with specific criteria is that they don't transfer outside a very narrow domain. More fundamentally this model does not consider alternatives or goals. Take the software example: however good it is, there might be another better. However bad, there may be *none* better, so you still need to recommend it.

Model 2: Using general evaluation criteria

Here the same criteria are used to evaluate different things, say care plans and healthy-eating policies. Strengths and weaknesses is the simplest model; opportunities and threats can be added to create the 'SWOT' analysis often used in business studies. Simple graphic organisers can be created to brainstorm ideas or to present conclusions.

Strengths	Weaknesses
Opportunities	Threats

If used literally these models are astonishingly weak despite their widespread use. It is fun to get students to see the weaknesses of the SWOT and other evaluation models, and to get them to improve the model with 'cognitive conflict' questions such as:

Question: Which is best, a Ferrari or a Ford Transit van? (student: 'a Ferrari')
Answer: No, a Ford Transit van because I'm moving furniture.
Moral: We need to consider goals when we evaluate and then consider fitness for purpose. (instead of 'goals' you might prefer objectives, purpose, aims, intended outcomes, intention, etc.)

Question: Is a bus or a car the cheapest vehicle for everyday transport? (student: 'a bus')
Answer: No, a bicycle!
Moral: We need to consider *all* alternatives for a really meaningful evaluation.

These are not trick questions irrelevant to everyday life. We considered in Chapter 1 a teaching strategy being advocated because it had many strengths and few weaknesses compared to common practice. But what if there is *another* method that has even more strengths, and even fewer weaknesses? And in any case, what are our goals?

'Alternatives' must usually include the status quo. For example, a business may consider the alternatives of spending money on computer training, or on buying more office space, ignoring the status quo and therefore the costs and benefits of *not* training and not increasing office space. Not training might be expensive if staff make errors on a system they don't understand.

You probably don't use SWOT and other models literally; you will intuitively consider goals and alternatives, but will your students? We need a model that teaches good practice explicitly, but what is it?

Model 3: Fitness for purpose or 'means to ends'

You can ask your students to improve the SWOT approach to evaluation, perhaps by asking them to devise an evaluation frame. These can be sketched out in rough when needed, and then students 'bullet point' their views into the boxes. There is hardly a better way to come to understand something than to evaluate it, so this is a great activity to learn new content, especially if students work in groups and then present their views to the class.

Don't forget to bridge the evaluation procedure with 'How did we do that?' and 'Where else could we use that process?' You can help them with the last question by giving them a range of tasks, and by asking them if the 'evaluation' process they have just used would help with them. For example:

- Describe . . .
- Analyse the . . .
- Suggest improvements to . . .
- To what extent . . .

Goals: 1. 2.		Evaluation frame
	Strengths: how does it meet the goals?	**Weaknesses in relation to goals**
Subject of this evaluation		
Best alternative		

Unfortunately models 0 to 3 do not consider the points of view of everyone affected by the subject of the evaluation. For example, when evaluating a marketing strategy one should consider the points of view of the management, customers, workers and investors. They will not agree. The model might cause students to miss other important 'spectacles' such as training.

It is possible to develop more complex evaluation frames to accommodate these extra criteria (see www.geoffpetty.com for some examples), but they soon get complex and cumbersome.

Model 4: The mountain model of evaluation

Earlier we saw that the mountain model can assist creative thinking. But it can also assist evaluation; why is this? Because to evaluate often means to determine whether what is being evaluated is the best path to certain goals. Also, evaluation is actually a *part* of the creative process, as we saw above.

The model can be used for any purposeful activity with a clear goal. In the case of expressive or artistic work the goals are the brief given, or are the intentions of the artist, that is 'clarification' in the model of creativity above. Artistic work is often exploratory, the goal being clarified during the work, but the model still works for this.

Suppose students were evaluating an experimental procedure, or a marketing policy. They could determine first what the goals should be for this, then ask themselves: Does it achieve these goals? Could it be improved? Is there a better alternative route to these goals?

In some cases the mountain model is improved, for both creativity and for evaluation, if spectacles are used to represent the different stakeholders (e.g. investors, managers, customers, etc.) and perhaps important factors such as costs. This model, then, overcomes all the difficulties so far considered, even if stakeholders disagree about which is the best path to the goal.

The model only works well, however, if goals are clear and uncontested, though this suits many subjects well. Like all models it can suffer the weaknesses of 'utilitarianism' considered below.

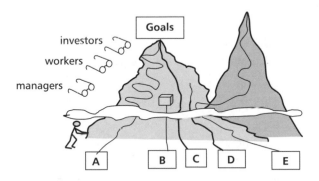

What happens if goals are contested (the investors want to expand the business but the managers don't), or if they are not clear (do we want to expand north or south?)?

Two or more goals create a 'conflict of interests' and to conceptualise this students need to understand values, and to use the next model. This opens Pandora's box, and out fly the monsters of right answer syndrome, relativism, post-modernism, and fundamentalism, and the real fun starts! Students will usually be very deeply motivated to debate these issues and if you can focus their debate on the content, as well as the philosophical issues you can create some very lively and useful lessons, and teach very transferable thinking skills too.

Model 5: Conflict of interests

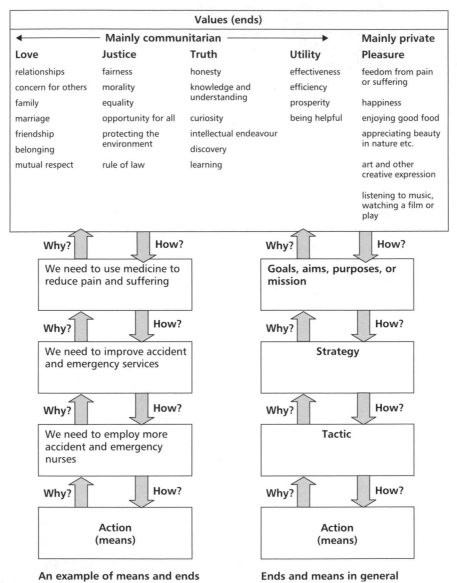

Values (ends)				
◄─────── Mainly communitarian ───────►				Mainly private
Love	**Justice**	**Truth**	**Utility**	**Pleasure**
relationships	fairness	honesty	effectiveness	feedom from pain or suffering
concern for others	morality	knowledge and understanding	efficiency	
family	equality		prosperity	happiness
marriage	opportunity for all	curiosity	being helpful	enjoying good food
friendship	protecting the environment	intellectual endeavour		appreciating beauty in nature etc.
belonging		discovery		
mutual respect	rule of law	learning		art and other creative expression
				listening to music, watching a film or play

Why? **How?**   **Why?** **How?**

We need to use medicine to reduce pain and suffering   Goals, aims, purposes, or mission

Why? **How?**   **Why?** **How?**

We need to improve accident and emergency services   Strategy

Why? **How?**   **Why?** **How?**

We need to employ more accident and emergency nurses   Tactic

Why? **How?**   **Why?** **How?**

Action (means)   Action (means)

An example of means and ends   **Ends and means in general**

Values as goals

As the diagram above shows, if you ask 'why' an action (such as employing more nurses) is being carried out, and then ask 'why?' of the answer, then eventually the answer is in terms of values. If we are behaving freely and rationally, values are our ultimate reasons for action. Free rational behaviour is an attempt to realise values by deciding 'how', as the same diagram shows.

Sociologists have shown that we pick up many of our values from our family and neighbourhood as part of 'enculturation'. Neighbours are not identical in their values, however – we must *choose* our values, as there is no agreed set, though values like friendship and fairness, and others on the diagram above, are common to many individuals and cultures.

Many disagreements and conflicts are due to a values clash, where there may be no simple 'right answer'. Suppose someone wants to build a factory that many people think ugly and noisy. Asking 'why?' of those for and against the factory may lead to a value clash between 'prosperity and jobs' on the one hand, and 'an attractive peaceful environment' on the other. Of course some people have interests: those who want jobs; those who must suffer the noise; those who will own the factory. But even disinterested people may find the decision difficult. Students often expect there to be a 'right answer' in such cases that everyone ought to agree with, and they need to understand why this may not be the case.

'I am not young enough to know everything.'
Oscar Wilde

Pluralism: 'You can't have it all'

Isaiah Berlin, a great 20th-century philosopher, argued that values could not be objectively *compared* as they were not measured on the same scale. Two people in an office might both value 'efficiency' and 'opportunities to learn', but disagree when they conflict. One might believe that an apprentice should do certain filing in order to learn; the other that she should not, on the grounds she would not do it efficiently. If these views are sincerely held, there may be no proving one side wrong in their values. How can 'learning' be weighed against 'efficiency' in a way that everyone would accept?

By flippant analogy, you can't argue a person into preferring broccoli over peas if they have tried them both and think the reverse. Values are our life choices, and people choose differently. Such conflicts happen every day of our lives, and almost every news item can be seen in terms of value conflict. However, preferring broccoli to peas is a choice that hardly affects others, while preferring personal prosperity to *fairness* does. We will pursue this distinction between private and communitarian values later.

There can of course be conflict over one value: workers may argue about who gets the nice office, or who gets the good job. But there can also be conflict *between* values – we often can't have them all at once. Students must recognise that circumstances can force us to choose between:

- spending time with a friend, or watching television at home
- telling the truth, and being loyal to a friend
- prosperity and a peaceful and beautiful environment.

Even for one individual the opposing pairs of values above may be exactly matched. Cruelly, life forces us to choose, and our choice shows the sort of person we are.

Even for an individual there is no simple hierarchy of values. In one situation I might choose beauty over prosperity, and in another the reverse depending on the degree of prosperity and beauty involved. Context counts. Charles Taylor, a celebrated modern philosopher, says 'the concrete situation is almost everything'.

For example, what has more value: personal freedom or public good? Most people will try to answer this question, but it has no general answer. Consider both these situations where they conflict:

- *Driving on the left*: Here the loss of personal freedom to drive on the right is trivial, but everyone driving on the left creates a great public good.
- *Killing those who are troublesome to the state*: Here the loss of freedom for troublesome people is very great, and the benefit to the public good small.

There are different *degrees* of every value, so everything 'depends' on the context; hence the need to analyse the situation carefully before making a judgement.

William Perry showed that students often start by believing that in any conflict, one side must be objectively right and the other wrong. Eventually they may realise that people differ in what they value, that values conflict, and that there is no simple route to a 'right answer' that everyone should agree with. Then they throw up their hands in horror and swing to the other extreme of 'naive relativism'. This is the belief that values are all just a matter of taste and enculturation, so everybody's values are different and equally valid. As you can't prove things either way, it doesn't really matter what you value.

Martin Hollis has criticised this simplistic form of 'relativism' as 'liberalism for the liberals; cannibalism for the cannibals'. And Terry Eagleton, a highly regarded cultural critic, asks if our only response to fascism is to be that it is 'not the way we do things in Sussex'.

Values are not like a choice of socks. Our values are the core of our identity, they determine how we live, and crucially they affect others, which gives values an inescapable moral dimension. They are the root difference between Ghandi and Hitler.

Debate about this issue has lately returned to the ancient Greek view outlined by Aristotle and Socrates that values (virtue) are knowledge about what is best for humanity. Abraham Maslow discovered what we value empirically, and expressed this in his well-known hierarchy of needs: we value personal safety; security; respect for ourselves and others; the need to belong; and the need to give and receive affection. And ultimately, the need to express ourselves by pursuing those values we most cherish.

The values on the left of the diagram on page 340 are mainly communitarian. If everyone in our community holds these values, then we all benefit. So morally we ought to value fairness, or the rule of law for the sake of this mutual benefit. So these values, which Berlin argued were objective in that they conferred real benefit, are 'right' in the ethical rather than the logical sense. Other values, such as our taste in music, do not affect others much or at all.

> *Most philosophers follow Hume and argue that you can't use reason alone to determine what we ought to value. However, reason is not our only toehold on truth, or the best. We can also use experience, and empirical methods and ask, as a matter of fact, what do people value? This is my approach here, as I am concerned with practical reasoning.*

Let's look at some models for handling conflicts of interest; these are useful in history, literature, business studies and indeed any vocational subject.

Ends and means comparison

I pinched the following table from a dissertation on dyslexia by Zoë, a Baccalaureate student. She uses this format to contrast the objectives, strategies and methods of the parties involved in a conflict.

Such a conceptual device can help students make sense of a value conflict. Another model Zoë was taught was the 'win-win' model of conflict. Let's take an example. Aunty Joan sends the twins Albert and Bertie a radio-controlled car as a present; there are five possible outcomes

- *Lose-lose:* e.g. the twins fight over the car and break it.
- *Win-lose:* e.g. Albert hides the car so Bertie can't use it.
- *Lose-win:* Bertie bullies Albert into not using the car.
- *Compromise:* On any given day only one twin plays with the car.
- *Win-win:* Either can play with the car if they want, but if the other wants to play too, they play a cooperative game where they take turns to set an obstacle course for the other to negotiate.

	Government	Dyslexics
Objective	To have a successful economy, to have continuous economic growth and wealth.	To reach their potential – the top of Maslow's pyramid – self-actualisation.
Strategy	To have as highly trained a population as possible. Needs a highly literate and numerate population.	To make use of the special abilities and aptitudes possessed by dyslexics and to have these valued by society.
Method	To have an inflexible system of education, focusing on the average person and on academic intelligence. This benefits the academically able.	To receive an education adapted to their individual needs and potential – an education likely to put more emphasis on creativity, visual thinking and spatial skills.

Win-win solutions

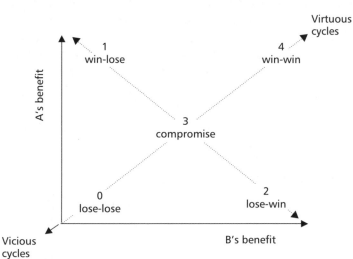

People involved in the conflict tend to see the situation as win or lose, so they only consider outcomes along the line 1 3 2 in the graph above. This is called zero-sum reasoning, where one side only gains if the other loses. It is ideal to resolve the conflict with a win-win situation, by concentrating on the line 0 3 4. Students can use this graph as a graphic organiser to write possible outcomes and to consider others.

In negotiating a conflict it helps not to focus on the *positions* of the parties – 'I want the car' – but to ask 'why?' and step up towards *desires* or values: 'I enjoy playing with the car.' It is then easier to find compromises and win-win solutions.

Conflicts are not necessarily between people or groups; one individual can encounter conflict. For example, a designer may have to cope with a conflict between the functionality of a piece of electronics and its cost; the models considered here can help with that too.

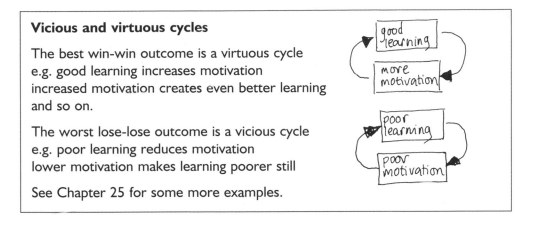

Vicious and virtuous cycles

The best win-win outcome is a virtuous cycle
e.g. good learning increases motivation
increased motivation creates even better learning
and so on.

The worst lose-lose outcome is a vicious cycle
e.g. poor learning reduces motivation
lower motivation makes learning poorer still

See Chapter 25 for some more examples.

The three-legged stool

You can develop an opinion by establishing the supporting facts, values and beliefs, and the connection between these and the opinion. You can attack an opinion by criticising the three legs, and their connection to the opinion. The three-legged stool makes a good graphic organiser, though it needs to be more detailed than that below. (See *Teaching Today*, Chapter 38.)

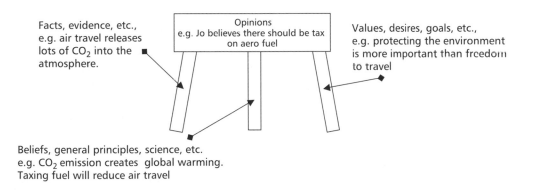

Facts, evidence, etc.,
e.g. air travel releases
lots of CO_2 into the
atmosphere.

Opinions
e.g. Jo believes there should be tax
on aero fuel

Values, desires, goals, etc.,
e.g. protecting the environment
is more important than freedom
to travel

Beliefs, general principles, science, etc.
e.g. CO_2 emission creates global warming.
Taxing fuel will reduce air travel

Mind-sets for critical thinking

Do we sincerely want the truth? Many people use their powers of reasoning to support self-interest, not to discover the truth – especially when the truth is unpalatable! This is a trait we recognise in others, but not in ourselves. R. W. Paul, quoted in Moseley (2005), suggested the affective traits or mind-sets required for good-quality critical thinking. These were intellectual humility; courage; empathy, integrity and perseverance; along with faith in reason, and fair-mindedness. We must share these aspirations with our learners whilst recognising that we may never achieve them, especially when our self-interest is challenged.

Ethics

It is not possible to teach students to negotiate conflicts of interest without also teaching them ethics, even if you don't mean to. Students often see ethics as just a system of prohibitions, but the ancient Greek view that it is what works best for everyone long term in the pursuit of the 'good life' and human flourishing is more accurate. Consequently ethics figures largely in politics, economics, vocational studies, the environment, indeed any subject that affects people's lives.

The school curriculum only nods at ethics, so it is now up to you and your rational curriculum to teach it. This is a huge responsibility, which potentially facilitates fully functioning individuals, friendships, families, communities, societies, and, most probably, the future of the planet. The reach and power of transferable thinking here is frightening.

Students need to consider ethics in very many topics; here is a sprinkling of examples:

How should we treat customer complaints?

How should conflicts between reducing unemployment and other treasury objectives be managed?

Was the Suez crisis well handled?

Is there a difference between legal and moral rights in a nursing home, and what if they conflict?

If you teach such topics you teach ethics, whether you like it or not, as I show below. And your ethical teaching will transfer to every domain of human activity. You might say that families should teach it; true, but how many families are equipped for the complexities below? Or that religious leaders should. But only 7 per cent of us attend religious services, which only rarely deal with these issues. It's up to teachers, and we should grasp the opportunity with both hands for human and for narrowly educational reasons.

When thinking about conflicts of interest there are four common 'ways of seeing' (spectacles), all of which are useful in some contexts and misleading in others. These are self-interest, utility, legal rights and moral rights. Students need to be aware of the value, and limitations, of each spectacle, and to use them all when appropriate. In other words students need to fit the spectacles together into a conceptual framework such as that shown on page 352 – which will make more sense after we have considered the spectacles separately.

A major difficulty, to put it mildly, in handling these spectacles is bias, rationalisation, and all the other bogies that self-interest puts in the way of rational thought.

The struggle is *not* between reason and emotion. For example, 'concern for others' is an emotion, as are most of the values on page 000 that rational thought attempts to realise. The struggle is between reason, and two adversaries: firstly a self-interest that is very narrowly and egotistically conceived (win-lose); and secondly negative emotions which are often 'tribal' in nature – dislike of people not like ourselves, for example.

John Rawls' *A Theory of Justice* (1971) is widely regarded as the greatest book on ethics since Kant. Rawls was an American political and moral philosopher, and showed that his ideas could be used by any political party. He used the theory of rational choice to determine how to resolve conflicts of interest. To eliminate self-interest from choices, he used a strikingly imaginative thought experiment, which suggests a great teaching method.

He imagined a representative group of people who knew about the world, but who did not yet know their place in it – for example whether they would be rich or poor, black or white, living now or living long in the future, or American or Pakistani. He then asked himself how would these ideally disinterested people resolve conflicts of interest?

In a meticulous and brilliant way, Rawls shows that these people would argue as follows. Society is a cooperative venture for mutual advantage (win-win), better for all of us than living entirely separately. However, the advantages of cooperation have to be shared fairly if the more advantaged expect cooperation.

Some people start life with a social advantage (e.g. born to a wealthy family), or natural endowment (e.g. good health). These advantages were due to historic causes and luck. So the advantaged had no right to a cooperative scheme that provided them with even further economic and social advantages *at the expense* of the less fortunate (win-lose). Meritocracy tends to do this, leaving the less advantaged behind.

People want liberty to be as extensive as possible, so long as there are like liberties for all. Present social and other advantage should be accepted, but not increased. The hypothetical people making these decisions were disinterested and representative and so their ideas do not presuppose any political belief.

Rawls concluded two ethical principles that would guide their thought during conflicts of interest:

1. There should be equality in the basic assignment of rights and duties and other social benefits (e.g. equality before the law).
2. However, inequalities, for example in wealth and authority, should be allowed only if *everyone* benefits from them, including the least advantaged. (For example, if paying surgeons more than cleaners benefits everyone, then that would be permitted.)

He called his system 'Justice as Fairness'.

Fair test

Rawls's thought experiment creates a brilliant teaching method to explore a conflict of interest. Suppose, for example, you were exploring a conflict between environmental and economic factors.

First tell students that they have full knowledge of the world from a former life, and are about to be reincarnated. Some will be rich, some poor, alive now, some will be born in the future, but they don't know which they will be yet. Try to include all interested parties. Then let them argue it out! When they have decided, give them a role, say a rich person alive now, a poor person alive in the future, and so on, and then let them argue it out again!

Four ways to look at a conflict of interest

Self-interest

This includes national interest and other group interests. It is entirely rational, ethical and just plain common sense for individuals or groups to pursue self-interest. However, when they affect the interests of others, then the 'higher' spectacles of utility and rights are needed. This is to avoid conflict, but also to realise self-interest most effectively, for example through cooperation, compromise or win-win solutions. Failure to think beyond an egocentrically conceived self-interest leads to conflict and possibly oppression.

Utility

This 'way of seeing' strives for the greatest good for the greatest number. This maximises 'utility', i.e. the advantages of whatever action is being considered, minus its disadvantages. This sounds like common sense, but if your students tell you so, try the following cases on them to create a 'cognitive conflict':

1. *The washing-up case.* Four students share a flat and none of them like washing up, which is making all four miserable. Three of them decide that the fourth, Jim, should do *all* the washing up, as this will make three of them very happy, and only one (Jim) unhappy. Jim complains that the others are being immoral, and picking on him because he is the smallest. But the other three argue that all four of them were unhappy before, and now only one will be. What's more it is a moral decision, as it delivers the greatest happiness for the greatest number.

2. *The baby case*. You are in charge of transplants in a hospital where a baby is born whose mother dies in childbirth. The child now has no relatives. Three other babies in the hospital are awaiting transplants, each of which will save their lives and greatly relieve their parents and other relatives. The orphan is a perfect match for these transplants. Should you kill the baby and use its heart, liver, and kidney to save the other four babies whose families are suffering terribly? Utilitarianism says you should. (If students agree ask 'What if the baby were you?')

3. *The India case*. Those in charge of British India in the 19th century were concerned that some Indians were plotting against their rule; this they considered a real threat to India and to utility. They rarely had enough evidence against these suspects, but decided to 'shoot them to be sure'.

Ask your students what we can conclude from these cases, and help them to recognise that utility only 'sees' maximum benefit, not whether it is *distributed fairly* (the washing-up case) or even *legally* (the baby case). They need to realise that utility can lead to tyranny, unless it is trumped by moral and legal rights (the India case). Stalin and Hitler were utilitarians! You will know of others.

The India case also shows that if the calculation of utility is left to the person considering the action, they may lack the judgement, the ability to foresee unintended consequences, or the inclination to avoid rationalisation. There is a grave danger that egocentric self-interest will be palmed off as the majority good, or even as a moral imperative. This difficulty occurs in all 'advantages versus disadvantages' thinking. Stalin was a utilitarian, and killed millions, ostensibly in the pursuit of the majority good.

Utility considers each case on its merit, and this creates another difficulty. For example, many decisions in the United Nations Security Council are made on the basis of national interest or at best utility. So in some cases where one nation has invaded another the UN has taken very concerted action, but in similar cases it has taken none. This is because the calculations of utility are different in different situations. Outsiders to these decisions see them as inconsistent and so unfair, and trust in the UN is damaged. Also the UN cannot be a strong deterrent to a would-be invader if its reaction cannot be predicted. This problem is not peculiar to the UN. Whenever decisions are made on the basis of self-interest or utility, and not on the basis of law or rights, there will be more inconsistency, less deterrence, erosion of trust, and perceived unfairness.

But there is another more subtle, and strikingly topical, difficulty with utility.

'But what happens if everybody does it?': the tragedy of the commons

If ten farmers each graze ten cattle on common land, the grass grows at the same rate as these 100 cattle can eat it, so the situation is 'sustainable'. But if a farmer puts eleven cattle on the common he will get a larger share of the grass, and so more milk and meat. But if all farmers do this, the pasture becomes overgrazed and all the cattle and farmers suffer. Even then, a farmer gets a bigger share of the grass with eleven cattle than with ten.

The latter was a widespread problem in 14th-century England and has been called 'the tragedy of the commons'. It occurs whenever there is a shared resource and people are unfair about the benefits and burdens.

> A teacher decides to give all her students A grades regardless of the quality of their work as then happiness will be maximised.

Another asset held in common is culture. For example, if there is a culture of truth telling, everyone benefits, but this requires that everyone accepts the burden of truth telling. An individual 'free rider', however, can lie in their own short-term interests, but this only works if almost everyone else tells the truth, so that truth telling is expected. If everyone lied there would be no culture of truth telling and we would all lose the benefit. There are very many other examples of such cultural assets.

At root the tragedy of the commons is about people not taking their fair share of the benefits and burdens of a collective asset. The only solution is to require that resources held in common should be managed for the long term. In practice this requires law and policing (*legal rights*). Managing a culture requires that we all accept our fair share of the burden of confronting free-riders, for example by insisting on our *moral right* to be told the truth.

This is a very current challenge. For example, rich countries release more carbon dioxide into the atmosphere than poor countries, and the rate of CO_2 emission cannot be sustained long term. The arguments *against* legal action to limit emissions – it will damage the economy or prevent us being re-elected, etc. – are based on 'utility'. But utility should not trump legal and moral rights in rational thought.

Rawls showed the weaknesses of utilitarianism, and the main purpose of his 'Justice as Fairness' was to fix them.

Legal rights

Legal rights can trump utility and self-interest, that's what laws are for. The baby case is an example of this. New laws are developed all the time to deal with the weaknesses of self-interest and utility as a means of delivering collective interests.

Moral rights

Laws sometimes offend moral rights, and then the law is often changed; for example, recently laws have been introduced requiring local authorities to ensure that their services are more accessible to people who are disabled.

The realities of power ensure that the trumping process does not always take place, of course, but the arguments above still stand from a rational and moral point of view. Indeed Rawls and Dworkin (1977) have shown that ethical behaviour *is* rational behaviour, in that they both consider how to deliver the long-term interests of ourselves and our communities.

In Plato's *Protagoras* Socrates argues that good values ('virtue') are knowledge about what is best for humanity. Aristotle's *Nichomachean Ethics* argues similarly, and this view has gained a great deal of ground in ethics and in political philosophy recently. Alisdair MacIntyre has been influential here, as has 'virtue ethics'. The psychologist Abraham Maslow discovered what we value using empirical methods, and expressed this in his well-known Hierarchy of Needs, showing that we value personal safety, security, respect for ourselves and others, the need to belong and to give and receive affection, and the need to express ourselves by pursuing those values we most cherish. This he called self-actualisation, and he discovered that when people self-actualise they tend to pursue communitarian values. See for example the diagram on page 367.

The trumping diagram

The diagram on the next page summarises what has gone before and is based on the work of Ronald Dworkin (1977), a first-rank political and legal philosopher. He argues that 'trumping' is what actually takes place in modern liberal democracies (when they work well!) and is implicitly accepted by peoples of almost any political persuasion.

Our crazy curriculum

The curriculum is what is taught. To decide what is taught we must be clear on the purpose of education, which can be seen as three overlapping goals. Ideally we should seek compromises and win-win solutions to any conflicts between these goals.

1 The learner as a means to economic ends

To make the learner employable and give them skills that are valued by the job market, and by the economy. This includes numeracy, literacy science, ICT, and the subjects offered by the standard curriculum, and also includes vocational courses.

2 The learner as an individual and as an end in herself or himself

The aim is to enhance the learner's life in ways that are not primarily economic. The happiness of individuals is highly dependent on the first few factors especially.

- Emotional intelligence: how to get on with others (also useful under I above)
- Parenting and other family relationship skills (to help people create rich, fulfilling and effective relationships)
- Pursuit of interests such as hobbies, their own music, literature, dance, theatre, etc.
- Problem solving, creativity, decision making and other thinking skills, including learning to recognise bias and self-deceit (also useful for I above)
- Health knowledge: maintenance of personal health and fitness
- Opportunity for everyone to exercise, and to learn physical skills that interest them. This would include sport, but also manipulative skills, handcraft, engineering skills, etc.
- Opportunity to get out and see the world
- Opportunity to follow their own interest, even if it is rap, and to discover and express your interest in it
- Voyage of self-discovery to follow interests that are not primarily academic or economic.

'What trumps what' in conflicts of interest (read from the bottom up)

Spectacle	Blind-spot for that spectacle
Moral rights: 'Do as you would be done by' Give equal concern and respect to all those affected, at least in terms of any changes in their conditions of life. Government and the highest courts can use moral rights to challenge the status quo, and for example change policy or the law. E.g. recent improvements in the rights of disabled people, children and women. Rawls showed that disinterested reason requires that the most disadvantaged should not suffer from any change.	Moral rights can conflict. E.g. your right to party, and your neighbours' to sleep. Rights depend on context, even right to life. E.g. police would shoot someone who went beserk with a gun denying their right to life. Moral rights 'see' the paths we should *not* take, but not those we *should* take. See 'legal rights' below. One person's right is another's duty. Where do rights stop, and personal responsibility start? We may not notice the moral rights of the least advantaged who sometimes don't express their interests.
Legal rights: the rule of law Laws protect individuals against others (e.g employers or the state) who might unreasonably use them as a means to their own ends, e.g. health and safety legislation and consumer rights protect individuals against unscrupulous businesses; freedom of information protects individuals against the State, etc.	Blind-spots: Doesn't 'see' moral rights. For example a court may decide against the fair treatment of a disabled person on the grounds that no law was broken. The law of course, is imperfect, and evolves due to legislation, and to the action of the higher courts. Like moral rights, legal rights do not 'see' the majority good or utility. They tell us what paths we should *not* take, not those we should. Only utility shows us how to realise our values.
Utility: greatest good for the greatest number Looking for the greatest good for the greatest number. 'Utilitarianism'. Shows how to realise our values. Works well if legal and moral rights are not an issue, but if they are, can lead to conflict and oppression. Stalin was a utilitarian!	Doesn't 'see' how good is *distributed*. This allows the legal and moral rights of individuals and minorities to be sacrificed for the majority good. Relies on the judgement of decision makers, e.g. their ability to anticipate and weigh all csequences. Falls easy prey to rationalisation and wishful thinking. The 'tragedy of the commons'.
Self-interest: greatest good for me An individual, or group considers how best to achieve their own interests. E.g national interests. Works well if others are not affected by your decisions or actions. But if they are, can lead to conflict and oppression.	Doesn't 'see' the interests of others or the mutual advantage in cooperation, compromise or win-win solutions. 'Enlightened self-interest' which does do this, involves utility, and the legal and moral rights of others, as described above.

Trumped by (between Moral rights and Legal rights)

Trumped by (between Legal rights and Utility)

Trumped by (between Utility and Self-interest)

3 The learner as a citizen

This includes:

- Valuing others, ethics, justice, taking responsibility.
- Citizenship: the nature and functioning of democracy, the roles of central, county and local government
- The aims of the political parties.

How well does the curriculum meet these overlapping needs? Any fair account would be bound to conclude that the curriculum gives an overwhelming priority to 1 – economic ends. The topics under 2 and 3 are barely covered by the curriculum; yet many would actually develop skills vital to the economy and society such as the rational curriculum, our emotional intelligence, etc. It is difficult to know whether this failure is due to political incompetence or to the unapologetic use of learners to further economic ends – that is, to unalloyed utilitarian thinking. In either case the curriculum is in need of a revolution, ideally one that puts the students' needs, the rational curriculum and emotional intelligence at its centre.

Our curriculum's relentless stress on academic 'book and biro' learning means that a third or more of students are made to fail compared to their peers. Vocational subjects are often conceived in a 'book and biro' manner too, giving little time for manual, personal and other real work skills.

It is a grotesque immorality to sacrifice the dignity and self-worth of a third of our children in the pursuit of narrowly conceived economic ends. Ironically the social costs caused by this curriculum, which include a high crime rate, drug abuse, and despair, make it counterproductive.

We can see from the trumping diagram earlier that the moral rights of low attainers to dignity, respect and self-worth should have trumped the narrowly utilitarian arguments that created our present curriculum. Ethics is not just a set of puritanical prohibitions. It is the Newton's laws of social behaviour, which guide us to the win-win and virtuous circle solution that make society work best in the long term.

I wonder if the architects of this corrupt curriculum ever suffer at the hands of its victims. Have they ever been burgled? Have they been mugged by an addict intent on feeding their drug habit? Have they had trouble finding a plumber?

We should seek a win-win curriculum that puts the needs of individuals on equal terms with economic and other factors.

This chapter continues on www.geoffpetty.com

References and further reading

Dworkin, R. (1977) *Taking Rights Seriously*, 2nd impression, London: Duckworth.

Moseley, D. *et al.* (2005) *Frameworks for Thinking: A Handbook for Teaching and Learning*, Cambridge: Cambridge University Press.

Petty, G. (1997) *How to Be Better at Creativity*, London: Kogan Page. See also www.greenfields.u-net.com.

Petty, G. (2004) *Teaching Today: A Practical Guide* (3rd edition), Cheltenham: Nelson Thornes.

Rawls, J. (1999) *A Theory of Justice* (revised edition; first published 1971), Oxford: Oxford University Press.

Part 10 Management and leadership

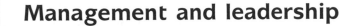

25 | Management and leadership

'If you want to make enemies, try to change something.'
Woodrow Wilson (1856–1924), American President

The strategic evidence-based approach versus custom and practice

How can you ensure that the students in your charge succeed, and how can you help improve the teaching of those in your team? You will have an important influence here whether you are a member of a teaching team or its manager.

Just like your teaching strategies, your management strategies can be based on what most people do, or they can be evidence based. Too often the 'custom and practice' management approach is to:

- collect information on student progress, drop-out rates, pass rates, and at the end of the course, student satisfaction
- give staff forms to fill in to keep them on their toes and to provide you with the information above
- discover areas of weakness, such as weak teachers or units on a course, and to suggest and require improvement here
- require teachers and managers to write self-assessment reports which include action plans for improvement in these areas of weakness.

This may seem like common sense, but it doesn't work, not by itself anyway. It is a 'systems approach', relying on administrative procedures to effect change; it is 'top down' in that the manager suggests most improvements. It is also a 'deficit model' in that it tries to improve by focusing exclusively on weaknesses (deficits), leaving what is 'good enough' alone – which invites mediocrity.

Sir Bernard O' Connell tried a similar 'systems' approach with great vigour in Runshaw College where he was principal, and despite Herculean efforts the college failed to improve. So he dumped the strategy (very evidence based!), and instead focused on the values, beliefs and expectations of staff as described below. This created one of the very best colleges in the country, indeed in Europe. Other award-winning 'Beacon' colleges and schools have independently arrived at a very similar approach. O'Connell (2002) gives the detail; we only have space for an outline here.

An evidence-based approach requires the realisation that teachers are very busy, and that some of what they do makes a big difference to student achievement, but some does not. Take another look at Hattie's effect-size table in Chapter 3 and you will see that school or college effects are very small compared to teacher effects.

If it is feedback on work towards challenging goals that makes students learn, then this needs to be your focus as a manager or team member, as we will see. If you expect teachers to fill in a new form, they usually have to make time for it by doing less lesson planning or marking. The result will often be a *decrease* in achievement. So let's concentrate on what makes a real difference to achievement: high-quality challenging goals, student activity, feedback, and the other principles in Chapter 14. Let's work smarter, not harder!

Hattie is not our only evidence here; we saw in Chapter 22 that research reviews on improving schools, and effective schools, all stress that the first priority in these successful institutions is not systems, but the student experience and especially learning and teaching. We also saw that exceptionally effective teachers work in supportive faculties that share teaching ideas and materials.

Let's look at three ways to prioritise learning: effective meetings; active schemes of work, and supported experiments.

> *Twenty per cent of what you do makes 80 per cent of the difference.*

Effective meetings

Effective meetings do not focus on institutional issues. The first item on the agenda is always learning and teaching. Are any students falling behind, and if so why? What topics or modules are causing difficulty and why? Would our students do better with a different exam body? What teaching strategies might improve achievement? Do our students have the necessary numeracy skills for a forthcoming topic, and if not, what can we do about it?

These and a million other issues like them, including welfare, well-being, and tutoring issues, decide whether our students flourish or crumple, whether they pass or fail. If there are problems in these vital areas we need to find and fix them fast, before they do damage. This is often best done in meetings, if possible with the

whole teaching team and some visiting student representatives, but if this is not possible, by a manager or their delegate raising the issues in smaller groups, or even with individuals one by one.

It's best if these meetings are short and frequent, so that they can respond quickly to events. It is amazing what can be achieved in a ten-minute meeting – if people attend punctually, and focus on what counts. Meetings are often used to disseminate information, but if everyone can read that's a waste! Why not use email or pigeon-holes to disseminate information, and then use the meeting time you save to discuss substantive teaching and learning issues? Try to balance discussion time between finding and discussing the problems ('Review' in the diagram on page 358), and discussing solutions to these problems and other ways forward ('Apply' in the chart). Improvement requires action.

Whether you lead or just contribute to the meeting try to avoid the temptation to blame or whinge. However irritating the problem think positively, suggest strategies to fix it, and/or to avoid it happening in the future. Show an unshakeable belief that it is what you do as a teaching team that makes the difference; you have a mountain of evidence on your side.

However, many teachers believe that improvement is unnecessary or impossible because of what I once heard Paul Martinez call 'the 5 Ds':

Denial   'It's not that bad really.'
Displacement   'It's someone else's fault.'
Deference   'Only management can improve achievement.'
Despair   'Nothing can be done.'
Destiny   'It's all a matter of social class, genes, luck, IQ . . .'

'Given the choice between changing, and proving that change is not necessary, most people get busy with the proof.'

J. K. Galbraith

In a brilliant empirical study, Maynard and Martinez (2002) concluded that:

'in the main, teachers on programmes with relatively poor student outcomes in terms of retention and achievement tended to explain these in terms of factors beyond their control while teachers on courses with high retention and achievement attributed their results to their own agency.'

This is 'attribution' and Dweck's theory of motivation again, only this time operating on teachers. Notice how the 'five Ds' all show teachers attributing success or failure to factors outside their control.

Meetings can help to sell the idea that the teaching team has a huge influence on student success rates, often just by the assumptions made in discussion. This is a major part of what is called 'culture management', a defining characteristic of all exceptional colleges and schools. 'Culture' here means positive beliefs, attitudes, values, and 'attributions' about what can be achieved and how, and subsequent high expectations of both teachers and students.

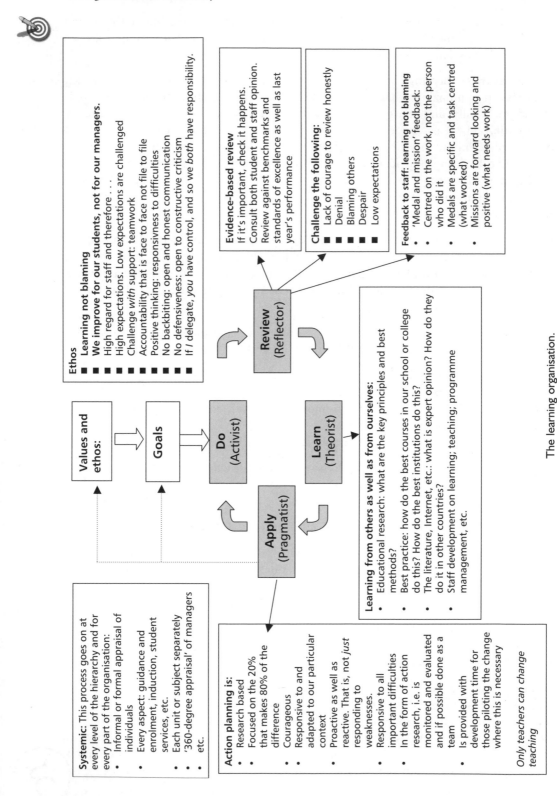

Ethos

- **Learning not blaming**
- **We improve for our students, not for our managers.**
- High regard for staff and therefore . . .
- High expectations. Low expectations are challenged
- Challenge *with support*: teamwork
- Accountability that is face to face not file to file
- Positive thinking: responsiveness to difficulties
- No backbiting: open and honest communication
- No defensiveness: open to constructive criticism
- If I delegate, *you* have control, and so we *both* have responsibility.

Evidence-based review
If it's important, check it happens.
Consult both student and staff opinion.
Review against benchmarks and standards of excellence as well as last year's performance

Challenge the following:
- Lack of courage to review honestly
- Denial
- Blaming others
- Despair
- Low expectations

Feedback to staff: learning not blaming
- 'Medal and mission' feedback:
- Centred on the work, not the person who did it
- Medals are specific and task centred (what worked)
- Missions are forward looking and positive (what needs work)

Values and ethos: → Goals → Do (Activist) → Review (Reflector)

Apply (Pragmatist) → Learn (Theorist)

Learning from others as well as from ourselves:
- Educational research: what are the key principles and best methods?
- Best practice: how do the best courses in our school or college do this? How do the best institutions do this?
- The literature, Internet, etc.: what is expert opinion? How do they do it in other countries?
- Staff development on learning; teaching; programme management, etc.

Systemic: This process goes on at every level of the hierarchy and for every part of the organisation:
- Informal or formal appraisal of individuals
- Every aspect: guidance and enrolment, induction, student services, etc.
- Each unit or subject separately
- '360-degree appraisal' of managers
- etc.

Action planning is:
- Research based
- Focused on the 20% that makes 80% of the difference
- Courageous
- Responsive to and adapted to our particular context
- Proactive as well as reactive. That is, not *just* responding to weaknesses.
- Responsive to all important difficulties
- In the form of action research, i.e. is monitored and evaluated and if possible done as a team
- Is provided with development time for those piloting the change where this is necessary

Only teachers can change teaching

The learning organisation.

Active schemes of work

If you want to keep any group of teachers talking productively almost indefinitely then just ask them for the best way to teach a given topic. If you then steer the discussion onto what is the best student activity for that topic, and how to ensure that students and teachers get good feedback from it, then your discussion really will be productive! You are now talking about 'the 20 per cent that makes 80 per cent of the difference'.

A systematic use of such a discussion is to create or improve an Active Scheme of Work. This is a scheme that includes a student activity or two for every topic or subtopic, along with signposting to any necessary resources.

There is no need to agree identical activities for every teacher who teaches the topic; alternatives can be included so long as they are equally effective. Indeed an altern-ative approach, which works better for some subjects that are not so content focused ,such as mathematics or English literature, is to create a 'Best Methods Manual'. This involves the team suggesting, researching, discussing and agreeing the best methods for teaching their subject, and writing this up. These methods can then be used on any appropriate topic.

However you decide to do it, I have found that creating active schemes of work or best methods manuals is remarkably popular with staff and ensures that:

- the best methods are available to all, and that resources are shared
- if expert teachers leave your team they leave their methods and resources behind!
- repetitive use of the same method in different classes or topics is detected and can be addressed.
- new teachers or those covering for absent colleagues are greatly helped
- it gets people talking and deciding about the most important aspect of learning: active learning.

Student activity *is* the 20 per cent that makes 80 per cent of the difference, so this is a brilliant way to improve other people's teaching. It can also help advanced prac-titioners, quality managers, and others charged with improving teaching to improve what goes on in classrooms.

Supported experiments

The research on excellence we considered in Chapter 21 found that when 'normal' people learn a skill they begin on a steep learning curve but then find methods that work reasonably well, say 'That'll do fine' and stick to these. Then their skill plateaus, because 'If you always do what you've always done – you'll always get what you've always got.' So if we want to improve, we must change what we do.

But how can we get the teachers on our teams to experiment? One way is to involve teachers in mini action-research projects called 'supported experiments'. You can start your team off by doing one yourself (this is called leadership!); any teaching method in this book that is new to you would do as a basis. Try the method out, collect evidence on whether it worked or not, perhaps some examples of students' work, and then tell your team about it. Be careful to mention any problems you had, and to ask how you could have done it better. You will not be short of advice! Then try your experiment again using some adaptations suggested by your team. Then report back again, admitting weaknesses and asking for more suggestions.

The aim is not just to experiment, but also to create a blame-free culture that supports learning from such experiments, like the ground rules we considered for students in Chapter 15.

Once you have shown the way, like a true leader, you can encourage others to try these supported experiments. (You don't need to be a manager to be a leader, just someone with vision and tact, prepared to stick your neck out and show a way forward!)

Try to stress that:

- Everyone should choose a strategy that interests them and experiment with it. Later you can try to steer your team or individuals towards experiments that address known weaknesses.
- Evidence should be collected on whether the experiment has worked, for example by asking students, or looking at their work.
- Supported experiments are done for the *team* not the individual, and outcomes are shared by all, for example by putting them on the Active Scheme of Work or in the Best Methods Manual.
- The team should support the experimenter. Learning new methods can be a real challenge, and discussion with others can really help. (Action research rather than control-group experiments is the most appropriate model.)

It helps to give supported experiments a high profile if you arrange in advance a staff development event or a meeting where everyone in your team will be asked to describe their experiments to another team or department. This is a great way to share best practice, especially if reciprocal.

If supported experiments continually improve your active schemes of work, then you have a culture of continuous improvement on the factors that have the greatest impact on student achievement. You will also have everyone improving, not just the weakest links; indeed the best teachers will often produce some of the most productive supported experiments. This is not a deficit model and it is bottom up rather than top down, and unlike many systems-based approaches it *creates* improvement, rather than simply identifying where improvement is needed and asking for it.

Course management: keeping a learner focus

Paul Martinez oversaw many hundreds of action research projects designed to improve student retention and achievement (that's ensuring students don't drop out, and do pass). These projects were very substantial and carefully evaluated. Putting their findings together, Martinez and his colleagues were able to point to those factors that had the greatest impact on retention and achievement.

This is the best synthesis of research evidence on course management I am aware of. There is not enough space here to do the work justice, and his references are strongly recommended.

I summarise some of Martinez's key findings below. (His research was in further education, including sixth form colleges, etc.) The ideas are very likely to apply in schools, where similar advice is often heard. The first section below does not apply to pre-16 education, however.

Ensure that students choose/enrol on the most appropriate course/subject/units

The best evidence for the future success of a student on a post-16 course is not how many C grades or above they achieved at GCSE, but their average GCSE score (Martinez, 2000c). Arguably, the very best evidence is the entry qualifications of your own successful students.

'Recruitment with integrity' requires that you simply say 'no' to a student who insists on doing a course they are not qualified for. Then there is a good chance that they can later be guided to a more sensible decision. Alternatively they will fail elsewhere, or be told 'no' there too.

It is unethical to enrol students who are not likely to pass just to make up course numbers. Neither does it make good business sense. If a student is wrong for your course they will be right for someone else's. Successful students are your best recruiters in the community – unsuccessful ones tell people to go elsewhere.

Initial guidance is crucial to success post-16; schools and colleges that get it right achieve pass rates of over 90 per cent, even with students suffering the greatest social and economic deprivation (Martinez 2000a). Success pre-16 is harder to achieve, as qualifications are not usually matched to the student's prior achievement.

Mind the gap

Even if good choices are made, your students may not have the precise prior learning and skills required for success on your subject/course. GCSE results are too crude a measure – a student may have a good maths GCSE but still be unable to use the percentages you need in module 3. Similar arguments hold on other courses: can your pupils give a map reference? Do your students have the dexterity required for hairdressing, the literacy for A levels?

An initial diagnostic assessment can determine key weaknesses early, so that they can be addressed before real damage is done. If the standard diagnostic tests don't discover what you need, devise your own, or devise a questionnaire:

'What is the map reference for Dewsbury Station?'

'Can you calculate molar concentration as done below?'

There is more detail on this and on what follows in *Teaching Today*.

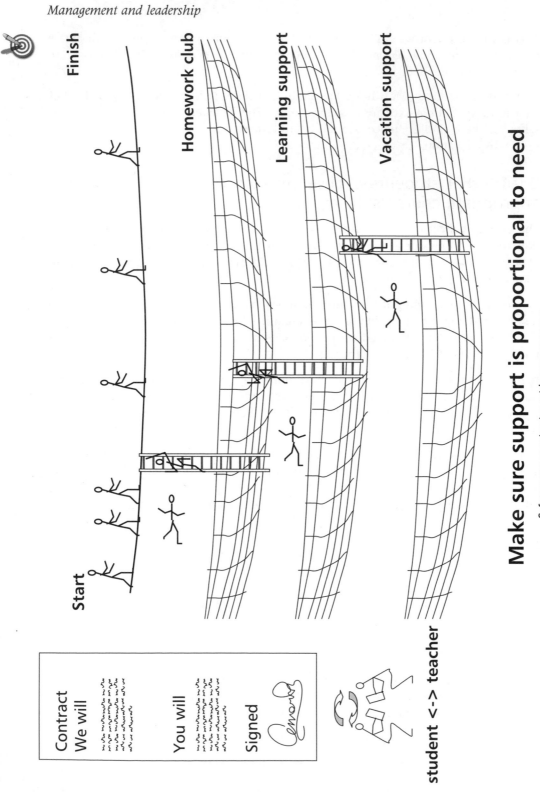

Start

Finish

Homework club

Learning support

Vacation support

Make sure support is proportional to need

Safety nets: monitoring with consequences.

Contract
We will

You will

Signed

student <-> teacher

Catch them before they fall

The 'Tutorial action planning' chart on the next page shows how initial diagnostic assessment and self-assessment lead to the discovery of weaknesses, which are addressed in one-to-one tutorials. An action plan is devised to address priority issues, and any support necessary is negotiated. The aim is not just to monitor progress and provide support but to ensure that the level of support is sufficient for each individual student. The arrows are the most important aspect of this chart, but are often missing in schools and colleges that boast the disconnected parts. Beacon colleges usually provide a series of safety nets (see the diagram above). If a net is not sufficient the next one kicks in.

One-to-one or small-group tuition has an effect size of about 1.0; Marzano showed that this is often enough to improve a pass rate from 75 per cent to 100 per cent (see page 73). B. S. Bloom (1984) quotes an astonishing effect size of 2.0!

> *The Basic Skills Agency found that students on learning support are more likely to achieve than those who don't need it.*

Few teachers and fewer students are aware of the transforming effect of individual tuition aimed at known difficulties, and they soon lapse into despair rather than face them. We must teach our students, and ourselves, to have more belief, especially as this is self-fulfilling.

This is 'attribution' and 'culture management' yet again.

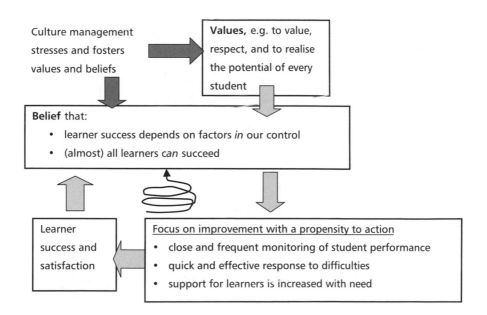

Tutorial action planning: 'Catch them before they fall'

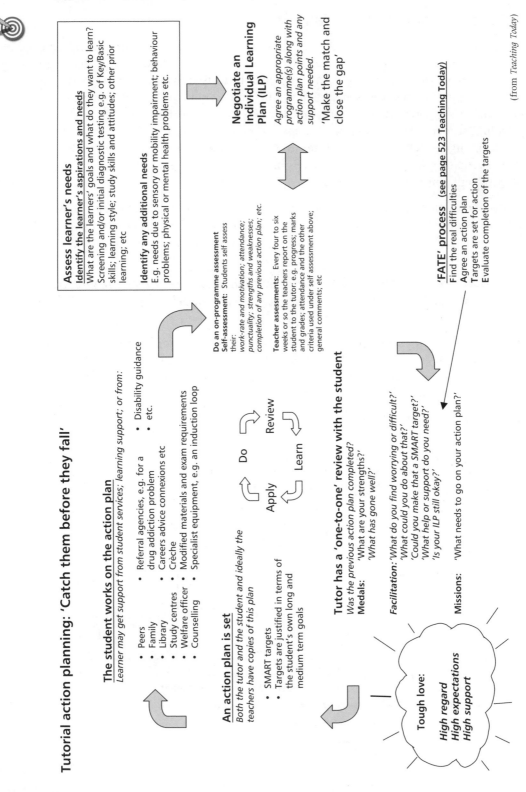

Assess learner's needs

Identify the learner's aspirations and needs
What are the learners' goals and what do they want to learn?
Screening and/or initial diagnostic testing e.g. of Key/Basic skills; learning style; study skills and attitudes; other prior learning; etc

Identify any additional needs
E.g. needs due to sensory or mobility impairment; behaviour problems; physical or mental health problems etc.

Negotiate an Individual Learning Plan (ILP)

Agree an appropriate programme(s) along with action plan points and any support needed.

'Make the match and close the gap'

The student works on the action plan
Learner may get support from student services; learning support; or from:

- Peers
- Family
- Library
- Study centres
- Welfare officer
- Counselling

- Referral agencies, e.g. for a drug addiction problem
- Careers advice connexions etc
- Crèche
- Modified materials and exam requirements
- Specialist equipment, e.g. an induction loop

- Disability guidance
- etc.

Do an on-programme assessment
Self-assessment: Students self assess their:

work-rate and motivation; attendance; punctuality; strengths and weaknesses; completion of any previous action plan; etc.

Teacher assessments: Every four to six weeks or so the teachers report on the student to the tutor: e.g. progress; marks and grades; attendance and the other criteria used under self assessment above; general comments; etc

'FATE' process (see page 523 Teaching Today)
Find the real difficulties
Agree an action plan
Targets are set for action
Evaluate completion of the targets

An action plan is set
Both the tutor and the student and ideally the teachers have copies of this plan

- SMART targets
- Targets are justified in terms of the student's own long and medium term goals

Do

Apply → Review

Learn

Tutor has a 'one-to-one' review with the student
Was the previous action plan completed?
Medals: 'What are your strengths?'
'What has gone well?'

Facilitation:'What do you find worrying or difficult?'
'What could you do about that?'
'Could you make that a SMART target?'
'What help or support do you need?'
'Is your ILP still okay?'

Missions: 'What needs to go on your action plan?'

Tough love:

High regard
High expectations
High support

(from *Teaching Today*)

This 'virtuous cycle' is at the heart of culture management. Systems that focus on improvement are not likely to work if these values and beliefs are not in place.

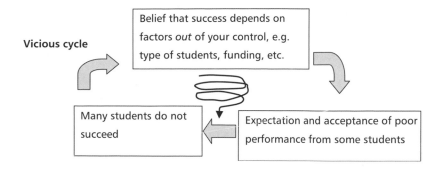

Taylor, reported in O'Connell (2002), studied a number of Beacon colleges and found that their systems did nothing that could not be found in a good manual – but that they did do it! Reviews of research on effective and on improving schools find much the same (Gray *et al.* 1999).

This 'did do it' rigour is not due to a controlling management style, but fundamentally to culture management, which stresses and develops positive values, beliefs, and expectations in staff, and consequently in students. See the virtuous cycle above, which is self-fulfilling. The vicious cycle, also self-fulfilling, is despairing and self-defeating, and corrosive of morale and of learners' life chances.

Institutions with a prodding, form-filling and aggressive management style don't attain Beacon excellence. It appears that if staff don't have the right values and don't believe that their actions can make a difference, they won't act effectively to make a difference, regardless of what managers or systems might require of them.

This 'culture management' approach has produced average post-16 pass rates of over 90 per cent even in catchment areas of the greatest social and economic deprivation, confirming the beliefs in the virtuous cycle above (Martinez, 2000a).

> *Post-16 colleges are able to put students on courses appropriate to their prior attainment; this makes their pass rate less sensitive to the nature of their intake than is the case for pre-16 education. It is therefore easier to identify good post-16 provision than good pre-16 provision, making this a useful source of evidence for this chapter.*

O'Connell (2002) described how Runshaw College achieved Beacon College status in *The Runshaw Way: Values Driven Behaviour*. Values were agreed, such as:

'teaching and learning are our first priority'

'opportunities for all'

'striving for excellence', etc.

Why this stress on values? There are two reasons a teacher might do something useful and productive: because they have to, or because they want to. Guess which is most motivating! When pursuing your own values you are doing what you regard as most important, and you don't feel controlled.

Teachers who are value driven and who believe that their students can achieve inculcate these same beliefs in their students. Their students now experience a very similar virtuous cycle to that shown above.

Even if your college is system and hierarchy driven, you can still use a value-driven culture management approach in your team to some extent. Stress the values and beliefs in everyday encounters and use them to justify and encourage change, rather than appealing to the administrative hierarchy, or to systems: 'The students would benefit if . . .' rather than 'The quality manager says we have to . . .'

> 'To put our ethos into action we must realise that values are ineffective without processes and structures that implement the values. Talk is not enough; a bias for action is necessary: we need to be practical, hands on, focusing on implementation.' (Runshaw College, 2002)

So for each value Runshaw staff agreed a separate set of related beliefs and attitudes for managers, teachers and students. Procedures were developed to ensure that these values were realised (O'Connell, 2005).

Hang on! Haven't we seen this stress on values and beliefs before? Yes, it's the value-expectancy theory of motivation again (Chapter 3), only this time for staff rather than students. If you take on board this last point it will help you towards an extended abstract conceptualisation as described in Chapter 2.

The value-driven approach creates a win-win virtuous cycle like that below (top facing page). This is based on Maslow's theory of management, which greatly influenced most of the major management gurus of the 20th century.

Maslow (1970) showed that people make a meaning and purpose for their lives by self-actualising, that is by pursuing their own values. However, this only occurs if the lower needs, such as belongingness and esteem needs, are at least partly met. So managers must ensure that teachers feel a sense of belonging, and feel respected and valued (esteem); then staff will tend to self-actualise. If values are articulated and agreed, and if ways of realising them are established, staff are motivated to realise these values. This improves student learning and college performance. It enables managers to recognise new staff successes, and so to strengthen esteem further, thus releasing more self-actualising, and so on in a virtuous cycle.

This is not easy to achieve in practice, and some staff will not respond in this way. They will need a more controlling management style. However, the virtuous cycle above is probably the most motivating approach for most people.

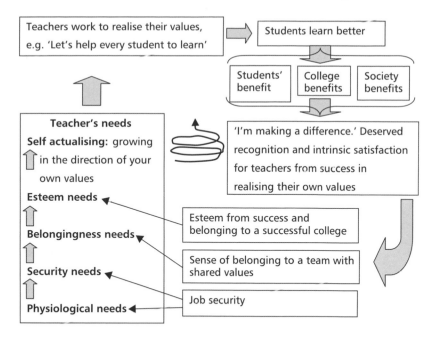

References and further reading

Bloom, B. S. (1984) 'The 2 sigma problem: the search for methods of group instruction as effective as one-to-one tutoring', *Educational Researcher*, 13, 6: 4–16.

Gray, J. *et al.* (1999) *Improving Schools: Performance and Potential*, Buckingham: Open University Press.

Martinez, P. (2000a) 'Raising achievement: a guide to successful strategies', LSDA Online.

Maslow, A. H. (1970) *Motivation and Personality* (3rd edition), New York: Harper Collins.

Maynard, J. and Martinez, P. (2002) *Pride or Prejudice? College Teachers' Views on Course Performance*, London: LDSA.

O'Connell, B. (ed.) (2002) *The Runshaw Way: Values Drive Behaviour*, Leyland: Runshaw College.

What is important in life is life, and not the result of life.

Johann Wolfgang von Goethe (1749–1832),
German writer and scientist

Bibliography

Adey, P. and Shayer, M. (1994) *Really Raising Standards*, London: Routledge.

Anderson, L. W. and Krathwohl, D. R. (eds) (2001) *A Taxonomy for Learning, Teaching and Assessing: A Revision of Bloom's Taxonomy of Educational Objectives*, New York: Longman.

Ausubel, D. P. (1968) *Education Psychology: A Cognitive View*, New York: Holt, Rinehart & Winston.

Ayres, P. *et al.* (2004) 'Effective teaching in the context of a Grade 12 high-stakes external examination in New South Wales, Australia', *British Educational Research Journal*, 30, 1 (February).

Bereiter, C. and Scardamalia, M. (1998) 'Beyond Bloom's taxonomy: rethinking knowledge for the knowledge age', in A. Hargreaves, A. Lieberman, M. Fullan and D. Hopkins (eds), *International Handbook of Educational Change* (pp. 675–92), Dordrecht: Kluwer. Download from: ikit.org/people/bereiter.html.

Biggs J. and Collis, K. (1982) *Evaluating the Quality of Learning*, New York: Academic Press.

Biggs, J. (2003) *Teaching for Quality Learning at University*, Buckingham: Open University Press/McGraw Hill.

Black, P. J. and Wiliam, D. (1998) 'Assessment and classroom learning', *Assessment in Education: Principles, Policy and Practice*, 5, 1: 7–74. See also QCA (2001). A very readable summary and a full reference is given at www.pdkintl.org/kappan/kbla9810.htm and www.qca.org.uk/ca/5–14/afl.

Black P. *et al.* (2003) *Assessment for Learning: Putting it into Practice*, Buckingham: Open University Press.

Bloom, B. S. (1984) 'The 2 sigma problem: the search for methods of group instruction as effective as one-to-one tutoring', *Educational Researcher*, 13, 6: 4–16.

Bowerman, M. (1978) 'The acquisition of word meaning', in N. Waterson and C. Snow (eds), *The Development of Communication*, London: John Wiley.

Boruch, R. *et al.* (2003) *A New Guide on Evidence Based Practice: Identifying and Implementing Educational Practices Supported by Rigorous Evidence*, Washington: US Department of Education. Downloaded from: www.ed.gov/about/offices/list/ies/reports.html.

Bransford, J. D. *et al.* (2000) *How People Learn: Brain, Mind, Experience and School*, Washington: National Research Council.

Bibliography

Brown, G. and Atkins, M. (1988) *Effective Teaching in Higher Education*, London: Routledge.

Bruner, J. (1977) *The Process of Education*, Cambridge, Massachusetts: Harvard University Press.

Carroll, W. M. (1994) 'Using worked examples as an instructional support in the algebra classroom', *Journal of Educational Psychology*, 83: 360–7.

Chizmar, J. and Ostrosky, A. (1998) 'The one-minute paper: some empirical findings', *Research in Economic Education*, Winter 1998. Download from: www.indiana, edu/~econed/pdffiles/winter98/chizmar.pdf.

Clarke, S. (2001) *Unlocking Formative Assessment: Practical Strategies for Enhancing Pupils' Learning in the Primary Classroom*, London: Hodder & Stoughton.

Clarke, S., Timperley, H. and Hattie, J. (2003) *Unlocking Formative Assessment: Practical Strategies for Enhancing Pupils' Learning in the Primary and Intermediate Classroom* (New Zealand edition), Auckland: Hodder Moa Beckett.

Coffield, F., Moseley, D., Hall, E. and Ecclestone K. (2004a) 'Learning styles and pedagogy in post-16 learning: a systematic and critical review' (LSRC reference). Download from: www.lsda.org.uk/research/reports.

Coffield, F. Moseley, D., Hall, E. and Ecclestone, K. (2004b) 'Should we be using learning styles? What research has to say to practice' (LSRC reference). Download from: www.lsda.org.uk/research/reports.

Cohen, L., Manion, L. and Morrison, K. (2000) *Research Methods in Education* (5th edition), London: RoutledgeFalmer.

Desforges, C. (2000) 'Review of reviews'. Download from: www.tlrp.org/pub/acadpub/Desforges2000b.pdf.

Desforges, C. and Fox, R. (2002) *Teaching and Learning: The Essential Readings*, Oxford: Blackwell. See particularly K. Ericsson's piece on deliberate practice.

Dienes Z. P. (1960) *Building up Mathematics*, London: Hutchinson Educational.

Donovan, M. S. and Bransford, J. D. (2005) *How Students Learn: History, Mathematics, and Science in the Classroom*, Washington: National Research Council.

Dweck, C. S. (2000) *Self-Theories: Their Role in Motivation Personality and Development*, Philadelphia: Psychology Press.

Dworkin, R. *et al.* (eds) (2001) *The Legacy of Isaiah Berlin*, New York: NYRB.

Dworkin, R. (1977) *Taking Rights Seriously*, 2nd impression, London: Duckworth.

Eagleton T. (2004) *After Theory*, London: Penguin.

Ericsson, K., Krampe, R. and Tesch-Romer, C. (1993) 'The role of deliberate practice in the acquisition of expert performance', *Psychological Review*, 100, 3: 363–406. For a shorter summary of this see Ericsson's 'Attaining excellence through deliberate practice: insights from the study of expert performance' in Desforges and Fox (2002). See also my paper at www.geoffpetty.com.

Eyesenck, M. W. and Keane, M. T. (2000) *Cognitive Psychology: A Student's Handbook* (4th edition), Hove: Psychology Press.

Feather, N. (ed.) (1982) *Expectations and Actions*, Hillsdale, New Jersey: Erlbaum.

Gibbs, G. (1981) *Teaching Students To Learn*, Milton Keynes: Open University Press.

Gibbs, G. (1992) *Improving the Quality of Student Learning*, Bristol: Technical & Educational Services.

Ginnis, Paul (2002) *The Teacher's Toolkit*, Carmarthen: Crown House Publishing.

Glass, G. V. and Smith, M. L. (1978) Meta-Analysis of Research on the Relationship of Class-Size and Achievement, San Francisco: Farwest Laboratory

Good, T. L., Grouws, D. A. and Ebmeir, D. (1983) *Active Mathematics Teaching*, New York: Longman.

Gray, J. *et al.* (1999) *Improving Schools: Performance and Potential*, Buckingham: Open University Press.

Green, M. (2002) *Improving One-to-One Tutorials*, London: LSDA.

Gunning, R. (1968) *The Techniques of Clear Writing*, New York: McGraw-Hill.

Halpern, D. F. (1997) *Critical Thinking Across the Curriculum: A Brief Edition of Thought and Knowledge*, Mahwah, New Jersey: Lawrence Erlbaum Associates.

Halpern, D. F. (2002) *Thinking Critically about Critical Thinking* (4th edition, workbook), Mahwah, New Jersey: Lawrence Erlbaum Associates.

Hall, J. (2005) 'Neuroscience and education: a review of the contribution of brain science to teaching and learning', Glasgow: SCRE. Download from: www.scre.ac.uk/resreport, and in summary form from: www.scre.ac.uk/spotlight/spotlight92.html.

Harris, J. R. (1995) 'Where is the child's environment? A group socialization theory of development', *Psychological Review*, 102, 458–89.

Hattie, J. A., 'Influences on student learning'. Download from Professor John Hattie's staff home page: www.arts.auckland.ac.nz/staff/index.cfm?P=5049.

Hattie, J, A. (2003) 'Teachers make a difference'. Download from: www.arts.auckland.ac.nz/staff/index.cfm?P=8650 and follow the download links to 'Influences on student learning'.

Hattie, J., Biggs, J. and Purdie, N. (1996) Effects of learning skills interventions on student learning: a meta analysis', *Review of Educational Research*, 66, 2: 99–136.

Herrmann, N. (whole-brain approach) See: www.leonardconsulting.com/Whole%20Brain%20Learning2.htm.

Hillier, Y. (2002) *Reflective Teaching in Further and Adult Education*, London: Continuum.

Hyerle, D. (1996) *Visual Tools for Constructing Knowledge*, Alexandria, Virginia: ASCD.

Bibliography

Jones, B. F., Pierce, J. and Hunter, B. (1988/9) 'Teaching students to construct graphic representations', *Educational Leadership*, 46, 4: 20–5.

Kluger, A. N. and DeNisi, A. (1996) 'The effects of feedback interventions on performance: a historical review, a meta-analysis, and a preliminary feedback intervention theory', *Psychological Bulletin*, 119: 254–89.

Lai, P. and Biggs, J. B. (1994) 'Who benefits from mastery learning?' *Contemporary Educational Psychology*, 19: 13–23.

Lenz, B. K. *et al.* (1992) 'The effects of curriculum maps and guiding questions on the test performance of adolescents with learning disabilities', Institute of Academic Access, Research report 11.

Maynard, J. and Martinez, P. (2002) *Pride or Prejudice? College Teachers' Views on Course Performance*, London: LDSA.

Martinez, P. (1998) '9000 voices: student persistence and drop-out in further education', LSDA Online. Download from: www.isneducation.org.uk/pubs

Martinez, P. (2000a) 'Raising achievement: a guide to successful strategies', LSDA Online. Download from: www.isneducation.org.uk/pubs

Martinez, P. (2000b) 'Raising achievement: managing the learning pathway', LSDA Online. Download from: www.isneducation.org.uk/pubs

Martinez, P. (2000c) 'Value added in vocational qualifications', LSDA Online. Download from: www.isneducation.org.uk/pubs

Martinez, P. (2001) 'How colleges improve', LSDA Online. Download from: www.isneducation.org.uk/pubs

Martinez, P. (2002) 'Raising achievement at levels 1 and 2', LSDA Online. Download from: www.isneducation.org.uk/pubs

Marzano, R. J. (1998) *A Theory-Based Meta-Analysis of Research on Instruction*, Aurora, Colorado: Mid-Continent Research for Education and Learning. Download from: www.mcrel.org/topics/productDetail.asp?topicsID=6andproductID=83.

Marzano, R., Pickering, D. and Pollock, J. (2001) *Classroom Instruction That Works*, Alexandria, Virginia: ASCD.

Maslow, A. H. (1970) *Motivation and Personality* (3rd edition), New York: Harper Collins.

Maslow, A. (1971) *The Farther Reaches of Human Nature*, London: Penguin Arkana.

Maslow, A. (1998) *Maslow on Management*, New York: John Wiley (first published as *Eupsychian Management*).

Maynard, J. and Martinez, P. (2002) *Pride or Prejudice? College Teachers' Views on Course Performance*, London: LDSA.

Mazur, E. (1997) *Peer Instruction: A User's Manual*, Upper Saddle River, New Jersey: Prentice Hall.

McGregor, D. (1960) *The Human Side of Enterprise*, New York: McGraw-Hill.

Miall, H., Ramsbotham, O. and Woodhouse, T. (1999) *Contemporary Conflict Resolution*, Cambridge: Polity Press. Download extracts from: www.polity.co.uk/ccr/contents.

Morgan, G. (1986) *Images of Organisation*, London: Sage.

Moseley, D. *et al.* (2004) 'Thinking skill frameworks for post-16 learners: an evaluation'. Download from: www.lsrc.ac.uk/publications.

Moseley, D. *et al.* (2005) *Frameworks for Thinking: A Handbook for Teaching and Learning*, Cambridge: Cambridge University Press.

Muijs, D. and Reynolds, D. (2000) 'School effectiveness and teacher effectiveness in mathematics: some preliminary findings from the evaluation of the Mathematics Enhancement Programme (Primary)', *School Effectiveness and School Improvement*, 11, 3, 273–303.

Muijs, D. and Reynolds, D. (2001) *Effective Teaching: Evidence and Practice*, London: Paul Chapman.

O'Connell, B. (ed.) (2002) *The Runshaw Way: Values Drive Behaviour*, Leyland: Runshaw College.

O'Connell, B. (2005) *Creating an Outstanding College*, Nelson Thornes: Cheltenham.

OECD (2002) *Understanding the Brain: Towards a New Learning Science*, Paris: OECD. See www.sourceoecd.org.

Palinscar, A. S. and Brown, A. L. (1984) 'Reciprocal teaching of comprehension-fostering and comprehension-monitoring activities', *Cognition and Instruction*, 2, 117–75.

Rosenshine, B. V. and Meister, C. (1993) 'Reciprocal teaching: a review of 19 experimental studies', Technical Report No. 574. (See 'References and further reading', Chapter 14.)

Petty, G. (1997) *How to Be Better at Creativity*, London: Kogan Page. Sec also www.greenfields.u-net.com.

Petty, G. (2004) *Teaching Today: A Practical Guide* (3rd edition), Cheltenham: Nelson Thornes. See also www.geoffpetty.com.

Pinker, S. (1997) *How the Mind Works*, London: Penguin.

Pinker, S. (2004) 'Why nature and nurture won't go away', *Daedalus*, 133, 4: 5–17.

Pintrich, P. R. (2000) 'The role of goal orientation in self-regulated learning', in M. Boekaerts, P. R. Pintrich and M. Zeidner (eds), *Handbook of Self-Regulation*, London: Academic Press.

Pollard, A. (2002) *Reflective Teaching*, London: Continuum.

Powell, R. (1997) *Active Whole-Class Teaching*, Stafford: Robert Powell.

QCA (2001) 'Assessment for learning: using assessment to raise achievement in mathematics: a research report'. Download from: www.qca.org.uk/6311.html.

Bibliography

Ramsden, P. (1992) *Learning and Teaching in Higher Education*, London: Routledge.

Rawls, J. (1999) *A Theory of Justice* (revised edition; first published 1971), Oxford: Oxford University Press.

Reynolds, D. and Farrell, S. (1996) *Worlds Apart? A Review of International Studies of Educational Achievement Involving England*, London: HMSO.

Roger, T. and Johnson, D. W. (1994) 'An overview of cooperative learning'. Download from: www.co-operation.org/pages/overviewpaper.html.

Rosenshine, B. V. and Meister, C. (1993) 'Reciprocal teaching: a review of 19 experimental studies', Technical Report No. 574. (See 'References and further reading', Chapter 14.)

Rowe, M. B. (1986) 'Wait time: slowing down may be a way of speeding up', *Journal of Teacher Education*, 37, 1: 43–50.

Sadler, R. (1989) 'Formative assessment and the design of instructional systems', *Instructional Science*, 18, 119–44.

Savinainen, A. (2001) 'An evaluation of interactive teaching methods in mechanics: using the force concept inventory to monitor student learning'. Download from: www.kotisivu.mtv3.fi/physics/downloads.html. This paper deals with 'peer instruction' or peer checking.

Schön, D. (1983) *The Reflective Practitioner*, San Francisco: Jossey-Bass.

Sharron, H. and Coulter, M. (1996) *Changing Children's Minds: Feuerstein's Revolution in the Teaching of Intelligence*, Birmingham: Imaginative Minds.

Shayer, M. and Adey, P. (2002) *Learning Intelligence. Cognitive Acceleration Across the Curriculum from 5 to 15 Years*, Buckingham: Open University Press.

Swann, M. and Green, M. (2002) 'Learning mathematics through discussion and reflection' (CD-ROM, video and print materials), London: LDSA.

Torrance, H. and Pryor, J. (1998) *Investigating Formative Assessment: Teaching, Learning and Assessment in the Classroom*, Buckingham: Open University Press.

Vygotsky, L. S. (1962) *Thought and Language*, Cambridge, Massachusetts: MIT Press.

Westwood, P. (2003) *Commonsense Methods for Children with Special Educational Needs: Strategies for the Regular Classroom* (4th edition), London: RoutledgeFalmer.

Some links worth exploring

www.arg.educ.cam.ac.uk: the Assessment Reform Group website

www.ascd.org: US organisation that is very evidence based

www.clcrc.com: useful for cooperative learning

www.ericdigests.org/pre-922/role.htm: gives an interesting account of the importance of review in teaching

www.geoffpetty.com: website linked to this book and many downloads, including Chapter 26 on evidence-based approaches to classroom management and discipline

www.intermep.org: whole-class interactive teaching in maths

www.loopcards.net: 'decisions, decisions' being used in mathematics

www.mapthemind.com/research/research.html: research on thinking maps

www.mindgenius.com: software that enables you to create mind maps

www.mind-map.com: Tony Buzan's website

www.openphoto.net and pics.tech4learning.com: copyright 'friendly' or free photographs and images

www.qca.org.uk/7659.html: Assessment for Learning on the QCA website

www.tech-head.com/fog.htm: for the FOG index

www.thinkingmaps.com: website for thinkingmaps Inc in the US

Index